Converting the Saints

Converting the Saints
A Study of Religious Rivalry in America

Charles Randall Paul

GREG KOFFORD BOOKS
SALT LAKE CITY, 2018

Copyright © 2018 Charles Randall Paul
Cover design copyright © 2018 Greg Kofford Books, Inc.
Cover design by Loyd Isao Ericson

Published in the USA.

All rights reserved. No part of this volume may be reproduced in any form without written permission from the publisher, Greg Kofford Books. The views expressed herein are the responsibility of the authors and do not necessarily represent the position of Greg Kofford Books.

ISBN 978-1-58958-756-4 (paperback); 978-1-58958-747-2 (hardcover)
Also available in ebook.

Greg Kofford Books
P.O. Box 1362
Draper, UT 84020
www.gregkofford.com
facebook.com/gkbooks
twitter.com/gkbooks

Library of Congress Cataloging-in-Publication Data

Names: Paul, Charles Randall, author.
Title: Converting the saints : a study of religious rivalry in America / Charles Randall Paul.
Description: Salt Lake City : Greg Kofford Books, 2018. | Includes bibliographical references and index.
Identifiers: LCCN 2018000266| ISBN 9781589587564 (pbk.) | ISBN 9781589587472
    (hardcover)
Subjects: LCSH: Missionaries--United States--History--20th century. | Missionaries--United States--Biography.
Classification: LCC BV2775 .P38 2018 | DDC 277.3/082--dc23 LC record available at https://lccn.loc.gov/2018000266

In appreciation for my wonderful teachers and readers,
David Tracy, Martin Marty, Harold Bloom,
and my intrepid partner, Jann Paul.

Contents

Scriptural Abbreviations Guide	ix
Acknowledgements	xi
Prologue	xiii
Introduction	xv
1. The American Lively Experiment: Sustaining Religious Rivalry and Peace	1
2. Violent American Religious Conflicts: Three Strong Cases	19
3. American Religious Climate 1900–1925: A Christian Nation?	41
4. Rival Stewards Of The American Promised Land	59
5. The True Church Challenge: Counterfeit Vs. Real Christianity	81
6. John Danforth Nutting, Nondenominational Preacher At Large	121
7. William Mitchell Paden, Presbyterian Polemicist	141
8. Franklin Spencer Spalding, Episcopalian Diplomat	167
9. Comparing Mission Methods Of Nutting, Paden, And Spalding	193
10. Contestational Rivalry Without Coercion Or Violence	221
Bibliography	235
Index	255

SCRIPTURAL ABBREVIATIONS GUIDE

Parenthetical scriptural references in this volume use standard LDS abbreviations.

Hebrew Bible

Gen.	Genesis
Ex.	Exodus
Lev.	Leviticus
Num.	Numbers
Deut.	Deuteronomy
Josh.	Joshua
Judg.	Judges
Ruth	Ruth
1 Sam.	1 Samuel
2 Sam.	2 Samuel
1 Kgs.	1 Kings
2 Kgs.	2 Kings
1 Chr.	1 Chronicles
2 Chr.	2 Chronicles
Ezra	Ezra
Neh.	Nehemiah
Esth.	Esther
Job	Job
Ps.	Psalms
Prov.	Proverbs
Eccl.	Ecclesiastes
Song	Song of Solomon
Isa.	Isaiah
Jer.	Jeremiah
Lam.	Lamentations
Ezek.	Ezekiel
Dan.	Daniel
Hosea	Hosea
Joel	Joel
Amos	Amos
Obad.	Obadiah
Jonah	Jonah
Micah	Micah
Nahum	Nahum
Hab.	Habakkuk
Zeph.	Zephaniah
Hag.	Haggai
Zech.	Zechariah
Mal.	Malachi

New Testament

Matt.	Matthew
Mark	Mark
Luke	Luke
John	John
Acts	Acts
Rom.	Romans
1 Cor.	1 Corinthians
2 Cor.	2 Corinthians
Gal.	Galatians
Eph.	Ephesians
Philip.	Philippians
Col.	Colossians
1 Thes.	1 Thessalonians
2 Thes.	2 Thessalonians
1 Tim.	1 Timothy
2 Tim.	2 Timothy
Titus	Titus
Philem.	Philemon
Heb.	Hebrews
James	James
1 Pet.	1 Peter
2 Pet.	2 Peter
1 Jn.	1 John
2 Jn.	2 John
3 Jn.	3 John
Jude	Jude
Rev.	Revelation

Book of Mormon

1 Ne.	1 Nephi
2 Ne.	2 Nephi
Jacob	Jacob
Enos	Enos
Jarom	Jarom
Omni	Omni
W of M	Words of Mormon
Mosiah	Mosiah
Alma	Alma
Hel.	Helaman
3 Ne.	3 Nephi
4 Ne.	4 Nephi
Morm.	Mormon
Ether	Ether
Moro.	Moroni

Doctrine and Covenants

D&C	Doctrine and Covenants
OD	Official Declaration

Pearl of Great Price

Moses	Moses
Abr.	Abraham
JS–M	Joseph Smith–Matthew
JS–H	Joseph Smith–History
A of F	Articles of Faith

Joseph Smith Translation

JST	Joseph Smith Translation

Acknowledgements

I am truly grateful for the inspiring teachings as well as the helpful criticism of my PhD dissertation reading committee: Harold Bloom (Yale and NYU), Martin Marty (University of Chicago), and David Tracy (University of Chicago). The excellent instruction and inspiration of my professors at The Committee on Social Thought at the University of Chicago where I studied in the early 1990s has guided my thinking in this work and beyond. I owe much to the late Brigham Young University professors Truman Madsen and Hugh Nibley who inspired my scholarly passion to probe the histories of religions, and especially the questions of understanding and dealing with intra- and interreligious conflicts over truth and authority.

I look back with affectionate gratitude at my Catholic, Jewish, and Protestant high school friends in Millburn, New Jersey, in the early 1960s. They inadvertently opened my mind and heart to the reality that people can live happily even in religious traditions that "fall short" of mine! More, they showed me uniquely inspiring religious practices and ideas that could improve my tradition's way—without requiring that I denounce it. Thus early in life my friendships outside my religious community spurred me to think about theological pluralism: Why had a just and loving God of revelation not re-revealed the same truth obviously and pervasively to all people at all times? Further, after rare but intense religious arguments with friends I sensed that religious conflicts are perennial and unresolvable by compromise. As I aged, influenced by social psychological training and life experience, I came to ponder the most important religious and ideological question of our time: "How does God—or our ethical standard—inspire us *to feel and behave* when critics and rivals challenge our most cherished beliefs, purposes, and allegiances?" These questions drive my scholarship and propel this book through its histories, theories, and meliorating prescriptions.

In writing this book I realized a Protestant scholar needed to edit my work, which attempts to interpret the Protestant voices that played such a prominent role in the history I explore here. John Morehead, MA, carefully read the entire text and provided many hours of thoughtful analysis to help organize the whole presentation. He enabled more accurate interpretation of the Protestant protagonists and their doctrines, helping me re-write sections of the text where my limited experience in studying Protestant theology resulted in incorrect readings of normal Protestant positions. I deeply appreciate his work on this book and our continuing friendship. He is convinced the highest way toward divine light is not the road I follow, and I am persuaded that he is wrong about that. A lively tension of co-resistance and collaboration informs our love for each other. We tend to symbolize the pragmatic potency of trustworthy rivals engaged in a serious contest over the purpose of life and the best way to live.

My wife, Jann Waid Paul, and my son, Jeron Paul, carefully edited early drafts of this manuscript. Jann and my children all sacrificed greatly while I worked over eight years to complete a mid-life doctorate that provided the basis for this book. I will always be thankful for their loyal and patient endurance.

Prologue

Stephen said, "You stiff-necked people . . . are forever opposing the Holy Spirit just as your ancestors used to do.". . . and they became enraged and ground their teeth at Stephen. And he said . . . "Look—I see the heavens open and Jesus, the Son of Man, standing on the right hand of God!" Then they covered their ears . . . and rushed together against him, and began to stone him: and the witnesses laid their coats at the feet of a young man named Saul [Paul].

Acts 7: 51, 56–58

Later as Saul [Paul], still breathing threats and murder against the disciples of the Lord . . . was approaching Damascus, suddenly a light from heaven flashed around him. He fell to the ground, and heard a voice saying to him, "Saul, Saul, why do you persecute me?" He asked, "Who are you, sir?" And the reply came, "I am Jesus whom you are persecuting.". . . And afterward Saul [Paul] preached Jesus in the synagogues, saying that he is the Son of God. And all those that heard him were amazed, and said, "Is this not the man who made havoc in Jerusalem among those who invoked the name of Jesus?"

Acts 9: 3–5, 15, 19–21

Thomas More referred to the above passages in his following final response to the judges that condemned him to death for refusing to consent to Henry VIII's claim to regal supremacy over the authority of the Roman Catholic Church:

"Paul . . . was present, and consented to the death of St. Stephen . . . and yet they are now both Holy Saints in heaven, and shall continue there friends forever. So I do trust . . . and pray, that though your lordships have now here in earth been judges to my condemnation, we may yet hereafter in heaven merrily all meet together to our everlasting salvation."

Anthony Kenny (1983, 88)

Introduction

Saving the world is complicated. Missions to do so are attacks no matter how benign the motive. The history of religious missions is replete with complex social, political, economic, and religious conflict. This study of how Americans have managed or mismanaged past religious conflicts can provide practical wisdom today when so many of our modern conflicts are strongly influenced by religious factors. We live in local and global societies that are deeply troubled by the perennial problem of religious and ideological conflict between uncompromising rivals that often justify political or economic coercion in their missions to save the world. Rival secular world-saving ideologies partake of the same problem.

More interesting is the less-observed fact that the primary offensive to save the sinful or enlighten the ignorant shifts toward a defensive war to eliminate rivals. Then religious adversaries, whose traditions criticize the use of violence over persuasion, often seek to justify coercive treatment of rivals by blaming them for supposed economic or political injustices. In either case, it is commonplace to reduce the diagnosis of social conflict to a struggle over political and economic power. However, this reduction is a fatal flaw in both political and religious policy formation. Not only do policy makers disregard the religious aspects of social conflicts, but both secular and religious thinkers have incorrectly presumed that resolution of religious conflict is both desired by the parties and a key to achieve social stability. The social-psychological fact is that humans desire to distinguish themselves in relationships of co-resistance as well as collaboration. The key to sustaining peaceful social relations is not found in overlapping consensus. The key to peacefulness is the desire in rivals to contest without coercion. Much of our global future depends on how we feel about our religious and ideological rivals. If we become trustworthy rivals who doubt not each other's good will, and if we can include the tension of contestation within our religious and political ideals of peacefulness, then we can face our difficult global problems with realistic hope that new collaborations between rivals will bless the earth and that violence between them will decrease.

Without reducing any conflict to one cause, there are cases where religious rivalry has been, and is today, the primary impetus. Rivals in these conflicts would prefer the peaceful conversion of their opponents that would create a more righteous and moral environment, which would bring divine blessing on all. They do not primarily desire the other's money or votes. Heart-to-heart conversation replaces hand-to-hand combat as the preferred method of engagement when persuasive conversion is the end goal.

This study is an attempt to demonstrate that our attitudes about the motives and capacities of our rivals substantially influence the methods we use to engage in conflict and vice versa. Congenial attitudes and methods are as potent as or more potent than common interests and beliefs in sustaining peaceful contestations and collaborations among rivals. When it is generally understood from experience that the best way to do religious battle honorably is in heart-felt contestation between respectful free agents, then our political and religious worlds will be liberated from wasteful violence. In America, this understanding was first manifested both socially and legally in the 1640s in Rhode Island, and a century and half later it was enshrined in the First Amendment to the United States Constitution. While there are notable exceptions that will be discussed in this study, for the most part the only legitimate way of engaging in religious conflict in America has been by verbal means of persuasive contestation. Still, to desire and know how to honorably engage with trustworthy rivals is not instinctual. Every generation must learn this desire and skill from experience. The current situation in American politics and religion show this learning is in danger of being forgotten. One of the purposes of this book is to revive this skill and pass it on.

This volume focuses on early-twentieth-century Protestant missions to convert Mormons in Utah to traditional Christianity. Although Mormons by then had already acquiesced to federal laws against polygamy and federal pressure to secularize Utah's governance, the religious conflict over Mormon legitimacy within the Christian world remained unresolved. This was a religious conflict that was engaged primarily as a contest to persuade the human heart. Both religious rivals understood this, and while they were disturbed by their aggressive mutual criticism, they did not think it wrong or even strange for their rival to engage them. This fact marks the crucial understanding at the center of the American experiment: that persuasive contestation over religion, ideology, or founding principles is normal in our secular state; and that contestation is even healthy for free citizens to flourish within a diverse society.

The general nineteenth-century presumption was of religion being entwined in all aspects of everyone's life; religious contestations were to be expected between intelligent rivals of different persuasions. In such an environment, persuasive missionary work was a normal and legitimate activity that took place in respectable venues for engaging in conflicts over beliefs and values between societies. During the twentieth century this changed drastically. It became unfashionable, if not improper or even illegal, for intelligent, practical people to engage in public religious or ideological contestation over inevitably unresolvable questions. Social and institutional places for engaging in conflict over economic and political security became the world order. But there are billions of people, religious rivals, who find no legitimate place for engaging the contests their integrity requires. World-changing terrorist strategies proliferate in the absence of an honorable venue to contend over religion. The religious voice is not respected nor welcome in the current public venues. Where could a respectable religious disagreement over social values or policies take place today? Not in the courts, the legislatures, the academy, the board room, the cyber street, or any sacred place of worship. The cultural wars over values are decreasingly fought between trustworthy rivals who respect each other. As a result, there are few models for this behavior and little inter-religious space for congenial contestation and collaboration between rivals. Americans can tell of the great ideological/religious adversaries, John Adams and Thomas Jefferson who developed into respectful friends without coming to consensus. The great military enemies, Ulysses S. Grant and Robert E. Lee, also provide moving examples of rivals who treated each other with honorable appreciation at the end of the Civil War.

The relevance of this study to national and world politics and religion should be clear: Without a legitimate and honorable place for religious and ideological persuasive contestation, frustrated advocates for change will find other means to contest seemingly unresolvable matters—including turning to inter-tribal or international wars or disruptive violence against civilian order.

To be forthcoming: I am a committed Latter-day Saint that dwells in Utah among my people. However, unlike many of my fellow Saints, I have found compelling warrants within Mormon orthodoxy and orthopraxy to seek divine influence from rival traditions that potently refute various LDS beliefs and practices. I thrive in the stimulating tension between different visions and suppose in my imagination that the God I revere does as well. I project from my own experience with critics I have come to respect that billions of people, now distrusting critics of each other, can learn to enjoy a kind of continual peaceful tension as trustworthy rivals. The God I worship could make things obviously clear to all of us by massive interventional revelation—and has chosen out of practical design not to do so. I believe that love is best proved in irreconcilable conflicts over things we value most—thus the radical pluralism provides a Providential, pragmatic way to develop more love. I imagine this condition to continue in any life-after-death that includes social persons of some kind.

This study of the conflict between a new revealed religion and older, established religions also founded on divine revelation and authority provides an interesting case study of non-negotiable, intractable, theological, ecclesiastical, and social religious conflict. Conflicting religious authority is a perennial problem. Revealed religions that answer the big questions regarding the true purpose and activity of the human soul now and after death provide the most important information there is.[1] Naturally, religious groups that claim an exclusive revealed break-through on these all-important questions are prone to antagonistic rivalry with those who contradict them.[2]

The methods of proselytizing that are of core interest in this book can best be grasped in the social-religious milieu that gave rise to them. The method of interpretation for this study is an analysis of historical texts and context.[3] To use Paul Ricoeur's term, I have "guessed" at the purposes of the protagonists after gathering as much information as seemed relevant and available.[4] At the end of this study I will employ several disciplinary

---

1. Hugh W. Nibley, *Approaching Zion*, 538–540, 554.
2. Scott Appleby, "Missions and the Making of Americans," in John D. Sarna, ed., *Minority Faiths and the American Prostestant Mainstream*, 232–278. For a book length treatment regarding rivalry in the contemporary Middle East, see R. Scott Appleby, *Spokesman for the Despised: Fundamentalist Leaders of the Middle East*.
3. Hans-Georg Gadamer has linked interpretation with understanding as if they were synonymous because language seems to be the very form of human interrelatedness and identity. However, that all humans grasp some form of language does not mean they understand each other as particular persons. I employ Gadamer's hermeneutical method with the critique that linguistic universality is analogous to biological universality. Hans-Georg Gadamer, *Truth and Method*, 364; Richard Bernstein, *Beyond Objectivism and Relativism: Science, Hermeneutics and Praxis*, 131–3; Mary Ann Stenger, "Gadamer's Hermeneutics as a Model for Cross-Cultural Understanding and Truth in Religion," 159–61.
4. See Paul Ricoeur, *The Conflict of Interpretations: Essays in Hermeneutics* and *Interpretation Theory: Discourse and the Surplus of Meaning*. On this point, Bruce Lincoln has said one cannot become an insider socially, religiously, or existentially,

lenses from the social sciences to elucidate aspects of the complex story. I will take positions with which readers can clearly argue. However, my primary bias is usually that of a social conflict theorist in the ever-open mode of radically pluralistic William James, not in the deterministic, materialistic mode of Karl Marx.

One over-riding purpose of this study is to persuade readers that certain ethical methods of inter and intra-religious contestation, if employed with skill, patience, and true care for the well-being of the rival or critic, will benefit the contestants and the societies in which they reside.[5] Today, conflicts over the purpose and destiny of humanity—religious and ideological in nature—exacerbate suspicion and contempt between billions of people facing economic and political stress over unevenly shared social and material resources. Mine is an ambitious goal for our tempestuous era: to provide the thoughtful desire—or passionate thought—that moves people towards a desire to experiment with new attitudes and healthy ways of engaging their critics and rivals in contests over what matters most. The evidence of history as I read it demands that we disenthrall ourselves from the desire to end conflict: rather, it is beneficial to cultivate the desire to sustain continual persuasive contestations over fundamentally unresolvable questions that guide our social order. I hope to engender among religious communities and secular enclaves serious desire to experiment with more fruitful ways of engaging in collaborative contestations.[6]

I theorize that particular forms of persuasive religious contestation can be healthy for both religions and societies; and more, that peacefulness in a pluralizing world depends on normalizing engaged contestation and col-

---

but one can do so linguistically. A language insider learns by imaginative trial and error guessing, not by belief. Bruce Lincoln, "Commentary on *Genealogies of Religion* by Talal Asad." I will examine later the close mutual influence between imagination and belief with respect to inter-religious differences and conflicts.

5. One description of the basic pragmatic method I have adapted here can be found concisely in Richard Rorty, *Objectivity, Relativism, and Truth: Philosophic Papers* 1, 110.

6. Throughout this study I will use the term competition, which in Latin means to seek or try to obtain along with another, in contrast to the term, contest. The former denotes a situation whereby several competitors are seeking similar ends without impeding or even being aware of each other. The latter, contest, is a form of conflict in which the contestants are aware of each other, and desire to surpass each other more than attain a goal. Where competitions allow shared ends, contests allow only one unsurpassed winner. See Georg Simmel, *Conflict and The Web of Group-Affiliations*, 57–58.

laboration between trustworthy religious or ideological rivals. In studying religious conflict, one faces the enormity of scope that is involved, and the uncanny dilemma of gaining precision by analytical reduction while losing the sense of inexhaustible vastness that the terms religion and conflict connote. While I occasionally employ traditional power/interest negotiation theory and conflict resolution theory, they are both inadequate for understanding fundamental religious conversion contests. They are based on a comparative scarcity of resources—the social, economic, and political power resources that a successful religion procures. Whether the end game is win-lose or win-win, the presumption of these theories is a resolution via some new power arrangement. We need a new theory that reflects the basic human desire for comparative supremacy even amid over-abundance of powerful resources. This theory observes the continual desire that is never resolved because it is not based on a lack, but on a gain achieved only if a close rival creates value for the gain.

Any difference brings with it an evaluative comparison and a desire for experiencing relative supremacy, in some form. In religious or ideological modes, it leads rivals for supremacy to face the frustrating problem that places success beyond their control: they cannot force conversions of the hearts and minds of their rivals. The very presence of the adamant rival calls into question the innate power of their religion to appeal to the whole of humanity. This causes a tension for resolution that many cannot patiently bear. So often we humans decide to free ourselves from disturbing, destabilizing criticism—once and for all—ironically by coercively eliminating the very people we had desired to freely join us.

This theory has interesting ramifications. Most presume peace is the positive result of social harmony. If we could see our critics in a broader context and understand their views, harmonic differences would blend, and peace would reign. This is a fundamentally incorrect assumption. Observe how human desire for uniqueness, originality, and comparative superiority intrudes on harmony. We desire close co-resistance as much as close collaboration. We thus need a conflict engagement theory based on disharmony, disagreement, and unresolvable, continual contestation over that which we value most: our unique values, passions, and purposes.[7]

---

7. James Duke lists the following ways conflicts can be terminated: a) disappearance of the object of conflict; b) complete victory and defeat (annihilation, exile, forced absorption); c) compromise; or d) conciliation. See James T. Duke, *Conflict and Power in Social Life*, 111. My theory adds a new termination category called conversion. It is a mutual victory of the vanquished

The theory I espouse, collaborative contestationalism, asserts the social and psychological benefit of sustaining conflicts over ideals in the mode of mutual persuasion contests between rivals that desire neither compromise nor final resolution.[8] The struggle to convert rivals to acknowledge one's superior position can never be final because supremacy is only manifest and maintained through the dynamic experience of engaged contestation. Ordinary power conflicts are compromised and resolved when interests are measured to mutual agreement. Conflicts of misunderstanding are resolved when parties are mutually aware of each other's real meanings, needs, and values.

Finally, this study aims to show that understanding the other does not always lead to resolution of conflict. Some conflicts are enhanced with a very clear understanding of irreconcilable differences. No enlightened intelligence or cosmopolitan sophistication will eliminate rival contests over ultimate truths of eternal importance, especially when they involve social change. Even in highly-educated societies, serious ideological or religious differences will continue to yield difficult conflicts. Just as a person may fear getting sick from someone contaminated with a disease, many are concerned that they and their communities might become infected by rivals who hold beliefs and values that they deem to be socially or eternally dangerous. To remain spiritually healthy, they attempt to avoid interaction with their rivals. The concern for tribal health increases in pluralistic societies where laws do not allow for the beliefs of rivals to be quarantined or expelled. Any assessment of the twenty-first century must look at this squarely.

Conflict over cultural contamination—without coercion—is a reasonably optimal outcome for society. My prescription for this public health problem of spiritual contamination is neither to find or found a new universalism, over-religion, meta-language, or meta-praxis that

---

and the victor. However, it is only a temporary termination, as it gives rise to new intra-group conflicts of heretical persuasions.

8. Social theorist Chantal Mouffe has promoted the idea that uneven distribution of social-economic power is a continual fact of political life manifest by agonistic subgroups seeking, but never finally achieving, hegemonic political supremacy. Her theory of managing with limited violence the continual engagement of rival challengers reflects James Madison's insight that rival interpreting factions will inevitably emerge from any perceived consensus, and thus peace cannot seriously be conceived as tranquil unity of factions, but as dynamic contestation without violent disorder. See Chantal Mouffe, *Agonistics: Thinking the World Politically*; James Madison, *Federalist Papers* 10 and 51.

will convince everyone that our differences are not dangerous. This approach feels like arrogant effrontery, even if well-intended. The effective prescription is mutual contamination by means of principled advocacy. This allows healthy interreligious contestation and collaboration without precipitating resentment, coercion, and violence. I appreciate the desire that many share for social-spiritual convergence in a philosophical religious universalism, but argue that the very hope for peaceful community that such universalism implies is unfounded. I suggest that humans would inevitably invent conflict if they had to live in harmony for very long.[9] The Christian Bible provocatively reveals there was war in heaven (Rev. 12:7). So how on earth can the cultural and religious inheritors of that sacred text expect tranquility?

---

9. William Blake sets the tone for positive conflict. From Blake's *Milton* we learn that Contraries are Positives. A Negation is not a Contrary. From *The Marriage of Heaven and Hell* we learn that reality consists never of One and the Other in Complete Harmony, but always One or the Other in Free Necessity to Love or Not. For a reading of Blake's ironic disparagement of Eternal Harmony and his celebration of the "eternality" of marriage of contraries that has influenced my study, see Robert Gleckner, "The Road of Excess," 114–17.

CHAPTER ONE

The American Lively Experiment: Sustaining Religious Rivalry and Peace

America's foundational document proclaimed that the Creator endowed all people with life and the liberty to pursue happiness. Their political order was an experiment to test whether millions of different people, together in one society, could freely pursue their conflicting, often mutually exclusive, ideals and programs for happiness without frustration and anger leading to coercion and social destruction. There is no fixed American creed or ideal for happiness upon which legitimate social order rests. The American experiment is based on mutual trust between citizens who agree not to resort to coercion or violence in their pursuit of happiness. The legitimacy of their governing order is not vested in the rule of law, but in a cultivated respect—if not love—for free rivals. Foremost, this applies to rivals that unceasingly challenge and contest our idealistic or religious purposes and programs for happiness. Breaking with thousands of years of tradition whereby social order was based on a given heavenly order mediated through priests, oracles, kings, and emperors, the American founding affirmed that the Creator gave men and women the unmediated responsibility to rule themselves. The foundation for their decisions was the human conscience influenced by both divine inspiration and natural reason. This required each citizen to learn from past sources and decide how to interpret and receive their influence without coercion from outsiders. This individual freedom opened the door to perpetual disagreements over the true or best purposes and methods that would bring happiness in our social union. To repeat for emphasis, America is not founded on a unifying Ideal or Truth, but on a way of embracing unresolvable never-ending contestations between rivals who actively influence others to follow their way toward happiness, first through socialization of their children, then exemplary living, and finally by various modes of public persuasion. This dynamic social process of continual contestation was constrained as orderly collaboration in two ways: first by civil laws that allowed no coercion of belief or practice—legal or physical—to be employed by rivals or opponents; and second by the cultivated habitual attitude of patient engagement that allowed critics or rivals a full voice—not just to ensure the reciprocal right for oneself but, crucially, to receive the influence of an opponent who is not necessarily an enemy. For many American believers this meant that God, their divine governor, provided the perfect social model, restraining himself from imposing coercive sovereignty on human consciences, preferring to win the contest for the soul by means of inspirational persuasion—at least until the Final Judgment.

By contrast, during the same epoch, Napoleon took the French crown from the Catholic bishop's hands and placed it on his own head. His action let God and religious institutions know they were no longer needed in Europe except perhaps for sentimental reasons. The French aimed to end centuries of violent conflict over religion by denouncing all quarreling acolytes. The unifying mission was to civilize the world as enlightened French people. America's founders were more collegial with their Creator, claiming He wanted them to be grateful for the freedom He granted them to sincerely worship Him as their consciences allowed. They gratefully acknowledged that God had granted all humans radical sovereignty to choose their own religious and social order. Further, leaning on Jesus's pronouncement to make disciples of all the nations, Christians came to believe God did not intend for each person to maintain primary allegiance to their family and culture. They did not think it strange to engage actively in intramural evangelizing contests. No people or country had come to so highly value the individual choice of religious belief—indeed, it was the national pastime well before baseball. Americans kept their rowdy peace by containing it as a persuasion contest between free and sovereign consciences that simply could not be coerced. More, for their society to thrive, the free give and take of this contest of conscience had to be invigorating rather than exhausting and had to be coupled with an attitude of patience in the freedom of a rival to resist persuasion.

The Enlightenment fight against the church especially in France had turned into a conflict with God. Citizens of the secular religion of the French Revolution replaced the authority of the Roman Catholic Church with the state. The American Revolution did not need to overthrow any religious authority because Americans had, from the early years of colonization, been separating themselves from the influence of a State church; they had no dominant religion common among them. They were far from a unified nation of believers in a single form of Christianity.

God and Humans: Co-Sovereigns in America

Most early Americans possessed a self-confident Protestant spirituality derived from their understanding of a New Testament emphasis on personal salvation attained by responding faithfully to the Biblical testimony of witnesses of Jesus as divine redeemer—whether pre-determined or not. Protestants rejected the need for sacerdotal mediation between God and men. To be sure, the early Puritans had made a covenant to be upheld in a congregation of similar believers, but eventually the authority of the leaders or the congregation became less important than the integrity of the individual vis-à-vis God. In the tug of war between loyalty to community and integrity of conscience and between salvation as a group and salvation as an individual, the Americans have struggled without resolution to the present day. Individual spiritual integrity required each person to freely choose to follow the innate good conscience provided by the Spirit of God. But the Spirit seems to inspire dissociation as much as unity. This inner call, in many if not most cases, was more compelling than family, tribal, political, or ecclesiastical loyalty. It was the custom still to join a group of like-minded souls as a free act of Christian fellowship, but the divine right to follow one's God-given conscience in switching—among Christian religious denominations initially and then among all philosophies—became the American norm. For believers this placed each person in a powerful negotiating position with a God who desired to save him or her. Whatever our philosophy or religion, the social-psychological and cultural power of resistance and attraction between co-sovereign free lovers is at the heart of American sensitivity.

The tension over the true provenance and destiny of each human person has been at the heart of Euro-American culture. The can-do Americans found a liberating story of the divine within them more inspiring than these distancing alternatives. Rejecting the notion they were just enlightened apes without a connection to the divine, they reversed the focus of theology toward understanding why and how humanity could conceivably be the unique beloved subjects of the Divine Loving Parent that Jesus had revealed to the world. In the nineteenth century many Americans resonated with the Christian scriptures in which the divine Jesus called his human disciples no longer servants but friends who were one with him and the Father (John 15:15).[1] This provided spiritual confidence that God

---

1. This book will employ the gender specific usage of the earliest New Testament texts with reference to God and Jesus. Late in the twentieth century, many

designed humans to choose to love and believe, freely making their lives true unforced testimonies of what they valued most. Crucially, this provided the theological approval for a social-political system assuring that all humans are free to accept or reject any religious beliefs—and to love God as a sincere loving friend does free of compulsion.

The belief and attitude that religious lives should be uncoerced produced unique religious political leaders like Roger Williams in the seventeenth century and social theorists like James Madison in the eighteenth century who acknowledged the priority of their fellow citizens' God-given and godlike freedom of conscience. This attitude, in turn, allowed a lively experiment in government that encouraged perpetual persuasive contestations over fundamental questions of truth, ethics, religion, goodness, and purpose. In sum, the Christian God that identified with uncoerced love of persons found its first political expression in America. Love made unfettered individual choice inevitable; the moment we love another person, we face the ever-open and never final question of how best to do so.[2]

When eternal salvation and damnation are at stake, religious disagreement among persons with integrity always creates strong dissonance over

---

Protestant and other theologians have employed gender-neutral or affirmative female gender language to scripture. Gendered language with respect to God in Christian theology is controversial. Protestants have no doctrine regarding a female deity. The Roman Catholics had affirmed a feminine alternative to the mediating aspect of the God-*Man* Jesus in Mary, The Bearer of God, who was born without taint of sin and was assumed bodily into heaven at the end of her mortality where she pleads to the Father for the forgiveness of humanity. (The Immaculate Conception and Assumption of Mary became formal doctrines in 1854 and 1950 respectively.) Still, no *She* is a member of the traditional Christian Godhead. However, Mormons in the nineteenth century affirmed the material body of God, the Heavenly Father, and that an unnamed material female divinity called Heavenly Mother was the wife of the Heavenly Father.

2. The tension between the idea of absolute sovereign control of God and an open divine and human freedom arises with the idea that virtue or love cannot be coerced or predetermined to be real. This tension over divine control and human freedom was at the heart of the American founding. See Paul V. Murphy, *The Rebuke of History: The Southern Agrarians and American Conservative Thought*, 42–44, esp. note 52. In the seventeenth century, John Milton examined this tension in *Paradise Lost* where Adam and Eve's fall was affirmed as a condition for freedom. We will see in this study that Protestants elevate absolute divine sovereignty and Mormons extol free agency in this disagreement over whether humans are liberatingly fettered by the fall.

who is right. Remarkably, some Americans faced it by finding uncanny enjoyment in the attractive intelligence and integrity of their religious rivals who might, nonetheless, be heading for damnation in their view. The unsentimental love of an honorable rival sprouted with Roger Williams in the 1600s and eventually bore fruit in the way Americans tend to view their prior enemies after wars—especially after their vicious and most costly Civil War. Such is expressed in these nineteenth-century stanzas of Henry David Thoreau. Thoreau's sentiments could stand as the theme for any realistic hopefulness as we face irresolvable religious and political conflicts in the twenty-first century:

> Let such pure hate still underprop
> Our love, that we may be
> Each other's conscience,
> And have our sympathy
> Mainly from thence.
>
> We'll one another treat like gods
> And all faith we have
> In virtue and in truth, bestow
> On either, and suspicion leave
> To gods below.[3]

Thoreau's "pure hate" derives from the conflict between people whose pure love for each other requires their paradoxical mutual opposition. To engage in persuasive mutual contestation with integrity is to honor the unfettered freedom of the other to present their highest ideals without any desire to coerce conversion. Only "gods below" think they can, and thus try and fail, to influence a change of heart by force.

The innate authority to follow conscience in the contestation over truth provided the basis for individual sovereignty as a founding tenet for the new nation. Whether conscience meant the spirit of God telling the mind the truth or illuminating the soul to hear the truth, humans were responsibly free to follow or not follow their inner voice.

Since many religions have existed in America—and since personal religious experiences produce no universal basis for resolving disagreements—conflicts over God's opinions have been frequent. Those who announce they have experienced two-way communion with deity on a public issue offend those who claim contradictory revelations, or who feel

---

3. Henry David Thoreau, "Let Such Pure Hate Still Underprop."

left out of the divine conversation. All doubt the others' reliability, and most conclude that no one should speak officially for deity.

The fallback position is one-way communication *to*, not *with*, deity. Denominations may still privately believe that they have a special relationship with God in which they experience God's specific directions, but the scandal of divisive religion is generally overcome—at least enough to keep the peace—by the social philosophy of "one nation under God." In terms of civic religion, Americans quasi-officially trust in a God of public prayer, pledges of allegiance, and mottos on coinage, yet many have developed rich, localized, religious lives that they balance against their national religious expression of pious humanism or deism that unites them enough for the government to govern.

The Great Code for Correct Conflict

Even though the government they established had no official religion, the self-identity of the founders and other early Americans was still deeply rooted in the Bible, perhaps the most powerful moral narrative to ever influence humanity. After many centuries, it had come to provide a code or way of thinking about all aspects of life, but especially social conflicts over the right way to live under the divine Eye.[4] Although twenty-first-century Americans are hardly as conversant in Biblical lore as their eighteenth-century ancestors, they have inherited an unwritten code of conduct heavily influenced by the Biblical narrative. From the Hebrew Genesis to the Christian Apocalypse, the theme resounds of conflict between God and his chosen people, between the chosen people themselves, and between the chosen people and their surrounding cultures. In response to the demands of a God who is jealous for the love of all humanity, the chosen people must confront and challenge those who do not worship the True God, which would inevitably lead to conflict—not only with strangers and enemies, but also with family and friends. While some Biblical stories denounce conflict over material or political power, conflict over ultimate questions of purpose and righteousness are shown to be humanity's main event—a sign that divine truth and goodness are continually at work expanding and resisting falsehood and evil.

Aware of the violence that has erupted over religious difference, America's founders recognized themselves as a new chosen people with a social order that would require authority to contain the inevitable conflicts

---

4. Northrup Frye, *The Great Code: The Bible and Literature*.

within their kingless society. They experimented with a unique way to sustain religious conflicts with as little violence as possible by normalizing contestation in the persuasive mode. Evangelizing and counter-evangelizing, shouting your different views of truth out loud in speeches, sermons, newspapers, and pamphlets normally without resorting to coercion, became the American way of religious, political, economic, and social life.

In America, the state accepts that its citizens disagree about ultimate reality or religious authority, and that non-violent contestations over them can be appropriate. American constitutional democracy provided a scaffolding to sustain religious and ideological conflicts, not eliminate them. It is no coincidence that religious freedom was included among the first of freedoms in the Bill of Rights—along with the freedom of speech, a free press, and the right to assemble, which are necessary for people to engage in persuasive contests over truth and ultimate purpose.

However, even as the government affirmed the right to persuasive contestation, the deep Biblical code provided a different, darker precedent—preemptive violence (a massive flood, a Canaanite genocide, capital punishment for false preaching) allegedly sanctioned by divine representatives to assure uncontaminated growth of truth and righteousness. A main narrative theme throughout the Bible is of God speaking through human mediators, and of the intended recipients often strongly disagreeing with the message's validity. Thus, religious conflicts derive often from disagreements over who is authorized to represent God's will to humanity, or over the actual merits of different doctrinal claims or ethical programs coming from self-proclaimed authorized representatives.

Despite the all-powerful sovereign threat of annihilation, the Biblical code affirms that the Creator King desires company, a kingdom of human beings that honor and even love Him. Theologically speaking, there is no absolute authority—it has its limits in the divine desire for subjects to freely choose to follow the King without threatening compulsion.[5] In the desire to be loved by free agents, the King radically shifts the foundation of authority to a living mutual relationship of trust instead of the absolute power of a Creator to do whatever He desires with His creations. Without any threats or bribes, authority is thus granted by loving consent of followers to the leader.

---

5. Hannah Arendt's analysis of political authority is germane. See Hannah Arendt, *Between Past and Future: Eight Exercises in Political Thought*, 93, 102–3, 128–29.

To avoid social chaos, some leadership is required, but why do people grant authority to one person or group and not another? Governments or religions whose leaders can gracefully obtain uncoerced authority have the best chance of flourishing. Because of this, religious conflicts that challenge authorized leadership are extremely serious. They not only call into question who should be leading that society, but they also threaten the order that assures salvation in worlds to come. The conflict-engendering dilemma we inherit from the Biblical code is provoked by the divine injunction, "Choose you this day whom you will serve" (Josh. 24:15).

Even Deeper than Morality and Law

The term "mores" denotes the typically religious social understandings that lead to unquestioned practices that provide a society its identity, values, and deep purposes. Mores, which are taken for granted, undergird a society's enduring institutions, laws, and traditions. Most cultures have invoked the divine as the earliest foundation for social and political legitimacy.[6] The longest lasting social organizations on the planet also sustain legitimacy by appealing to divine constancy through centuries of change. Religious and ideological groups that spread throughout the globe can survive cross-cultural conflicts through their unifying mores and foundational myths.[7]

Religious doctrines reflect and develop the mores of social cohesion in a way that formal law can never replicate. Traditionally, a society that lasts learns to interweave the oughts and ought nots of its common mores with its laws. When citizens share similar mores, they develop positive programs enforced by laws that they think are appropriate. However, when there is a conflict over the authoritative foundations of society—that is, a conflict over the mores that undergird the law—schism arises as people disagree over the correctness of their laws. Religious differences that display a conflict of mores can severely test the ability of any society to remain intact. As we shall see in the next chapter, on three occasions in American history, religious piety directly led to a snap of the limits that common mores could bear—with violent results.

The First Amendment was an attempt to leave to the individual states and churches the problem of religious conflicts over mores that developed

---

6. For a classic theoretical treatment of this, see Georges Dumézil, *The Destiny of a King*.

7. See the theoretical basis for this claim in Alexis de Toqueville, *Democracy in America*, 292–93 and Antonio Gramsci, *Selections from the Prison Notebooks*.

within their borders and congregations. By the late nineteenth century, all of the states had ended their legal support for a particular religion, so the government's remaining task became establishing, by court ruling or legislation, those religious behaviors that offended American mores enough to require negative sanctions. In the case of social conflicts of interest, since these types of disputes are typically quantifiable and fungible, compromises are usually effective in maintaining stability. But in the case of conflicts of identity, compromise seems impossible—hence cries in times past and present that even one slave is too many, or two wives is too many, or one interracial or homosexual marriage is too many. For those holding fast to certain mores, compromising the moral truth even once would concede that their truth does not really matter. In short, Americans can be tolerant of conflicting *beliefs* but not of conflicting *mores* that influence behaviors, especially if those mores are held by a group that is a geopolitical competitor for cultural power. If a subculture's mores come to differ from the majority culture's mores, a secession crisis can occur; it means that the main culture has failed to persuade the subculture that it is wrong, or vice versa. At that point, the use of some form of coercion is inevitable.

Morality may be legislated, but mores always precede law. For this reason, republican democracies with identical systems of law function very differently in societies with different mores. Because they operate at such a core level, conflicts over mores are often seen as religious in nature—such as when Southern mores like slavery, or Mormon mores like polygamy, or Native American mores regarding property, family, and sacred practices conflicted with majority mores. As evidence, each of these conflicts was viewed first as conflict over right and wrong and only secondarily as conflict over power and interest. In these cases, when the tensions between mores could no longer be sustained, the majority imposed negative legal sanctions before ultimately using force to keep the United States intact. The immediate result was the creation of three major geographic reservations—the South, Utah, and Indian reservations—the existence of which allowed the divergent groups that formed the greater American society to feel unified by comparison.

Though religion generates contests that separate communities, it also generates mores of solidarity and loyalty that are often stronger than allegiances to kith, kin, nationality, or ethnicity. The social power a religion holds is derived from the pervasive, uncoerced, continuous authority that members of that group grant to their leaders. A community can become a very powerful force if it can generate a strong degree of solidarity. Religion is the best example of genuine social power created through common mores that are not enforced by totalitarian or democratic means. As we can see in today's world, the largest faith traditions have each attained enough authority across cultural and international borders that disparate peoples, races, nation/tribes, and even states share purposes and allegiances beyond local interests. Viewed internationally, religiously authorized cross-cultural mores are the most powerful cultural influences in today's world.

Many early Americans inherited the belief that sharing the right Protestant religious ways played an important community-building role in establishing norms for personal, social, and political life. Hence Alexis de Tocqueville's observation: "I have known Americans to form associations to send priests out into the new states of the West and establish schools and churches there; they fear that religion might be lost in the depths of the forest and that the people growing up there might be less fitted for freedom than those from whom they sprang."[8] In describing this phenomenon, Tocqueville is focusing on the overt unanimity of Protestant Christian mores—not belief in doctrines per se—that sustained the free institutions in America. He writes: "No one in the United States has dared to profess the maxim that everything is allowed in the interests of society" because "American revolutionaries are obliged ostensibly to profess a certain respect for Christian morality and equity, and that does not allow them easily to break the laws when those are opposed to the execution of their designs."[9]

Tocqueville's theory that common religious mores make it possible for people to uphold laws together is the essence of the problem at the heart of the American experiment with pluralism. When religious mores are truly diverse among large sectors of society, will there yet be enough social cohesion for a nation to stand undivided? Designed to evade the violent confrontations between social, religious, and political rivals that had caused years of bloodshed in Europe, America was and still is a precarious experimental contest in the practical limits of cooperation among voluntary associations. While the American Founders anticipated these contests for religious supremacy, they hoped to prove that the continual contestation between various factions would check and balance the overwhelming power of any individual faction.

While a broadly popular religion is a powerful political force for stability, the desire to keep true religion from being contaminated usually

---

8. Tocqueville, *Democracy*, 292–93.
9. Tocqueville, 292.

provokes criticism between factions who see each other as heretical. When this occurs, their desire to keep order and purity often leads them to exercise religious coercion, which, in turn, often leads to counter-coercion and, at times, violence.

Fairly understood, freedom describes a dual capacity to persuade and be persuaded. Freedom increases only as those two capacities increase. The freedom to change oneself, to become a convert, is as radical as the freedom to advocate change in others. Persuasion is never finished. This is the other experimental aspect of the American way: once converted, we can be converted again. It is the search for truth, or the continual testing of truth already found, that is the key to the American experiment. When American Protestants decided that they could no longer get along with heretics within their ranks, they would split in schism. There was no need to create laws against that. But as Tocqueville saw, since social cohesion and the rule of law arise from general acceptance of ethical and religious mores, when substantial numbers of people in a society hold very different ethical and religious mores, the social order might reach its limits to sustain cohesion though persuasive contestation. For instance, while he believed that Catholics, who shared similar enough mores, would eventually be assimilated successfully among Protestants, he did not think Native Americans, African Americans, nor charismatic prophet/leaders would be assimilated as equal citizens among white Anglo-Saxon Protestants.[10] As we shall discuss, history proved him partially right in his predictions.

Whose Promised Land Is This?

From the earliest colonies, American political and religious contests were engaged by clustered communities of people holding similar beliefs, mores, and interests; and in American democracy, social-political power was obtained by voting majorities in geo-political concentrations. As a result, large aspects of the American experiment were engaged as continual contests for land control. Religious beliefs and political interests melded in questions over the purposes that various groups had for gathering on particular sections of land as the nation expanded. Different groups from Europe settled each colony for a different purpose, establishing separate cultures with divergent values.[11] For early New England colonists, the

---

10. Tocqueville, 317, 341, 435.
11. Colin Woodard, *American Nations: A History of Eleven Rival Regional Cultures of North America*, 1–3.

"empty" continent was a savage place, not holy in advance of their arrival. In their view, it was they, the people of divine promise, who made America the "promised land." Massachusetts became the land of promise when John Winthrop declared it so.[12] Although the Mormons believed that Jackson County, Missouri, was the locale of the eschatological New Jerusalem, they nimbly followed Brigham Young to Utah where they created another promised land. Since the days of the earliest colonies, contests ensued over which religious group—including the Indians—would make the promised land of the Americas holy. To the European Christians who chose to settle here, the land north of Mexico seemed to be void of the important forms—such as temples, churches, and permanent cities—that belie an eternal order. Hence, it seemed to be waiting for them to take or purchase it from the nomads already present on it, whose ownership claims seemed to them to have false legitimacy compared to the colonists' divine right to establish an orderly kingdom based on true religion that was to spread to all nations.

Is one nation destined to inherit the earth, along with the meek? Who decides whether one culture should expand or not? Does prior occupancy of land justify continued occupancy or expansion on it? It is an uncomfortable fact that every culture exists in tension with other forms of life, and historically cultures have exploited or displaced those who have allowed them to grow. Violent pushing and shoving have usually, if not always, occurred when a new nation is established on any previously inhabited land.[13] There were missionaries like Roger Williams who evangelized while respecting the consciences, religions, and cultures of the na-

---

12. The chosen people motif did not begin with the Massachusetts Puritans. The new American continents were claimed by the Roman Catholics as well. In 1493, Pope Alexander VI enunciated the Spanish/Catholic responsibility to colonize the world with true religion and declared the right of missionaries to acquire new land and converts with their free consent and fair payment. However, tellingly, most of the Christian colonizers believed they were warranted in taking the land by force if the native peoples would not allow evangelizing or promise to avoid violent resistance to them. See Paul Gottschalk, *The Earliest Diplomatic Documents of America*, 21; Ward Churchill, *Struggle for Land: Indigenous Resistance to Genocide, Ecocide, and Expropriation in Contemporary North America*, 47–48, 64n8.

13. While I disagree with Rene Girard's thesis that all cultures are built on a ritual order that regularly sacrifices the weakest to placate the general pent-up envy that, without the scapegoat, would lead to violent destruction of the group, it is nonetheless difficult, if not impossible, to historically discover human cultures that do not experience violent conflict due to their own expansion or

tive populations, but they were not the majority. While Cortez was more direct in his military approach to seizing control of land than Winthrop, European Americans, drawing upon the Biblical *herem* (holiness) code of Israel in Canaan as justification for their acts, eventually usurped the best land, killed or exiled the indigenous tribes, and established their sacred promised land. American Christians thought their mission was affirmed by geo-political expansion, while at the same time felt threatened by the cultures and religions they were trying to convert.

Peaceful Conflict is Not an Oxymoron

The American founding documents did not confront social conflicts between religious rivals directly. However, the framers handled the matter discretely behind the facade of the preamble to the Declaration of Independence that promoted vague deism as the safest way to publicly discuss religion without eliciting sectarian revolts. The Declaration's language encompassed any religion that believed God was the creator of human beings, appealing to "the separate and equal station to which the Laws of Nature and of Nature's God entitle them, . . . that all men are created equal, that they are endowed by their Creator with certain unalienable Rights."[14] With its lack of doctrine and clergy, and its emphasis on a deity uninvolved in human affairs, deism was a poor proselytizer; but it included a powerful lay priesthood of all-citizens-under-God. As James Madison proclaimed, "Before any man can be considered a member of civil society, he must be considered as a subject of the governor of the universe; and every man who becomes a member of a civil society does it, saving his allegiance to the universal sovereign."[15] Madison, nevertheless, knew better. He knew from history that people see "their Creator" from such different perspectives that they would inevitably call each other's views blasphemous perversions of the divine. No motto on a nation's currency would ever negate the fact that in America, as elsewhere, millions of people believe their religious rivals are dangerously spreading falsehoods that will do damage to individual souls as well as the greater society.

Since Madison believed that religious conflict was inevitable, his focus went to containing, not constraining it:

---

that of others. See Rene Girard, *Violence and the Sacred* and *Things Hidden From the Foundation of the World*.

14. Thomas Jefferson, *The Declaration of Independence*, first published July 4, 1776.
15. Sidney E. Mead, *The Nation with the Soul of a Church*, 67.

> There are two methods of curing the mischiefs of faction: the one, by removing its causes; the other, by controlling its effects. There are again two methods of removing the causes of faction: the one, by destroying the liberty which is essential to its existence; the other, by giving to every citizen the same opinions, the same passions, and the same interests. It could never be more truly said of the first remedy that it was worse than the disease. . . . The second expedient is as impracticable as the first would be unwise. . . . The diversity in the faculties of men, from which the rights of property originate, [is an] insuperable obstacle to a uniformity of interests. . . . The latent causes of faction are thus sown in the nature of man; and we see them . . . [as] a zeal for different opinions concerning religion, concerning government, and many other points. . . . The causes of faction cannot be removed and [therefore] relief is only to be sought in the means of controlling its effects. . . . A religious sect may degenerate into a political faction in a part of the [nation]; but the variety of sects dispersed over the entire face of it must secure the national councils against any danger from that source. . . . Any other improper or wicked project, will be less apt to pervade the whole body of the Union than a particular member of it.[16]

The government, therefore, was to set limits on religious behavior that disturbed the peace, but it would not attempt to mediate religious conflicts. Religions, like other ambitious factional interests, would check each other by critical scrutiny and public antagonism. Madison knew there were no disinterested congressmen, judges, presidents, or priests. He concluded that the only hope for lasting, orderly freedom was, ironically, an optimal amount of continuous, pervasive, interactive factionalism.

Whenever a society seeks to establish some great reform to correct a prior regime or to benefit a particular group for any reason, a clash of ideological or religious beliefs about the status quo is inevitable. The question remains, though, about which religious groups or ideological movements should survive the continual conflicts between them and, by surviving, establish their ways of life among the American people and beyond. The Constitution forbids Congress to establish a religion or to limit its free exercise, but it provides no way of determining the best ideology or religion. As a result, the Supreme Court has had to develop a body of precedents to help determine when the government is justified in using force to curtail religious practices that threaten national unity by challenging broadly held cultural norms and mores.[17]

---

16. Jacob E. Cooke, ed., *The Federalist*, 52.
17. Jace Weaver, ed., *Native American Religious Identity: Unforgotten Gods*, 224–27.

From Wounded Knee to Waco, from peyote to polygamy, the legal use of state force over sacred activity has been controversial in America because of the conflicts that arise from the diverse mores among legislators and interpreters of the law. The First Amendment religious exercise clause was tested in the 1878 decision *Reynolds vs. The United States*. In justifying its decision, the court essentially declared that Mormons were not Christians—at least of the stripe who founded the United States and whose values provided its stability. Using religiously-charged language, the court unanimously upheld a bigamy law that outlawed Mormon polygamy as "contrary to the spirit of Christianity and of the civilization which Christianity has produced in the Western world. . . . The state has a perfect right to prohibit polygamy, and all other offenses against the enlightened sentiment of mankind."[18] However, in a 1940 ruling, *Cantwell vs. Connecticut*, the high court held that it was legal for religions to proselytize even if their activity might lead to public disorder. Ninety-six years after *Reynolds*, in *Wisconsin vs. Yoder*, the Supreme Court decided that the Amish could defy state schooling laws on religious grounds. In rendering that decision, Justice William Douglas opined, "*Reynolds* said the state could punish even deep, sincere, long-lasting convictions—*Yoder* opens the way, and even promises, that in time *Reynolds* will be over-ruled."[19] Because of the court's ability to create new precedent as circumstances and mores shift through time, the American experiment has survived most of its religious conflicts without having to use direct force.

What has emerged today is a general feeling that for the government to act for or against religion, the justification must rest on some compelling state interest that supersedes any particular religious interest. America thus relies on decisive legislation or court directives to govern religious conflicts. Any doctrine of neutrality admittedly swerves back and forth across the neutral centerline.

Although Madison believed interreligious conflict was a sign of a healthy, pluralistic society asserting its inevitable cross-purposes, the three violent religious conflicts discussed in the next chapter were too divisive to feel healthy, even within a diverse society. Perhaps embarrassed by this failure to mediate without violence, religious differences in the twentieth century were played down in attempt to create greater tranquility. Further, secular humanism became a sign of sophistication in many sectors of educated society. As a result, it became indelicate to discuss religious dif-

---

18. *Reynolds vs. The United States* (1878).
19. Edwin S. Gaustad, *Dissent in American Religion*, 99–141.

ferences in public, and cultured people typically looked down on overt proselytizing as a dangerous vestige or a time when naive people believed God cared about religious affiliation.

Historians have described the seventeenth-century founding of an American Zion as an experiment in toleration of diversity, one designed to avoid the violent religious conflicts Europe experienced, including the additional blood spilt through its various attempts to end such conflicts once and for all by establishing a secular-utopian worldview based on Enlightenment ideals.[20]

To claim an invisible unity of Christians and soften their schisms to nominal differences, Protestant Americans developed the strategy of calling different churches "denominations." The denominational system permitted hundreds of small churches to compete for an eventual spot in the oligopoly that became known as the Protestant mainstream, consisting primarily of Baptist, Methodist, Presbyterian, Lutheran, Congregationalist, and Episcopalian churches. By the early twentieth century, Congregationalist and Unitarians were waning, and Roman Catholicism and Judaism were becoming strong contenders for a place within the oligopoly. Schisms and mergers took place between Pentecostal churches, Church(es) of Christ, and others. However, in the nineteenth and early twentieth centuries, Mormons and Native American religions were not considered acceptable prospects for mainline religious acceptability.

The First Amendment effectively legitimated the conflicts between and within sects that claimed mutually exclusive correctness. The main danger, it was assumed, was establishing one national religion supported by taxes. The idea was to maintain a salutary conflict of religions by allowing aggressive, nonviolent intolerance. Initially, a state could not legislate a citizen's belief, but still allowed legal coercion to support the state's established church. In its essence the political strategy was to use the comforting language of unity while systematically planning for interminable local conflict. While European leaders tried to replace religious establishments with adamant scientific skepticism, American leaders emphasized the freedom of conscience to choose one's religious way. The American Protestant sects, though frequently trying for converts, had de-

---

20. For example, eschewing religious conflict, the French Revolution proclaimed the replacement of moribund Christendom with an ideological secular Zion that would unite a new European culture with a *telos* of beauty and progress. See Robertson and Chirico "Humanity, Globalization, and Worldwide Religious Resurgence: A Theoretical Exploration," 240–41.

cided "sheep stealing" between them caused too much resentment, so they preached patience in awaiting the ultimate eschaton when the triumphant flavor of divine religion would be clearly revealed. Until then, inoffensive, government-sponsored deism would suffice for most public discourse.[21] However vague it might be, Americans developed a sense of national inclusive religious feeling that Europe had lost through its efforts to end the kinds of violent clashes over religion that had so dominated its past.

Patience is a complex American trait.[22] One must be patient with the free conscience of any citizen to resist our truth. However, we sometimes feel called to impatiently proclaim the truth as we see it. In the case of Joseph Smith, the Mormon prophet, both his expansive originality and his critical closeness to Christianity provoked antagonism and stretched patience to the breaking point. We will now explore war with Mormons and two other groups that Americans could not accommodate let alone absorb into normal society.

---

21. Mead, *The Nation with the Soul of a Church*, 22.

22. Martha Nussbaum extols the virtue of Patience to bring Peace and Truth together without coercion and violence in her excellent analysis of liberty of conscience and the value of equal political treatment for all religions. Adopting Roger Williams's personification of Patience, Peace, and Truth, she notes how human pride and the desire to be surely and safely right about religion will assure continual conflicts. However, she seems disinclined to acknowledge that continual religious conflicts will also result from the virtuous desire to help others—a desire that motivates many to proclaim the superiority of one religious way over others out of sincerity of conscience not arrogance of personality. See Martha Nussbaum, *Liberty of Conscience: In Defense of America's Tradition of Religious Equality*, 360–63.

CHAPTER TWO

Violent American Religious Conflicts: Three Strong Cases

Geographer and historian D. W. Meinig categorized the United States as an empire containing sub-nations, which he defined as large ethnic and religious groups who are geographically concentrated and intra-marry in large numbers. From within each sub-nation's geographic and ideological space, the empire is viewed as a foreign power. They may view their connection to the empire as important to their own interests, but if forced to choose between allegiances, members within these smaller nations have higher loyalty to their own group and its mores and ideals than to that of the larger empire.

Using Meinig's model, the three most provocative geographically-centered sub-nations in the history of the United States empire have been the antebellum Southerners, Mormons, and Native Americans.[1] The empire's theoretical plan for these sub-nations was to reform their unacceptable tribal behaviors, make them conform to the majority's mores by converting the people to correct religious beliefs, and legally coerce conformity even if they were not converted ideologically. If nonviolent coercion failed, legal violence such as incarceration or war was next. The South, Utah Territory, and the various Native American reservations acted as temporary holding areas until the religious and ethnic solidarity of each group dissolved, transforming these distinct people into "ordinary American individuals" who would cease voting as a bloc or resisting as a group—their loyalty to the State having become more important than their ideological, religious, or ethnic interests.[2]

---

1. Roman Catholics and Jews also were sub-nations, at least initially, but were dispersed quickly and did not make clear geographical claims on the land.

2. It took more than one hundred years for individuals in the South to be infiltrated by enough Northerners to make the geopolitical bloc more diverse. It took about one hundred years for the Mormons in Utah to be diluted by roughly fifty-percent through immigration of others. Native Americans still hold mostly to their reservations. As a matter of convention, in this book I use the term

In each case, when the majority began fearing that the sub-nation possessed enough power to influence prevailing mores, they forced the issue. For example, Reconstruction followed the Civil War, the 1887 Edmunds-Tucker Act dissolved the Mormon Church's legal right to own property, and the Dawes Act ended tribal ownership of land. These legal acts were all distinctively harsh displays of imperial power. As Meinig states, these actions were evidence of the "refusal to accept geopolitical territories defined essentially in ethnic or religious terms."[3]

For both these sub-nations and the larger empire, their conflicts were primarily religious: conflicts over the right way to live, justified by religious authority that overrode the opponent's political power and social mores. Even for Americans who were disinterested in religious differences, there remained economic and political concerns that potential shifts of power represented. The religious aspects of the Civil War, the Mormon battles, and the Native American wars were also deeply intertwined with economics and politics.

As discussed, America's founders assumed that sectional factions would play a major role in national politics, giving equal representation to each state regardless of population. However, the government could not function if a significant number of states, united on sectional issues, refused to budge. There was no mechanism in place to force the people to compromise. In the end, the Civil War, the Mormon wars, and the Indian wars were each fought because neither side could convert these sub-nations to allegiance to a national unity of belief. At the extreme, refusal to engage on core issues becomes secession; and these nations' uncompromising bloc voting or group resistance to social norms of the majority ultimately troubled Americans enough to use violence to keep these factions from splitting the empire.

Religious, social, and economic issues sparked the conflicts, but ethnic and geopolitical separation made violence a realistic option. Granted the equal weight given to each state by the U.S. Senate, it is biased towards region rather than population and allows effective government shutdowns through filibusters. Given the importance of geographical isolation as a prime factor making government-sponsored violence a more realistic option, it is interesting to

---

Native American instead of Indian to describe the indigenous people that were overwhelmed by the coercive European migratory occupation. The only uses of the term "Indian" herein come in quotations or in references to the "Indian wars" or other events or policies in which the use of that term is the standard convention.

3. D. W. Meinig, "The Mormon Nation and the American Empire," 47–48.

speculate that if all those who believe in abortion rights and same-sex marriage lived in the eastern states and all those who do not lived in western states, we might today be seriously discussing secession again—or worse.

Three American Wars of Religion

After all the social and economic reasons for the Civil War are weighed, the political decision to fight—for both the North and South—derived from a religious belief in the righteousness of their own cause and the unrighteousness of the other's cause. As Tocqueville aptly said, "Slavery does not attack the American confederation directly, through interests, but indirectly through mores."[4] Granted the perennial motives of material interests and power, still, the American Civil War was an intra-religious war between schismatic Protestant denominations that were at deep moral odds over slavery. In addition to that great civil conflict, I study two inter-religious wars here—one with the Mormons and the other with Native Americans—fought against non-assimilated American religious groups.[5] Both of these wars ended in 1890 with Protestant-supported victories imposed by force. In Salt Lake City, federal action that threatened to disfranchise every Mormon and confiscate all church property—including its sacred temples—psychologically crushed the Saints leading to Mormon prophet and president Wilford Woodruff's issuing "The Manifesto" that

---

4. Alexis de Tocqueville, *Democracy in America*, 376.

5. For a similar reading of American cultural history, see Richard Hofstadter, *Social Darwinism in the United States, 1860–1914*, 12–15. The Spanish-American War might be added to this list of religious wars due to the accompanying anti-Catholic feeling and the international missionizing aspect of it by Protestants. Kenneth MacKenzie's theory that imperialism needs evangelism for legitimacy, and evangelism needs imperialism for staying power, is controversial. See Jon Miller, "Missions, Social Change, and Resistance to Authority: Notes Toward and Understanding of the Relative Autonomy of Religion"; Paul A. Varg, "Motives in Protestant Missions, 1890–1917." However, there is good evidence that Protestant missionaries to Mexico, Puerto Rico, Cuba, and the Philippines wanted the mission fields opened to non-Catholic proselytizing, to allow one-way conversions of Roman Catholics. See Kenton J. Clymer, "Methodist Missionaries and Roman Catholicism in the Philippines, 1899–1916;" Karl M. Schmitt, "American Protestant Missionaries and the Diaz Regime in Mexico: 1876–1911." The French and Indian War also had religious aspects as French Catholic missionaries collided with the Protestants over proselytizing Native Americans. See Frederick E. Hoxie, *Encyclopedia of North American Indians*, 671.

withdrew Church support for any new plural marriages.[6] At Wounded Knee, the last major effort at asserting Native American religious[7] and political authority was crushed with bloodshed.[8] Before succumbing to massive force, both Latter-day Saints and Native Americans sought an escape from the expanding American Empire but to no avail.[9]

These three wars outline the conditions of acceptable coercion and violence in American religious conflicts: (1) the foundations of the American way of life—the economic, political, social, aesthetic, and moral progress of American society—are deemed to be at risk; (2) the danger is immediate—a moral plague is spreading its contaminating influence and must be stopped; and (3) the enemy is either a non-Christian or a counterfeit Christian and not a fellow member of an acceptable American religion. Southerners and Mormons were effectively excommunicated counterfeiters; Native Americans were pagans.

In each of these wars, the federal government sided with a majority Protestant coalition that argued war was justified as a defense of Christian righteousness that was under attack or being diluted by the opponents. The minority opponents also justified their positions by an appeal to religious correctness. In these three cases, a stalemate of conflicting integrities made a peaceful compromise too difficult. The South, which could not

---

6. Thomas Alexander, *Things in Heaven and Earth: The Life of Wilford Woodruff, a Mormon Prophet*, 261–68.

7. The three hundred-plus Native American cultures would no doubt make important distinctions among their various religious beliefs. I apologetically group them because the mainly European peoples of United States treated them all as heathen Indians without true religion or correct culture. For a much more nuanced treatment, see Lee Irwin, "Native Voices in the Study of Native American Religions."

8. Jack Utter, *Wounded Knee and the Ghost Dance Tragedy*.

9. Like the Native Americans who were not welcome in the Europeanized society of North America, no matter where they turned the Mormons' diplomatic efforts to find a possible new home for the entire church in Canada and Mexico were rebuffed due to their practice of polygamy; see Dee A. Brown, *Bury My Heart at Wounded Knee*. Moreover, Mormons were wary of any further exodus solution. The human and financial cost of migrating with hundreds of thousands of people in 1890 seemed unbearable—and they feared that the need to move because of social rejection would never end. They had been violently encouraged to leave Kirtland, Ohio; Jackson and Clay counties, Missouri; and Nauvoo, Illinois. They decided to make their stand in Utah. Interview with Thomas Alexander, July 22, 1993. In author's possession. Also see Edward Leo Lyman, *Political Deliverance: The Mormon Quest for Statehood*, 69–95.

compromise on slavery; the Mormons, who could not be disloyal to God's call for them to practice polygamy; and the Native Americans, who could not abandon their religious ways of life, were each large enough reason to threaten disruption of the Republic. The geographic concentration of these nations made physical battle lines clear. Fighting the South, the Mormons, and the Native Americans, was facilitated because each group gathered apart from its opponents.

Given these factors, the empire decided to protect itself and force the regional iconoclasts into conformity. The Civil War killed and maimed hundreds of thousands in direct battle. In the case of the Mormons, although an army of 5,000 troops was dispatched to Utah in 1857 to quell a supposed rebellion, the violent interactions from the 1830s to 1900 resulted in, perhaps, a thousand Mormon deaths—a few from direct battle with state militias and vigilante mobs, but the majority from privation and disease caused by forced dislocation.[10] The post-colonial Indian wars from 1776 to 1890 killed scores of thousands in battle and many more by privation and disease from forced dislocation.[11]

The Religious Civil War

The morality and legality of slavery remained unresolved issues at Independence Hall in 1787. A religious issue with economic ramifications, the debate was finally dropped as neither side made any converts. There was no apparent room for compromise: either someone was a slave or free. A gradual phase-out plan offered some promise, but others resisted, claiming that slavery was a morally acceptable solution to economic realities. The Civil War completed this unfinished business from Philadelphia.

James McPherson said, "Because the American Civil War was not a war of religion, historians have tended to overlook the degree to which it was a religious war."[12] Observed Randall Miller: "By casting the slavery issue in moral terms of good and evil, Americans made it non-negotiable. . . . In the end, neither side dared yield, for to do so would invite not only political defeat but, surely, also God's wrath."[13]

---

10. Leonard Arrington and Davis Bitton, *The Mormon Experience: A History of the Latter-day Saints*, 56–57; Daniel Ludlow, *Encyclopedia of Mormonism*, "Missouri Conflict."

11. Hoxie, ed., *Encyclopedia of North American Indians*, 500–502.

12. Randall M. Miller, Harry S. Stout, and Charles Reagan Wilson, eds., *Religion and the American Civil War*, 409.

13. Miller, Stout, and Wilson, 5.

To understand how the Civil War was understood as a deeply religious and moral war by those who fought it, three scholarly studies are crucial. First, in his book *Redeemer Nation: The Idea of America's Millennial Role*, Ernest Tuveson explained the religious imperative held by many Americans is that their country has a special mission to redeem other countries and peoples from their inadequate ways of life, preparing them for the final utopia established by Christ's Second Coming.[14] A chosen people on such a serious mission cannot tolerate dangerous traitors and saboteurs—which is how the North and the South came to see each other. James Moorhead claimed something similar, noting that, especially for the northern churches, the war was a millennialist prophecy being fulfilled. In their view, the North would scourge the South and usher the Second Coming. The religious tone and content of "The Battle Hymn of the Republic" makes his point: "Mine eyes have seen the glory of the coming of the Lord!"

C. C. Goen's *Broken Churches, Broken Nation: Denominational Schism and the Coming of the Civil War* recounted the history of pre-war denominational schisms along regional lines.[15] The war's religious nature became clearest when opponents felt they had to excommunicate one another before killing each other. Just as the slaveholder could not see a slave as a fellow human being, so too Northerners and Southerners had to view their future military victims as traitors to the fellowship of Christ that had once unified them. Religious schism and excommunicating those on the other side provided a way for each to "honorably" answer this personal offense and opened the way for former compatriots to kill one another.[16]

Drilling deeply into the contemporary religious reasoning that supported schism and civil war, Michael Snay's *Gospel of Disunion* analyzed the many sermons and other public religious rhetoric during the period.[17] This study demonstrated how both sides used biblically orthodox interpretations to defend their moral and sectional disputes over slavery. Each side claimed to be the true Israel leading the world to a Christian order of

---

14. Ernest Lee Tuveson, *Redeemer Nation: The Idea of America's Millennial Role*.

15. C. C. Goen, *Broken Churches, Broken Nation: Denominational Schisms and the Coming of the Civil War*.

16. Dante saved the lowest spot in hell for traitors—those who pretended to be insiders but are truly outsiders. One recent study shows that sixty-one-percent of 186 different linguistic groups value violence against outsiders. No group values violence against its own community. See Marc Gopin, "Religion, Violence, and Conflict Resolution," 204.

17. Mitchell Snay, *Gospel of Disunion*.

righteousness while the other was schismatic.[18] From 1787 forward, the decision to bar slaveholders from moving into new U.S. territories implied the South's moral inferiority. Upholding the moral sanctity of slavery became the most important element in the Southern states' consensus for secession and war.[19] There could be no living in social-religious unity if the price were impurity.[20] Northerners claimed that human freedom was God given; Southerners countered that Northerners were atheistic humanists who were tampering with a God-given system of Christian masters teaching industrious workers the true freedom that comes from correct belief. To them, the slaves who wanted manumission were heretics who broke the religious bond of master and slave. Ultimately, however, there were too many violations of the ideal plantation for Southerners to justify the system as righteous. Consequently, they explained the ultimate loss of the war as divine punishment for abuse by wicked individual slaveholders, not as punishment for the system of slavery itself.[21]

Abraham Lincoln surmised that the war was a divine scourge to bring all Americans to repentance for supporting a program that unjustly enslaved their fellow men. Lincoln's unifying wisdom came in understanding the religious and moral aspects of the conflict. He understood that although the North held the high moral ground on the issue of slavery, it did so while using soldiers who were no more righteous than the Southerners they were fighting. Their willingness to risk all for a cause they felt was worthy of their own lives showed great moral strength on both sides. But Lincoln knew, too, that both sides would be punished for their inability to avoid violence. In his most famous moment, Lincoln at Gettysburg used religious, sacrificial language to honor "the brave men living and dead" who fought in the Civil War: the dead had not died in vain but had "hallowed and consecrated" the promised land.

---

18. Snay, 148.

19. Snay, 213–15.

20. Snay, 209. The evidence is clear that religious beliefs overrode purely sectional interest. Remarkably, one-fourth of the Fast Day sermons given in 1860 in the North contained pro-slavery diatribes against the liberal atheistic abolitionists.

21. Snay, 217. For more on the moral ambivalence among some Southern slave-holders about slavery, see R. E. Beringer et al., *Elements of Confederate Defeat: Nationalism, War Aims, and Religion*, 160–65.

The Mormon Wars

From the very founding of the Church of Jesus Christ of Latter-day Saints, its members were considered by the Protestant majority to be counterfeit Christians[22] possessing dangerous, potentially contaminating ideas that could threaten the salvation of the nation's other citizens. Because of this, Mormon attempts to claim large tracts of North American land were considered threatening enough that legislative bodies countenanced preemptive force in subduing or exterminating them. Referring to the 1880s, one historian described, "for all practical purposes, what amounted to a state of war between religion and the state stretched across the Great Basin."[23] Given that the Saints had applied for statehood six times between 1850 through the 1880s, this seems a peculiar statement. However, Utah's petition was denied each time because Congress sensed the Saints hoped only for the right of autonomy to run their own affairs without the federal meddling that accompanied territorial status.[24] Offended by polygamy and politically influential prophets, Congress felt the Mormons were already too autonomous as a quasi-theocracy. The moral critique of their religious beliefs was as infuriating to the Mormons as the moral critiques of slavery were to the Southerners. While Mormons may also have expressed the desire to secede, they lacked resources and numbers to fight the government.

Unlike the wide cultural differences that played a part in conflicts with Native Americans, neither race nor cultural background were alienating issues between Mormons and Protestants. Despite attempts by Protestant America to paint Mormons as religious aliens, the Saints

---

22. Many Protestants also considered the largest single religion in the United States, Roman Catholicism, counterfeit Christianity, while Judaism was an unappreciated, though tolerated, non-Christian group. Many other religious outsiders were variously ignored, tolerated, or persecuted non-violently. See Philip Jenkins, *Mystics and Messiahs: Cults and New Religions in American History*, 34–38; and Edwin Scott Gaustad, *Dissent in American Religion*, 92–100. Gaustad typified American religious outsiders as schismatics, heretics, and misfits. He placed the Mormons among the misfits who managed their dissent by exile from the greater society.

23. Jan Shipps, "Difference and Otherness: Mormonism and the American Religious Mainstream," 98.

24. James H. Moorhead, "God's Right Arm? Minority Faiths and Protestant Visions of America," 351.

were mostly English and Scandinavian with Protestant progenitors.[25] Like their forebears, the Saints were industrious, pious, and devoted to personal and social progress.[26] While their ethnic background should not have been alienating, their heresy was.[27] The Mormon-Protestant conflict stemmed from the founding doctrines of Joseph Smith, who began as early as 1830 to plan the political and spiritual conversion of the world—if not to Mormonism, then to unified friendship—prior to the Second Coming of Christ.[28] Of course there are always multiple causes for social religious conflicts, and in the Mormon case the social, economic, and political ramifications of theological differences greatly exacerbated the problem. In Missouri (1833–39) and Illinois (1840–47), Mormons took a very offensive stance by laying out their sacred space in the actual dirt of the American heartland.[29] Their serious plans to build Zion outward from there made local inhabitants defensive. Add to this their theology as a chosen people, a large standing militia, secret rites, rumored strange

---

25. On the history of racial issues among the Mormons, see W. Paul Reeve, *Religion of a Different Color: Race and the Mormon Struggle for Whiteness*.

26. Leonard J. Arrington, *Great Basin Kingdom*, 5–7, 96.

27. On ethnicity in connection to Mormons, Dean May argued that Mormons should be construed as a religio-ethnic group in his entry on "Mormonism" in Stephan Thernstrom, Ann Orlov, and Oscar Handlin, eds., *Harvard Encyclopedia of American Ethnic Groups*. Approaching the topic from a different perspective, Martin Marty has described Mormons as a special "people" group in "History: The Case of the Mormons, a Special People," in Martin E. Marty, *Religion and Republic: The American Circumstance*.

28. Joseph Smith declared, "I calculate to be one of the instruments of setting up the kingdom of Daniel by the word of the Lord, and I intend to lay a foundation that will revolutionize the whole world." Joseph Fielding Smith, *Teachings of the Prophet Joseph Smith*, 366. As to the role of friendship, see 316. Elsewhere I have written that Joseph Smith saw himself as a founding father of a new civilization of new humanity, fulfilling the promise on the Great Seal of America: *Annuit Cœptis Novus Ordo Seclorum*. See Charles Randall Paul, "Four L.D.S. Views on Harold Bloom: A Roundtable," 196–97.

29. Just north of Independence, Missouri, is a farming area—a wilderness when Joseph Smith in 1835 called it Adam-ondi-Ahman, referring to the place where Adam prayed to God after being ejected from the Garden of Eden. According to Mormon teachings, America was thus the real Old World which Noah left by boat. Just prior to the Second Coming of Christ, resurrected Adam and all the ancient and modern prophets will meet with Jesus at Adam-ondi-Ahman. Symmetrically, the Garden of Eden and the New Jerusalem are in Missouri. *Encyclopedia of Mormonism*, "Adam-ondi-Ahman."

sexual mores, an aggressive proselytizing program, their abolitionist bias in a border state,[30] and the preferred trading status they gave to insiders. Serious trouble was inevitable.[31]

Mormons wanted to be a separate religious people, not like the Amish who quietly let the world go by, but more similar to Evangelical Protestant groups who also designed to convert the world. Even after capitulating on their overt practice of polygamy, Mormons still maintained their exclusive claim to divine authority over any other Christian denomination. Ironically, Mormon goals were too much like militant Protestants' goals to allow compatibility, thus creating a collision of similarities. There could be only one American Zion, so like ancient Israel, Mormons moved aggressively to usurp the Pilgrims' claim, outrageously calling the Christian variations of Wesley, Calvin, Luther, and Augustine apostate.[32] By 1846, Mormons had been mobbed out of the Midwest by people they associated with Protestant Christian community who could not stomach the Saint's exclusive religious claims and social tribalism.[33] Mormon Apostle Orson Pratt's anti-Protestant "history lesson" given in 1849 is a classic seething counter-counter-attack. Asking rhetorically why God had stopped communicating clearly with the human race, he leveled this excoriating indictment:

> It is because he has had no subjects to converse with; all have turned away from him and advocated other governments as being the rightful and legal authority. They killed off, and utterly destroyed, every true subject of his kingdom, and left not a vestige of it upon the earth; and, to add to their guilt and wickedness, they have introduced idolatry in its worst forms, and utterly turned away from the true and living God. They have introduced a "God *without* BODY, PARTS OR PASSIONS." They have had the audacity to call this newly-invented god by the same name as the God of the ancient

---

30. The Saints were not all abolitionists, but the threat of voting in block was real on the volatile issue of slavery in any case. See Newell G. Bringhurst, *Saints, Slaves, and Blacks: The Changing Place of Black People Within Mormonism*.

31. Annette P. Hampshire, *Mormonism in Conflict: The Nauvoo Years*, 41–53, 91–93.

32. Though there was little proselytizing interaction between Mormons and Roman Catholics in America in the early twentieth century; many American Catholics were focused on a strategy for their own manifest destiny to first reform European Catholicism and then the Christian and greater world beyond. See Thomas Wangler, "The Birth of Americanism: Westward the Apocalyptic Candlestick."

33. See Max H. Parkin, *A History of the Latter-day Saints in Clay County, Missouri, from 1833 to 1837*.

Saints. . . . No wonder that they have received no communion from him! No wonder that he has not honored them with a visit.³⁴

. . . [W]ho in this generation has authority to baptize? None but those who have received authority in the Church of Jesus Christ of Latter-day Saints: all other churches are entirely destitute of all authority from God; and any person who receives baptism or the Lord's Supper from their hands will highly offend God, for he looks upon them as the most corrupt of all people. Both Catholics and Protestants are nothing less than the "whore of Babylon" whom the Lord denounces by the mouth of John the Revelator as having corrupted all the earth by their fornications and wickedness.³⁵

Although Pratt's rhetoric was some of the most volatile, a core belief for Mormons was the apostasy of all existing Christian churches.

Eventually both sides lost in the Protestant-Mormon theological and political contest to establish the kingdom of God on North American soil and beyond. The Saints were legally forced to abandon their offensive religious and political practices. Protestants lost hegemony by having to share it among their own schismatic ranks as well as increasingly strong Catholic and Jewish communities. Simultaneously, a social progressivism rose within Protestantism and secular society replacing faith-based initiatives with government welfare, disturbing their sense of unique mission to serve and save the world.

In 1890, Mormon prophet Wilford Woodruff announced a change that ensured their continued existence.³⁶ Legal, not armed, combat with the United States left the Saints still united although economically and politically disabled. Mormon civil disobedience had not drawn public sympathy for their minority cause; and when the twelve apostles in Utah faced the nine justices on the Supreme Court, the court ruled in favor of the majority's higher civilization. Brigham Young's spacious State of Deseret, founded in 1847, became, in 1896, another state—Utah. The melting pot theory of assimilation of minorities into a single national culture has been problematic in America up to the present day. However, in the early twentieth century the reigning policy was what Meinig called a

---

34. Orson Pratt, *The Essential Orson Pratt*, 51.
35. Pratt, 255.
36. As president and prophet, Woodruff had authority to speak for the Church, although his decisions were not binding until ratified by the consent of the members. In the LDS Church's October 1890 General Conference, a majority of those voting accepted his proclamation to desist from entering new polygamous marriages.

sub-nation's forced submission to an aggressive assimilating empire.[37] As the conflicts with the slave states, Native Americans, and Mormons show, this is the method of choice when the U.S. government engages in serious religious conflict.

The Native American Religious Wars

Henry W. Bowden observed, "Historians today busy themselves with many dimensions of the [Native American] conflict, but the religious aspects often go neglected."[38] Martin Marty has viewed America's Native American conflicts as battles joined under the moral aegis of religion. He wrote: "Many of the anti-Indian moves took place with religious justifications. Whatever the terms used to define the land, whether God's New Israel, Zion, the Lord's vineyard, God's city set upon a hill, or still others, it was clear that the newcomer had taken of the continental neighborhood in the name of God."[39]

From the arrival of Columbus to the end of the nineteenth century, more than a thousand battles between the Europeans and indigenous North and South Americans resulted in the deaths of thousands of Europeans and hundreds of thousands of natives from direct attack or war-related disease and privation.[40] Europeans justified their aggressive attacks by their obligation to spread Christianity to the benighted heathen. While most Christian missionaries may have been sincere in their intent to save souls, the genocidal results were the same. American Indian theologian and historian George Tinker pointed out:

> Christian missionaries . . . were partners in genocide. Unwittingly no doubt, and always with the best of intentions, nevertheless the missionaries were guilty of complicity in the destruction of Indian cultures and tribal social structures—complicity in the devastating impoverishment and death of the people to whom they preached. . . The blurring [of the gospel of salvation and their own cultures] invariably resulted in the missionary's culture, values, and social and political structures, not to say political hegemony and control, being imposed on tribal peoples, all in the name of the gospel. . .

---

37. Meinig, "The Mormon Nation and the American Empire," 50–51.
38. Henry W. Bowden, *American Indians and Christian Missionaries: Studies in Cultural Conflict*, ix–x.
39. Martin E. Marty, *When Faiths Collide*, 41.
40. Hoxie, *Encyclopedia of North American Indians*, 670–71.

and [under an] illusion of white self-righteousness as it was internalized and acted out by the missionaries themselves.[41]

As Christian missionaries, and certainly their political constituency, did not want to be genocidal oppressors, "rather than crush outright those who were unwilling to accept Anglo-Saxon civilization, the federal authorities decided simply to erode their ability to withstand it."[42] Andrew Jackson thought he was doing right by the natives to ship them away,[43] but Alexis de Tocqueville saw the bigger picture:

> The Spaniards let their dogs loose on the Indians as if they were wild beasts, . . . but the remnant of the Indian population, which escaped the massacres, in the end mixed with the conquerors and adopted their religion and mores. On the other hand, the conduct of the United States Americans toward the natives was inspired by the most chaste affection for legal formalities. . . they did not allow [Indian] lands to be occupied unless they had been properly acquired by contract; and if by chance an Indian nation cannot live on its territory, they take them by the hand in brotherly fashion and lead them away to die far from the land of their fathers. The Spaniard, by unparalleled atrocities which brand them with indelible shame, did not succeed in exterminating the Indian race and could not even prevent them from sharing their rights; the United States Americans have attained both these results with wonderful ease, quietly, legally, and philanthropically, without spilling blood and without violating a single one of the great principles of morality in the eyes of the world. It is impossible to destroy men with more respect to the laws of humanity.[44]

Tinker also attributed the cultural genocide of the Native Americans to Christian missionary attempts at conquest. From the earliest days in

---

41. George E. Tinker, *Missionary Conquest: The Gospel and Native American Cultural Genocide*, 4–5.

42. Henry W. Bowden, *American Indians and Christian Missionaries*, 193.

43. Andrew Jackson's 1837 farewell address defends his policy of forced relocation as benefitting the natives: "The States which had so long been retarded in their improvement by the Indian tribes residing in the midst of them are at length relieved from the evil, and this unhappy race—the original dwellers in our land—are now placed in a situation where we may well hope that they will share in the blessings of civilization and be saved from that degradation and destruction to which they were rapidly hastening while they remained in the States . . . the remnant of that ill-fated race has been at length placed beyond the reach of injury or oppression, and that the . . . Government will hereafter watch over them and protect them." See Francis Paul Prucha, ed., *The Indian in American History*, 74.

44. Tocqueville, *Democracy in America*, 339.

the colonies some missionaries respected the integrity of Indian culture,[45] Roger Williams being an early example of this.[46] However, despite usually benign long-term intentions, European American Christians religiously oppressed the natives first by denigrating their traditional way of living and belief and later by legal attacks on their religious rites. From such disrespect followed political marginalization with patronizing representation, social dislocation through frequent forced moves and segregation, and economic isolation.[47]

Taking a different angle on the missionary encounter with Native Americans, Robert Berkhofer, Jr. concluded that, perhaps unknowingly, the diverse Protestant denominations sowed much discord among the indigenous peoples by creating conflicting denominational enclaves within the same tribe.[48] Within these competing religious enclaves nests yet another conflict with some converts believing they should adopt white Protestant culture and others resisting it.[49] Yet as Berkhofer observed, even Native American converts who desired to assimilate were thwarted by a refusal to accept people of color on equal terms in social life and marriage within white society. The white population's negative racial attitude kept the Native Americans from desiring assimilation and "guaranteed the failure of the missionary program."[50] Native Americans became spiritually divided between Christian and native traditions; they also became segregated from the majority culture.

However, there was another trait common among Native Americans that the Christian American government planners, operating from an eth-

---

45. Stephen Neill, *A History of Christian Missions*, 191–194; Kenneth R. Mulholland, "Indian Carried Christianity: Wampanoag Christianity on Martha's Vineyard, 1643–1690."

46. For an exploration of Williams' complex relationship of deep respect for and eventual antagonism with the Native Americans see John M. Barry, *Roger Williams and the Creation of the American Soul*.

47. Tinker, *Missionary Conquest*, 6–8; 18–19.

48. Robert Berkhofer, Jr., *The White Man's Indian: Images of the American Indian from Columbus to the Present*, 75–78.

49. Prucha, *The Indian in American History*, 83. Chief Joseph of the Nez Perce tribe reportedly said he did not want Americans to school his people because they would teach the people to quarrel about God: "We may quarrel with men sometimes about things of this earth, but we never quarrel about God." U.S. Commission of Indian Affairs, Annual Report 1873, 527 in Dee A. Brown, *Bury My Heart at Wounded Knee*, 318.

50. Berkhofer, *The White Man's Indian*, 84.

nocentric paradigm, couldn't really grasp. The natives were resistant to assimilation because their own spiritual lives were fulfilling. As Bowden states, each tribe was a deeply religious community that possessed a "wellspring of inner strength not easily affected by superficial changes. As long as independent religious vitality survived, it filled the Indians with a sense of their own identity and importance, with a power that defied alien control."[51] Hence, proselytizing took place on both sides, and both failed to convert the other. Natives could not convince most whites to respect the spirits of nature, and whites could not persuade most natives of the superiority of Christianity.

There is no more obvious indicator of the religious nature of the Native American conflict than President Ulysses S. Grant's Peace Policy, which in 1868 placed the administration of Indian affairs in the hands of religious leaders.[52] In theory, these clergy would replace corrupt military and political appointees with fair and honest leadership—teaching Christian principles by word and example,[53] educating the Native American farmers,[54] and thus preparing them to leave savagery and become American citizens.[55] In practice, however, the religious leaders assigned to direct Indian affairs did

---

51. Bowden, *American Indians and Christian Missionaries*, 194.

52. Grant's policy toward Native Americans was also sometimes referred to as the "Quaker Policy" because it was first urged by Quaker representatives and because of the high proportion of Quakers who eventually took part in administrating the policy. The roster of religious leaders employed in the program disproportionately slighted Catholics, Jews, and Mormons.

53. Government aid to church mission schools was considered normal at the time, a better alternative to the political spoils systems, though perhaps a clear violation of the First Amendment as it would be interpreted by twentieth-century courts. See Robert H. Keller, Jr., *American Protestantism and United States Indian Policy 1869–1882*, 176, 213.

54. The link between an acceptable economic way of life and religion is almost unbreakable. The Southerners' plantation, the Mormons' isolationist communalism, and the Native Americans' nomadism were economic contradictions to capitalism. Further, these groups geo-politically blocked the fluent interstate commerce envisioned as necessary for national security. It is not mere coincidence that these three major groups attempted to assert economic independence from the United States, in two cases with new separate money systems: Confederate dollars and Deseret (Utah territory) currency.

55. Hoxie, *Encyclopedia*, 474; William T. Hagen, *American Indians*, 121–24; Bowden, *American Indians and Christian Missionaries*, 192–93.

not honor Native American religious ways any better than government officials had. As Michael C. Coleman wrote:

> Quakers, Methodists, Episcopalians, and all the other Protestants fighting for the religious liberty of their own groups on the reservations, made no move to grant so much as a hearing to the Indian religions. The record of the Catholics was no better. They criticized Protestant bigotry and called for freedom of conscience, but that freedom did not extend to native religions, which were universally condemned. By religious freedom the missionaries meant liberty of action on the reservations for their own missionary activities.[56]

When the Peace Policy ended in 1882, it had fallen far short of its purpose. Natives had resisted conversion and had been forced onto lands that were unsuitable for efficient farming. Since settlers and miners continued to encroach on the reservations, wars between whites and Native Americans were as frequent as ever.[57] The Peace Policy period brought into focus the religious nature of the conflict. After centuries of decline and the final devastation at Wounded Knee in 1890, most of the approximately 300,000 surviving North American Indians remained isolated from the enveloping white society.

Why, after slavery had ended, did so many Americans who claimed all men were created equal support cultural genocide of the Native Americans? The justification could lie in the commonly accepted belief that the biblical God calls his chosen people to establish a righteous nation and gives warrant to those acting on his behalf to convert or displace those who refuse to believe. The biblical code was interpreted in such a way as to allow religious "cleansing" as a justification for American Christian imperialism. In 1870, an editorial in a Wyoming newspaper reflects this tone: "The same inscrutable Arbiter that decreed the downfall of Rome, has pronounced the doom of extinction upon the red men of America. To attempt to defer this result by mawkish sentimentalism . . . is unworthy of the age."[58]

Echoes of manifest destiny for a superior race and culture were clearly displayed in Theodore Roosevelt's policies for displacement of the Native Americans by European Americans. Whether Anglo-Saxon Americans fought indigenous natives now, or Russian settlers who were displacing

---

56. Michael C. Coleman, *Presbyterian Missionary Attitudes Towards American Indians, 1837–1893*, 58.

57. Hoxie, *Encyclopedia*, 674.

58. Hagen, *American Indians*, 128.

the Natives in Alaska later, Roosevelt believed there would need to be a fight to secure "our continent and our religion" under one government.[59]

> Of course our whole history has been one of expansion. . . . That the [American Indians] recede or are conquered, with the attendant fact that peace follows their retrogression or conquest, is due solely to the power of the mighty, civilized races who have not lost their fighting instinct, and which by their expansion are gradually bringing peace into the red wastes where the barbarian peoples of the world hold sway.[60]

Latter-day Saints and Native Americans

When Mormons came to the Great Basin in 1847, they, like other expansionist Americans, assumed their right to farm and urbanize the irrigable land that Native Americans were using for hunting. The Book of Mormon taught the Saints that Native Americans were descendants of Israelites, destined to convert voluntarily to the Mormon version of Christianity in the last days before the Second Coming of Christ. Brigham Young benevolently remarked, "We are now [the Indians'] neighbors; we are on their land, for it belongs to them as much as any land ever belonged to any man on earth; we are drinking their water, using their fuel and timber and raising our food on their ground."[61] Yet Young also claimed that the land belonged to no man, telling his followers not to pay "the Indians for their lands, for if the Shoshones were to be thus considered, the Utes and other tribes would claim pay also. The land belongs to our Father in Heaven and we calculate to plow and plant it; and no man shall

---

59. The tone Roosevelt used no doubt reflected the preponderance of American opinion: It is unfortunate that those who wanted to hold land apart would be overrun. "To recognize the Indian ownership of the limitless prairies and forests of this continent—that is, to consider the dozen squalid savages who hunted at long intervals over the territory of a thousand square miles as owning it outright— necessarily implies a similar recognition of the claims of every hunter, squatter, horse thief, or wandering cattleman. . . . Our difficulties . . . were partly caused by our own misdeeds, but were mainly the inevitable result of the conditions under which the problem had to be solved; no human wisdom or virtue could have worked out a peaceable solution. . . . With the best of intentions, it was wholly impossible for any government to evolve order out of such chaos without resort to the ultimate arbitrator—the sword." Theodore Roosevelt, *The Winning of the West*, Vol. 1, 257–61.

60. Theodore Roosevelt, *The Strenuous Life*, 25.

61. Gustive O. Larson, "Brigham Young and the Indians," 178.

have the power to sell his inheritance for he cannot remove it; it belongs to the Lord."[62]

As a result of this attitude, Mormons attempted to trade with the natives[63] and instruct them in farming, but there were too few resources and too little will on either side to turn hunters into farmers.[64] There followed numerous violent Mormon-Native American clashes before the latter were relegated to government-sanctioned reservations. The Saints and the Native Americans were usually reluctant to fight; the Utah chiefs respected Brigham Young and he them.[65] The tribal leaders knew of the Mormon ambivalence about the Great Father (the American president) in Washington. When the natives eventually signed the final treaties with the federal government in 1865, Brigham Young accepted the chief's request that he oversee the final ceremony.

Mormons and Native Americans were in competition for the same "promised land"; however, they at times colluded against the greater threat: Protestant-influenced US government. The Mormons did not collude with the southern States against the Union during the Civil War, perhaps because both sides saw the irresolvable problem each would have were they to join ranks. The Saints would have had to fight to protect slav-

---

62. Larson, 176.

63. As Stephen P. Van Hoak has chronicled, the trade included human beings. The Utes stole (or forced parents to sell) children of the weaker Paiutes to sell them as slaves to New Mexicans. When Mormons arrived in the 1850s, the Utes tried to sell these children to Mormons, who refused until the Utes learned that threatening to kill the children usually resulted in a purchase. As a result, several hundred Paiutes were raised in Mormon families, but not as slaves. See Stephen P. Van Hoak, "And Who Shall Have the Children? The Indian Slave Trade in the Southern Great Basin, 1800–1865," 4–17.

64. Battles occurred in 1849, 1850, 1853, 1860, and from 1865 to 1868 with Chief Black Hawk. Native Americans were forced to the reservations in 1872. See Daniel Ludlow, *Encyclopedia of Mormonism,* "Native Americans." For the Mormon wars with Native Americans, see Howard A. Christy, "Open Hand and Mailed Fist: Mormon-Indian Relations in Utah, 1847–52;" Howard A. Christy, "The Walker War: Defense and Conciliation as Strategy"; Howard A. Christy, "A Book Review of John Alton Peterson, *Utah's Black Hawk War*"; John Alton Peterson, *Utah's Black Hawk War*; Ronald W. Walker, "Toward a Reconstruction of Mormon Indian Relations, 1847–1877," 32–38; and Arrington and Bitton, *Mormon Experience,* 145–60.

65. Francis Paul Prucha, *The Great Father: The United States Government and the American Indians* 1, 374–80.

ery, which they politically did not embrace, while the Southerners would have had to protect polygamy, which they abhorred.

The Results of American Religious Coercion

The losers of each of these three American religious wars interpreted their defeat as a disaster for the winners. The Southerners, the Latter-day Saints, and the Native Americans each feared for a haughty and debauched American society that had rejected their attempts to transform and save it.[66] Neither the Southern way of biblical social harmony (allowing slavery), nor the Mormon ways of Zionism (allowing polygamy and theocracy), nor the Native American ways of tribal spirituality and natural communality (allowing paganism) were congenial to the morality of most Americans. But the losers believed their ways would have been a blessing for the winners. It was not just a question of territory but of a higher way of living that had been at stake.

The Civil War ended with the slow transition of enmity beginning with the Reconstruction. The North and the South did not truly reunite until cross migrations after World War II made it possible for Americans to elect a Southern Baptist with a Georgia accent, Jimmy Carter, to the Presidency. But the religious rifts have never fully healed. The Northern and Southern Protestant churches have remained separate.

The Mormons thrived. The Saints were willing to compromise on polygamy in order to maintain a strong economic foundation from which to launch an aggressive proselytizing and propagation effort. Like conservative Jews, Mormons attended public schools while attending afternoon or early morning religious classes. Although they married their own in private temple ceremonies, they went to romantic movies and danced with "Gentiles" to popular music. They volunteered for two years as proselytizing missionaries and attended Church-owned colleges, but they also served in the armed forces and attended secular graduate schools. Ethnically, they looked and acted like northern European Protestants and they began to disperse from their intermountain enclave.

---

66. For a discussion of the call felt in the Southerner's theology to restore the correct spiritual order, see Snay, *Gospel of Disunion*, 10–14, 40–70; for discussion of the same attitude in LDS theology, see Ludlow, *Encyclopedia of Mormonism*, "Protestantism"; for the same in Native American theology, see Bowden, *American Indians and Christian Missionaries*, 195.

By contrast, the Native Americans were organic people who felt welded to the regions and ways of life that had been wrenched from them. Their promised lands had been replaced with reservations that felt more like prison camps than new homes. Further, to embrace modernity seemed like heresy, while rejecting modernization also meant economic marginalization. Exiled and powerless, they did not attempt to build a modern economic base or to counter-proselytize. They looked and behaved, and in many ways still do, like an outsider ethnic group that did not fit within a northern European country like America.

Noting the Anglo-Saxon refusal to intermarry with people of color, Tocqueville declared American slavery the moral blight of the United States. Freed slaves, unlike elsewhere, could not be assimilated as social equals for intermarriage. They would remain socially second-class as long as the Anglo-Saxon majority reigned. So, too, Native Americans accept that they, Tocqueville thought, would be annihilated before becoming a significant stable minority.[67] Though some intermarriage did occur, neither African Americans nor Native Americans have fully meshed with European-American society. Until just the past several decades, blacks and Native Americans have been excluded politically, economically, socially, and religiously. The South did rise again as somewhat having its own identity through opposition to the North and the urban-dominated coasts. In 2004, American national politics showed blatant religious clefts between what might be called the southern temperament of church-oriented traditionalism and the northern temperament toward secular progressivism. Modern American Mormons have participated politically and economically but have stood apart socially and religiously—seen as strange by their countrymen, but within acceptable limits. During the Mitt Romney campaigns for the presidency, the so-called Evangelical block of American voters was only willing to support a Mormon for president as the last right-wing alternative.[68]

My reading of history concludes that there is no way to end religious conflict. Even if rival believers are eliminated by sincere conversion or by violent annihilation or exile, heretics quickly emerge from the united community to reignite the conflict of rivalry again. Further, while assimilation strategies end the immediate fighting, they tend to feel like a form

---

67. Tocqueville, *Democracy in America*, 325–26.
68. For a broader look at the Mormon image in recent decades, see J.B. Haws, *The Mormon Image in the American Mind: Fifty Years of Public Perception*.

of slow annihilation to religious or cultural purists who inevitably rise up to resist dilution.

We are wise to expect continual religious conflicts and to develop practical attitudes and methods for engaging in perpetual contests of persuasion between dynamic rivals. These American religious wars were unsuccessful if creating religious or cultural unity was the goal. No social-political melting pot can eliminate the human desire to resist or improve the status quo—especially in the comprehensive life-ordering realm of religion. Neither the South, nor the Mormons, nor the Native Americans ever recanted their religious beliefs, even though almost all of the defeated parties changed behaviors. Each chose to hope for future victory or vindication.

Coda

The history of American religious or ideological coercion and violence is not necessarily at an end. In the twenty-first century, religions are continuing to provide the vital motivation to most cultures in diverse regions of the world. Religions, as comprehensive systems of social order and life purpose, continue to influence social, economic, and political conflicts. Since humans will continue to differ on the great religious questions, there will continue to be conflict over the highest purposes and methods to attain them. With no common metric for determining the truth of our ultimate claims, major religious or ideological conflicts cannot be resolved by negotiating compromises. Groups or societies that attempt to bring unity between all religions may begin with benevolent intent, but often end in totalitarian coercion and violence. Even if one way creates temporary hegemony, the orthodox soon feel under siege by new heretics. No one way of life has ever lasted without conflict.

Even in times of relative social tranquility there remains some contest under the surface of orderliness. Passive coexistence is a common goal, but this call to tolerance usually reflects a tentative, condescending, or apathetic regard for "the other" that cloaks deeper contempt and resentment. Explosions of violent antipathy erupt within as well as between merely tolerant groups, especially when breeches of social or economic justice can be blamed on a religious or ideological rival. When a final solution is attempted—by forced conversion, expulsion, or annihilation—it takes little time until a new heresy develops to create new conflicts. Violent expulsion and annihilation are strategies that are tentatively effective but have never brought lasting resolution of conflict. Importantly, unifying conversion inaugurates a new round of mutual persuasion contests as members of the same tribe begin to fine tune and then persuasively resist each other's interpretations of the pure unadulterated Way or Truth.

This leaves coercion-free conversion as the only peaceful strategic aim for rivals engaging in contests over the hearts and minds of humanity: a patient approach that demands honest engagement but does not demand final resolutions to conflicts over our deepest values.[69] Americans and all citizens of this shrinking planet need to establish new conventions—congenial to diverse cultural sensibilities—for respectfully engaging in religious-type conflicts as patient, persuasive, conversion contests. Although current social power asymmetry matters, the ebb and flow of historical change proves no religious hegemony lasts forever. I will discuss this in greater detail in the final chapter.

---

69. Many people consider any form of expression that offers a judgment or attempts at persuasion to be a form of undesirable intrusion, and thus coercive. In this book, we acknowledge the gradient between persuasion and coercion is difficult to measure especially when social power relations are substantially unequal (as with parents and young children). However, we define coercion as the use of legal or material force that is unwanted. Thus when a party can voluntarily cease communicating with the "verbal intruder," and assume equal access to political and social discourse, this is not a case of coercion but unwanted persuasion. The lack of certainty amid growing pluralism that sprouted in American mainstream culture in the early twentieth century has bloomed into strange flowers. A broad fear of being personally challenged has led to influence avoidance generally. It is affecting the norms of a supposedly open society, free inquiry, and expression, especially at American universities. See Jonathan Haidt and Gregg Lukianoff, "Why It's a Bad Idea to Tell Students Words Are Violence." Tellingly, Haidt has co-founded The Heterodox Academy movement to encourage a provocative idea: teaching diverse intellectual points of view at universities.

CHAPTER THREE

American Religious Climate 1900–1925: A Christian Nation?

For many at the turn of the twentieth century, religious affiliation provided the only comprehensive and reliable way for understanding and judging reality.[1] Religion, after all, spoke about the one issue of universal interest: death.[2] In 1910, a majority of Americans still assumed that their major focus should be preparation for what awaited souls following death. Whether one entered the afterlife saved or damned was an important question. It was not merely an academic exercise for people to discuss earnestly distinctions between reincarnation and resurrection, soul sleep and annihilation, or eternal bliss and eternal damnation. Truth was oriented toward otherworldly salvation—the ordering frame of all other

---

1. This is very different from the contemporary period in American and the West. There has been a shift in interest in institutionalized forms of religion toward internal and subjective expressions of spirituality. Robert Wuthnow has referred to this as a shift from a "spirituality of dwelling" in churches to a "spirituality of seeking" involving an individualized quest. See Robert Wuthnow, *After Heaven: Spirituality in America Since the 1950s*. This phenomenon may also be seen in "The Nones," those who, in response to a 2012 Pew Forum Survey, stated that their preference was for no religious affiliation. While this does include a rise in the number of people identifying with atheism, overall it signals a shift toward individualized and alternative forms of spirituality and away from institutionalized religion. See Elizabeth Drescher, "Yet Another Survey Shows 'Nones' Growth at Record Levels."

2. This too has changed as increasing numbers of individuals are more interested in how religion and spirituality help in the mortal world than after death. Many believe that traditional institutional religions emphasize life after death at the expense of considerations related to a "lived spirituality" and well-being in this lifetime. This may be one reason "subjective-life spiritualities" are on the rise. See Paul Heelas and Linda Woodhead, *The Spiritual Revolution: Why Religion is Giving Way to Spirituality*.

experience.³ In short, most people believed if they were right with God, nothing else—neither success nor failure nor even death—really mattered. Although skeptical uncertainty was part of the scene, religious convictions still provided most people the grand context for valuing human experience, action, and purpose.

Yet from Asia to Europe to America, the early twentieth century was also a time of fundamental revolutions—scientific, artistic, ideological, and religious. Influenced by new ways of looking at both the world and scripture initiated by the work of Charles Darwin, scholars promoting the insights of higher Biblical criticism, and the energies of the proto-feminist movement, were becoming impatient with religious answers to the world's problems.⁴ Although religious discourse was still respected within established institutions of society, many teachers promoting agnostic worldviews hoped their critical influence would encourage students to rely on reason and empirical evidence more than trust in traditional religious stories about supernatural things. In reaction to the prospect of Protestant Christian authority slipping away, the Protestant missionary

---

3. Wolfhart Pannenberg said the religious history of humankind is "a competition between the religions concerning the nature of reality, a competition grounded in the fact that the religions have to do with comprehensive views of reality. Only in this way can they provide a basis for the orders of human existence or . . . mediate salvation to man. . . . The gods of religion confront man as realities distinct from themselves because they are experienced as powers over the whole of man's existence including the world." Wolfhart Pannenberg, *Basic Questions in Theology: Collected Essays*, Vol. 2, 88, 104.

4. Although Leo Strauss claimed one could not with integrity cross the line between belief in intelligible revelation (religion) and belief in continual skeptical criticism (philosophy), he discoursed seriously over the similarity of focus between religious eschatology and philosophical teleology. See Leo Strauss, *The Rebirth of Classical Political Rationalism: Essays and Lectures by Leo Strauss*, 167–68. Religion and philosophy take us to the end of our limits as we seek a *telos* in pondering the ultimate divine or human purposes. This ultimate seeking-in-questioning has often made philosophy look religious and religion look philosophical. In its earliest practice, Pythagorean philosophy apparently came very close to becoming a religious practice, influencing Plato among others to go beyond contemplation to implement his spiritual-political-philosophy. See Plato, *Plato: The Collected Dialogues Including the Letters*, 1574–98; James Redfield, "The Origins of Philosophy." However, most modern philosophy is self-consciously a method of skeptical criticism, not a way of faithful dedication to some ultimate reality and purpose.

crusade in North America that began during this period was part of a broader, though disjointed, movement to resettle the teleological questions that influence the direction of society.[5] For its proponents, religion not only offered answers to the question of how to face death, but was also essential to the social stability needed for living with purpose in the here and now. Religion was still the main authoritative public discourse behind public policy, and its champions wanted it to stay this way.

World War I also arrived amid these other upheavals, and its impact on the early-twentieth-century worldview is difficult to overestimate. Historian Kenneth Latourette dated the ideological end of general Western optimism and beginning of the spirit of the twentieth century in 1914, when the Great War began.[6] The supposed war to end all wars marked the end of an impressive century of Christian expansion, the end of the expectation of continuous progress, and the commencement of broad-based cynicism, skepticism, nihilism, and pessimism over the evils of human society.[7] With the arrival of the war, the variety of possibilities for valuing human nature and purpose had finally overstressed the modern soul. In the face of rapid and shocking change, massive creative efforts—both secular and religious—were born. As historian Jacques Barzun observed about this period: "In science, art, technology, philosophy, social and political thought, all the new principles were set forth with finality, from aviation, wireless, and motion pictures to abstract art, city planning, aesthetic simultaneity, quantum physics and genetics, relativity and psychoanalysis."[8]

Further, it was not the theoretical language of church-state division within the First Amendment in 1789, but the actual separation between various believers and non-believers in the early-twentieth century that marked the real disestablishment of religion in America. This social shift opened the cultural gates to contestation of values and mores among and

---

5. Any authoritative claims about teleology leading to a social order of ethical action are religious claims whether or not a person believes in active divine involvement in the world. Defining this connection as religious in nature has the benefit of allowing the inclusion of atheistic traditions—such as Buddhism, which claims to grasp the true nature of reality—as a "religious" tradition. In this sense, Russian communism was also religious.

6. Latourette's comment is mentioned as cultural context in Gerald H. Anderson, "American Protestants in Pursuit of Mission: 1886–1986," 391.

7. Robert Wiebe, *The Search for Order, 1877–1920*, 16–22.

8. Jacques Barzun wrote the trenchant historical review of the twentieth century in John A. Garraty and Peter Gay, eds. *The Columbia History of the World*, 1162–63.

between religions and ideologies that remain open to this day. In 1900, religious status mattered greatly in American society, sometimes determining if one obtained credit at the bank or could be elected to the U.S. Presidency.[9] Yet, as conflicts within established social/religious society reshuffled authoritative power into more diverse hands, a space was created for pluralism and secular relativism. A century-and-a-quarter after the American founders evaded violent religious conflicts by constitutionally relegating religious practice to a right instead of its earlier status as a foundational mandate, religion had finally lost its cultural primacy as the unquestioned authoritative anchor in many Americans' personal lives.[10]

Still, for deeply religious Americans who believed in the unity of Divine Truth, religious pluralism was a scandal that presented competing and unworthy "truths." They craved religious unanimity to prove that religion was not like every other ephemeral human science or project. They desired to re-establish the priority of revealed truth over all other types of human knowledge. Even though the times required them to acknowledge multiple allegiances, their prime allegiance was still to religious authority.

Denominationalism, the accommodationist strategy that declared it mattered not to God or neighbors where one attended church (as long as it was mainline Protestant) had once helped American Christians feel a sense of unity with each other. But denominationalism was now failing to act as a unifying religious authority. As Thomas Jonas described the Christian denominational mindset of this time, they were living in a subtle tension between religious responsibility and social civility, trying "to be absolute in their convictions, but tolerant of other beliefs; strict in their internal discipline, but accepting of a diversity outside it; evangelistic, but

---

9. Theodore Roosevelt's Progressive Party theme song was "Onward Christian Soldiers" with the full hymnal connotation intended. Robert Dallek argues that U.S. foreign policy from 1898 to 1920 "is best understood as reflecting the Evangelical faith and ideals of Theodore Roosevelt and Woodrow Wilson—themselves representatives of two opposing parties." See Robert Dallek, "National Mood and American Foreign Policy: A Suggestive Essay," 229–61. See also Alexis de Tocqueville, *Democracy in America*, 287–97 and Max Weber, *From Max Weber*, 305–11.

10. See Wolfhart Pannenberg, "How to Think about Secularism," 28. Only in the final decades of the twentieth century have sociologists of religion had resources like the University of Chicago's National Opinion Research Center (NORC) or the Pew Trust Surveys to measure religious opinions over time on the same questions to trace what "many" actually think. Nevertheless, prior to such surveys respected historians have read personal journals, church sermons, and public newspaper articles to corroborate their opinions many of which being expressed herein.

not exclusivist; critical of other beliefs, but ecumenical in their relations to other faiths."[11] Theirs was a difficult dance, to be sure.

But these new challenges to religious certainty had also revitalized their desire to theologically argue that they were right to believe—that they were acting in body, mind, and heart, according to the will or love of God. For those espousing the social gospel, the Holy Spirit affirmed that service to the needy was the quintessence of God's love. In contrast, those who came to be called Protestant Fundamentalists determined that to love God was to love the perfect, inerrant Word of God in the Biblical text. For them, prayerful pondering and heeding of scripture that "clearly meant what it said," a doctrine known as the clarity of scripture,[12] led to salvation.

In 1907, Walter Rauschenbusch, a Baptist theologian and social activist, led many Protestant church leaders to emphasize social action over doctrinal accuracy and personal piety. This was the birth of the *social gospel* movement that stood in contrast to the *fundamentals* movement. Rauschenbusch said the following:

> No one shares life with God whose religion does not flow out, naturally and without effort, into all relations of his life ... Whoever uncouples the religious and social life has not understood Jesus. Whoever sets any bounds for the reconstructive power of the religious life over the social relations and human institutions, to that extent denies the faith of the Master.[13]

In 1908, thirty-two Christian communions in sympathy with the social gospel emphasis met in Philadelphia to form the Federal Council of Churches to coordinate church social welfare as a primary Protestant mission.[14]

Redesigning American Visions

The challenges of reconfirming belief centers and religious identity were not the only tensions facing early-twentieth-century religious believers. The Progressive Era in America (roughly 1890 to 1920) was typified by strenuous efforts to replace religious institutional powers with secular controls in a war against threatening otherness. There were more cases of class, religious,

---

11. R. Scott Appleby, "Missions and the Making of Americans," 267.

12. Evangelicals continue to hold to the clarity or perspicuity of Scripture, defined as meaning "that the Bible is written in such a way that its teachings are able to be understood by all who will read it seeking God's help and being willing to follow it." Wayne Grudem, *Systematic Theology*, 108.

13. Walter Rauschenbusch, *Christianty and the Social Crisis*, 48–49.

14. See the website of the National Council of Churches, https://nationalcouncilofchurches.us/about-us/history/.

and racial violence during this period than any other period in American history.[15] During the first quarter of the twentieth century, the role of women in society was both deeply questioned and adamantly reaffirmed. Sexual gender ambiguity commonly acquainted with the late twentieth century has its roots in the earlier part of the century. Open affirmations of homosexuality, transgressive by common mores, led to the creation of anti-sodomy laws. Both celibacy and free love were avant-garde feminist ideas that were countered by a reaffirmation of conventional family mores. Polygamy in Utah, still publicly contested despite official declarations that the practice had ceased, looked to some like a mix of the worst extremes of libertine and reactionary mores.[16] Elaine Showalter chronicled and interpreted these events as social, political, and religious power struggles—early-twentieth-century culture wars.[17] It becomes easy to see how Warren Harding could have won the 1920 presidential election with the bland motto, "Not nostrums but normalcy." After twenty years of intense cultural questioning and several years of world war, folks wanted no change for a change.

Immigration also produced huge challenges for Christians whose theology and teachings had, until then, dominated American social discourse. Seventeen million new foreigners (fifteen-percent of the entire U.S. population) arrived in America between 1880 and 1910—and only very few were raised in ways that American Protestants found compatible with their practices. A civil war over slavery had left the country with a minority black population that was not accepted as full citizens because, as Tocqueville presciently decried, the general European distaste for intermarrying with races of darker color made equal assimilation impossible.[18] Bringing into American society more red, yellow, black, and brown peoples threatened white people who responded by enacting laws that limited immigration. Racial purity was conflated with religious purity as many American Christians argued that social stability depended on all citizens following their Christian mores. Politically, the Protestant label was still very powerful. Both major-party Presidential candidates in 1896—

---

15. Richard Hofstadter, *Social Darwinism in the United States, 1860–1914*, x–xiii.

16. Along with the present volume, these two works discuss in detail various (usually negative) ways the American media often characterized Mormons in the early twentieth century: Terryl Givens, *The Viper on the Hearth: Mormons, Myths and the Construction of Heresy*; and Kathleen Flake, *The Politics of American Religious Identity: The Seating of Senator Reed Smoot, Mormon Apostle*.

17. Elaine Showalter, *Sexual Anarchy: Gender & Culture at the Fin de Siècle*, 12.

18. Tocqueville, *Democracy*, 340–43, 356–58.

William McKinley and William Bryan—were self-identified Evangelicals, and presidential rhetoric remained Evangelical for another twenty years.[19] Ritual recitation of the Pledge of Allegiance—penned in its original form by Francis Bellamy, a Baptist minister, and adopted in 1892—used a religious form to solidify the national community.

Even while Protestant ideologies maintained some claim to continued relevance in national discourse during these quickly changing times, factions within the Protestant movement were forcing discussions on several fronts. These centered around five questions:

1. What do we do about *economic diversity*—or who determines what is valuable and controls the distribution of wealth?[20]
2. What do we do about *race differences*—or is intermarriage the answer to homogenize natural biases against color and cultural otherness?
3. What do we do about *sexual differences*—or does biology require social role differences and separate ethical expectations?[21]
4. What do we do about *value conflicts*—or are there higher purposes for our society than preserving healthy human biological life?
5. What do we do about *religious conflicts*—or is there one true religion and way of life that might help answer the above four questions?

---

19. Sidney E. Ahlstrom, *A Religious History of the American People*, Vol. 2, 243; Robert T. Handy, *A Christian America: Protestant Hopes and Historical Realities*, 122.

20. This question ran deeper than socialism vs. capitalism. Tocqueville noted that American inheritance laws disallowed dynasties. See Tocqueville, *Democracy*, 51–53. The significant wealth of early-twentieth-century business magnates was preserved intact only by bequeathing it to independent foundations that today wield substantial economic power (the top five each has a net worth of more than four billion dollars). Should churches also be rich? For the most part, they did not save and centralize their funds to last for generations, the Catholics and Mormons being notable exceptions—a fact that very much bothered the decentralized Protestant congregations. See Leonard J. Arrington, *The Mormon Experience: A History of the Latter-day Saints*, 262–83.

21. The avant-garde began discussing "free love with certain precautions," and even the rear guard began challenging traditional ways by suggesting that celibacy would give women more freedom. In response, President Theodore Roosevelt railed against "race suicide" by any form of social or personal contraception. Showalter, *Sexual Anarchy*, 63–78.

These social questions of the last century are still with us.[22] The fourth has lately been politically and socially easier to discuss in America than the fifth because it does not require an authoritative response beyond one's own sense of what is right. But the fifth question, which seeks an authority from outside human limitations, is the most powerful and potentially useful, as well as potentially dangerous. Nearly a century ago, it was the salient question for most religious Americans because they believed that religion provided the most reliable foundation on which to base social mores and policies. Hearing religious teaching was the main way to develop personal virtue. Religious training was thought to correct the natural soul, providing the guidance to answer all major social questions. If proper religious teaching could change a person, then prudential education could change a society. Hence, suffrage, prohibition, labor reform, ethnic purity movements, and muckraking were all highly energized efforts during this period. Both with and without specific religious energies behind it, the progressive mood brought with it a moral commitment to social intervention.[23]

No matter which side one was on, activism for change or against it was normal and considered a public good. Matching the spirit of these times, Protestant denominational assemblies organized their disparate congregations for social service and missionary work.[24] Knowing that official unity would create an even more powerful effect, comity agreements were signed between Presbyterians, Dutch Reformed, and Congregationalists in the 1890s. In 1908, almost all Protestant denominations agreed to charter the Home Missions Council to coordinate their missionary efforts in the United States.[25] In the same year, the Federal Council of Churches began a great fundraising effort to establish a permanent body of multi-denominational

---

22. These American questions contrast with Europe at the turn of the century in which the salient questions were the following: how different ethnic groups should organize within the state and the interaction of ideologies such as nationalism, racism, socialism, and political Catholicism for power. See Mikuláš Teich and Roy Porter, eds., *Fin de Siècle: Its Legacy*, 80–97. Of course, many of these issues can be seen in the ongoing debate in America and the West in terms of wealth distribution, and in our post-9/11 world, religious conflicts remain front and center in political and cultural issues of foremost concern.

23. Robert L. Buroker, "From Voluntary Association to Welfare State: The Illinois Immigrant's Protective League, 1908–1926," 643–660; Ferenc M. Szasz, *The Divided Mind of Protestant America, 1880–1930*, 42–44.

24. John A. Smith, "Ecclesiastical Politics and the Founding of the Federal Council of Churches," 122–23.

25. Smith, "Ecclesiastical Politics," 126.

leaders. While the Home Missions Council succeeded into the 1920s, the Federal Council never raised enough money to survive beyond a year.

Missions, Missions, Missions!

Although Christian missions began during Jesus' lifetime and continued in monastic movements during the Middle Ages as well as the Renaissance, the greatest Protestant missionary ardor began in England and the United States following the Civil War in the form of voluntary societies.[26] Supported primarily by middle-class women, they sprang up to bridge the organizational gaps between local denominational administration and the need for a unified force to convert a world whose problems, they believed, derived from false religious foundations.[27] Typifying this sentiment, the closing speaker of the 1901 national synod of the Protestant Episcopal Church cried out: "We bid you to carry away from our great synod as the watchword of our battle: missions, missions, missions!"[28]

Militant enlistment of young and old to the gospel cause began in earnest.[29] C. Atkins has characterized 1900 to 1915 as "the Age of Crusades" in which "there was a super abundance of zeal, a sufficiency of

---

26. One historian of the Protestant missionary movement listed the following motives for missionary work during the nineteenth and twentieth centuries: to proclaim the glory of God, serve with love and compassion, save the lost millions who know not Christ, plant new churches, warn of the Second Coming, establish a new world order, stem the decline of culture, convert the Jews (or Mormons, or others), and obey the "Great Commission" of Christ to preach the gospel unto all the world until the Second Coming. A. Wind, "The Protestant Missionary Movement, 1789–1963," 241.

27. Andrew F. Walls, *The Missionary Movement in Christian History*, 241–53.

28. Handy, *Christian America*, 130.

29. Though they lacked central coordination for all denominations, great efforts were made to enlist college students for foreign missions. The Commission on Cooperation and Promotion of Unity for the World's Missionary Conference stated in 1910 that lack of coordination of the home support system with the field proselytizing effort was causing a breakdown. See Henry C. McComas, *The Psychology of Religious Sects*, 228–29. One leader called for a unified mission center where new missionaries would learn foreign languages and cultures, simplified doctrines, and agricultural and health basics. See Handy, 230. Ironically, more than ninety years later, the Mormons (still not quite acceptably Christian) have implemented such a program in several training centers for more than 58,000 full-time missionaries who serve eighteen-month and two-year missions in various parts of the world.

good causes, unusual moral idealism, excessive confidence in mass movements and leaders with rare gifts of popular appeal.... The air was full of banners, and the trumpets called from every camp."[30] At the 1908 meeting of the Federal Council of Churches of Christ in America, a keynote speaker claimed the following:

> This council stands for the hope of organized work for speedy Christian advance toward World Conquest.... It is marvelous how the presence of the common enemy in heathen lands has brought Christian men to realize their need of unity in thought and work. Face to face with the corruption and degradation of heathenism, they realize this world is lost apart from Jesus Christ.[31]

Lewis F. Sterns, a prominent Evangelical preacher of the period, avowed

> The future of the world seems to be in the hand of three great Protestant powers—England, Germany, and the United States. The old promise is being fulfilled; the followers of the true God are inheriting the world ... We have no question of Christianity's universal conquest. No other religion can vie with it. There is no likelihood that any religion will ever rival it ... The facts are manifest.[32]

Such rhetoric was symptomatic of the Protestant struggle for religious authority. Just as a foreign war often rallies domestic consensus, national reform and international missionary work mobilized Protestants who saw the competition for truth and power eroding their traditions. Though most of the Protestant focus was on so-called heathen nations in Asia and Africa, the major home mission drives targeted American heathens: Native Americans and the Utah Mormons. There were also home missionary efforts among Chicano Catholics in the southwest, the Appalachian hill people, urban Catholics, and Jews.[33] As discussed, the Native Americans, who did not convert and assimilate, were destroyed in battle or exiled to reservations.

---

30. Handy, *Christian American*, 128.
31. Handy, 148.
32. Handy, 105.
33. My main sources for the history of Protestant missionizing in this period are Kevin J. Christiano, *Religious Diversity and Social Change: American Cities 1890–1906*, which provided a demographic count of the changes in denominations over several years in various towns; Mark T. Banker, *Presbyterian Missions and Cultural Interaction in the Far Southwest, 1850–1950*, which analyzed the Southwestern missionary effort; Robert T. Handy, *We Witness Together: A History of Cooperative Home Missions*, which documented activities of home mission boards; Martin E. Marty, *Modern American Protestantism and its World: Missions*

My sense is that all of these domestic missions, including the Utah crusade to convert Mormons that is discussed in this book, can be understood in part as an overall movement among Evangelical Protestants to firmly re-establish their moral/political leadership in the face of evidence from within and without that true Protestant hegemony in America no longer existed.[34] Scott Appleby concluded that the Protestant missionary effort was ultimately successful in culturally and religiously differentiating Protestants from other American religious groups, especially the fast-growing Catholics and Jews; but he concludes, as have others, that it was less successful in halting the eroding cultural hegemony.[35]

Similar to the fact that the several voluntary societies that sprung up following the Civil War were primarily supported by women, the same holds true of the Protestant missionary movement. Historians have calculated that in 1910 more than two million American women were involved in the missionary movement.[36] The entire U.S. population at that time was about 75 million. If half were women and a third were over eighteen, then approximately sixteen-percent of all adult women were enlisted in missionary support work. Women, more than men, were concerned about reforming family and society; they accepted as their moral mission the eradication of drunkenness, infidelity, sloth, vulgarity, and impiety.

From 1890 to 1920, middle-class homemakers and single women from the township to the national level religiously devoted much of their

---

and Ecumenical Expressions, which analyzed the missions in respect to broader religious and cultural elements; Ferenc M. Szasz, *The Protestant Clergy in the Great Plains and Rocky Mountain West, 1865–1915*, which focused on efforts in New Mexico, Colorado, and Arizona; and Timothy Yates, *Christian Mission in the Twentieth Century*, who wrote a comprehensive history of mainline Protestant missions during the twentieth century.

34. Some religious historians claim that due to Protestantism's fragmented localism there was never any real Protestant hegemony in America. See Robert Booth Fowler, *Religion and Politics in America*, 14–16; R. Laurence Moore, *Religious Outsiders and the Making of Americans*, 207. But more agree that there was, and that it declined after the North-South schisms of the Civil War, finally ending completely following the first decades of the twentieth century. See Robert T. Handy, *A Christian America: Protestant Hopes and Historical Realities*, 55; Martin E. Marty, *Modern American Religion II: The Noise of Conflict*, 24.

35. R. Scott Appleby, "Missions and the Making of Americans," 233, 266, 269.

36. Gerald H. Anderson, "American Protestants in Pursuit of Mission: 1886–1986," 387; Susan M. Yohn, *A Contest of Faiths: Missionary Women and Pluralism in the American Southwest*, 9.

time and resources to charitable activities, missions, and reform movements.[37] No Protestant denomination ordained women to clergy status, but the mission schools, the backbone of many proselytizing efforts, were typically staffed with young women; and hundreds of thousands of young women raised the lion's share of mission funds at home to support the field staffs. It became normal for young Protestant women to volunteer after high school years to take up the noble cause of social reform through missionary support work, and in some cases by serving as missionaries. In fact, the powerful ad hoc missionary boards staffed by women began to encroach so much on the ordinary activity of the denominations themselves that pastors took back the reins of missionary work, thereby causing the missions to lose their major fundraising source.[38]

By about 1920, however, fewer women were employing domestic servants, which forced them to focus more on family maintenance. More significantly, at this time, the notion of who should attend to social salvation shifted from the religious sphere and volunteerism to that of educated, paid professionals.[39] Female volunteers and missionaries, men included, began to be considered too sentimental and unprofessional to render social services and administer public welfare. Backed by a more secular twentieth-century society, they were soon replaced by social scientists and government administrators. The scientific welfare state was being born out of social gospel service programs, and the ardor for voluntary mission was being replaced by concerns for finding ways that educational proficiency might be applied usefully in society. Some scholars consider the assertion and rejection of female public leadership in the extensive Protestant missionary program as the first major projection and rejection of a mass feminist movement in America.[40]

---

37. Mary Ann Glendon, "The Man Who Loved Women and Democracy," 41.

38. Gail Bederman, "'The Women Have Had Charge of the Church Long Enough': The Men and Religion Forward Movement of 1911–1912 and the Masculinization of Middle Class Protestantism," 432–465; David G. Hackett, "Gender and Religion in American Culture, 1870–1930," 145–49; Handy, *We Witness Together*, 24–38.

39. Barbara Welter, "She Hath Done What She Could: Protestant Women's Missionary Careers in Nineteenth-Century America," 111–125.

40. The belief in an all-loving, fair, and forgiving God at the final judgment began to subtly take hold, diminishing the urgency of missions to heathen. This highly influenced the shift from viewing missions as instruments for "snatching the heathen from hell" to vehicles for improving economic welfare. See Rev. James Dennis, *Christian Missions and Social Progress: A Sociological Study of Foreign*

This sense that people could not change the world or themselves without secular, professional help doused the enthusiasm for missions. Without the financial, personal, and moral support of the voluntary women's groups, Protestant missions diminished greatly. In 1925, a multi-denominational survey and critique of Protestant missionary work published under the sponsorship of John D. Rockefeller Jr. and William Hocking urged a shift in focus, including an end to Protestant triumphalism: "The real battles are to be fought in the great transverse areas where spiritual and altruistic forces contend against materialism and cupidity, so Christianity needs to collaborate, not compete with other world religions."[41] The figurative/literal Protestant split epitomized by the spectacle of the Scopes Trial over teaching evolution in the schools, combined with the implementation and repeal of national Prohibition, further contributed to the decline in Protestant social prestige and America's new distaste for overt dogmatic moralizing in both religion and politics. As a result, religion was rendered a taboo topic in polite society during the next seventy-five years. Spared a bloody Thirty Years War that disgraced religious authority so much that it led to a secular Europe, America had instead an embarrassing Thirty Years Debate that ended in the mid-1920s and led to a practical disestablishment of religion in public life. The fundamentalists and the progressives solidified their polar differences, making it finally obvious that Protestant Christianity could not unify itself, let alone be the vehicle to unite a more diverse nation under a single moral authority.[42]

Missions, referenced in Marty, *Modern American Protestantism,* 12. However, as late as 1946, John Mott, a moderator between soul proselytizers and preachers of social welfare, received the Nobel Peace Prize for organizing Protestant college-age gospel-spreading missionaries. See Yates, *Christian Mission,* 28. Historian Susan Curtis maintains that the social gospel plan religiously backfired by professionalizing and commercializing and politicizing the community integrating efforts of lay religious proselytizing done by common unprofessional people. See Susan Curtis, *Consuming Faith: The Social Gospel and Modern American Culture.* Susan Yohn adds that the backlash of the fundamentalists against the liberal social Gospel was the beginning of the American dissatisfaction with "big government that taxed much but did little to solve social ills." See Yohn, *A Contest of Faiths,* 250.

41. William R. Hutchison, "Christianity, Culture, and Complications: Protestant Attitudes toward Missions," 90.

42. Robert T. Handy, *Undermined Establishment.*

Who Is Christian—Really?

Although the idea of finding *the true church* seems irrelevant to many people today, this quest was very much on the minds of laymen and scholars during the early twentieth century. In fact, religious historian Jonathan Z. Smith's research generally supports the claim that most of the professional biblical scholarship done by Christians in the last two centuries was polemically aimed at proving one or another contemporary denomination to be a bone fide successor of the supposed original church.[43] These questions were rarely asked publicly by religious seekers, but they were rhetorically asked by those who desired to differentiate their authoritative truth from rivals' claims to maintain distinct boundaries between groups.[44] As a result, one important drive during the Protestant missionary heyday was the search for counterfeit Christians who needed to be exposed and converted.

This quest is ongoing today, with religious conflict still flourishing between certain Evangelical Protestants and those, such as the Mormons, they consider to be non-Christian or pseudo-Christian groups. Interestingly, the arguments used today have not been substantially modified since the early twentieth century,[45] even though some of the churches espousing

---

43. The rivalry between orthodox adherents to any religion or ideology spring into life almost as soon as a new movement is born. For a history of this phenomenon pertaining to Christianity and classic pagan religions, see Jonathan Z. Smith, *Drudgery Divine: On the Comparison of Early Christianities and the Religions of Antiquity*.

44. Historian Jan Shipps noted that the question of a true religion is most frequently asked by Evangelical Protestant groups who have ambiguous boundaries. They are usually not seeking a clearer categorical understanding of religious movements but are attempting to engage in boundary maintenance between their group and others. See Jan Shipps, "Is Mormonism Christian?: Reflections on a Complicated Question," 461–63.

45. Within Evangelicalism, a group of individuals and ministries known as the "counter-cult" apply an apologetic approach that seeks to identify and refute the false teachings of "cults" in contrast with "historic Christendom" and Protestant Evangelicalism in particular. A handful of these "new religious movements" have received special attention by counter-cult groups, with Mormonism receiving a large majority of the critique. For a sociological analysis and critique of the counter-cult see Douglas E. Cowan, *Bearing False Witness? An Introduction to the Christian Countercult*. A new movement within Evangelicalism should also be noted, one that still disagrees with Mormon teaching and which evangelizes its adherents, but which eschews several aspects of the counter-cult apologetic approach. The first published volume setting forth this missiological approach

them have been.⁴⁶ Contemporary readers who read missionary messages from a century ago will note a quaint strangeness to them. They were fervently self-confident. Missionaries were called by the Spirit to proselytize and were supported by American religious orthodoxy and theological degrees from religiously oriented seminaries and universities. They emphasized disputatious arguments constructed on propositional logic. Such arguments assumed that a singular truth actually existed that was both non-contradictory and comprehensible to honest interlocutors.⁴⁷

---

was Irving Hexham, Stephen Rost, and John W. Morehead II, eds., *Encountering New Religious Movements: A Holistic Evangelical Approach*.

46. After the 1920s, conservative branches continued to proselytize though with less funding support. See Handy, *A Christian America*; Martin E. Marty, *Fundamentalism and Evangelicalism*; Ferenc M. Szasz, *The Divided Mind of Protestant America, 1880–1930*. Even with the growth and strength in Evangelical movements, the mission to Mormons is still alive in the twenty-first century, although counter-cult apologetic efforts in general, as well as its particular focus on Mormonism, seem to have waned since its peak in the 1980s. See Earl Parvin, *Missions U.S.A.*; Francis J. Beckwith and Stephen E. Parrish, *The Mormon Concept of God: A Philosophical Analysis*; Jerald Tanner and Sandra Tanner, *Answering Mormon Scholars* 2 Vols.; Carl Mosser and Paul Owen, "Mormon Apologetic, Scholarship and Evangelical Neglect: Losing the Battle and Not Knowing It?" The best outlines of the issues of conflict today can be found in the Northern American Mission Board of the Southern Baptist Convention's 1997 pamphlet, *The Mormon Puzzle: Understanding and Witnessing to the Latter-day Saints*, and its detailed review in Daniel Peterson, "Shall They Both Not Fall in the Ditch? What Certain Baptists Think They Know about the Restored Gospel"; as well as Craig L. Blomberg and Stephen E. Robinson, *How Wide the Divide?: A Mormon and an Evangelical in Conversation*; and more recently, Robert L. Millet and Gerald R. McDermott, *Claiming Christ: A Mormon-Evangelical Debate*.

47. George Lindbeck described two widespread modes of religious discourse among cultural interpreters of religion in George Lindbeck, *The Nature of Doctrine: Religion and Theology in a Postliberal Age*, 132–140. He notes an "expressive-experiential" discourse, which avoids propositional truth arguments in favor of sharing personal experiences of God that was just beginning to be recognized in 1910. At this period, William James focused seriously on varieties of religious *experience*. See William James, *The Varieties of Religious Experience*. The "cultural-linguistic" interpretation of the world that situates truth in human language and tradition and assumes knowledge of ultimate ontological reality to be incommensurate with human epistemic capacity, was not yet typical of religious thinkers at that time. Without a cultural-linguistic method of interpretation, Protestants and Mormons, finding they had different meanings for the same

As discussed, American denominationalism had offered a creative answer for those Christians who could not wait for the Second Coming to unify Christendom.[48] To those who were willing to go along with the denominational model's compromise, the various Protestant churches all possessed the same true religion within them.[49] In the interest of religious peace, these Protestants promoted preference for their own denomination's emphases and worship forms while still publicly affirming a belief in the indivisible and invisible true church. This view bridged the denominational competition created by the disestablishment of state religions, and comity agreements between them allowed each group to recognize the baptisms of the other denominations.[50] By 1910, however, this fiction of mainline Protestant unity was growing too thin to face the aggressive truth claims from other sources, both secular and religious, particularly when groups began to engage each other more vigorously. Despite the creative compromise of denominationalism, Protestantism was sliding inevitably toward schisms. The final efforts to establish Christian unity that established the National Federation of Churches in 1900 and the World Council of Churches in 1910 ultimately exacerbated the figurative and literal schism already latent in all Protestant denominations, and set up clear bounds between Catholics, Protestants, and Jews. The early-

---

Christian terms, continually accused each other of purposely missing the point so they could teach a false Christianity for personal gain.

48. Timothy Weber documents the interpretative range of opinions about the Second Coming during the past hundred years. See Timothy P. Weber, *Living in the Shadow of the Second Coming: American Premillennialism, 1875–1925*. Premillennialists believed that Christ would inaugurate his thousand-year reign with the abrupt destruction of the wicked; thus, anything but proselytizing was a waste of effort. Postmillennialists believed that Christ would not return until the world was converted. Hence, social work, local prosperity, and international peace were the best strategies. Weber also pointed out that premillennialists in the early twentieth century appropriated postmillennialism by arguing that they must proselyte to create a world that desired peace; however, only Christ's power, unleashed at his return, could effect conversion. Social improvement programs were therefore still a waste of energy and resources. See Weber, *Living in the Shadow*, 104.

49. Many Roman Catholics, Orthodox, Protestants, and Mormons still describe themselves (though usually not each other) as "the church." In Rome, several eastern capitals, and Salt Lake City, this "true religion" has physicality, but Protestants assume a unity and what is now a waning hegemony based on their common belief on a common body of faith and doctrinal confession.

50. Robert T. Handy, *A Christian America*, 3–5, 8–14.

twentieth-century crusade against Mormonism occurred on the brink of pending Protestant schisms. In a last grasp for solidarity, if not hegemony, Protestants—progressive and fundamentalist alike—answered the exclusive question, "Who, really, is Christian?" with the unifying answer: "Well, certainly not the Mormons."[51]

---

51. It is helpful in building group solidarity if internal factions can concentrate their criticism clearly on foreign enemies. By the late nineteenth century, Roman Catholicism had become the largest religious community in America, and a formidable invading force of "false Christianity" that worried Protestants. Protestants concentrated on converting them initially, but ultimately, these efforts brought a unifying resistance among immigrant Catholics who felt confident solidarity in their growing numbers. The Protestants eventually focused more on smaller populations of heretics and heathens, including the Mormons. Jenny Franclot, *Roads to Rome: The Antebellum Protestant Encounter with Catholicism*, 11–12; Christiano, *Religious Diversity*, 144–49. The Protestants also targeted Jews for conversion, but they, too, responded by consolidating Jewish Americanism as an internally diverse subculture willing to participate in the larger society. See Nancy T. Ammerman, "Fundamentalists Proselytizing Jews," 114–17.

CHAPTER FOUR

Rival Stewards of the American Promised Land

In 1702, the prolific Puritan minister and pamphleteer Cotton Mather announced his decidedly religious view of the Promised Land's divine history:

> The God of Heaven served as it were a summons upon the spirits of his people in the English nation stirring up thousands with almost unanimous inclination to leave all the pleasant accommodation of their native country, and go over a terrible ocean, into a more terrible desert, for the pure enjoyment of his ordinances. . . . [They gathered to New England on these purposes:] First, it will be a service unto the Church of great consequence, to carry the Gospel into those parts of the world, and raise a bulwark against the kingdom of antichrist, which the Jesuits labor to rear up in all parts of the world. Secondly, all other Churches of Europe have been brought under desolations; and it may be feared that the like judgments are coming upon us; and who knows but God hath provided this place to be a refuge for many whom he means to save out of the General Destruction.[1]

In an almost uncanny echo from 1869, Mormon apostle Lorenzo Snow used the same imagery of a bulwark and a refuge to spell out the duty of converts to gather to Zion. According to Snow, the Mormon message was:

> "I have come in the name of the Almighty, in obedience to a call from God, to deliver you from your present circumstances. Repent of your sins and be baptized, and the Holy Ghost shall rest upon you, and you shall know that I have authority to administer the ordinances of the Gospel . . . Gather out from this nation, for it is ripening in iniquity, there is no salvation here. Flee to a place of safety." And as the messenger who went to Sodom said to the family whom he found there, so says the Elder of Israel, telling them, as

---

1. Cotton Mather, *Magnalia Christi Americana: or the Ecclesiastical History of New England, from its First Planting in the Year 1620, unto the Year of our Lord, 1698*, Vol. 1, 69–70.

Moses did the children of Israel, "to go to the land that the Lord God has appointed for the gathering of his people."[2]

Religious conflicts often concern real estate: earthly Zions need to take place somewhere. Nothing could have predicted the Protestant-Mormon conflict more clearly than the simultaneous framing of the rival groups' answers to the question: Who is the rightful steward of the American Promised Land?[3]

Protestants had been, from their colonial American beginnings, modest communities with immodest dreams. They aimed to lead the whole nation to adopt their Christian-American way, including an acknowledgement of divinely sanctioned Protestant leadership. However, Reformation culture had provided no single legitimate human authority to rally the diverse believers. The mostly-Protestant Founding Fathers claimed no divine authority for their political action, invoking instead the humble wish that Providence might smile on their best efforts. Still, desiring some authoritative foundation greater than mere human whim for their revolution, they adopted the Protestant notion of a higher, invisible, spiritual reality that was surely true. As discussed, they acted as political prophets, asserting as self-evident the radical equality of all men and their inalienable rights. Upon this invisible, quasi-religious authority of the rational spirit, they rejected any individual right over another—even if it were a king with an ancient divine right—and founded their state on the rightful "priesthood" of each believer or citizen.

---

2. Lorenzo Snow, "Column Article."

3. Jan Shipps, *Mormonism: The Story of a New Religious Tradition*, 41–65 and Truman G. Madsen, ed., *Reflections on Mormonism*, 84–91 discuss the Mormon self-image as that of the true Israel, at last restored to its proper place—geographically, in America. Joseph Smith claimed the New Jerusalem would be established in Missouri to jointly rule with the Old Jerusalem during the millennium. Why Missouri? Smith had announced revelations identifying it as the place where Christ would meet with the prophets of the past and present and that it was also the location of the Garden of Eden (D&C 27:5–15; 84:1–4, 99–102; 116). God would thus end the world where he began it. The Mormon vision thus reclaimed the American continent; they were righteous stewards of the promised but lost paradise, the builders of a new Zion, co-inheritors with the resurrected righteous citizens of Christ's kingdom who would arrive during his Millennial reign. After they triumphantly announced this news to Protestant farmers living nearby, it was only a matter of time before the Saints were thrown out of Missouri.

Mormons had similar desires to leaven the American loaf and beyond. They saw themselves as the true Israel, with the Book of Mormon extolling the American continent as the Promised Land. As such, from the very inception of the Church of Jesus Christ of Latter-day Saints, its missionaries aggressively proselytized Protestants throughout the United States and beyond.[4] From the Protestant point of view, the large Mormon enclave that had risen in Utah was dangerously spreading by the turn of the century. For them, Mormonism was a religious tumor between the Rockies and the West Coast that might metastasize if not cut out soon. Protestants saw Mormons as heretical Christians who looked and sounded in many ways like stalwart Protestants, but in reality were dangerous wolves clothed in prophetic enthusiasm that invigorated naïve seekers with false hope in new apostles teaching devilish doctrines. Their missionary efforts in Utah were, in large part, a defensive containment plan to protect the Christian flocks in the east from Mormon sheep stealing.[5] The most potent reason for their

---

4. The early twentieth century conflict studied here derived from a continuous seventy-five-year conflict between the upstart Latter-day Saints religious movement and established Protestant religious groups. The renowned historian, Eduard Meyer, after writing his *History of Antiquity,* chose to study the beginnings and development of what he deemed a nascent American Christianity in an Islamic mode: "Mormonism is one of the most instructive phenomena in the whole area of religious history. . . . Students of religions have kept themselves strictly aloof from Mormonism and disdained the rich instruction it has to offer. . . . It is not just another of the countless sects, but a new revealed religion, [with] an exceptionally rich contemporary store of documents; . . . what in the study of other revealed religions can only be surmised after painful research, is here directly accessible in reliable witnesses. Hence, the origin and history of Mormonism possesses a great and unusual value to the students of Religious History." Eduard Meyer, *The Origin and History of the Mormons, With Reflections on the Beginnings of Islam and Christianity,* i–iv.

5. Two inter-denominational missionary coordinating groups reported on missionary work in Utah: the Utah Interdenominational Commission (meeting annually) and the Utah Home Mission Workers' Council (meeting semi-annually). They adjusted overlapping efforts and planned cooperative activities. Participants were the Baptists, Congregationalists, Episcopalians, Methodists, and Presbyterians. See Robert T. Handy, *We Witness Together: A History of Cooperative Home Missions,* 48–49. This study is not a complete history of all the Protestant efforts but analyzes the specific, different proselytizing methods of an Episcopalian, a Presbyterian, and a Congregational/non-denominational minister. For the activities of the separate Baptist and Methodist missionary efforts through 1900, see Joseph Clark, *Leavening the Nation: The Story of American*

conflicts, however, was that both groups desired religious supremacy. The early Mormon plan for establishing and expanding a righteous empire, at such odds with American Protestant hegemony, was on its last legs entering the twentieth-century. Mormons viewed themselves as a chosen pilgrim minority, a spiritual Israel, separate from the worldwide "Gentile" majority that required conversion.[6] However, the reverse was the case in Utah. Protestant missionaries were the lonely pilgrims, surrounded by heretical Saints who needed to repent. Conflict was inevitable.[7]

Protestant missionaries had been working to convert Mormons in Utah since the early 1870s. During Utah's statehood struggle in the 1880s and early 1890s, the relationships between the two groups were especially

---

Home Missions, 235–39; and T. Edgar Lyon, "Evangelical Protestant Missionary Activities in Mormon Dominated Areas, 1865–1900." By the mid-twentieth century, the evangelical community of churches that focused on conversion from one false church to a true one were distinct from the social gospel oriented community that aimed on bringing people to God through service and devotion with little emphasis on conversion to a particular church (or even to Christianty). For a brief missiological review of twentieth-century methods employed by the "liberal" Protestant churches that associated as the World Council of Churches in the late 1920s see the Global Ministries website at http://www.globalministries.org/college_of_mission_missiology_models_of_mission.

6. I use "Protestant" and "denominations" to apply to the largest denominations in the United States at the turn of the century: Baptists, Congregationalists, Episcopalians, Lutherans, Methodists, and Presbyterians. "Evangelicals" distinguishes members of these denominations who were actively proselytizing both heathens and heretics at the time, usually supervised and supported either by their denominational or by a cooperative multi-denominational association. "Mormon" means members of the Church of Jesus Christ of Latter-day Saints headquartered in Salt Lake City, Utah.

7. The Saints were serious proselytizers beginning in the 1830s with missions to Western Europe, and then South America, the South Pacific, and Asia. An equal-opportunity religion, Latter-day Saint outreach was organized to eventually include Africa and all humanity including the billions of earthlings who had and would die without ever hearing their true gospel. Through vicarious temple rites, Mormon baptisms for the dead gave all dead persons, now dwelling alive in a parallel spirit world, the opportunity to accept the true (LDS) gospel by acknowledging the vicarious baptism prior to the end of the world and final resurrection (D&C 128; 1 Cor. 15:29; 1 Pet. 3:18–20, 4:6). Latter-day Saints have amassed the largest genealogical research library in the world to help perform this task of gathering the records of all the worlds' people in order to perform these ordinances.

strained as Protestants strongly backed the federal government's sanctions against polygamy and Mormon theocracy. The incarceration of polygamists and the escheating of Church properties can be seen as a Protestant religious and political triumph.[8]

Even after Utah attained statehood in 1896, questions remained about just how much the Mormons would be willing to bend to American law. Most Protestants close to the situation were quite suspicious; and, tellingly, their most aggressive missionary efforts occurred immediately after Mormons had disbanded their political party and withdrawn official sanction for new plural marriages. Most of the nation was relieved to see the messy social, political, and economic sanctions and pressures against Mormons resolved through the lengthy Senate hearings (1904–1907) that finally seated Mormon Apostle-Senator Reed Smoot, while many Protestants were not.[9] When Harvard's president, Charles Elliot, declared in 1892 in Salt Lake City that the Mormons were "the new Pilgrims" and that, since they had put polygamy behind them, they had every right to stand precisely in the same position as any other American religion, there was a great outcry among Protestant missionary and moral reform communities.[10] In response, Evangelicals launched even more energetic counter-proselytizing activities among the Mormons.[11] Their feelings were

---

8. On the aftermath of polygamy and the Mormon transition into acceptability as American citizens these texts are enlightening: Thomas G. Alexander, *Mormonism in Transition: A History of the Latter-day Saints, 1890–1930*; Howard R. Lamar, "National Perceptions of Utah's Statehood," 42–65; Gustave O. Larson, *The "Americanization" of Utah for Statehood*.

9. The potential conflict between evangelizing Protestant denominations over mission territories was resolved in the Western states by comity agreements that recognized as valid any baptisms performed by denominational parties to the agreement. The denominations also agreed to restrict proselytizing to exclusive territories to avoid wasting Protestant resources. These comity agreements helped to define the mainline Protestant churches at the time. See Andrew M. Greeley, *The Denominational Society*; Lyon, "Evangelical Protestant Missionary Activities"; Sydney E. Mead, "Denominationalism: The Shape of Protestant America"; Ferenc M. Szasz, *The Protestant Clergy in the Great Plains and Rocky Mountain West, 1865–1915*.

10. Author unknown, "Elliot Patronizes Mormons."

11. Jan Shipps has documented a decrease in periodical literature on the Mormons after the Smoot dispute, but their polemical religious content increased until the mid-1920s when the trend shifted toward more neutral or even pro-Mormon content. Shipps concluded that the higher the negativity of an article,

clear: Accepting Utah into the Union did not mean that Mormonism should be accepted among the nation's respectable religions. Claiming that polygamy had merely been a symptom of the deeper Mormon disease, several zealous missionaries warned Americans about the "Mormon Mohammedan Menace."[12] Protestants in Utah, who resented being a minority group with relatively little political and economic power, were particularly alarmist.[13] Mormonism's geographical concentration was a scandal to a Christian nation, they trumpeted. It had to be crushed or converted before it could be legitimized by Utah's recent statehood.[14]

These Utah Evangelicals sensed, correctly, that Mormons did not plan to be ordinary loyal Christian citizens. Beginning with the un-redressed Missouri expulsion in 1838, the relationship between the Mormon Kingdom of God and the United States was decidedly ambivalent. Although today's Mormons are known for their staunch patriotism, early Mormons took a more nuanced view, valuing their American citizenship as long as the government nurtured nascent Mormonism, but finding it a corrupt morass when it did not protect them. Their first loyalty

---

the greater the probability that its author was a Protestant minister. Jan Shipps, "In the Presence of the Past: Continuity and Change in Twentieth Century Mormonism," 18–21; see also Ethan Yorgason and Chiung Hwang Chen, "Geopolitical Imaginations about Mormons in News and Popular Magazines."

12. "Mohammedan" was a frequent epithet in the Protestant proselytizing materials. Exotic, barbaric images of Muslim and Mormon harems commonly caricatured both religions in novels, newspaper cartoons, and pornography. See Gary L. Bunker and Davis Bitton, *The Mormon Graphic Image: 1834–1914*; Craig L. Foster, "Victorian Pornographic Imagery in Anti-Mormon Literature." For a less prurient diatribe, the best example is Bruce Kinney, *Mormonism: The Islam of America*. An editorial in *The Missionary Review of the World* displays the general tone of Protestant attitudes at the turn of the century: "Islam is a dry rot, but the robe of Mormonism is rank, and smells to heaven." See Bruce Kinney, "The American Mohommedanism," 844.

13. In Utah in 1906, the Protestant denominations combined had a total of about 11,200 members. The breakdown is approximately as follows: Baptist, 1,800; Congregational, 900; Disciples of Christ, 300; Lutheran, 600; Methodist, 2,800; Presbyterian, 2,300; Episcopalian, 2,100; and others, 400. See Herbert Ware Reherd "An Outline History of the Protestant Churches of Utah," 650. Bruce Kinney estimated that in 1912 only about 3,000 Utah Protestants had converted from Mormonism and into some Protestant denomination. See Kinney, *The Islam of America*, 172.

14. Lamar, "National Perceptions," 58–62; Jan Shipps, *Mormonism*, 29.

was to their earthly Kingdom of God, not to any secular government.[15] Mormons believed, almost as an article of faith, that their theodemocratic utopia would outlast the Republic; and that the Utah pioneers would, within a generation or two, return east to re-inherit their lost properties and redeem a dissolute secular American democracy.[16] The Republic had relinquished its divine calling by rejecting Mormonism, by snubbing the Saints' appeals for redress for persecution in Missouri and Illinois and by murdering their prophetic leader.[17] They viewed their new statehood status ambivalently and ironically. Though some among them, especially the young, were ashamed of their peculiarity and craved to be accepted as normal Americans, many found U.S. citizenship an imposed accommodation, a temporary testing until the political New Jerusalem in Jackson County, Missouri, rose above the unrighteous realm in Washington, DC.[18] Protestant missionaries to Utah may not have understood the totality of

---

15. Laurence Moore describes Zionism as a kind of intentional isolationism from competing cultures that encourages orthodox teaching in the schools and media and discourages inter-marriage with backsliders and infidels. R. Laurence Moore, *Religious Outsiders and the Making of Americans*, 32–33. Thus, like Mormons, the Catholics, Jews, Southern Baptists, and American Indians have developed large enclaves. Edwin Scott Gaustad categorized American religious dissenters as schismatics, heretics, and misfits. This study confirms his placement of Mormons among the misfits who were managed by exile from the larger society. See Edwin S. Gaustad, *Dissent in American Religion*, 92–100.

16. Dean C. Jesse, "Joseph Smith's 19 July 1840 Discourse," 392–394.

17. After being forced out of Ohio, Missouri, and Illinois, and almost being disenfranchised in Utah, twentieth-century Mormons replaced their literal Zion with a metaphoric Zion that consisted of the "pure in heart" wherever they were found. But Mormon scripture still makes it offensively clear that it was just a matter of time before the country came running to Zion for help: "And it shall come to pass that every man that will not take his sword against his neighbor must needs flee unto Zion for safety. . . and the righteous shall be gathered out from among the nations, and shall come unto Zion. . . And Zion shall flourish and the glory of the Lord shall be upon her. . . And the day shall come when the nations of the earth shall tremble because of her, and shall fear because of her terrible ones. The Lord hath spoken it" (D&C 45:69, 71; 64:41, 43).

18. Two histories emphasizing the Mormon hope for eventual large-scale political influence are Klaus J. Hansen, *Quest for Empire: The Political Kingdom of God and the Council of Fifty in Mormon History*; and Robert B. Flanders, *Nauvoo: Kingdom on the Mississippi*.

the Mormon vision of the nation's future, but they nevertheless recognized this sense of religious differentiation and identity and found it alarming.[19]

Unifying Authority and Persecuting the Peculiar

Joseph Smith originally aimed to unify all Christianity. Channeling Smith's life-long abhorrence for angry bickering between supposed loving brothers and sisters in Christ, the Saints adopted a critical attitude toward the Protestant tendency to argue contentiously over doctrine and practice with a marked lack of charity. For later Mormons, unification was achieved through modern revelation from twelve living apostles whose senior member was honored as a living prophet. Whenever Church members disagreed over individual revelations, they deferred to the most authoritative voices among their divinely approved oracles. Protestants had left Rome over this very controversy about authority, and to have Mormons protesting their divisiveness sounded to them like an old argument for the Papacy. Though this study does not look at the Protestant-Catholic conflicts that occurred during this same period, it is important to note that there was still a strained relationship. Immigrant American Catholics, scattered throughout the larger cities of America, were by sheer numbers in a position to challenge a would-be Protestant hegemony.[20] When it came to proselytizing to the Protestants, Mormons, with their prophet, were more aggressive than Catholics with their Pope. The Saints seemed more dangerous as religious counterfeiters—although they wanted to centralize authority like Catholics, they looked like Protestants protesting the Protestants.

For hundreds of years Protestants had been used to divisiveness as a badge of their independence from any central imposition of authority. Over the centuries they had each separated into denominations because they found their critical disagreements on doctrine and practice to be serious, and it was normal for the various denominations to maintain that mutually critical attitude—especially behind closed doors. Nevertheless, most of the sects had agreed to speak civilly about each other in public, trade together equally, accept each other's baptisms, attend school together, and allow

---

19. Claton Rice, *Ambassador to the Saints*, 97–103; Szasz, *Protestant Clergy in the Great Plains*, 169.

20. These historic works treat American religious bigotry, including Catholics, Jews, and Mormons: Gustavus Meyers, *History of Bigotry in the United States*; Henry F. May, *The End of Innocence: A Study of the First Years of Our Own Times, 1912–1917*; and Martin E. Marty, *Righteous Empire: The Protestant Experience in America.*

their children to inter-marry.[21] Mormons were excluded from this compact, however. They wanted respect from their enemies, equality before the law, and fairness in adjudicating disputes; but even without those, contempt and persecution acted to usefully confirm their status as the peculiar people mentioned in the New Testament letter of 1 Peter 2:9. They were outsiders chosen as emissaries to the corrupt establishment.[22] Of course, Protestant denominations believed the same about themselves and that the Mormons' peculiarity disclosed only the LDS counterfeit usurpation of truth.

In 1911, Theodore Roosevelt, about to run for a third term, published an article in *Collier's* magazine to defend what some criticized as his previous vote-courting of the Mormons. In doing so, he expressed what was likely the national majority opinion on the Mormon-Protestant conflict at that time. If the Mormon Church tried to revive polygamy, he pointed out,

> it would be doomed. . . . Any Mormon who advocates disobedience to . . . the manifesto forbidding all further plural marriages . . . is doing his best to secure destruction of the Church. . . . If on the other hand, the Mormon Church shall turn its face to the future . . . the Church will be treated precisely on an equality with all other churches. The Mormon has the same right to his form of religious belief that the Jew and the Christian have to theirs, but, like the Jew and the Christian, he must not practice conduct which is in contravention of the law of the land . . . [Among Mormons I have known] . . . the standard of sexual morality was unusually high. Their children were

---

21. Perhaps there is no greater indicator of tribal defensiveness in hopes of maintaining purity than separation from any serious engagement with outsiders. According to John Fulton's analysis of contemporary troubles in Northern Ireland, neither Catholic and Protestant groups have the power to impose order. They both employ enclave strategies: they oppose outside religious parties, maintain segregated schools, and discourage mixed associations that might lead to intermarriage with outsiders. Identity is thus determined by their relation to outsiders. See John Fulton, *The Tragedy of Belief: Division, Politics, and Religion in Ireland*, 24. Social theorists have observed the important role of conflict with external groups, imagined or real, in maintaining identity. However, when a group's major strategy is to focus on an outside threat, it betokens internal disunity and eventual collapse.

22. Laurence Moore persuasively argues that American culture appreciates the dynamic movement from the outside to the inside, the foreigner to the citizen, the strange to the familiar, the persecuted to the proclaimed. However, this means no group can stay still in America—the continuous movement between outside and inside is what matters. This is counterintuitive in religious realms where the unchanging is presumed to reflect divine perfection. Moore, *Religious Outsiders*.

numerous, healthy, and well brought up; their young men were less apt than their neighbors to indulge in sexual dissipation . . . and they were free from that vice, more destructive to civilization than any other can possibly be, the artificial restriction of families, the practice of sterile marriage . . . which ultimately means the destruction of the nation.[23]

Anticipating what historian Jan Shipps would conclude some seventy years later, Roosevelt identified Mormonism as a genuinely new religion that he welcomed into America's fold—but not into Christianity.[24] Roosevelt's notice was politically acceptable to Mormonism's critics because he avoided the religious issue and instead positioned Mormons as a separate people, much like orthodox Jews.[25] An overtly religious candidate whose campaign song was "Onward, Christian Soldiers," Roosevelt would not have risked losing votes among Protestants, which he would have done had he made gestures toward accepting Mormonism as a Christian denomination. Bringing Utah fully into the national life made good economic and political sense. Roosevelt was banking on the American penchant for forgiveness that allowed enemies to quickly become profitable allies. It would have been economically inefficient for Americans to quarantine a state with strong market potential in the middle of the Western trade route.[26] However, Roosevelt did not appeal to either of these economic or political motives; instead, he cancelled out Utah as being a political problem and successfully framed the "Mormon question" as a First Amendment issue. In so doing, he tapped into America's deeply ingrained religious individualism whereby salvation comes to one person at a time, even in resistance to family or tribe solidarity. This made the basic social unit the individual. A brief excursus will be helpful here.

As Harold Bloom incisively observed, individual sovereignty derived from something deeper than a political right.[27] It was the foundation

---

23. Theodore Roosevelt, "Mr. Roosevelt to the Mormons," 28.

24. Jan Shipps, *Mormonism*.

25. Max Weber reasoned that Jewish resistance to Christian proselytizing was their reverence for their prophets, disdain for polytheism, and stable traditional family and congregational life of religious education and ritual. They accepted their status as a pariah (but pure) people. See Max Weber, *Ancient Judaism*, 424. A similar analysis could be made of the Protestant-Mormon missions.

26. In 1910, Utah's total population was about 400,000, geographical lying between Colorado at 800,000 and California at 2,500,000.

27. Harold Bloom, *The American Religion: The Emergence of the Post Christian Nation*, 32.

that Tocqueville identified, and Lincoln memorialized in the Gettysburg Address, as the sovereignty of people—a God-given sovereignty of each individual. In its most radical strain, it claimed co-eternal divine un-created status for the personal soul and God without collapsing the two into one.[28] Athenian democracy was a group majority system; the group in power granted a portion of power to individuals in the service of the group. But in American democracy, authority lay inherently in individuals, which individuals conferred upon "the people" (the government) to act on individuals' behalf.[29] The Constitution's Bill of Rights asserts ten rights—and all of them granted to individuals. The Constitution's preamble implies a unity that has never really existed in this nation of individualism, but it has been a useful myth that American sovereigns have appropriated from time to time to persuade the minority that they are out of step.[30]

The image of the lone individual standing up for his or her political rights is closely linked to the lone prophet who stands up for righteousness against the fallen tribe. This individualism resonates with the fundamental Protestant doctrine that people can personally commune with the divine. While God spoke, leaving a singular text, the Holy Spirit speaks the meaning of the text through the mediation of millions of individuals. Lonely Luther hammering his criticisms on the door at Wittenberg is an archetype. The Protestant sovereign soul and the American individual had a common derivation and shared the same penchant for self-confidence. The question of radical soul competency or radical free agency of souls produces the theological conundrum at the heart of the Hebrew and Christian Bibles: who is responsible for what happens including what we

---

28. Alexis de Tocqueville, *L'Ancien Regime*, 397.

29. Sidney Mead, *The Nation with the Soul of a Church*, 105; Wolfhart Pannenberg, "How to Think about Secularism," 28–29.

30. Democracy or rule of the majority without harming the dissenting individuals or minority groups is not applied or valued in the same way in all cultures. Indeed, it shifts within the same nation over time. The dynamic interpretation of the American Constitution reflects the changing cultural value of individualism compared to social cohesion. According to Benjamin Constant, Athenian democracy (fifth century BC) gave each male citizen an active role in approving the laws; but majority rule was weighed against any law's too strong positive empowerment of any particular citizen. The group was protected from individual interests. In American democracy, "the people" weigh the majority's laws against their negative infringements on individual interests. The individual was protected from group interests. Benjamin Constant, "The Liberty of the Ancients Compared with that of the Moderns," 321–27.

choose to think, feel, and do? It must be God if God created human souls in an instant out of nothing. But it must be the individual soul if souls are not created by God, but are un-created entities as old as God? Further, who is responsible for the environment in which we exist? It must be God if the universe is created ex nihilo by an independent act of an ultimately inscrutable deity. It must be all of the souls, not just God, if the universe was organized out of pre-existent, un-created matter in accordance with the collective decision of un-created souls that dwell in it. These theological conundrums have had lively social political ramifications in American society.

As the founding myth undergirding American democracy we have two rival plots: one based on the world-saving act of a singular Divine Sovereign, and the other based on the collective decisions of infinite numbers of equally Sovereign Souls. This mythic rivalry derives in part from the tension within traditional Christianity as it embraced and resisted the divine peerage of humans akin to God that were also abjectly powerless in facing ignorance, evil, and death. Joseph Smith's Mormonism unequivocally affirmed that the tension would never be resolved as long as divine beings were radically free to love or not and find new ways to create. Thus the rival tension between two social-political-theological ideals—finding the true self in pleasing or uniting with The Almighty Creator, Redeemer, and Sustainer of everything versus discovering and expanding on the infinite, free, uncreated, and indestructible self—by association with other similar infinite souls including God.

The old Protestant idea rejected the Popish hierarchy and thereby acknowledged each soul's direct connection to God and salvation. But they did not make it clear that the connection was one of mutual influence. God was more of a Popish King than a malleable Father. God was an Absolute Sovereign with absolute power and never asked real questions, knowing all. They tended to worship the definition of divine omnipotence, not the love of a Divine Father conditioned by the free acts of His children beyond His control.

Under the cloak of top-down hierarchical political or prophetic authority dwells the deeper eternal source of bottom-up authority of the people, by the people, and for the people. American democracy is unabashedly based on collaboration between personal sovereigns, and this derives from the Protestant impulse toward soul sovereignty that in Mormonism bloomed into an explicit doctrine of divine anthropology based on the Christian insight that God can take human form as Jesus did; through that humanity of Jesus, God saw Himself in human eyes as a loving Dad with great expectations for his mature children. The American ideal of progressive improvement derives from a more ancient source than the Renaissance or the Enlightenment. No aspect of current techno-wonder epoch, no sci-fi imagination has revealed more impressively the potential destiny of humanity than the texts of St. Paul and St. John—and the expansions on them by such as Joseph Smith. But mere progressive capacity—to live forever as an individual—is empty without the pains and joys of family and friends. Counter to individualism, the eternal plan in Mormonism is for advanced human-like souls to increase in others their desire and capacity for more joyful and ever-original experiences together eternally.

The Protestant spirit guaranteed the inevitability of religious schism. The Protestant way of receiving inspiration from the Holy Spirit individual by individual alone weakened church unity. The way to resolve disagreements ultimately led to schisms between those whose constituencies could not sustain a majority vote. Moses's wish that all the Lord's people would be prophets was realized in Protestantism, but it meant doing away with Moses (Num. 11:29). Denominational comity was as close to union as the Protestants would get—at least up to the present.

Joseph Smith, a radical proponent of the eternal, uncreated individual, proposed counterweighting Protestant-type schismatic individualism with heavy doses of Jewish-type tribal loyalty and Roman Catholic-type centralized ecclesiastical authority. Even with these counter-measures, Mormon schisms over prophetic succession following Joseph Smith's untimely death were still on the minds of many older LDS members at the turn of the twentieth century. There was a strong tendency to lean toward organizational unity under the direction of the prophet-president when spiritual individualism pressured the Saints to change. Mormon reformations had occurred, but they were led from the top, allowing the Utah church to renew its values while maintaining both its authority and organizational integrity.[31] The Mormon way of church governance allowed central apostolic authority to oversee a universal lay priesthood of individual mini-prophets who, in turn, checked the autocratic revelation from above by subjecting it to sustaining voter approval. Prophecy, whether from the top or from

---

31. Leonard J. Arrington and Davis Bitton, *The Mormon Experience: A History of the Latter-day Saints*, 206–61.

the grassroots, was not allowed to run amok.[32] But this church unity was purchased at a price that looked dangerously like Papism.

Proselytizing Rivalry

Missionizing was as inherent in Protestantism as schism. Although American Protestants were individualists, they were rarely hermits or solipsists. The crisis over religious authority was ultimately a social crisis. Inspired individuals felt impelled to share the Holy Spirit's message as a universally important truth, and the community either validated individual faith experiences or not. Joseph Smith, for example, took the Protestant approach by reading the Bible, feeling deeply motivated by a passage of scripture (James 1:5), which encouraged him to pray for guidance.[33] He asked which church he should join and, in a theophany of the Father and the Son, was instructed to join no church, that "all their creeds were an abomination" in God's sight.[34] He forthwith shared with a Methodist minister whom he respected the good news that Protestantism was corrupt and was startled by the hostile reception (JS–H 1:21–26). Smith's later reflections on this episode reveal his earlier disappointment with the established denominations and their ministers:

> At about the age of twelve [in 1817] my mind became seriously impressed with regard to the all important concerns for the welfare of my immortal Soul which led me to searching the Scriptures . . . [and] thus applying myself to them and my intimate acquaintance with those of different denominations led me to marvel exceedingly for I discovered that they did not adorn their profession by a holy walk and Godly conversation agreeable to what I found contained in that sacred depository this was a grief to my Soul . . . until age fifteen, I pondered many things in my heart concerning the situa-

---

32. With prophecy open to all while only an elite can interpret prophecy for all, the polarized organizational tensions between the Weberian priests and prophets is somewhat diffused in Mormonism. See Weber, *Ancient Judaism*, 169–93, 297–320.

33. There are other similarities between Mormon and Protestant approaches to spiritual practices, particularly in connection with the Methodist tradition. The work of Christopher C. Jones is particularly interesting in this regard. See Christopher C. Jones, "We Latter-day Saints are Methodists: The Influence of Methodism on Early Mormon Religiosity"; Christopher C. Jones, "The Power and Form of Godliness: Methodist Conversion Narratives and Joseph Smith's First Vision"; and Christopher C. Jones, "The Worst Fights are Behind Relatives: Mormons and Methodists in the Nineteenth Century."

34. Dean C. Jesse, "The Early Accounts of the First Vision," 280.

tion of the world of mankind. My mind became exceedingly distressed for I became convicted of my Sins and by searching the Scriptures I found that mankind did not come unto the Lord but that they had apostatized from the true and living faith and there was no society or denomination that built upon the Gospel of Jesus Christ as recorded in the New Testament.[35]

The very name of the fledgling church, Latter-day Saints, launched a similar attack on traditional Christianity.[36] In other words, the original first-century saints had been followed by the dark ages until new revelation burst on the scene with original scriptures revealed by angelic means to a modern prophet in the early nineteenth century.[37] Mormonism blithely disregarded eighteen hundred years of Christian tradition upon which Western and American Protestant culture relied. Unsurprisingly, Protestants resented this non-cordial Mormon insistence on their inherent corruption.

Mormonism's founding story is somewhat similar in its original impulse to that of Protestantism. Martin Luther, after all, had desired only to reform Catholicism and was only reluctantly forced toward a radical schism. It was not until he came to believe that the Holy Spirit overrode Rome's authority to excommunicate, and then declared Rome criminally heretical, that a new religion began. Though Luther and Zwingli briefly attempted to form a unified Protestantism, they could not agree on the Holy Spirit's interpretation of doctrine. After years of religious wars in Europe, the strategy of overt tolerance and covert criticism became increasingly workable. Major Protestant leaders began to consider their churches as appendages in the Pauline body of Christ, with universal unity being postponed until the final eschaton. This strategy of expecting eventual harmony became, in America, the shibboleth for acceptance into mainstream Protestant denominationalism. Mainstreamers believed that their sacraments, or saving ordinances,[38] were fungible between de-

---

35. Jesse, "First Vision," 279.

36. Bruce Porter, "Church of Jesus Christ of Latter-day Saints," 277.

37. Mormon history leaps from ancient to modern worlds. In 1829, Joseph Smith and his associate Oliver Cowdery received the keys of their Christ-bestowed priesthood authority from resurrected apostles Peter, James, and John, who thus bypassed centuries of popes, priests, pastors, reformers, and revivalists (D&C 27:12–13). In 1830 Joseph Smith, having recently published the Book of Mormon and received this priesthood ordination, organized the body known today as the Church of Jesus Christ of Latter-day Saints.

38. The two terms—sacraments and saving ordinances—are not identical. Catholics and most Protestants call the sacred rituals instrumental to personal

nominations, and that proselytizing should focus on those outside of the mainline denominations.[39]

By the early twentieth century, a minimalist Protestantism had merged with American individualism. To be mainline, one followed his or her own conscience in protesting against evil, heresy, and abuse without attempting to proselytize those of other mainstream Christian groups. Protestants who found this position too weak departed for more authoritative religions or affiliated with Protestant fundamentalists who affirmed that the authority of orthodoxy was worth fighting over.[40]

Joseph Smith, a product of New England Protestantism, had three hundred years of heretical precedent on which to found his new beginning. His claim of restoring the original New Testament church, however, was an all-American leap beyond the Protestant Reformers.[41] His was a

---

salvation "sacraments." Other Protestants such as the Southern Baptists, and the Latter-day Saints call them "ordinances." Some Christian groups believe that neither sacraments nor ordinances are important to attaining salvation. My study has led me to believe that the term "ordinance" was developed as a middle way between sacerdotal/sacramental salvation and universal salvation of the good-hearted. Very briefly, a sacrament was an authorized ecclesiastical ritual that God required to make a person acceptable in His kingdom. An ordinance was an authorized ecclesiastical ritual that humans needed to help them change sufficiently to enter God's kingdom. Sacraments were public acts of submissive obedience to please God. Ordinances were acts to teach correct order and allow an overt commitment to change. A sacrament was a legal act that pleased God. An ordinance was a learning experience necessary for progress toward God. In either case, salvation came from being good and practicing the sacraments or ordinances. Mormons and Catholics believed sacerdotal authority was also required for the ritual to be efficacious. On this point, to avoid handing the keys of salvation over to the ordained priesthood, Protestants were less strict.

39. Martin E. Marty, *Modern American Religion I: The Irony of it All*, 88.

40. Martin Marty and Scott Appleby demonstrated that religions that do not actively criticize other religions and secular cultures often lose membership to those that do. See Martin Marty and Scott Appleby, eds., *Fundamentalisms and Society: Reclaiming the Sciences, the Family, and Education*. Ironically, if the critique becomes the main aspect of religious life, the religion becomes a political movement that does not satisfy the deeper desire for otherworldly worship that provides purpose to human endeavors. The successful groups have thus found an optimum balance of the worldly and otherworldly.

41. Another restorationist, Alexander Campbell (1788–1866), challenged Joseph Smith's restoration as well as all Protestant denominations that relied on any tradition other than what could be found in the Christian Bible and did not

claim for an original Catholicism—earlier than Rome, earlier than Jesus even—a religion taught by God and angels to Adam with authority that trumped all other religions. By fusing his modern version of Israel's prophetic authority with the ubiquitous Protestant experience of the Holy Spirit's private whisperings to individuals, Joseph Smith attempted to meld the authority of inspired office with the authority of the individual inspired conscience. He tried to accomplish the very thing Protestant Evangelicals wanted; namely, to create a strongly unified Christian community that could militantly proselytize and still allow for personal freedom in religious expression.

Who Should Lead?

Just as brothers irritate each other and fight over the things they have in common, they often also battle for supremacy in the family's pecking order. As discussed earlier, I believe the primary reason behind the early-twentieth-century Protestant-Mormon conflicts was both groups' desires for religious supremacy and hegemony; and their belief that they were called to lead the nation—and even the world. Protestant hegemony would be attempted by encouraging Americans to vote for Protestant candidates. Their religious influence on culture came before the candidates were elected, but was to be sustained by keeping Protestants in the top seats of power. Even though Americans had told themselves they had separated church and state, the church had maintained a deep, almost unnoticed, and lasting influence on the state. Protestant denominationalism itself was a model of maintaining at least an image of unity amid a substantial Christian diversity. It seemed quite compatible with the American political system. The similarity of mores among the various Protestant groups was not threatening because denominational divisions gave no impression of monolithic power. Catholics and Mormons, on the other hand, were assumed by the majority of the nation to achieve unity by top-down political and religious control by pope or prophet.

Mormons foresaw their triumphal theodemocracy in America and the rest of the world as something that would occur following Christ's Second Coming, during which Zion would be reestablished in Jackson County, Missouri, near the site of the Garden of Eden. Smith's restoration was to

---

seek to return to the simplicity and "primitivism" of the first century church. Richard T. Hughes, "Two Restoration Traditions: Mormons and Churches of Christ in the Nineteenth Century."

go beyond returning the first-century church to earth. The earth and all its peoples were to be restored to pre-lapsarian paradisiacal glory. The U.S. Constitution, though divinely inspired, was a preparatory regime to be replaced by a Millennial world theodemocracy. In contrast, Protestants feared that any kind of theocracy would turn to tyranny. They hoped to make the state merely their moral ally by assuring that most state officials would be Protestant. As we see in this history, the Protestant majority actually did enlist the power of state law to restrict religious practices of their competitors.

In contrast to their nineteenth-century counterparts, the early-twentieth-century Saints stopped expecting an imminent Second Coming and concentrated on purer living and more ardent proselytizing to prepare the whole world as a righteous Zion *before* the Second Coming.[42] They had a vast mission to limit the apocalyptic destruction of the earth and its people through social, political, economic, and spiritual programs that would uplift mankind, including all who have ever lived on the planet.

Hegemonic Underdogs

Given the diversity of American religious groups—and the American penchant for checks and balances on social power of any kind—it appears naive for any religious group to believe it could attain supreme cultural influence. However, if the group believes that God is on their side, then all things seem possible. For both Protestants and Mormons, even setbacks were read as progress—and on very good authority: "For whom the Lord loveth he chasteneth, and scourgeth every son whom he receiveth. If you endure chastening, God dealeth with you as with sons: for what son is he whom the father chasteneth not?" (Heb. 12:6–8).

Even though both groups could read themselves into scripture this way, Mormons had received not only chastenings—their legal and political defeats that led to their agreement to cease the practice of plural marriage—but had also experienced many successes. As Theodore Roosevelt

---

42. Carmon Hardy has analyzed the excuses given to protect God from His seeming unresponsiveness to Mormon pleas for divine help. Abuses of the system of plural marriage and selfishness of some in communal living efforts were given as reasons. See B. Carmon Hardy, "Self Blame and the Manifesto," 43–56. To this day many Mormons believe the Church members have been living on a lower spiritual plane than that required for the establishment of a true Zion in which the Second Coming may happily occur. See Hugh W. Nibley, *Approaching Zion*, 54–59, 366–71.

had sensed, being a minority religious group with audacious truth claims, moral discipline, and Zion-building dreams, the Saints were positioned as the quintessential American underdogs. They articulated iconoclastic dissent against classic Christian history, had appropriated American history, and had stood immovable for their beliefs. As refugees to the West, they had come close to establishing their own nation. They promoted economic self-sufficiency; at one time even established a new calendar of holidays (July 24th remains a Utah state holiday, commemorating the Mormon pioneers who entered the Salt Lake valley); coined their own money; and developed a Deseret alphabet to set their language apart.[43] What the South attempted with cannons, the Mormons attempted with calculated isolation and sheer creativity, usurping the pilgrim story of founding the American Zion. Laurence Moore has elucidated this incisively:

> That one way of becoming American was to invent oneself out of a sense of opposition. . . . The American religious mainstream never meant anything except what competing parties chose to make of it. . . . In defining themselves as being apart from the mainstream, Mormons [for example] were in fact laying their claim to it. By declaring themselves outsiders they were moving to the center. . . . It was the impulse which the Mormons represented that made their story important. Nineteenth-century historians, and many who followed them, got the meaning of American religious experience almost exactly backwards. The trend was never toward unity. *American religious experience began as dissent, and invented oppositions remained the major source of liveliness in American religion both in the nineteenth and twentieth centuries.*[44]

Mormons were the new Protestant underdogs—the purists against the old corrupt American Protestant establishment.[45] The fact that Mormons had adopted a Protestant strategy did not, however, endear them to these brothers. The two groups' overlapping desires to become the saviors of America and the world produced a subtle envy and overt resentment of any gains that the other might achieve in social power or church membership. Both were attempting to build a new Zion, and both were ambiva-

---

43. Ferenc M. Szasz, *The Protestant Clergy*, 166.

44. Moore, *Religious Outsiders*, 45–46; my emphasis.

45. This strategy of healthy tension against the enveloping culture has recently been found just as successful for Protestants as it was for Mormons. According to Christian Smith, successful American Evangelical churches maintain a distinct sub-cultural identity by emphasizing its antagonism with dissimilar Christian, secular, and other religious groups. Christian Smith, *American Evangelism: Embattled and Thriving*, 118.

lent towards modernizing trends in American culture. Some Mormons felt they should become a small nation on their closely guarded Utah reservation, acting as a beacon to the corrupt American empire that surrounded them. Others believed they should be the leaven in society and freely disperse among the Gentiles. Evangelicals also attempted to gather in mass urban meetings as an alternative to a growing urban society that was becoming increasingly secular and increasingly Catholic. Both Protestants and Mormons wanted to weld a nation of individualists into a righteous Christian community, but each thought the other lacked the bona fide doctrine and authority to do so.

Their religious contest was not a conflict based on miscommunication. These opponents rationally comprehended each other's concepts, methods, and claims, but they had difficulty empathizing with each other and thus respecting the core imaginative ideals that gave their respective religions their unique appeal. They believed that their fundamental religious rivalry stemmed not from different viewpoints, but from dark motives or deception by the devil. Their mutual and similar critique of the surrounding culture could not outweigh their suspicions that their critics were willing dupes dealing in bad faith. Despite similarities in Christian terminology and many moral matters, they denounced each other for believing in God wrongly and not just differently.

They also baffled each other by the religious life they chose. Both assumed that the other's religion repressed their capacity to learn a better truth. Each believed that their own missionaries' teachings were clear and attested by God's spirit. Therefore, their religious differences could not be innocent communication errors, for God would not affirm irreconcilable doctrines and practices on matters of ultimate salvation. As a result, they sensed that neither would seriously consider another religion's appeal as long as they held their own as the divine truth. Thus, their proselytizing and counter-proselytizing approaches were to attack the misplaced faith of the other: they had to persuade a potential convert to doubt.

Evangelical historian Paul Jesse Baird has described well the Protestants' feelings and reasons for aggressive efforts to proselytize in Utah:

> [T]he Mormon Empire in the Great Basin presented to non-Mormons a formidable wall of separation: anthropomorphic in its doctrine of God, and thus anti-spiritual in its view of faith and life; polygamous in its view of family life, with carnal attitudes toward sex and marriage which still affect the life of the area; materialistic in its value system, which bent thrift and

industry into a life-system of salvation by works and material substance; and overpowering in its political and societal dictation and discrimination.[46]

To recap, the never-solid Protestant cultural hegemony in America was faltering in early-twentieth-century America. At the end of the nineteenth century, as the nation was importing diverse cultures and ideas, Protestants tried to unify to protect their powerful borders from erosion, and a religious-nationalist wave hit the country strongly.[47] Protestants believed they were the foreordained stewards of the Providentially blessed continent and ached to assert their moral authority. As the greater society looked to their religious leadership less, one group took them extremely seriously—as rivals! Mormons made a direct theological and missionary attack on them that was galling and embarrassing when successful. Hence, Protestant missionaries counter-attacked the Mormons' claim of sole religious authority as arrogant, their concept of God as blasphemy, and their emphasis on industriousness as materialism. They tried to persuade the Saints to humbly accept that Protestant authority—granted to clergy by the Holy Spirit—was adequate, that the Trinitarian concept of God was true, that grace was the only way to ultimate salvation, and that salvation was found in unity with God, not in some ever-progressing social evolution of married divinities.

Mormons counter-counter attacked, claiming their Protestant antagonists to be blindly or stubbornly bound to corrupt traditions. They mirrored each other in their penchant for combat through scriptural text-proofing and discrediting the motives of their opponents' leaders. Each group charged the other with prideful and irrational heresy and apostasy from true Christianity.[48] Although both shared a desire to lead American society for good, they knew the other could not do it with erroneous doctrines and practices. With integrity, they each believed the highest good was to eliminate heretical Christianity that would mislead rather than save the world. The method of elimination is central to this story. Both sides shared a conviction that the human conscience should not be coerced, and this dissuaded them from desiring to violently destroy their rivals.

---

46. Paul J. Baird, *The Mystery of Ministry in the Great Basin*, 92.

47. Josiah Strong, *Our Country: Its Possible Future and Its Present Crisis*; Luther Tracy Townsend, "Manifest Destiny from a Religious Point of View."

48. The claim that Mormons were simply not Christians was made consistently and earnestly as the twentieth century began. See David M. Williams, "Will the Mormon People Become Christians?" and Elizabeth B. Vermilye, "Non-Christian Faiths in America."

Further, the American way of sustaining social order through persuasive rather than coercive conflict engagement was a powerful part of their common cultural context. Fighting over God had to go on among free people that inevitably disagreed over religious truth, but they had persuasion not coercion as the goal; and that makes things inefficient—especially if one is used to wielding power by other means. Although some American religious conflicts went all the way to violence, this time the conflict was by other means, which makes it both very interesting as history and very relevant as prophesy.

CHAPTER FIVE

The True Church Challenge: Counterfeit vs. Real Christianity

In this examination, I have chosen the following categories to compare the claims and practices of my protagonist communities: *narratives, doctrines, symbols and rites, and styles of religiosity*. I aim to clarify the differences and similarities that produced such a deep and lasting rivalry between Protestants and Mormons and provide a keener understanding of why their social-political-religious contestation has endured almost two centuries.

There is no such thing as *the* Protestant point of view on any subject, because there are millions of such points of view with no centralized authoritative voice. Still, it is possible to consider the range of Protestant viewpoints on doctrine and to arrive at a general understanding of views among adherents. Even within Mormonism, usually viewed as a unified system of belief and practice through a hierarchical leadership, there exists no authoritative systematic theology despite its centralized apostolic authority. Nevertheless, one can obtain an understanding of the most accepted beliefs through reading texts by venerated leaders and scholars. In the discussions of the doctrines of God and salvation that follow, with the editing assistance of an Evangelical scholar, John Morehead, I have attempted to convey an accurate summation of Protestant views in reaction to Mormon claims and vice versa during the early twentieth century.

Narratives

Andrew Greeley wrote: "Religion is story, story before it is anything else, story after it is everything else, story born of experience coded in symbol, reinforced in the self and shared with others to explain life and death."[1] He claimed that the sociological study of any religion requires first learning its poetic narrative that predates its systematic prose.[2] This comparative

---

1. Andrew M. Greeley, *The Denominational Society*, 40.
2. See Leonard J. Biallas, *World Religions: A Story Approach*.

study of persuasive conflicts between these religious rivals is described as "narrative contests"—the battle of one sacred story against another.[3]

Religious stories usually include a cosmogony, a theogony, a theology, an anthropology, and a theodicy that explain how God relates to creation, including human beings and their sustenance, improvement, and destiny. The narratives' images are not exact doctrinal statements, but expressions of possibilities that believers expand on through their own thoughts and desires. Religion provides the story of ultimate reality that gives human beings an orderly basis for hopeful and purposeful living. When conflicts arise over *the* story of ultimate reality, they are usually engaged as a contest between groups who are deeply invested in defending the truth of their own stories.

The great Christian story is simple: humans are candidates destined for divinity through the loving gift of God. New Testament stories describe Jesus of Nazereth as a man who was also God—fully man *and* fully God. Christian theologians for centuries have worked to avoid dragging The Almighty down into human imperfection, or raising man too high toward divine perfection. To traditional philosophers, the idea that the singular creator and sustainer of the universe could become a mortal man in history seemed incomprehensible. Paul and John affirmed that Jesus was both divine and human (Rom. 8:14–19) and became man to perfect humanity.

The story climaxes here: Almighty God loves each human creation as would a parent and friend. God lifts His child and friend to the highest state of joy with Him—and somehow changes humans to become as He is. This doctrine of theosis is the glorious, mysterious end game for all who are saved. Theosis came via Jesus, the man-god, who out-loved us all—and thus secured both his and our eternal joy and divine glory (Heb. 12:2). Christianity is the great optimism. However, Protestant and Mormon versions of this optimistic narrative presented drastically different versions of the divine and human mystery.

The Protestant grand story emphasized the Christological link between the sovereign deity and the creatures he created, sustained, and redeemed. Man could never forget that dependency, nor rely on any other person or thing for ultimate happiness in this life or the life to come. God was fundamentally different from humankind, but nevertheless offered eternal bliss to a depraved humanity by His loving grace and through the gift of faith in Christ. In contrast, the Mormon story was based on

---

3. Gerald Bruns, *Hermeneutics, Ancient and Modern*, 248.

an ontological anthropology of equality between God and His offspring. On the theological stage in early-twentieth-century Utah, Protestant and Mormon grand narratives about the provenance and destiny of humanity were locked in unresolvable conflict.

The Protestant Sacred Story in America

The basic Protestant understanding of the overarching biblical narrative comes by way of appreciation of what may be called God's Grand Story. Protestants follow this narrative thread woven through Genesis to Revelation. It may be understood as the unfolding of the divine drama in which God is the primary focus and humans play an important part within the cosmic backdrop. This drama involves six acts including creation, catastrophe, covenant, Christ, church, and consummation.

The Protestant Christian view is that God chose out of love to create the cosmos, and creatures who could freely choose to be in relationship with Him. Through disobedience, humanity fell, inclining human nature toward sin (although Protestants disagree about the extent of the influence of the fall on human nature and its impact on free will and choice). Through God's love, He promised to redeem humanity from sin and began the process through Abraham by calling a people who would become Israel, eventually culminating with the life, death, and resurrection of Christ. Jesus preached a message of the Kingdom of God, which was present and began with his coming; and which would one day come in totality with his Second Coming. Until then, his disciples were to be involved in expanding and demonstrating the Kingdom in various ways, including both social action and the sharing of the gospel message of the work of Christ.

Various speculative scenarios may be found in Protestantism in regards to the last days, but in general there is a hope for the return of the resurrected Christ, a Millennium of peace, the resurrection and judgment of humanity at the end of the ages, and a restoration of all good things with the creation of New Heavens and a New Earth where the blessed dwell for eternity.[4] More than on the nature of and purpose for eternal life with God, the focus on the Protestant story is on how heavenly safety is secured.

---

4. Although Evangelicals tend to emphasize doctrine in terms of propositions and systematic theologies, a narrative theology is also helpful. It provides a way for Evangelicals to reconnect their doctrinal truths to the broader story of God in the Bible, and this form of theologizing connects more readily to Mormon culture

Due to heavy persecution from the Church of England, the Puritans (a Calvinist branch of the Protestant tradition) came to America where they could establish a righteous people to wait for the Lord's Second Coming. After years of disputation and schism, the mainline Protestant sects developed a system of inter-congregational cooperation and sacraments that gave believers the freedom of affiliating with other Christians of similar temperament or cultural background. Though they might look like hundreds of different churches, all were considered the body of Christ, unified by several beliefs: the testimony of a triune God, the democratic priesthood of believers, the central authority of the Bible, the reality of Christ's death and resurrection, grace through faith as the only mechanism of salvation, and the Great Commission to share the Gospel with unbelievers throughout the world.

The grand Protestant story was a spiritual war story—and how the war is to be engaged and eventually won in this world. Twentieth-century Christian missionaries not only aimed to save souls, but also sustain the culture of Protestant Christianity that under-girded American society. As Christian soldiers, they brought converts into the ranks to invigorate a corrupt and worldly society. They were the Pilgrims' pride: the redeemed people of God with a mission to help save the wicked before the Second Coming. Their Christian lives leavened society. As the figurative Body of Christ, they were called by God to be His servants and the means to save America and the entire world from spiritual disaster. Dante in *The Divine Comedy* and Milton in *Paradise Lost* poetically expanded the traditional Christian narrative in great detail, both in future and past tenses. The Protestant grand narrative focuses on the middle of three acts while hinting at what was before and what is to come.

The Latter-day Saint Sacred Story

For Mormons, the purpose of God was to lead His creations to become more perfect divinities by experiencing the pain and joy of this world and the resurrection to come. The Gods as Heavenly Parents had clothed uncreated individual intelligences with spiritual form prior to our mortal birth in physical bodies. This spirit form enabled each person to have more experiences that

---

that emphasizes narrative. On narrative theology in traditional Christianity see Stanley Hauerwas and L. Gregory Jones, eds., *Why Narrative? Readings in Narrative Theology*; Gerard Loughlin, *Telling God's Story: Bible, Church and Narrative*; and Christopher J. H. Wright, *The Mission of God: Unlocking the Bible's Grand Narrative*.

enhanced their capacity for relational joy—the main purpose for existence. The mortal body form was designed to further enhance our capacity for joy. Everyone who has lived or will live on the earth is a courageous adventurer, freely choosing to enter mortality—a new and disorienting environment in which their pre-mortal experiences are forgotten and in which they acquire a body of flesh and blood that suffers and dies. Adam and Eve were two of God's most valiant collaborators, and they were the first to be given physical bodies, becoming the progenitors of humanity. A minority of spirit children refused to descend into this mortal human experience and, for reasons difficult to understand, these children were exiled from God's presence and became enemies of mankind alongside Lucifer, the devil.

Although human mortals live with a veil of forgetfulness concealing their prior life with their Heavenly Parents, they nevertheless are still connected to God through the whisperings of conscience that reinforces desires for beauty, love, and spiritual communion with God and each other. Throughout human history, God has also inspired prophets to teach humanity which way to go. These instructions are preserved in Holy Scriptures. Although temptation abounds, and evil may be chosen as freely as good, each human's inner core cherishes freedom and love, giving mortal beings an advantage in rising to meet the challenges and achieving a joyful, abundant life. The highest relationship among mortals mirrors that of the Heavenly Parents: the loving union of a man and woman who procreate new forms in which fellow spirits may also come to earth to experience life's hard lessons and joys.

After experiencing mortality, the physical body dies while the spirit body, now endowed with both its pre-mortal and mortal memories, moves on to another sphere to await the judgment and resurrection. The righteous will be resurrected at the time of Christ's Second Coming, with a general resurrection to follow at the end of the Millennium—a thousand-year period in which Christ will lead all earthly governments and oversee important work for the salvation of souls. Resurrection applies to all human beings who have ever lived on the earth, and is a function of Christ's conquering of death. In the resurrection, all will experience new and improved bodies with enhanced capacities and their future existence will expand infinitely before them. Those who have proven most loving will also be exalted, or endowed with the ability to procreate other bodily forms. When this parent-child relationship is formed, the couple will be gods to those who choose to become their children. The relation of Heavenly Parents with infinite lines of progeny is that of joyful friendship, including the sadness and happiness that interpersonal love always provides. Thus, each person on earth is born destined for enhanced divinity, though not all will choose to conform their lives (in this world or the next) to associate in heavenly society.

Although each individual is capable of choosing and living righteously, the truth has many counterfeits and the devil is a wily deceiver. In Mormon view, the scriptures chronicle repeated cycles of apostasy from the revealed truth beginning with the ancient patriarchs to the present. These cycles are the most important events in the history of the world. After the death of Christ's apostles, the Christian churches fell into apostasy and evolved through the centuries into weak approximations of the original apostolic church. Many truths about the nature of God and destiny of humans were obscured; and the authority to receive new scripture and perform salvific ordinances was lost. Religious reformations during these centuries were sincere but largely ineffective efforts to return Christians to the true path. For about seventeen-hundred years, no truly valid Christianity existed on the earth—then, in 1820, came the light.

In the Mormon scenario, the United States achieved political independence primarily to allow religious freedom to flourish, creating an environment in which the truth could be restored without being crushed or contaminated by entrenched religious/political cultures. In 1820, an upstate New York teenager named Joseph Smith prayed to know which of all the Christian churches was right and received a visitation from God the Father and Jesus Christ who assured him that the true church was not on the earth. This theophany painted a picture of sacred history in which Christ's return was imminent. Subsequent angelic visitations instructed that Smith would translate a record of the former inhabitants of the Americas that contained the fullness of the gospel of Jesus Christ—The Book of Mormon. From resurrected and glorified messengers, Smith received "keys" held by former prophets: Noah, Abraham, Moses, Elijah, John the Baptist, and Christ's three main apostles Peter, James, and John. This new-yet-old church would fulfill Daniel's prophecy—becoming a stone that would roll forth to break down all human kingdoms and establish God's kingdom in its place (Dan. 2:34–35) to prepare the world for the Second Coming of the Lord Jesus.

Doctrines

Doctrines explain how and why to live rightly within the context of the great narrative. Just as the grand stories, the doctrines of Protestants and Latter-day Saints were substantially different and seriously contested. The natures of mankind and their object of worship, God, mattered deeply to most people in the early twentieth century. People believed they could ascertain the truth about religious doctrine and live in accordance with it. Protestants especially focused on correct scriptural interpretation regarding doctrines and relied less on grand narratives or clergy than Mormons did.

William Paden, a Presbyterian missionary that labored in Utah from 1897 to 1931, accused the Mormons of denying the following orthodox doctrines: That God the Father was the creator, sustainer, and savior of the world; that God the incarnated human Son was the inexplicable mystery of the monotheistic Trinity; that humankind was innately prone to sin; that salvation comes only through a miraculous change in human nature brought about by grace; and that eternal rewards and punishments would be meted out at the final judgment awaiting each person.[5] Using Paden's indictment as a general guide, I will explore several of the major doctrinal controversies that undergird the mutual accusations of false or counterfeit Christianity.

Human Relationship to God

The seventeenth-century mathematician and theologian Blaise Pascal once observed: "Christianity is strange: it requires man to recognize that he is vile, and even abominable, and yet bids him to desire to be like God. Without such counter-weighting, man's pending exaltation would make him execrably vain, or his abasement would make him execrably despicable."[6] This summation of the paradox that underlies the Christian view of humans in relation to God also speaks to the heart of the doctrinal conflicts between Evangelical Protestants and Latter-day Saints at the beginning of the twentieth century. While each group acknowledged both sides of the paradox, Protestants emphasized humanity's miserable fallen state; the Mormons, its glorious eventual rise.[7]

---

5. Paul J. Baird, *The Mystery of Ministry in the Great Basin*, 26, 92.

6. Blaise Pascal, *Thoughts, Letters, and Minor Works*, 544; my translation.

7. William James also described this doctrinal polarity in terms of two different temperaments. For him, the "sick soul" feels the burden of evil in the cosmos as necessary and seeks God's love to endure the inevitable suffering it brings. The "healthy minded" soul feels that the universe was created for joy, and that evil is extraneous—something to be eliminated in good works inspired by a loving God. See William James, *The Varieties of Religious Experience*, 121–126. To put it in Jamesian terms, there were more sick souls among the Protestants and more

Beginning from a position as fallen beings, Protestants located their fondest hopes and joys in the mystery of how a God so great could care for a creation so weak. Human value was rooted in a God who created humanity in the divine image that remained and shone through even if tainted by the effects of the Fall. Contemplating God's great love for humans, despite their corrupt natures, inspired them to deep devotion and yearning for salvation securable through the completed work of Christ by grace alone, through faith alone, and extended into the afterlife with an immaterial God as they entered into relationship with their Heavenly Father by adoption as spiritual sons and daughters. Mormon hopes and enjoyment primarily came by contemplating that human souls were uncreated eternal beings that could grow in limitless capacity to love as God loves. Men and women, at their best, were mortal examples of physical, godlike, resurrected beings. That humankind could be related to God literally as a child to a parent inspired in them the hope for post-mortal family and social maturation into ever-fuller divinity.

From the foundational belief that God was infinite and eternal, while humans are finite beings created in God's spiritual image, Protestants were attracted to the hope of enjoying such divine love, power, and beauty as saved souls resurrected at the end of the ages and dwelling in God's presence either in heaven or a new earth. This entailed living now in the divine spiritual presence of the indwelling Holy Spirit; and, in the world to come, in the presence of the triune God. The Protestant believer's approach to worship combined the feelings of an awestruck, imperfect being gazing at divine perfection and, though pardoned from one's faults, bearing the guilt of remaining imperfections. By contrast, from a foundational belief that humans were eternal beings capable of infinite growth, and who saw this earth as a school for lessons in growing more godlike, they did not worship God in awe so much as in affection. At the crucial moment of returning to God after mortality, divine punishment for the Protestant was retributive, but for the Mormon, remedial. The Protestant knelt before a Divine King; the Mormon embraced a Heavenly Parent.

Neither Protestants nor Latter-day Saints dared to claim anything close to having a fullness of knowledge about the Godhead, but the Saints felt that humans could know more about a deity who was an exalted Man

---

healthy-minded souls among the Mormons, although each group contained numbers of the other temperament. This note is equally pertinent in the section to follow on Styles and Religiosity.

of Holiness than one of absolute Otherness.[8] Protestants would not say that deity was totally inaccessible, nor would the Mormons imply that God was a dad to pal around with. Even if Protestants did believe something akin to humans having godly potential, their emphasis on the virtue of humility meant that they kept such notions to themselves. They were more reticent than Mormons to discuss any ultimate divinization.

God: A Person or Personal?

Jesuit theologian Edward T. Oakes wrote, "if the gods have a genealogy, [that means] the world-womb out of which they were born is greater than themselves."[9] He suggested that gods with histories and personalities are inferior to a god that is beyond personal categories, and he used the various gendered gods of pagan myths as examples. These gods were "subject to sexual needs, desiring, and mating with each other; moreover, they eat and drink, fall sick and require healing, need and invent tools, etc."[10] Such limited gods of ancient Egypt, Mesopotamia, and Greece stand in contrast to a god that somehow self-exists (aseity) and is not dependent upon or limited to space and time.

Agreeing with this sentiment about the inferiority of a god who has a history and dwells in a spatial/temporal context, many theologians in the early twentieth century concluded that the Biblical passages that described the Almighty in anthropomorphic terms were esoteric symbols. Theologians affirmed the only *real* god was an all-powerful deity that created time and space itself. All existents and powers, natural and supernatural, mortal and immortal, were mere creations subject to their creator's unsurpassable power. God, the only eternal being, created everything *ex nihilo*, and everything (chaos, matter, space, time, ideas, laws, would-be demons, gods, humanity, et al) was upheld by the omnipotent and subject to the divine will. In contrast with the concepts of the ancient Near East, the only reasonable way for a worshiper to talk about such a deity was to laud God's transcendent Otherness. As Richard Neuhaus said, "God always remains other, the Ultimate Other, infinitely more than we can think or say. All our thought and language about God is analogical, and we must ever keep in

---

8. For a respectful crtique by a Protestant on the Mormon idea of Almighty God as Man of Holiness see John L. Bracht, *Man of Holiness: The Mormon Search for a Personal God*.

9. Martin E. Marty, "A God to End All Gods," 4.

10. Marty, 4.

mind the caution of the Fourth Lateran Council (1215) that 'No Similarity can be found so great but that the dissimilarity is even greater.'"[11]

Protestants believed that God was involved in the world as a pure act of unlimited love that amplified and culminated in the revelation of Christ, who was God in the form of a man on earth, but they could not say much more than that.[12] Trinitarian theology wrestled with the mystery of the relationship between the fierce monotheism of Second Temple Judaism and the church's understanding of the incarnated Christ and the Holy Spirit also as God in keeping with the affirmation of monotheism.

Joseph Smith and his Latter-day Saints faced the problem by claiming that God was a spacio-temporal person who was not the creator, redeemer, or sustainer of everything—at least not as Protestant opponents would define those terms. For Mormons, the matter was more complex. God was titular for the Godhead of the Father, Son, and Holy Ghost, which Mormons viewed as a social, not ontological, trinity of three distinct and divine persons. For them, the term "god" also described *any* eternal persons who had the power to organize matter into worlds and lead other eternal persons in creative experiences of expansion. Even though one might view Latter-day Saints as polytheists because they asserted that there are many persons with divine powers who exist in other realms, Mormons considered themselves to be monotheists inasmuch as they worshiped a single Godhead.[13] It didn't detract from the God they worshipped if there were other universes that had been organized by and were being led by other gods, for all the humans on this earth were subjects of this particular Godhead.[14]

---

11. Richard Neuhaus, "Christ and Creation's Longing," 24.

12. J. R. Dummelow, ed., *The One Volume Bible Commentary*, civ–v, cxiii–cxiv.

13. The Mormons aren't the only Christian group to have had their view of God criticized as polytheistic. Mainstream Christianity's own Trinitarian theology of a God-Creator, God-Man, and God-Holy Spirit was considered a scandal to Jewish and Muslim monotheists because to these traditions it elevated two of the Creator's "effects" (Jesus and the Holy Spirit) to full divinity with the Father Creator. The Holy Spirit was less of a problem, as they might imagine "it" as the Creator's power-substance or "spirit," but the bodily resurrected Jesus was a much more difficult matter. His existence in personal, bodily form meant that the Creator was not alone as God. For these critics, polytheism had returned.

14. The term "henotheism," the worship of one God while acknowledging the existence of other gods, was originally applied to Mesopotamian divinities that were believed to rule particular earthly regions; Van Hale, "Defining the Mormon Doctrine of Deity," 25–26. Joseph Smith's theology is a brand of henotheism that shifted those sectors of responsibility to different regions of the

Concerning the human incarnation of the divine Christ, both Mormons and Protestants believed it to be central to any understanding of the love of God. The issues for debate from a Protestant perspective were not the personhood of the incarnate Christ, or whether God could be within the time and space of His creation, but whether the Word/Son was part of a Trinitarian conception of God. Mormons seemed to hold a polytheistic (or henotheistic), finite conception of a social Trinitarian godhead. Differences also arose over whether God was immaterial or material; and whether a material body was essential to a proper definition of personhood in relation to God. Mormons had a very different understanding than did Protestants through their Biblical, systematic, and philosophical theologies. As philosopher Sterling McMurrin said: "The Latter-day Saint's prophet made a clean break with absolutist tradition. . . . But words like 'finite' and 'limited' don't go over well at the pulpit or in the publications of the pious."[15] The Mormon proclivity to use the absolutist language of mainstream Christianity (references to various "omni-" attributes of God), despite their belief about God being in space and time, irked Protestants. These critics engaged in theological polemics about Mormonism's finite God, but such subtleties seemed irrelevant to the Saints who felt their personal God was still all powerful enough to inspire sincere worship.

---

cosmos. The God of this earth, who was the Father of Christ and the Father of the spirit bodies of all human beings, had also organized innumerable other inhabited worlds (Abr. 3:12–14). Furthermore, God the Father of this cosmos likely had a Father who managed the affairs in His own universes, and so forth ad infinitum. Yet, as discussed in the text, each person, whether in this world-system or another, worshiped only one God and Savior for the cosmos in which he or she dwelled. See Keith E. Norman, "Mormon Cosmology: Can it Survive the Big Bang?," 23. Though I believe this theology was very much in the air during the early twentieth century, much of it, even then, was considered speculative theology and was not very often preached in Mormon church meetings. For various possibilities for interpreting multiple divinities under one God, see the discussion in Blake Ostler, *Exploring Mormon Thought: Of God and Gods*, 24–26. One interpretation, Ostler's favorite, is that there is a singular Almighty with no preceding parentage who rules all other gods. This he calls Kingship Monotheism with a hierarchy of royals under one almighty, always-extant King of Kings.

15. Sterling M. McMurrin, "Comments on the Theological and Philosophical Foundations of Christianity," 46.

Christian theo-anthropology: Ye Are Gods

Joseph Smith's view of God derived from his theophany in 1820 in which he claimed to have conversed with the Father and the Son, two separate personages in human form "whose brightness and glory defied description" (JS–H 1:17). In 1844, Smith elaborated on this revelation:

> God who sits enthroned in yonder heavens is a man like one of yourselves! . . . If you were to see him today, you would see him like a man in form—like yourselves in all the person, image, and very form as man. . . . It is the first principle of the Gospel to know that we may converse with God as one man converses with another, and that he was once a man like us; and that God himself, the Father of us all, dwelt on an earth, the same as Jesus did. . . . You have got to learn how to be Gods yourselves, and to be kings and priests to God, the same as all Gods have done before you, namely, by going from one small degree to another, and from a small capacity to a great one; from grace to grace, from exaltation to exaltation, until you attain the resurrection of the dead, and are able to dwell in everlasting burnings, and to sit in glory, as do those who sit enthroned in everlasting power. . . . God is not trifling with you or me.[16]

---

16. Andrew F. Ehat and Lyndon W. Cook, *The Words of Joseph Smith*, 344–61. Smith's doctrine of human divinization is not just another version of Eastern Orthodox theosis in which humans are lifted into a mystical union with deity. The uniqueness of Smith's doctrine is in the serial anthropology of an infinite regress of deities. Philosopher David Paulsen has written the most comprehensive comparative analysis of classical Christian and Mormon concepts of divine embodiment. See David L. Paulsen, "The Doctrine of Divine Embodiment: Restoration, Judeo-Christian, and Philosophical Perspectives." Also, James Faulconer, "Divine Embodiment and Transcendence: Propaedeutic Thoughts and Questions." For Joseph Smith's doctrinal development of infinite meliorism and polyanthropotheism prior to when Smith delivered the King Follet Discourse, from which this quotation was taken, see Van Hale, "The Doctrinal Impact of the King Follett Discourse," 209–23. For a history of the debates within Mormonism regarding theological interpretations of God and man, see Thomas Alexander, "The Reconstruction of Mormon Doctrine," 15–29. Joseph Smith was murdered in June 1844, two months after giving the King Follett Discourse, which has not been canonized, thus leaving room within Mormonism for more conventional Christian interpretations of deity and humanity. In this book, I am presenting Mormon belief as Joseph Smith taught it in his final years and as most Saints believed it in the early twentieth century. However, there are other views, which have been labeled variously as neo-orthodox or minimalist Mormon theology. On this subject, see the examples of Robert L. Millet, "Joseph Smith and Modern Mormonism: Orthodoxy, Neoorthodoxy, Tension, and Tradition"; Stephen E. Robinson, *Are Mormons Christian?*; O. Kendall White, *Mormon Neo-orthodoxy: A Crisis Theology*.

Protestants found passages such as this to be heretical if not blasphemous and idolatrous. Conversely, Mormons insisted that to worship a God who was beyond every category was to idolize an abstraction. To them, such a being could not be the same God who appeared as a human-like person to Abraham, Isaac, Jacob, and Moses.

When Jesus was challenged by some of his contemporaries for referring to himself as the Son of God, he defended himself by quoting Psalms 82:6, "I have said, Ye are gods; and all of you are children of the Most High" (John 10:34). To paraphrase this answer: if you humans can be thought of as gods, why be angry that I can be a son of god? Neither Protestants nor Mormons saw a problem with Jesus's statement, but they each viewed it very differently.[17] Protestants understood that Jesus was quoting a passage in Psalms that draws upon the word Elohim, which is interpreted variously as rulers, mighty ones, or gods, depending upon the context. The psalm is addressed to Israel's "mighty ones," or rulers, not divinities. Mormons found this passage pregnant with esoteric revelation. They believed that all human mortals are actually uncreated, intelligent, eternal beings as old as the God they worship, although certainly not as wise and loving (D&C 93:29).[18] They imagined an infinite regression of divine persons who organize innumerable worlds of existence over which

---

17. For studies that contrast the Mormon and more traditional Orthodox views of human divinization, see Keith E. Norman, "Divinization: The Forgotten Teaching of Early Christianity," 14–19; and Philip L. Barlow, "Unorthodox Orthodoxy: The Idea of Deification in Christian History," 15–18.

18. Joseph Smith's vision of divine love and freedom also necessarily required that no creation *ex nihilo* ever occurred, that all existence has always been everlasting including the slowly changing entities we call selves or persons. God could organize and reorganize intelligence-matter but could neither create nor annihilate it. Smith said man was "co-equal" with God: "God never had power to create the spirit of man at all. . . . It is a spirit from age to age and there is no creation about it. . . . God finds himself in the midst of spirits and because he saw proper to institute laws for those who were less intelligent that they might have one glory upon another . . . he took a hand to save the world of spirits." See Ehat and Cook, *Words of Joseph Smith*, 352. Mormons did not usually distinguish between everlasting-in-time, and eternal-beyond-time. From the context, Smith apparently meant that God and all things have always existed in an infinite regression and an infinite future of time, everlasting backwards and forwards. See Brigham H. Roberts, *The Autobiography of B. H. Roberts*, 37–43, cxxii.

they have influence.[19] The mysterious infinite regression and progression of divinity was the result of a theology and cosmology based on the eternal existence of matter, time, and space, in which uncreated divine entities organize and reorganize existing material.[20]

For Christians generally, the mysteries of provenance fade to irrelevance compared to the glorious destiny that God has for those who love Him. Paul provided support for their hopes: "The Spirit [of God] itself beareth witness with our spirit, that we are the children of God: And if children, then heirs; heirs of God, and joint-heirs with Christ; if so be that

---

19. A fundamental unanswered question in Mormon theology involves eternity and infinity. Some scriptural exegetes believe that eternal life is timeless (beyond duration or linear change), and thus all that appears "in time" is perspectively erroneous. It is the best explanation if all things are constantly before God. Other exegetes believe that infinity (eternal temporality) is more scripturally based. "Eternal" here means everlasting in both directions: time, space, and motion—change itself is eternal. God can see all things that exist, but the past and future do not exist except God's memory or imagination. Charles Hartshorne notes: "Heidegger [hinted in *Being and Time*] that not mere eternity but infinite temporality may be the key to the idea of God [which] I take, with Shubert Ogden, to point toward panentheism." See Charles Hartshorne, *A Natural Theology for Our Time*, 135. With an embodied pro-creative material deity Joseph Smith's infinite temporality included a kind of biogenetic panentheism (D&C 93:11–13). An excellent discussion of the "infinite regression" problem in relation to eternal materialism can be found in Blake T. Ostler, "Review of *The Mormon Concept of God: A Philosophical Analysis* by Francis J. Beckwith and Stephen E. Parrish."

20. The Mormons believe the Godhead organized the earth collaboratively with its future human inhabitants. The Gods "instituted" laws by which this universe is ordered, as Joseph Smith explained in the King Follett discourse. See Ehat and Cook, *Words of Joseph Smith*, 340–62; Van Hale, "The King Follett Discourse: Textual History and Criticism." Latter-day Saints debate whether the institution of laws by the Gods indicates a reconstruction or reorganization of existing elements under new laws or an implementation of eternally given laws in this new situation. If the former, eternal law is whatever law the eternal Gods choose, allowing for change in fundamental order itself. If the latter, eternal law is fundamental order to which the Gods are subject like everything else. The result is an immutable past with an open future. Thus, eternal law is both a given foundation for the Gods and a free construction of the Gods' future order. There is no necessary order to existence. Only existence itself—which implies some entity aware of some organization—is necessarily given. Gods are free to cease being Gods, and existence might shrink as the lessened awareness and influence of its inhabitants became less and less. There is no one outside existence observing and holding it together.

we suffer with him, that we may be also glorified together" (Rom. 8:16–17). The traditional Protestant interpretation of this text is that Christians enjoy a metaphorical child-father relationship with God, rather than one of prisoner-judge. The heir will somehow share the glory of God with and through Christ.[21] The saved person neither becomes ontologically one with Deity nor is separately elevated to equality with God.

On the Mormon side, Joseph Smith quoted John 14:2 which says, "In my Father's house are many mansions," and then announced, "It should be—'In my Father's kingdom are many kingdoms, in order that ye may be heirs of God joint-heirs with me.'. . . There are mansions for those who obey a celestial law, and there are other mansions for those who come short of the law, every man in his own order."[22] Smith then conjoined this text with Romans 8 to explicate a doctrine of human deification in which every person that desired it enough to act within his or her capacity upon the desire would receive all that God has, which entails becoming the organizers of new worlds (D&C 84:38; 130:1–2, 22; 132:20–24).

This Mormon belief that a god is an embodied person who exists in eternal relationality has an interesting extension to it—one that early-twentieth-century Latter-day Saints acknowledged as part of their theology but rarely spoke about in any depth—which is that for a being to be a father, there must necessarily also be a mother. As a result, nineteenth-century Mormonism developed the belief that every soul is spiritually the offspring of Divine Parents—God the Father and a Heavenly Mother. Mormons held that the Godhead consisted of the Father, Son, and Holy Ghost, but the Heavenly Mother remained a yet-to-be fully revealed partner in the divine organization. Going well beyond the Catholic elevation of Mary to quasi-divinity, Mormons believe God the Father is married to a female Goddess.[23] However, early-twentieth-century Mormons did not dwell on or attempt to develop the doctrine to any strong degree.

---

21. J. R. Dummelow, ed., *The One Volume Bible Commentary*, 876–77.

22. Ehat and Cook, *Words of Joseph Smith*, 368. Smith declaring that a biblical text should read differently than it does happened regularly and in addition to translating the gold plates into the Book of Mormon, Smith emended the King James text of the Bible, calling it an inspired revision. He did not claim to translate the Greek or Hebrew texts, but instead added and deleted words, sentences, and paragraphs, updating or clarifying the text as he felt prophetically inspired to do so.

23. This esoteric doctrine's most articulate expression is the Mormon hymn "O My Father" penned by poetess Eliza R. Snow (1804–1887). The hymn's key verse

Protestants tended to see Joseph Smith as a charlatan megalomaniac whose elaborate polytheistic Biblical interpretations offered equality with God and eventual Godhood to all the faithful. He supposedly mesmerized people who were greedy for autonomous power and perpetual carnality. It is difficult to grasp how outrageously hubristic Mormon theology appeared to Protestant sensibilities. It was not merely a question of personal or doctrinal hubris. A religion that truly reduced God to a mere holy man had also elevated humanity to unholy Promethean idolatry.

God Loves Freely vs. By Necessity

A difference in the understanding of divine love and divine freedom was a major cause of doctrinal conflict. Protestants agreed that God must have created the universe and humanity out of a desire to increase love. But God's divine love was a universal attribute, not a question of interpersonal relations, lest God might be tempted to play favorites. Biblical accounts of apparent divine favoritism were troublesome to many Christian theologians. Even though God later claimed to equally love all the Gentile nations (Acts 10:34), it seemed God spread His word and blessings unevenly throughout history.[24] Mormons were willing to face this problem

---

regarding Heavenly Mother states: "I had learned to call thee Father, through thy Spirit from on high. But until the key of knowledge was restored, I knew not why. In the heavens are parents single? No, the thought makes reason stare! Truth is reason, truth eternal tells me I've a Mother there." In Snow's hymn, and in most other affirmations about the existence of a Heavenly Mother, the doctrine seems to have first come through a logical inference from giving a literal interpretation to scriptural passages that state that humans are "children of God." Bruce R. McConkie, an influential Mormon apostle later in the twentieth century (1972–1985) wrote: "Implicit in the Christian verity that all men are the spirit children of an Eternal Father is the usually unspoken truth that they are also the offspring of an Eternal Mother. An exalted and glorified Man of Holiness (Moses 6:57) could not be a Father unless a Woman of like glory, perfection, and holiness was associated with him as a Mother. The begetting of children makes a man a father and a woman a mother whether we are dealing with man in his mortal or immortal state." See Bruce R. McConkie, *Mormon Doctrine*, 516.

24. Early Christians were well aware of the story of the War in Heaven referenced in obscure biblical and apocryphal fragments (Rev. 12:7; 2 Enoch 31) and culturally canonized in Milton's *Paradise Lost*. The story recognizes, even asserts, that evil is always an option because freedom is inalienable. Joseph Smith amplified this story into the polity of pre-earth heaven and the purpose of human life. In the Mormon version of the epic, all humans had existed in the pre-mortal

in order to preserve their notion of divine and human love as a radical decision. If God's love for a person (and vice versa) were to be worthy of the pain love requires, then both God and humanity must be free to reject or embrace each other's desire for loving friendship. No one wants a lover that loves by necessity instead of choice (D&C 121:34–46).[25] In the tension between freedom and necessity in a loving God, Protestants emphasized the certainty of divine loving grace over the uncertainty of divine freedom. They stood in trusting awe of a deity who could only love and who focused that love on His creation, particularly His human creatures. God loved by necessary definition no matter what else happened.

Protestants disagree as to the extent of the Fall and its impact upon free will. All are in agreement that the Fall is understood in negative terms and is contrary to God's desire for humanity, even while it was foreknown by God from all eternity. Protestants believe that the Fall impacted human nature so that there was a disposition to evil rather than good. They believe that human beings still had free will, but that this too was affected by the Fall. For Protestants on one end of the spectrum, such as the Presbyterians, human beings could not respond to the gospel without the work of the Holy Spirit on the individual. For those on the other end of the spectrum, such as the Methodists, the Fall did not do so much damage free will so as to make a response to the Gospel impossible, even if the Spirit was still involved in illuminating the human heart. One challenge for Protestant theology relates to its view of fallen human nature and its connection to human responsibility and free choice in responding to the

---

world as individual spirits—organized into a huge family by God. Lucifer who had been a brilliant leader in the pre-mortal presence of God, when everyone was still in heaven, aspired to godhood (a worthy goal, if God is love) by unrighteous means. The pre-mortal Jesus spoke for the Father's risky plan of free choice in the face of temptation (Moses 4:1–4). The Father, Son, and pre-mortal spirits freely debated and chose sides when Lucifer and the third part of the hosts of heaven claimed freedom would lose too many souls. They were cast out of heaven and descended to the earth to thwart the plan by tempting humanity to rebel against God on earth (Jude 1:6).

25. B. H. Roberts positioned divine free love as the motive in Christ's atonement. See Brigham H. Roberts, *The Truth, The Way, The Life: An Elementary Treatise on Theology*, xc–xci. But Mormons also entertained other theories of the atonement, some sounding quite Protestant. Mormons were pragmatically eclectic without much concern for philosophically systematic coherence. Sterling M. McMurrin, *Theological Foundations of Mormon Religion*, 82–90.

Gospel. James Neuchterlein, a contemporary Protestant theologian, captures the classic Christian dilemma:

> For if I was, quite literally, born in sin, how could I be responsible for it? If the wrongs that I did proceeded inevitably from the nature of my fallen being, then what [many call] the ineffable grace of God in Christ in saving me from the deserved consequences of my deeds [seemed] the superfluous action of an arbitrary, indeed quite absurd, deity. I should be grateful for being rescued from a situation for which I had no moral responsibility in the first place? I should love a God who created me a sinner then "saved" me from being what he had made me?[26]

In contemplating the Fall and its consequences, the question becomes whether God's desire overpowers all human desire, making human desire ultimately irrelevant to its final disposition or judgment. Most Protestants said yes, most Mormons, no. Leaning toward Luther, Calvin, and European pessimism, many, though not all, Protestants relied completely on God's work in human nature, providing an ability to respond to the inward working of the Spirit through regeneration. This was particularly true for Protestants who leaned toward Reformed theology, while those with Wesleyan views acknowledged God's grace but also strongly emphasized free will in the human response to God's inward call.[27] By contrast, believing in the uncreated self that freely collaborated with Divine Parents to become a child of God, Mormons challenged theologies that placed God's sovereign otherness ahead of parental likeness. Protestants, who believed that God was love, trusted that they were already saved by the impenetrable mystery of a loving God in the face of their complete unworthiness as fallen creatures through the completed work of Christ.[28] Mormons, who believed

---

26. James Neuchterlein, "Sin, Theodicy and Politics," 7.

27. Methodist and Holiness theology emphasizes human free will and assent to God's gift of grace. By contrast, Presbyterian and other Reformed views emphasize the divine call to salvation and the idea of "irresistible grace." See John Dillenberger, "Grace and Works in Martin Luther and Joseph Smith," 181–85.

28. Related to this are varying Protestant views on predestination. All traditional Christians believe that God has predestined various things. However, they disagree on the form this takes in regards to salvation, and the idea of election and those God has chosen to save. One view closer to Methodism says that God has predestined only those who freely accept God's offer of salvation, while the Presbyterian and Reformed view says that God predestines only the elect, a segment of humanity. In this way God is understood to offer pardon to some but not all, but all receive justice regardless. Although these views demonstrate differences of thought within Protestantism as well as historic Christendom, as Roger Olson has noted,

that God always desired and acted in love, trusted God to ease their suffering and burdens on their journey towards higher divinity if they followed the light they were given as best they could (D&C 19:15–20).

Because Mormon doctrine stated that primal person or intelligence was coeternal with God, that freedom of choice was inalienable from intelligent existence. Mormonism interpreted the fall of Adam and Eve as a *felix culpa,* a blessed, fortunate fall upward toward more life-expanding experience. In Mormon thought, mortality was a test of one's deepest desires, a battleground between short-term pressures and long-term purposes. The optimistic results of the divine collaboration would yield an improvement for all but a few.[29] Thus, the earth test, performed behind a veil of forgetfulness that shielded humankind from knowing their true divinity, was a benign set-up. Regardless of final test scores, all who suffered through mortality would receive resurrected bodies and the capacity to experience even greater joy.

Both Protestants and Latter-day Saints embraced a variety of theories of the Atonement, or Christ's mysterious acts of vicarious suffering, sacrifice, resurrection, and work of reconciliation. For Protestants, the need for redemption was caused by the rebelliousness of the creature against its creator, and the inability of the creature to make adequate restitution. Sanctification—a life-long process of becoming more godly—is a cooperative endeavor whereby the individual surrenders his or her life to the will of God and the transformative work of the Holy Spirit. The seeker's responsibility was to freely and gratefully accept the sanctifying grace of Christ. Humanity could not obtain the gift from God by their good works, as Protestants accused Mormons of trying to do. For them, the God of love saved all that God chose to save by His inscrutable will. It seemed silly for men to try to improve on or change the already perfect and loving mind of God, as incomprehensible as it is.

---

traditional "Christians all together believe that salvation as reconciliation with God and inward renewal from the corruption of inherited depravity and toward the restoration of the image of God is wholly and completely a work of God's grace while at the same time is also an event and process involving human agency. That is, for Christians, salvation is both gift and task." Roger E. Olson, *The Mosaic of Christian Belief: Twenty Centuries of Unity & Diversity,* 272–3.

29. Mormon theology is essentially a rebellion against the orthodox Protestant dogma of the unfortunate Fall and the resulting innate depravity of human nature. The radical optimism displayed in this rebellion may well be Mormonism's most distinctive characteristic. McMurrin, *Theological Foundation,* 66.

Salvation as Eternal Flourishing

Protestants and Mormons believed that Jesus came to give humanity abundant or eternal life, marking the way forward with his own resurrection. Salvation is existence in a heavenly state to come among immortals. The current church, scriptures, and world are temporary instruments for improving the prospects that eternal life or flourishing will be enjoyable.

Sociologist Georg Simmel observed that a religious community is not enhanced by holding a divine lottery view of who is saved or damned because such a view makes efforts toward achieving salvation futile. In contrast, a doctrine that teaches that salvation is achieved, at least to some degree, through personal merit assures that those who sincerely serve each other will receive a heavenly reward.[30] In short, a belief in salvation that requires persons to freely choose to serve others through good works enhances community life. As a result of their views of God's complete responsibility in saving souls, Protestant communities were democracies of individuals—saved one at time, as each person became an adopted child of God by being spiritually born-again. Mormons believed that each human was already a pre-mortal child of God no matter what he or she did with that birthright. The concept of a society of pre-mortal Divine Parents and children pervaded their sense that salvation was an improved continuation of pre-mortal and mortal social life. Social life provided the test that improved their souls. Thus, their community was both the means and the end of their religious quest. Although Protestants preferred to be saved with family and friends, eternal bliss was not contingent on a heavenly social life. The primary relationship was the asymmetrical one between the creature and the Creator. It was hard enough to love the Creator as a friend, but outrageous to do so as a peer.

Many cultures have believed in the necessity of spiritual solidarity with one's ancestors. Others have believed that the only form of life after death is in the memory of the living. Most believe that genetic inheritance is enormously influential on their present being and personality. Whatever the particular belief, cross-generational relations of families have had a quasi, if not explicitly, religious importance.[31] Christianity found ways

---

30. Georg Simmel, *Conflict and The Web of Group-Affiliations*, 69–70, 88.
31. Bryan Turner has argued that recent trends in sociology of religion neglect the social effects of religion while focusing on the subjective meaning of religion for the believer. Thus, he thinks Peter Berger's fine work on shared sacred meanings has missed "Marx's insight (and Aristotle's) that the person is an effect of an ensemble of social relations, which in turn reflect the complex structure of

to express individuality, kinship, and friendship through customs that allowed the believer to become valuable and distinctive, to have the security of genetic family ties, and to have the enjoyment of freely choosing loyal friendship. In contrast, religions that focus on individual enlightenment or salvation do not usually emphasize family or friendship. This tends to decrease concern for social interaction and change. Religions that emphasize kinship ties over friendships tend to remain insular tribes resisting change within larger cultures. Religions that emphasize friendship over kinship tend to grow by expanding elective relationships through proselytizing and assimilation.[32]

Like Western Christianity in general, mainstream American Protestantism—especially with its rugged individualism—leaned toward individual salvation and voluntary association of like-minded friends rather than toward natural associations of family and ethnic traditions.[33] The geo-social mobility of Americans is a Protestant penchant derived from the belief that one is called individually to salvation. Conscience, not the church or scripture, became the decisive authority regarding the will of God. The fungible denominational church system in America allowed individuals tremendous personal mobility. No matter where they went, they were still able to remain true to conscience within the Protestant fold. They

---

class positions." See Bryan S. Turner, *Religion and Social Theory*, 4. "The historical and sociological importance of religion in human life can only be grasped in the analysis of religion vis-à-vis the body, the family, and property. Meaning is material, not theoretical alone." I have tried to use both Berger's and Turner's insights in my analysis.

32. Commenting on the long-term trend in history of salvation toward emphases on the individual, Eric Voegelin says: "Salvation has definitely shifted from fulfillment in the people's history to the individual member of mankind. With this shift, however, eschatology has lost its meaning as the end of history; it has become the end of individual human existence." See Eric Voegelin, "History and Gnosis." Joseph Smith's theology combined social salvation with the existential freedom of individual originality.

33. There have been exceptions to individualistic salvation from the beginning. Acts 16:31 included the promise that the household will be saved with the individual, and many Christian intentional communal movements over the centuries were based on the desire for the group to be saved. Few Christians want to be alone in heaven. In differing cultural contexts, such as those of Asian and African Christianity, there has been less emphasis on individual and more on community concerns in salvation.

selected friends of similar conscience and temperament—the church was less important for salvation than for reading the scriptures conscientiously.

Latter-day Saints, on the other hand, more akin to Jewish tradition, emphasized salvation in the continuity of the faithful family and social solidarity of a tribe. The Hebrew Scriptures and the Book of Mormon were both stories of family dynasties that grew into a large, religiously political people. Joseph Smith founded his social-religious vision of Zion on the concept of a city economy consisting of units of like-minded families. If one came to Zion alone, they were spiritually adopted into one of the faithful families, even as an adult.[34] Growing their church from a small group of rural families to a large urban political block in the Midwest, and later in Utah, Mormons deeply troubled their primarily Protestant neighbors. Their proclivity to gather as a people into hierocentric cities in the middle of a democratic American economy was offensive to previous homesteaders who quickly became minority outsiders after hordes of Saints arrived.[35]

Joseph Smith said, "And if we [Mormons] go to hell, we will turn the devils out of doors and make a heaven of it. Where these people are, there is good society. What do we care where we are, if the society be good? . . . Friendship is the grand fundamental principle of 'Mormonism.'"[36] Mormons addressed each other with kinship titles of "Brother" and "Sister" as a continual reminder of each soul's past identity as common offspring from the same Heavenly Parents. Kinship in this earth life would only enhance that friendship in the world to come.

The doctrine of establishing an earthly Zion before the Second Coming appeared as utopianism that was too politically religious for most Americans by the turn of the twentieth century. The primacy of individual conscience was the foundation from which American Protestants rejected Catholic authority along with all other political entanglement with religious authority. Despite traditional beliefs in absolute divine sovereignty

---

34. Gordon Irving, "The Law of Adoption: One Phase of the Development of the Mormon Concept of Salvation," 305–6.

35. St. John said the New Jerusalem was to be a city where the Lord dwelled (Rev. 21:22), and the Mormon cities anticipated the Second Advent by building temples (each one inscribed "The House of the Lord"), as sociopolitical fortresses of religious solidarity against "the world," including the Protestant American world. God and Christ would ultimately be the temple of New Jerusalem; but until then, Mormons made temples—not capitols or office buildings—the foundation for social, political, and economic life.

36. Ehat and Cook, *Words of Joseph Smith*, 234.

and human predestination, many Protestants deemed the individual soul competent to judge for itself, to override ecclesiastical or other secular influences, and to choose salvation or damnation. Most of the first-generation Latter-day Saints had converted from Protestantism to Mormonism under the tutelage of that principle.

Given this emphasis, the great fear for American Protestants at this time was the possibility that another human being might command one's belief or vote by claiming an authority higher than unfettered conscience. Catholics, who bent their consciences to papal authority, had introduced this early evil in the body of Christ; the Latter-day Saints seemed even more willing to bend to their prophet's command. Protestants feared that when a Mormon leader spoke out about political issues or candidates then an entire people would vote accordingly, or that the leader would influence political and economic affairs. The democratic process could easily be turned against those living in areas controlled by the Mormon bloc vote.[37]

The Saints rejoiced in a prophet who could receive current revelation for the church and, at times, all people, but they also understood the Protestant critique about the danger of unchecked centralized power. In any large organization—the LDS Church included—there is tension at the intersection of the hierarchical commands and the individual member's conscience. Joseph Smith had attempted to ease the tension by saying that a prophet was to be followed when acting under the inspiration of the Holy Spirit—and that all should have access to confirmation of that Spirit.[38] This dictum honored individual free agency and required each person to interpret when a prophet might be acting prophetically. Individuality, freedom, and revelation created a necessity for all members to seek divine guidance—in essence, to become prophets themselves. This is a Protestant principle housed within a hierarchical ecclesiastical order. Mormons, for all their emphasis on personal free agency, were covert authoritarians—Catholics in Protestant clothing. This applies as well to their use of symbols.

---

37. Religious indignation coupled with fear-based politics had been a major factor in the conflicts with Mormons in the 1840s in Ohio, Missouri, and Illinois. The Mormons were beset with mobs that no doubt justified their lawlessness as vigilante prevention of an undemocratic take-over by growing hordes of fanatical theocrats. Leonard J. Arrington and Davis Bitton, *The Mormon Experience: A History of the Latter-day Saints*, 440–64; see also Annete P. Hampshire, *Mormonism in Conflict: The Nauvoo Years*.

38. Joseph Fielding Smith, ed., *Teachings of the Prophet Joseph Smith*, 278.

Symbols and Rites

Sociologist Andrew Greeley taught that symbols are "a much stronger predictor of world view than is doctrinal orthodoxy.... [They] also tend to correlate more powerfully with social behavior and attitude than do doctrinal propositions."[39] Assuming this is true, let us examine how different symbolic forms and sacred rites either reflected or elicited conflicting social behaviors and worldviews.

The Cross vs. Moroni

There is no more commonly recognized symbol of Christianity than the simple Protestant cross, which, unlike the Catholic crucifix, contains no effigy of Christ. The empty cross encourages the believer to ponder Jesus's life before his crucifixion, the tragedy of his agonizing death, and the triumph of his subsequent resurrection. The bare cross, compatible with any Christian denomination, had for centuries affirmed a religion that faces the soul's suffering and the body's death with bold hope. Nevertheless, the cross was also an ancient instrument of torture used to punish militant or criminal action against the state. Hence Christianity's defiant appropriation of the cross symbolized that the tables had been turned. The cross was also an apt symbol for the Protestant penchant for militancy in the fight against sin and error—not infrequently placed on the background of a battle shield on denominational flags. Although typically associated with Catholicism, the term crusade itself denotes a cross-led war for Christian victory.

By contrast Mormons did not emphasize the cross in their liturgy or architecture.[40] The most ubiquitous symbol glittering atop Mormon temples was a different resurrected being than the one who had perished on a cross. He was Moroni, son of the ancient American prophet Mormon, for whom the Book of Mormon is named, and the last historian of his people living in America in AD 400. As a resurrected being in 1823, Moroni directed Joseph Smith to the location of the gold plates upon which The Book Mormon had been inscribed. This event launched the LDS restoration movement, and today Moroni, trumpet raised with the Book of Mormon under his arm, stands atop Mormon temples around the world. He is a harbinger of the latter-days before the Second Coming—but more, he symbolizes the divine human bodies each will enjoy in the resurrec-

---

39. Andrew Greeley, *Religion: A Secular Theory*, 58–59, 98–99.
40. See Michael G. Reed, *Banishing the Cross: The Emergence of a Mormon Taboo*.

tion.[41] According to Joseph Smith, the resurrection that began with Jesus has continued ever since, with many of the righteous, such as Moroni, being selected for early resurrection. Smith learned that, in addition to Moroni, Abraham, Isaac, and Jacob "have entered into their exaltation according to the promises, and sit upon thrones, and are not angels, but are gods" (D&C 132:37, 49).

This good news of the Mormon gospel—that godhood is the destiny of all the righteous—was blasphemy to Protestants; and the golden angel looked to them as heretical as a golden calf. Their own symbol, the empty cross, was a subdued reflection of quiet confidence in their own salvation through Christ. They sensed arrogance in a trumpeting man, resurrected or not, as the goal for eternal life. The Protestant cross stood between the Catholic crucifix, showing the suffering God-Man, and the Mormon gold-leafed resurrected Man-God. The LDS enthusiasm for divine humanity did not reflect the meekness of souls saved to inherit the earth. Still, perhaps the subtlest symbols of Mormonism were the lay members of the church standing in front of the congregation in simple clothing giving talks or serving communion—each a divinity to be.

The Temple: The House of the Lord and Humanity

To Joseph Smith, the supreme symbol of the restoration of all things was the oldest anthropological building of all: the temple. For Mormons, the temple rituals provide the esoteric knowledge of human divinization, making Mormonism the one true religion that capped all others lacking the teaching of exalted salvation: the mystery of godliness. Rejecting ritual mysteries, Protestants saw Mormon temples as a profane mixture of stale Hebrew formality and heretical paganism.[42] Similarly, cathedrals—the temples that centered European culture for centuries—stood for despised oppression of the masses by the Catholic clerics.

Religare, the root term for religion, means binding together. In 1836, Joseph Smith recorded that, during the dedication of the Kirtland Temple,

---

41. Evangelicals and other Protestants, Roman Catholics and the Orthodox, conceive of angels as immaterial spirits and a different kind of being than humans. Resurrected humans will live among the angelic beings in heaven.

42. A scholarly critique of the historical desire for a hierocentric Christian temple to function analogously to ancient temples was written from a Mormon point of view by Hugh Nibley. See Hugh W. Nibley, *Mormonism and Early Christianity*, 391–434. For an Evangelical assessment of the Temple in connection with the early Jesus movement of the first century see Nicholas Perrin, *Jesus the Temple*.

the prophet Elijah, as a resurrected man, bestowed upon him the keys of sealing "the hearts of the fathers to the children, and the children to the fathers" (Mal. 4:5–6; D&C 110:13–16). In 1829, Joseph Smith had reported receiving the apostolic keys directly from a resurrected Peter that allowed him to bind together on earth what would be bound in heaven (Matt. 16:19). Smith felt empowered to unite the entire human family in the latter-day culmination of "the dispensation of the fullness of times . . . [when] a whole and complete and perfect union, and welding together . . . from the days of Adam until the present time" (D&C 128:15–18).

The Mormon temple was a sacred space where only Mormons in good standing could enter. This closed access made the Protestants suspicious, particularly since the memorized oral temple ritual was not available for open study. To Protestants, such policies showed that Mormonism was not only a heretical regression to distracting, empty ritualism, but it was also a secret society suspiciously like Masonry—non-Christian, conspiratorial, and undemocratic at the core. For Protestants, the Mormon temple symbolized a dark fortress more than a welcoming center to save and exalt everyone. Jesus could and did do that by himself.

Marriage and Family, Now and Forever

Latter-day Saints have identified their celestial marriage and eternal sealing rite as their most important difference from other religions. Protestants critically agreed, viewing the Mormons' esoteric liturgy as a pagan-like doctrine that elevated humans to divine status through sexual union and everlasting familial fecundity. This took the divine promise to Abraham of great posterity to the extreme, and equated divinity with marriage. Through the dramatic narrative presented in the temple, Mormons observed that God is a glorified human, that humans lived in bodies of spirit-matter with God in a heavenly society before entering mortal life as infants, and that human mortals had all participated in the planning of the creation of Earth as a site for them to experience growth.

The sacred temple narrative reenacted the Earth's primal organization from pre-existing matter, the existence of scarcity and death because of the fortunate fall, and the sacred knowledge to eventually achieve resurrection. The biblical Adam and Eve were not drawn as a romantic couple, however, and the marriages of the subsequent ancient patriarchs were discussed—the wives of the ancient patriarchs are not even named. Joseph Smith looked to the later narratives of Abraham and Sarah, Isaac and Rebecca, and Jacob and Rachel as icons of marriage (Gen. 12:1–3; 13:16; 15:5; 17:1–8, 16; D&C

132:30–33, 63). Controversially, this covenant could include more than one spouse in the heavens. Some form of polygamy was in store for couples who made the covenant with more than one spouse on Earth.[43]

It stands to reason that Protestants failed to be persuaded of the importance of continuous marriage in the eternities. To them, the concept of eternal marriage seemed a projection of man's proclivity for erotic union. They understood the Abrahamic covenant as part of the unfolding work of the *missio dei*, God's missional work to restore His relationship to a broken world. This work included the revelation of monotheism in a pagan world, not, as Mormons believed, to propagate family lines through which the divine power would descend. Polygamous practices by the patriarchs were permitted, though not ideal, and replaced by New Testament monogamy (1 Cor. 7:2–9; Matt. 22:23–33). Protestants despised as blasphemy the Mormon "god-making" doctrine, which demoted God Almighty into an embodied, passionate, polygamist while elevating human sexuality into a world-organizing divinity.[44] They were content to allow the Almighty to save His creatures into an eternal life that was beyond any anthropomorphic social arrangement that they could presently imagine.

Eternal marriage within Mormonism conspicuously lacked erotic symbols.[45] Though often caricatured by critics as libertines, Mormons

---

43. Joseph Smith reported this revelation from God: "[I]f a man marry a wife by my word, which is my law, and by the new and everlasting covenant, and it is sealed unto them by the Holy Spirit of promise . . . [they] shall come forth in the first resurrection . . . and pass by the angels, and the gods, which are set there, to their exaltation and glory in all things, as hath been sealed upon their heads, which glory shall be a fulness and a continuation of the seeds forever and ever. Then shall they be gods, because they have no end . . . because they continue. . . . This is eternal lives—to know the only wise and true God and Jesus Christ, whom he hath sent" (D&C 132:19, 20, 24). Within this notion of expansion, Joseph Smith, following the ancient patriarchs, included polygamy mainly polygyny, but some polyandry. For a general history of the practice, see Richard S. Van Wagoner, *Mormon Polygamy: A History*. For a analysis of Smith's revelation on polygamy, see William Victor Smith, *Textual Studies of the Doctrine and Covenants: The Plural Marriage Revelation*.

44. For two examples of this common Protestant critique, see John Danforth Nutting, "The Secret Oaths and Ceremonies of Mormonism: The Secret Temple Work Which Binds Mormons Together Under the Power of Their Priestly Leaders"; and William Mitchell Paden, "Temple Mormonism."

45. Colleen McDannell and Bernhard Lang, *Heaven: A History*, 318–21. One of the most perceptive and synthetic treatments of sexuality and religious

were not.[46] Couples were taught that the Holy Spirit enhanced their abilities to enjoy married pleasures, and that their sexual love was part of the greater love of God who Himself was an embodied being.[47]

Although critical of LDS emphasis on holy sensuality, Protestants were not pleasure-squelching prudes. Contrary to their reputation, the early American Puritans' prime desire was the joyful fellowship of community social life graced with the spirit of God. Individual purity and discipline were two means to that end.[48] Most twentieth-century Protestants enjoyed American-style romance: finding one's love, marrying for life, courting with dance and music in most cases, and looking forward to resurrected associations with loved ones—though not necessarily in marriage—in the afterlife. However, they were more circumspect in their celebration of worldly enjoyments, expecting them to be mere fringe benefits, if not superfluous, to a heavenly life centered in worshipful life with God.

Mormons believed that they could seal their children in an everlasting familial unity through their temple marriage rites. Such sealings were also vicariously performed for the ancestral marital couples that Mormons could identify through genealogical research, thus bonding each generation together and eventually the whole human family. By performing proxy baptisms and sealings, Mormons believed they were giving the spir-

---

controversy can be found in R. Laurence Moore, *Selling God: American Religion in the Market Place of Culture*, especially chapter five on "The Market for Religious Controversy." Summarizing, Moore points out that no American religion, including the Mormons, ever encouraged promiscuity, however unusual their marriage teachings. Mormons tried to carefully restrict their sexual conduct and roles to a rather bourgeois family model within the framework of polygyny at first, then with monogamy after 1890.

46. Moore, *Selling God*, 123.

47. It is instructive in comparing worship styles to use Andrew Greeley's typology of high church (formal liturgy) and low church (informal liturgy) types and Nietzsche's model of Dionysian (celebratory of passionate bodily enjoyments) and Apollonian (celebratory of contemplative beauty) social forms. See Greeley, *Denominational Society*, 18–25; Friedrich Nietzsche, *The Birth of Tragedy* and *The Case of Wagner*. The Protestants exemplified middle- to low-church Apollonian restraint in both doctrine and practice. The Mormon Church matched the middle- to low-church social profile of the Protestants with respect to practice, but displayed a tension between its Apollonian ritual and its Dionysian doctrine that allowed even God the enjoyments of bodiliness.

48. Rex Eugene Cooper, *Promises Made to the Fathers: Mormon Covenant Organization*, 14–42.

its of the deceased the chance to accept a universal salvation possible for all humanity who desire it.[49]

Protestants understood the significance of baptism as a public proclamation and symbol of union with Christ in his death and resurrection, however they rejected the Mormon view of baptism as the first step toward exaltation and divinizing in marital sealing. Protestants believed that a sovereign God did not need human assistance to save the human race. In previous centuries, they split with the Roman Church by rejecting indulgences and the need for priestly sacraments as requirements for salvation. In their understanding of New Testament theology, the Hebrew temple ritual laws have been fulfilled by the atonement and High Priestly work of Christ who served both as unblemished sacrificial offering and temple attendant (Heb. 7:11–19). Within the believer, the Spirit dwells with the body as a divine temple (1 Cor. 6:19–20).[50] The notion of Mormon elders performing salvific temple rites seemed a retrograde theology. Relying on God's grace and judgment to determine their status in heaven, Protestants rejected esoteric temple doctrines and mistrusted any policy that allowed ecclesiastical leaders to guard the door to salvation.

Styles of Religiosity

Protestants did not need an apostolic magisterial authority that could assure salvation or bind in heaven and on earth (Matt. 18:18). They craved instead a strong binding consensus of biblical interpretation on doctrine

---

49. No commentator inside or out on the religion of the Latter-day Saints has better grasped the palpable sincerity, intensity, and audacity of Joseph Smith's vision (D&C 128 and 132) than Harold Bloom, who commented on the Mormon program for vicarious baptismal work to save together the entire deceased human family as follows: "the really shocking spiritual ambition, indeed the aggressive drive, of Mormon baptism for the dead, is unlikely to find any true parallel to it in modern religious history." Harold Bloom, *The American Religion: The Emergence of the Post Christian Nation*, 122. To provide individual candidates for proxy baptisms, the Mormons have assembled by far the largest genealogical library of names, times, and places anywhere on earth. It is the closest thing to a catalogue of humanity that exits. Bloom, 121. *The American Religion* concludes that Mormonism, more so than even historian Jan Shipps proposed, diverged so strongly from Protestantism that it became a new religious tradition as far from Protestant Christianity as original Christianity was Islam. Bloom, *American Religion*, 123.

50. See Nicholas Perrin, *Jesus the Temple*.

and moral behavior. "The church" for Protestants became a catchall term for those called out of the world, and who followed the faith they found described in the Bible by Christ and his ancient apostles. Biblical text had become the main foundation of religious authority for those that rejected the Catholic priesthood. To sincerely believe the biblical truth was to have divine authority—that was Protestantism's strength. To sincerely differ in interpretation assured schism—that was Protestantism's weakness. Loyalty to Christ and the sacred text went with the believer wherever he or she decided to attend meetings. No priesthood of any affiliation could keep a good Protestant from being baptized by faith, confirmed by the Holy Spirit, sustained by the Word of God, and saved by Christ.

Mormons and Catholics used a complex organizational and liturgical structure to help limit schism.[51] Protestants disputed biblical interpretations knowing that they would win or lose converts to a consensus of meaning. Questions of liturgical correctness, sacramental authority, or moral rectitude were trivial compared to disagreement over textual meanings that often resulted in dissociation or schism. For the fervent Protestant missionary, correct expression of doctrine (orthodoxy) was as important as correct behavior (orthopraxy), if not more. Precision of interpretative accuracy provided surety of alignment with divine truth.

Religious Sociality

A beehive is centered on the Utah State flag. Deseret (dez-ur-ette) was the original name Mormons gave to the Utah territory to symbolize their social community. A term from the Book of Mormon, the beehive stood for industrious collaboration now and in heavenly life.[52] All religions are social organizations, but Mormons believed even God belonged to an

---

51. Of course, the original Christians bred the early schisms, with the great one of east and west now a thousand years old. The Catholics and Orthodox have sustained much fewer schisms than the Protestant offshoots, which from the Reformation have endured thousands of schisms. The Latter-day Saints since 1830 have experienced over two hundred splinter groups. The largest split occurred in the 1860s between the Reorganized Church of Jesus Christ of Latter-Day Saints, now with about 250,000 members, and the Church of Jesus Christ of Latter-day Saints, now with about 14,000,000 members. On the Mormon schisms, see Roger D. Launius and W. B. Spillman, *Let Contention Cease: The Dynamics of Dissent in The Reorganized Church of Jesus Christ of Latter Day Saints*.

52. Sociologist of religion, Armand L. Mauss, expands on this in his classic study *The Angel and the Beehive: The Mormon Struggle with Assimilation*.

industrious heavenly social collaborative. Utah Mormons experimented with collaborative economic communities in the late 1800s and organized their social lives around their local tribe members, the ward congregation. They believed heaven consists of social life (D&C 130:1–2), claiming that individual salvation as resurrected people without one's friends and family would be hellish. Without meaning to offend their Heavenly Father, it seems He alone was not enough eternal company.

Jesus's final recorded prayer with his apostles expresses a mystery: his desire "that they all may be one; as thou, Father, art in me, and I in thee, that they also may be one in us. . . . I in them, and thou in me, that they may be made perfect in one" (John 17:21, 23). What does it mean to be perfectly one, or to be perfect because of oneness? A traditional Protestant interpretation of this prayer is that Jesus is praying that Christians will develop perfect love for each other and become a single unified church.[53] While not disagreeing about the need for a unified church, Latter-day Saints read Jesus's prayer as the process of loving collaboration whereby human divinization and divine enhancement are produced through social unity.

To Protestants, Smith seemed to conflate knowing God with knowing one's spouse in his view that becoming one with God emulated a divine proclivity for bodily interaction. Sexual union and pluralistic expansion is revealed in Smith's paraphrase of St. John's record in John 17:

> This is eternal lives—to know the only wise and true God, and Jesus Christ, whom he hath sent. . . . If a man marry a wife by my word, which is my law, and by the new and everlasting covenant, and it is sealed unto them by the Holy Spirit of promise . . . [they] shall inherit thrones, kingdoms . . . all heights and depths . . . and they shall pass by the angels, and the gods, which are set there, to their exaltation and glory in all things . . . which glory shall be a fulness and a continuation of the seeds forever and ever. (D&C 132:24, 19–20)

Note the shift from John's Christocentric and God-focused "eternal life" to social procreative interaction implied by the "eternal lives" enjoyed by sealed couples who have offspring. How Heavenly Parents increase— whether it involves gendered sexual intercourse or not—was not revealed.[54]

---

53. Dummelow, *Bible Commentary*, 804.

54. From the moment his followers learned Joseph Smith had seen God the Father and Son in separate material humanlike bodies the question naturally arose, "how humanlike are they—do they have organs and passions and . . .?" When Joseph Smith saw a resurrected man, Moroni, he described his resurrected body

Nevertheless, gendered sociality seemed to be a form that God everlastingly desired.[55] This marked a stark difference with Victorian Protestantism.

As McDannell and Lang point out, most Christian traditions allow everlasting loving friendship a place in heaven, defining it as a shared beatific relationship of knowing and loving Christ and God. United with God, the saved soul can abandon earthly ties with kith and kin, especially when such relationships are viewed as primarily legal and functional.[56] The Apostle Paul separated salvation from pedigree, critiquing the idea of a chosen lineage and ancestor worship—perhaps the most pervasive form of spirituality in the world. Protestants noted that, except for the story of his own birth, Jesus's parents and siblings are only incidentally mentioned in the Gospels. There is no mention of his marriage in the canonized Bible. All could become part of his Father's kingdom, in which it was assumed marriage was unimportant if it existed at all (Mark 12:25). The social bonds of kinship were subordinate to the spiritual bonds of discipleship. Salvation required freely choosing Christ, a personal choice that often alienated one's family. The doctrinal focus was thus on the freedom of friendship, rather than the necessity of kinship. Friendship with spouses or children was a fringe benefit at best compared to the final knowing union with God (John 15–17).

Congregational Worship

For people with such voluptuous religious aspirations, Latter-day Saint Sunday service and chapel design were remarkably homely and spare—a liturgically low church. Protestant weekly worship had an air of formality and its clergy's homilies a certain cadence and tone not present in the comparatively informal Mormon main preaching service (sacrament meeting). At the turn of the twentieth century, Mormon meetings usually lasted an hour and a half to two hours long. The meetings included invocation and benediction hymns and prayers, the sacrament (communion—bread and water passed among the attendees), and typically an hour's instruction from

---

but did not discuss how the glorified body differed in function from the mortal one (JS—H 1:31–32). Joseph Smith revealed that the same "sociality" exists in heaven as on earth only in glorified bodies (D&C 130), and that marriage could be eternal (D&C 132), for God and the rest of glorified humanity.

55. One of the most perceptive and synthetic treatments of sexuality and religious controversy can be found in Moore's *Selling God*, especially chapter five on "The Market for Religious Controversy."

56. McDannell and Lang, *Heaven*.

three or four members of the congregation. Tellingly, Mormons avoided the formal term "sermon." With no comparable training to that of Protestant ministers, speakers typically offered optimistic homilies interspersing personal experiences and scriptural texts. A laugh or a tear was a more typical congregational response than a moment of deep reflection over a theological conundrum. Mormonism had its theologically-minded members, but the congregational pulpit was not typically the place for their expressions.

Hymns were important in both Protestant and Mormon worship services. However, the subtle differences in their respective lyrics illustrated their divergent spiritual temperaments. Arguably, the most famous Protestant hymn was Martin Luther's "A Mighty Fortress," sung with dignity and vigor:

> A mighty fortress is our God,
> A bulwark never failing;
> Our helper he amid the flood
> Of mortal ills prevailing.
> For still our ancient foe
> Doth seek to work us woe;
> His craft and power are great.
> And armed with cruel hate,
> On earth is not his equal.
> Did we in our own strength confide,
> Our striving would be losing;
> Were not the right man on our side,
> The man of God's own choosing;
> Dost ask who that may be?
> Christ Jesus, it is he;
> Lord Sabaoth his Name,
> From age to age the same,
> And he must win the battle.[57]

The LDS hymnal leads off with a classic celebration of the restoration, written by early Mormon apostle Parley P. Pratt. It is sung joyfully at a moving clip:

> The morning breaks, the shadows flee;
> Lo, Zion's standard is unfurled!
> The dawning of a brighter day,
> Majestic rises on the world.
> The clouds of error disappear
> Before the rays of truth divine;

---

57. This 1852 translation was Frederick Hedge's. See *The Hymnal of the Protestant Episcopal Church*, 551.

> The glory bursting from afar
> Wide o'er the nations soon will shine.
> Jehovah speaks! Let earth give ear,
> And Gentile nations turn and live.
> His mighty arm is making bare
> His cov'nant people to receive.
> Angels from heaven and truth from earth
> Have met, and both have record borne;
> Thus Zion's light is bursting forth
> To bring her ransomed children home.[58]

In his hymn, Luther's praise is inspired by God's sovereign strength to overpower the devil, to save men from their fallen state, and to triumph over the tragedy and misery against which human powers are impotent. Christ will unquestionably win the battle, but the faithful must endure unending trials until the kingdom of God is finally established at the end of the world. Pratt's exuberant declaration celebrates the union of God's people in a geo-political Zion, which, thanks to Jehovah and angels who speak again to living prophets, will rise supreme among the nations. The shadowed world is again bathed in divine light. It is not Christ's Second Coming that climaxes religious history; it is the gathering of the Saints in the Mormon Zion.

A group's founding narratives, doctrines, and symbols yield a general social temperament and religious lifestyle that, over time, can be observed across cultural and economic influences. Protestant religious temperament leaned toward anthropological pessimism: humans were created *ex nihilo* by a God that owes them nothing. Humans suffer from an inherited sinful nature that requires divine redemption from eternal punishment. Mormon temperament leans toward optimism: humans are already divine children of Heavenly Parents sent without memory to learn in mortality. They have always been uncreated social intelligences that freely inclined toward divine light together. We can see how these two temperaments might yield such conflicting styles of religious life that each group might call the other non-Christian.

---

58. For this and other quintessential Mormon hymns see Victor Ludlow, *The Encyclopedia of Mormonism*. Incidentally, Pratt borrowed his first line from Charles Wesley.

Church Governance and Schism

The very word Protestant denotes a defense against the errors of authority, and the Protestant movement was a critical venture that ultimately replaced clerical authority with the human conscience. Distrusting any central governing body, Protestants endured schism after schism as the heavy price of an unfettered conscience. Mormons also valued their freedom of conscience and they endured one major and many minor schisms up through the early twentieth century.[59] The largest body of Mormons under Brigham Young, however, came to expect members to sustain their prophet's inspiration and leadership should a conflict of conscience arise. Mormon loyalty to a group of apostles was troubling to Protestants who were suspicious of clerical authority.[60]

Although its worship services might appear informal, the Mormon Church was organized as elaborately as an army, with lay members being appointed (or "called") by their local ecclesiastical officers into posi-

---

59. Historically, although there have been hundreds of small schismatic groups among the Mormons, the only major schism occurred in 1845–46 when there was a major disagreement among church members over Brigham Young's succession to the presidency. The largest unreconciled minority group left the Church and later started the Reorganized Church of Jesus Christ of Latter-Day Saints in 1860, asking a surviving son of Joseph Smith to be their president. This church is currently headquartered in Independence, Missouri, and is now known as the Community of Christ with about 250,000 members worldwide. See Newell G. Bringhurst and John C. Hamer, *Scattering of the Saints: Schism Within Mormonism* on the history of LDS schisms.

60. The Protestants criticized the clandestine hierarchical forces controlling the Mormons, and the Mormons made fun of the Protestant penchant for disunity and schism. Historian Dean May, interested in comparing the methods of schism-avoidance in the more "Protestant" Reorganized Church of Jesus Christ of Latter-Day Saints and the Utah Mormon Church, analyzed the difference between the direct voting system whereby congregations determine their governance on issues and leadership in open forums, and the indirect system of sustaining leaders publicly while criticizing their leadership by merely disregarding it. The former was a typical Protestant method employed by the Reorganized Saints, the latter the typical Utah Mormon way. Though the latter had to find devious ways at times to influence change without disturbing surface harmony, their system avoided "the brittleness that public dissent and decision making often engender, leaving a powerful residue of flexibility and variety beneath the outward veneer of uniformity." Dean May, "Dissent and Authority in Two Latter-day Saint Traditions," 17.

tions designed to keep local congregations running smoothly. Similarly, beginning in their teen years, all active adult men were assigned in pairs and expected to pay formal monthly visits (called home teaching) to a specified list of families to assure their temporal welfare and deliver a spiritual message.[61] This was duplicated among adult women in a program titled Visiting Teaching. Tiers of priesthood leadership and accountability link the most recently called deacon, the lowest ecclesiastic office, to the Church President, the highest ecclesiastic office.

Protestant religious culture, from which most first-generation Mormons converted, taught that all true believers in Christ were priests in the service of their God. Nevertheless, depending on the denomination, each had a hierarchical clergy. Each congregation typically raised and spent its own funds, providing them with a very strong sense of local power and freedom. Twentieth-century Latter-day Saints, in contrast, paid a required tenth of their incomes to Church headquarters. Collected by local congregations, these donations were forwarded to the centralized administration, then dispersed back to local congregations as the general leaders saw fit. Unlike the Protestants, the local Mormon congregations felt comfortable with centralized control over the church funds.

Both Protestants and Mormons provided funds for church administration. However, with no professional clergy at the congregation level, and the Church's two-year missions being family or self-funded, Mormons could aptly describe their church as run by unpaid volunteers. Protestants criticized the Mormon system, claiming that its local lay leaders naively trusted enormous sums of money to corrupt prophets. Mormons counterclaimed that Protestant local missionaries were hirelings—spiritual bounty hunters rather than sincere ministers of the gospel.

---

61. Typically, the Latter-day Saints were assigned to attend a local congregation (called a "ward" by Mormons) in the neighborhood of their residence. Mormon wards provided the social basis for much of the members' recreation and friendship. Combining the always-changing home grown lay leadership with this method of assigning congregational attendance, the Saints came to develop relations and friendships from various walks of life that they would not have normally chosen themselves. Interestingly, contemporary Pentecostalism has been growing more rapidly than any other Christian religious tradition; and observers believe it is due in large part to the small local congregations where members are expected to take care of each other and to maintain high standards or civility, morality, and financial prudence as a sign of solidarity to the reputation of their local congregation. Martin Marty, "The Spirit Behind Pentecostalism," 6–7.

Spiritual vs. Material Authority

If a curious outsider asked a Latter-day Saint in 1910 what made her church different, she would have likely answered: "continuous revelation." Not only did the Mormon prophet receive revelation to direct the Church as a whole, but also each member confidently expected to receive inspired answers to prayers—and sometimes even supernatural visitations.

Mormons wondered at the Protestant subscription to an ancient religious text that described living oracles and miracles that Protestants themselves seemed to think they could not themselves experience. Indeed, the common Protestant application of Revelation 22:18 ("If any man shall add unto these things, God shall add unto him the plagues that are written in this book") was interpreted to preclude the possibility of new scripture being added to the established canon, rather than only to John's visionary epistle. To the Protestant, the Bible was complete and needed no further words of clarification. Protestant skepticism about new revelation seemed also to stem from a sense of history. Too often in the history of Israel (Deut. 18:20; Isa. 8:20) as well as the history of the New Testament church (Matt. 7:15–23; 24:24; 2 Tim. 4:3; 2 Pet. 2:1), false prophets and teachers, at times proclaiming new revelation even through angelic messengers (Gal. 1:8), had led people astray.

In an effort to mediate between divine directions revealed for the whole church and individual charismatic experiences, Mormonism developed two practical rituals that honored revelation of both types. The first was a formal encouragement for each Latter-day Saint to gain a personal testimony (or witness) of the real existence of Heavenly Father and Jesus, Joseph Smith's prophetic calling, and the continuation of divine authority among current Mormon apostles.[62] Every Mormon child baptized at

---

62. The early Mormon apostles implored God to allow them the same experience as Joseph Smith and Oliver Cowdery had, to see and talk with resurrected Christ and receive an ordination by literal laying on of hands from the Nazarene: "You have been indebted to other men in the first instance for evidence; on that you have acted; but it is necessary that you receive a testimony from Heaven for yourselves; so that you can bear testimony to the truth of the Book of Mormon, and that you have seen the face of God. That is more than the testimony of an angel. When the proper time arrives, you shall be able to bear this testimony to the world. When you bear testimony that you have seen God, this testimony God will never suffer to fall, but will bear you out; although many will not give heed, yet others will. You will, therefore, see the necessity of getting this testimony from Heaven. Never cease striving till you have seen God

age eight was encouraged to study, pray, and live worthy of this personal witness.[63] Every faithful Latter-day Saint, whether born Mormon or not, was ideally a convert, insomuch as they sought their own spiritual witness. The Church then formalized the importance of having this personal conviction by scheduling a monthly testimony meeting in which anyone in the congregation, young or old, might rise to share their witness from the heart.[64]

That a testimony of the Holy Spirit was available to all believers was not in question among Protestants. Still, to them, the content and source of the Mormon testimony was suspect. It focused too much on their allegiance to a prophet and on the apostasy of other Christians. It was too open to ecclesiastical abuse and personal self-deception. Furthermore, they suspected that these testimonies resulted more from socialization, autosuggestion during childhood and youth, or perhaps even demonic spiritual sources than from genuine inspiration from the Holy Spirit. Mormons were likewise suspicious of Protestant testimonies of a truth-affirming indwelling Spirit that had led to centuries of schismatic disagreement.

To Protestant ears, the Mormons' testimony that Jesus is savior of the world was overshadowed by their testimony that God and Jesus in material resurrected bodies had authorized a restoration of the primitive church ex-

---

face to face. Strengthen your faith; cast off your doubts, your sins, and all your unbelief, and nothing can prevent you from coming to God. Your ordination is not full and complete till God has laid His hands upon you. We require as much to qualify us as did those who have gone before us; God is the same. If the Savior in former days laid his hands on his disciples, why not in latter days?" See Parley P. Pratt, *The Autobiography of Parley P. Pratt*, 12. These were not figurative words for these apostles. Indeed, each Saint was told to seek to meet God as soon as possible—before his or her mortal death preferably (D&C 93:1, 19).

63. Jan Shipps, *Mormonism: The Story of a New Religious Tradition*, 52–65.

64. Not only a spoken report was expected. Mormons were encouraged to keep regular journals as Joseph Smith had done to record for future generations the testimony of their sacred experiences. Each Latter-day Saint thus symbolically and practically thought they were replicating the ancient prophets whose recorded written testimonies became the scriptures that benefited future generations. Mormons would read the journals of their ancestors to be inspired by their testimonies to keep the faith; Ludlow, *Encyclopedia*, 770–71. Of course, many Protestants kept similar written records of spiritual experiences, typically in the form of letters or journal entries. It was the methodical and ubiquitous responsibility of speaking "from the dead to the living" that made the Mormons unusual in this practice.

clusively to Mormon apostles and prophets. More brazenly, Joseph Smith and his associate, Oliver Cowdery, claimed that it was, in fact, the resurrected apostles Peter, James, and John who had ordained them with the priesthood authority that the three had themselves received directly from Jesus, but which had been lost in post-apostolic apostasy. The Latter-day Saints thus claimed to be the only people with leaders who could legitimately trace an unbroken line of authority back to Christ.[65] Material resurrected hands had touched material mortal heads to make this clear.[66]

Protestants thought the Mormon theology of a physical God was primitive and wrong. For them, God had appeared at various times in seemingly physical manifestations, but these were understood as "theophanies," an immaterial God temporarily appearing in a seemingly physical form so as to communicate with his physical creatures. Further, they understood the incarnation of Jesus as one in which the immaterial and eternal Word of God took a new physical nature, but not the implication that the Father or the Son were physical and material beings in the same sense as humanity. This flowed from the teachings of Protestant theologians and pastors who, in turn, had drawn this concept from Biblical passages where God was described by Jesus as a spirit; and that a spirit did not have flesh and bones as Jesus did after his resurrection (e.g., John 4:24; Luke 24:39).

According to Joseph Smith, he received the buried gold plates from the resurrected Moroni and returned them to him. This is a prime example of the material/spiritual *mélange* that made Joseph Smith such an uncanny, un-mystical, and—to Protestants—unbelievable, prophet. Smith claimed he had translated the plates in about seventy days, dictating to his scribe without erasure a five-hundred-page history of an ancient American

---

65. Worthy Latter-day Saint men at about age twenty were ordained to the Priesthood after the order of the Son of God, commonly called the Melchizedek Priesthood following the usage in the New Testament (Heb. 6:20, 7:1–3). Mormon men kept a written record of their line of priesthood authority tracing it from the one who ordained them back to first century apostles Peter, James, and John, and thus Jesus who had ordained them (John 15:16).

66. Much philosophical questioning has centered on the connection (if any) between empirical/material and rational/spiritual phenomena. William James attempted to describe all phenomena as empirical—the invisible world merely needed to be more clearly revealed by more precise perception with or without technical devices. While most theists in the nineteenth century were dualists positing a spiritual realm separate from the material one, Joseph Smith (before James) claimed spirit is matter, and we will all have the capacity to see it more clearly with improved resurrected bodies (D&C 131:7–8).

enclave of Hebrew immigrants. To Protestants, these material-historical claims sounded more like fabrications than actual visitations or translation. Even though there were eleven signers of affidavits verifying the reality and apparent antiquity of the golden plates, they were dismissed by Protestants who viewed them as unreliable insiders.

In summary, the differences that made Protestants and Mormons religious rivals included irreconcilable differences in grand narratives, doctrines, symbols, and religious styles of life. Better grasping these tensions explains why Protestants felt compelled to send missionaries to convert unaccepting Mormons in Utah. In the next chapter, we will examine closely the tactics and methods used by three of the most famous proselytizers employed to convert the Saints.

CHAPTER SIX

John Danforth Nutting, Nondenominational Preacher at Large

John Danforth Nutting was born at Randolph, Vermont, in 1854. His parents, Rufus and Sarah Nutting, raised him to become a minister of the Christian gospel. In 1881, he took a Master's degree at Wheaton College (Illinois) and for the next four years completed advanced studies at Oberlin Theological Seminary (Ohio). In 1885, he married Annie Miller; however, she died a year later. He then married Lillis Morley in 1890. Nutting's controversial decision to marry again broke the ministerial code some Protestants held during this period that strictly interpreted the injunction in Matthew 5:32 against divorce and remarriage, allowing no remarriage even when the first marriage did not end in divorce. Nutting was rebuffed in his attempts to obtain ordination from several conservative denominations, citing his second marriage as the reason for their refusal. The more liberal Congregationalist traditions accepted him and, after serving briefly in Ohio, Kentucky, and Missouri, in 1892, he was appointed pastor of the Plymouth Congregational Church in Salt Lake City, Utah. After six years as pastor in Utah, he began a mission to the Mormons that attracted funding support from several denominations that had previously refused him ordination.[1]

---

1. Kurt Van Gorden, Two telephone interviews in August and September 1993 with Charles Randall Paul regarding the life history of John Danforth Nutting. Van Gorden at that time was the President of the Utah Gospel Mission. He is the archivist for the unindexed papers of John Danforth Nutting. On Nutting's demise, his family assembled his unindexed files and subsequently gave them to Kurt Van Gorden of Orange, California, who was the mission leader of the Utah Gospel Mission in 1993. The information about John Nutting's personal life, and some details of his mission activity not in the files were provided in the two telephone interviews noted above. No biography of Nutting has been written. His writings herein cited date from several periods of his life. Most of his writings in the late 1920s were elaborations of his earlier thought, illustrating Nutting's constancy rather than his development. I have mixed citations chronologically when clarity of theme outweighed sequence.

If the biographical details about Nutting seem a bit sparse, that is because he didn't leave behind much in the way of personal information. No formal biography, even a short one, has been written. Nutting left behind a wealth of documents containing details about his missionary work in Utah, but very little of it was personal in nature as his writing was often geared toward audiences that he was appealing to for support of his Utah ministry. In what follows, we'll be meeting this highly energetic, devoted minister of the Christian gospel primarily through his polemical writings, which were designed to raise awareness of the ongoing danger to Christian souls posed by Mormonism's continued growth. Although Nutting comes across in these pages as strident and condescending toward Utah's Mormons—and what he believed to be the many heresies of the Church of Jesus Christ of Latter-day Saints—there is still much to admire about his devotion to a mission that lasted more than fifty years.

In the first six years following Nutting's appointment to pastor Salt Lake City's Plymouth Congregational Church, he immersed himself in serving his flock and in studying the Mormonism that surrounded him. In 1898, the Salt Lake Ministers Association selected him to launch a new inter-denominational proselytizing initiative: the Utah Gospel Mission.[2] This mission was designed to reach into Mormonism's small towns, mostly settled two generations earlier, with additional outreach to Protestants and those with no church affiliation in small mining towns. Protestant denominations could establish permanent congregations only when local funds adequately matched contributions from stronger congregations in the East. At the time, there were too few circuit riders and traveling Sunday School teachers to focus much effort on small Utah towns whose religious makeup was usually ninety-percent Mormon and ten-percent unchurched. To enlist workers for the Utah Gospel Mission ministry, Nutting would typically travel to the Moody Bible Institute of Chicago

---

2. The term "proselytizing" usually has described a one-way effort whereby the missionary taught the hearer with no expectation for the table to be turned. The most effective modern dialogue, I argue, can best be interpreted as two-way table turning proselytizing with conventions of civility and "open" listening added. The fact that the Protestants came to Utah to teach the Mormons who had already been teaching Protestants, and the fact that the Mormons usually wanted to turn the table on the Protestant missionaries, makes this a counter-proselytizing situation for both the Protestants and the Mormons. It is an early case of modern religious dialogue with the *de facto* convention of civility, but without in most cases the convention of "open" listening.

and the Bible Institute of Los Angeles (now BIOLA University) and recruit six to twelve young men to serve as Utah missionaries for a year in return for a modest expense reimbursement.

Nutting and his handful of missionaries were commissioned to represent all Protestants as interdenominational, face-to-face and door-to-door, evangelists. Within about three-and-a-half years, these emissaries visited almost all of the seven hundred small towns in Utah, southern Idaho, and northern Arizona that comprised "Mormon country."[3] They soon became known as the wagon missionaries because they traveled in three Studebaker-built horse-drawn wagons until roads improved enough to allow motorized vehicles. The missionaries repeated this long circuit into the late-1940s.[4]

Because they believed that regular church meetings and denominational affiliation were not necessary for individual salvation, these non-denominational missionaries did not find the lack of local congregations an impediment to their work. They encouraged converts they had won to attend Christian churches when they could, but regular affiliation was prohibitive, often barred by many miles of rough road between towns. The larger difficulty for these converts came in their trying to refocus their spiritual lives away from a tight-knit social community dominated by Mormon forms of worship into a loosely structured mode of individual scripture reading and personal prayer. Small-town Utah's social life was dominated by Mormon-sponsored activities—dances, weekly sermons, dramatic productions, and other enticements—that an occasional nondenominational meeting could not replace. A Mormon who converted to a more Evangelical form of the Christian faith would not only suffer social disapproval, they could grow bored with their new way of spiritual life in contrast with their former Mormon social experiences. As a result, these converts often followed their missionaries back to California or Chicago.[5]

In doing their missionary work, Nutting and his missionaries would request, and frequently receive, permission to use the local Mormon chapels to make a general presentation before making the rounds to each home. If there was no chapel, or if the local Mormon bishops (lay pastors)

---

3. Descriptions of these missionary methods are related in Edward L. Mills, "One Hundred Years of Mormonism," 918–19; Herbert Ware Reherd, "An Outline History of the Protestant Churches of Utah," 649–690; and Brendan Terry, "John Danforth Nutting and the Utah Gospel Mission," 32–41.

4. John Danforth Nutting, *Light on Mormonism* 1(1): 7.

5. Nutting, *Light on Mormonism* 1(1): 53.

were uncooperative, they would sometimes hold a tent meeting, following up with door-to-door activities. In 1922, Nutting reported that in an average year his missionaries amassed these statistics: house visits: 11,313; settlements visited: 67; meetings held: 222; average attendance: 114; pages of tracts distributed: 1,203,000; gospel songbooks sold: 236; miles traveled by auto or wagon: 1,095.[6] The circuit the missionaries followed was somewhat seasonal, focusing on northern Arizona during the months of coldest weather but roaming as far north as the Mormon colonies in southern Alberta, Canada, during the summer.[7]

Nutting published annual reports to his supporting community in the eastern states that included statistics like the ones listed above, as well as appeals for funds and reports about the rigors of proselytizing to Mormons. For instance, in one of these reports, he described how hard his six missionaries worked and noted the lack of local Protestants, the strenuous life of constant travel, and his own prolonged absences from his beloved home in Ohio. An excerpt:

> The work in Utah is of two kinds, denominational and the Utah Gospel Mission. The former is localized, and the latter is traveling—both are needed to the full. Both are undermanned and suffer from lack of permanence in their force. The field is difficult; it has been called the hardest field in the world because of its peculiar difficulties [Mormonism] added to those found elsewhere. . . . Those men who come usually do not stay long . . . Men go to foreign lands [and] . . . a sort of halo is thrown about the foreign field by its distance. The home missionary may do just as need[ed] and difficult work at equal risk in every way, and be thought far less of than the other; surely for no good reason.[8]

Nutting's complaint about the exotic appeal of foreign lands in attracting young missionaries was a just grievance. Some contemporary Evangelicals argue that this phenomenon continues today, with mission work overseas being perceived as more glamorous and necessary than domestic mission work. Setting the tone for missions at the 1886 Moody Bible Conference, Matthew Simpson, a Methodist bishop, proclaimed: "You may live to see the day every land is Christian. . . . God is making our land a kind of central spot for the whole earth. The eyes of the world are upon

---

6. Nutting, *Light on Mormonism* 1(1): 6.
7. Van Gorden, Interview, 1993.
8. John Danforth Nutting, *Light on Mormonism* 2(4): 1.

us."⁹ Another speaker at the same conference deliberately used military metaphors to appeal to the potential sacred soldiers: "The work of missions is not a wrecking expedition, but it is a war of conquest."[10] Utah mission recruiters attempted to forge parallels with glamorous foreign missions such as China and India. As to Nutting's statement about "equal risk" in foreign and domestic mission work, no record of physical conflicts in Utah is associated with Nutting's mission. It is likely that Nutting was speaking in terms of "spiritual warfare," a trope common within Evangelical thinking. There is, however, one newspaper account of a fistfight between Nutting and the son of the LDS prophet Joseph F. Smith in Buffalo, New York, where Nutting was giving an anti-Mormon fundraising lecture. Smith had issued a complaint against Nutting, but local authorities refused to arrest him.[11] Relations with Mormons were generally tolerant. Indifference was a larger obstacle to overcome than antagonism.

Strapped for resources, the congregations represented by the Salt Lake Ministers Association could not financially support the Utah Gospel Mission. Nutting generally spent from mid-November to May each year in his Cleveland office raising money.[12] Until the late 1920s, financially solvent eastern Protestant congregations would typically adopt western mission churches that had too few members to support a full-time pastor.[13] Using his family and church connections, Nutting arranged lectures at various denominations. Using hand-held stereo slide pictures, he illustrated the natural wonders of Utah, then described the rigorous conditions under which his missionaries labored, emphasizing the terrible plight of Utah's people who were in the thrall of Mormonism's corrupt heresies.[14] Congregations or individuals agreed to send money to the Utah Gospel Mission. Unfortunately, such commitments were often only for a year, forcing Nutting to fish for funds every year in the East before returning to fish for souls in the West.

Nutting's financial records spanning half a century provide a barometer of the interest in missions to Mormons. When Evangelical anti-Mormon sentiment reached its height in the late 1910s, Nutting obtained

---

9. Robert T. Handy, *A Christian America: Protestant Hopes and Historical Realities*, 69.
10. Handy, *A Christian America*, 112.
11. "Mormon Elder Attacked," 1.
12. Reherd, *An Outline History*, 650.
13. Colin B. Goodykoontz, *Home Missions on the American Frontier*, 38.
14. Van Gorden, Interview, 1993.

substantial gifts from crusading philanthropists. However, these sources seemed to dry up during the middle 1920s, forcing Nutting to launch mass mailing campaigns to Eastern congregations. Although Nutting's efforts never slacked, general Protestant interest in Utah missions apparently declined by 1923. His annual mission report that year listed only twenty-nine speaking addresses, which had reached a total of 3,628 listeners; distributing or selling 558,000 pages of tracts or books; and traveling over 3,000 miles by rail. Between Nutting's personal work and that of his fellow missionaries, he reported a total of $70,000 in expenditures over the previous twenty years of mission work, or an average of $3,500 per year. Comparing his system to the typical $4,000 annual salary of a denominational pastor at the time, in addition to the costs of meetinghouse construction and maintenance and salaries for a church staff, Nutting championed the cost-efficiency of his Utah mission. Yet, even as he made so much working with so little, Nutting described his treasury as being "in the poorest condition in years" and begged, "Please help. We are sure our work is telling in many ways."[15]

Nutting wrote more than forty articles and brochures about Mormonism, most supposedly for Mormon eyes, but more often aimed at Eastern funding sources. In his annual reports, he listed under "eastern work" the costs of printing his polemical newsletter *Light on Mormonism*, which Nutting published for twenty-six years.[16] Further, he flagged several of his brochures as inappropriate for Mormon readers, and listed highly critical literature or material that exposed his proselytizing strategy as "for discriminating use only."[17] There was a brotherly tone to brochures written directly for Mormons, but even disaffected Mormons reading *Light on Mormonism* would no doubt have been put off by its condescension.

Nutting's typical practice in attacking Mormon doctrinal concepts was to pair them with a self-conscious defense of the value of the work his mission was doing, along with describing his need for more missionaries and financial support. The rhetorical foe in his writings was often an imaginary skeptic who challenged the utility of proselytizing Mormons who now had monogamous families, worked industriously, and paid their taxes. Nutting cast his responses as calls to arms in a religious war with a subtle enemy to which others were blind. While he blamed the advance of Mormonism on

---

15. John Danforth Nutting, *Light on Mormonism* 3(3): 67, 83.
16. Nutting, *Light on Mormonism*, 1(1): 6.
17. John Danforth Nutting, "Mormonism Today and its Remedy," back cover.

the corruption and deceit of its leaders,[18] he once admitted that American secularism might also be a problem. Pointing out that the number of Protestants nationwide who had converted to Mormonism in 1925 had dropped from 7,500 to 6,400, he proposed that "the general laxity about religious things" might also have been a partial cause. But he also modestly attributed it to "our own work," reinforced by the work of another group, "the National Reform Association of Pittsburgh."[19] Nutting gleefully noted a drop in Mormon missionary effectiveness: even though the Mormon missionary force increased by 600 men, their annual harvest of converts had decreased by 1,200 in 1925. Bolstered by this, he asked his readers: "How about throwing still more reserves into the battle next year?"[20]

Despite this example of good humor, however, Nutting was perpetually disturbed that his Protestant countrymen so casually shrugged off a religion that not only kept its hundreds of thousands of members in spiritual darkness but aggressively searched for more proselytes. He believed that Mormon doctrines and social systems not only jeopardized the salvation of Latter-day Saints themselves, but also were spiritually threatening to all Christians within their influence:

> With some 2,500 men proclaiming [Mormonism] from door to door . . . no church is free from danger to some member; none can be free from the responsibility for letting souls . . . innocently be taken in error which Mormonism so plausibly presents and often really believes as truth. Probably three-fourths of all Mormon converts have been out of Christian churches, though generally backsliders, just because they did not know the facts about Mormonism and those of Christian belief in contrast.[21]

Nutting became convinced that Mormonism was a mixture of devilish paganism, selfish materialism, and aggressive imperialism, wrapped in a seductive package of exclusive claims to modern revelation and Millennial triumphalism. He worried that thousands of his countrymen would be seduced by its exotic story and submit to Mormon priesthood leaders who,

---

18. This same strategy is often employed by those in contemporary Evangelical counter-cult ministry. LDS Church leadership is conceived of as knowledgeable and purposefully deceptive, while rank and file members as ignorant and gullible. Thus, a harsh apologetic stance is seemingly justified against the institution and its leadership, while a softer stance is usually taken toward general membership.

19. John Danforth Nutting, *Light on Mormonism* 5(1): 131.

20. Nutting, *Light on Mormonism* 5(1): 131.

21. Nutting, *Light on Mormonism* 1(1): 6.

he was convinced, were corrupt power-seekers. He repeatedly reminded people in speeches and pamphlets:

> We need not think that only ignorant or mentally deficient people are in danger of Mormonism, neither need we assume that Mormonism is backed only by human power. . . . Supernatural evil craftiness and power are clearly evident. We must train all to know the Bible truths [that combat Mormonism]. Ten thousand or more converts every year fall to the peril. Blow the fog horn! Every church is in danger.[22]

Nutting was also irritated by the lack of outrage most Protestants showed toward Joseph Smith's claim that God had told him all other churches were false, and all clergymen corrupt. This belief—that all non-Mormons were apostates or dupes of apostates—demeaned other faiths, other beliefs, and other clergy. Furthermore, the Mormons seemed proudly aloof from and ignorantly prejudiced against Protestant proselytizing:

> Mormonism is armor-plated against ordinary methods of work . . . prepossessed of special difficulties . . . its terrible doctrines often borrowed from heathenism and unsuspectingly accepted, its aloofness often greater than that of the other fields, its lack of response seldom equaled anywhere in the world. . . . But chief most among hindrances is the systematic slanders of all [Christian] church work and workers as fraudulent, and the trained and often supervised absence of Mormons from [Protestant] services.[23]

Nutting and the young missionaries he recruited could not see how any intelligent Christian could be duped by Mormonism—an attitude that made it difficult to be anything but condescending toward the Saints. John Nutting sincerely claimed to love Mormons while hating their dearest possession, Mormonism. At the same time, Nutting ambivalently bemoaned the meager number of converts he and his team were able to win.[24] Perhaps his theological logic also communicated ambivalence: God had delivered him from darkness when Nutting sincerely sought Him, so God would do the same for all sincere believers—or, was it those that God had foreordained to salvation no matter their sincerity? He seemed to blame the ignorant, blind, or hardhearted Mormons for not responding, yet at the same time acted strangely surprised that such people did not heed him. Were they predestinated by God or by character to remain in the dark? Not knowing the will of God for each soul, he treated all as

---

22. John Danforth Nutting, *Light on Mormonism* 4(3): 87.
23. John Danforth Nutting, "Difficulties of Work Among the Mormons," 857.
24. John Danforth Nutting, "The Truth About God."

if they might be saved. Nutting presumed most Mormons were unknowing dupes that might be awakened if God so willed. Most of his clients felt his presumption was a less than optimistic affirmation of salvation—presaging one of the deepest perennial conflicts about the radical salvific optimism of the Saints that the Protestants thought dangerously prideful and naïve.

Nutting's Attitude toward Mormons

Nutting made a sharp distinction between loving the deceived Mormon and hating the Mormon system that put them in the dark. Nutting used the term "system" frequently to avoid elevating Mormonism to the status of religion. He instructed his prospective missionaries that a Mormon was like a proud drunk on a ledge, unaware that he was disoriented and risking suicide. Talking him back to safety usually required calmness and even flattery—not condescension or criticism. Nutting's plan to help Mormons come to the light appears in passages like these from various brochures instructing would-be missionaries:

> This is not a "scarehead paper" [yellow press] . . . not that there is any lack of fact which would not justify big headings and produce astonishment enough; but sensationalism is far from our object. We shall speak the truth in love . . . from careful and rational study of the facts. . . . Our only motive in years of work with Mormons is love.[25]
>
> [To understand a Mormon] first postulate that Joseph Smith was a true oracle of God; then hypnotize yourself with your own testimony. Say, "I know this work is true," on every possible occasion, in private, in public. Then pray to be true to your testimony. Never pray for light as to the real teaching of God's word independent of Latter-day Saint positions. Follow this plan and you will never leave the faith of your fathers . . . Like the [Muslim], the Mormon blinds himself to reason through the hypnosis of "prayer" or what he thinks is prayer.[26]
>
> [No Christians] can be free of responsibility . . . for the souls of those who have been innocently taken in the error which Mormonism so plausibly presents.[27]
>
> A person with small light on Mormonism may join it with sincerity; the writer believes that many Mormons who were born into the system would be condemned of God if they were to leave it now, because it is the best they know at present. It is the fault of the Christian people that they

---

25. Nutting, *Light on Mormonism* 1(1): 1.
26. Nutting, *Light on Mormonism* 4(2): 98.
27. Nutting, *Light on Mormonism* 1(1): 2.

have not long ago shed the light so fully that all might know the errors, even when presented cleverly by [Mormon] emissaries.[28]

The true attitude of the Christian ought to be that of deep sympathy [with people] who are being deprived of their gospel chance by an almost utterly false religion . . . [but] as to the *system* which enthralls them, we should have no sympathy at all for it is as far from the Gospel as can be imagined.[29]

Mormonism has been called Satan's masterpiece; and, with all due respect to its sincere adherents, there is no more fitting name.[30]

Although he chided fellow Christians for their neglect of missionary zeal toward the Saints, Nutting held Mormons themselves responsible for remaining in spiritual darkness once they were called to the light by the true Christian gospel. Nutting strategically used multiple causality to make the most of any outcome from his counter-missionary efforts. If few Mormons converted to Protestantism, he blamed inadequate funding. He also stressed patience along with the urgency of saving souls—if there were no way for someone to hear the gospel, God would judge only according to the light one was given. Nutting was vague in expressing what he believed to be the destiny of those who had no chance to hear the true gospel. He did not want to support Mormon practices of vicarious baptism for the dead that theoretically extended the saving gospel to everyone who ever lived; however, he did not want to preach that a loving God would condemn to hell all unbaptized souls.

In many ways, Nutting and other Evangelical missionaries were fighting a battle for the soul of the Christian movement that had already been lost. By the end of the nineteenth century, the wrathful and legalistic judge of heaven had, for most Christians, become an understanding God who would not punish any person for their sincere beliefs. Ironically, though Mormons claimed exclusive authority, they also fit comfortably with this emerging view of God's primary concern for sincerity and goodness, claiming that anyone who sincerely followed the dictates of his or her conscience would have every opportunity to learn the truth, repent of wrongdoing, and benefit from salvific ordinances in the next life. On this point, liberal Protestants agreed. As a result, many members on the Home and Foreign Mission boards felt that funds should be spent on social programs rather than indoctrination—threatening financial support for Nutting and others who still felt that missions were vital. For these

---

28. Nutting, *Light on Mormonism* 1(1): 2.
29. Nutting, *Light on Mormonism* 5(1): 131.
30. John Danforth Nutting, "Why I Could Never Be A Mormon," 1.

holdouts, the great missionary commission from Jesus to the apostles was anything but out of date (Matt. 28:19–20).

Nutting's strategy in appealing for support avoided any discussions of predestination. Salvation had to depend at least partly on human involvement or his donors' sacrifice would make no real difference. Nutting left the question ambiguous: God had called him as a witness to Utah, and if he didn't get to everyone quickly, it might be "too late" for those whom he had no means to reach. But by the 1910s, this appeal became less and less compelling as the Mormons, having moved beyond polygamy, appeared to most Christians to be sincere, though mistaken, believers.

Nutting fretted about "finding some means by which Christian truth can be brought into wide and kindly contact with the Mormon mind."[31] But even though he and his missionaries hoped to preach the true Christian gospel as brothers appealing to their beloved family members, it was almost impossible for them to teach those who thought they already had it without demeaning the potential convert's prior judgment. At some point, the missionaries had to set up a comparison demonstrating that Evangelical views were true while Mormon views were false. They seemed to find no respectful way to engage their mutually exclusive truth claims. The apologetic method Nutting employed (and one used by most Mormons as well) was confrontational debate with the presumption that the opponent was a blinded, prideful dupe.

Nutting's strategies were nevertheless attempts to be as non-threatening as they could be without shying away from the heart of the matter. He and his missionaries were to act as interdenominational, non-salaried travelers. By moving on without establishing formal churches in the small, Mormon communities in which he evangelized, Nutting hoped to convert individuals to Christ without seeming to be a competing church.[32] The Utah Gospel Mission was initially multi-denominational, or inter-

---

31. John Danforth Nutting, "A Study of the Present Mormon Problem," 934.

32. In the late twentieth century the term "proselytizing" has achieved such cultural opprobrium that it is rarely used except to describe asymmetrical social power relations in favor of a missionary over his or her "client." The term has also a connotation of unidirectional proclamation—preaching without listening to the benighted subject needing salvation. The term evangelizing has risen in popularity to describe a two-way conversation on more or less equal terms of social power and openness to learning. Evangelizing affirms the comparatively superior claims of the missionary's doctrine vis-à-vis the other, but not the missionary's wisdom or spirituality or goodness. Thus, the missionary is wise to

denominational; Nutting also started describing it as non-denominational by the mid-1920s to shield his ministry from denominational contamination.[33] Given Nutting's denominational connections, the term was an oxymoron that attempted to circumvent the scandal of sectarian divisions by creating a sect with no name. Avoiding a firm identity offered less against which to protest when significant differences arose.

Nutting's wagon missionaries used a basic three-pronged approach that was rational, empirical, and phenomenological. It contained a systematic theological argument, a comparison of the cultural fruits of different religions, followed by personal testimonials about God's saving grace. Nutting outlined his proselytizing plan as consisting of a six-point strategy:[34]

1. Use the opponent's text to lead into a discussion on the nature of God.
2. Show how all truth comes quickly to a true vs. false conception of God.
3. Explain the concept of the human fallen nature to show the need for Christ.
4. Argue against heathen idolatry as demeaning to all-powerful God.
5. Issue a call to immediate repentance.
6. Sound an urgent warning based on the imminent final judgment.

Having used similar techniques during their own missionary work, many Mormons understood these approaches and engaged the wagon missionaries with lively responses. Indeed, most of the grandparents of the Utah Saints had been converted to Mormonism by similar modes of persuasion.[35]

---

openly listen to the other to learn and be inspired even while evangelizing. In this historical study elements of proselytizing and evangelizing become obvious.

33. Lawrence Foster, *Defenders of God: The Fundamentalist Revolt Against the Modern Age*, 153–61; and Van Orden, *Interview*, 1993.

34. John Danforth Nutting, "Paul's Method of Dealing with False Religionists."

35. A competent analysis with bibliography of the appeal of Mormonism to its late-nineteenth-century converts is by Leonard J. Arrington and Davis Bitton, *The Mormon Experience: A History of the Latter-day Saints*, 23–41. The list of sales points includes 1) Restoration of the true church, 2) Creative Biblicism, 3) The Book of Mormon, 4) Modern revelation, 5) Millennial Eschatology, 6) Mythic potency, 7) Religious authoritarianism. "Mormonism's appeal was its combination of theological intelligibility and spiritual reassurance with a specific program offering material and emotional satisfaction in the present." Arrington and Bitton, 27–43. Also see Marvin Hill, *Quest for Refuge: The Mormon Flight from American Pluralism*, 155 on Mormonism as the premier primitivism gospel

As the twentieth century began, Christian apologetics continued to emphasize rational doctrinal arguments over personal experience. Historian Mario De Pillis has shown that the perennial quest for religious authority in America was exacerbated by Protestant denominationalism.[36] Protestants vied for authority internally and externally, while denouncing Catholics and Mormons and others. Where was the true church of God? This was the oft-contested Protestant question during the time Nutting and his teams did their work. Within early-twentieth-century missionary tracts and texts, matters of doctrinal truth and ecclesiastical authority were almost as lively a question then as they had been during the Second Great Awakening period that Mormonism was born into.

The Mormon view of the Christian apostasy contrasted the Evangelical view that the Mormons themselves were the new apostates. If Joseph Smith had merely denounced abuses of ecclesiastical authority, he would have joined a company of illustrious Protestant Reformers. But in rejecting the authority of the entire Christian tradition, while simultaneously proclaiming a restoration of the original church, Smith manifested an audacious pride. To them, the Mormon message was that Christ had bypassed all other Christians to communicate with a few men in Salt Lake City. Accepting such a premise would mean that God had repelled the worshipful prayers of millions of sincere Christians for centuries. Was Joseph Smith the only person of faith since the death of the Biblical apostles who had prayed to know the right Christian way? For Protestants, this was egregious. Nutting interpreted the battle as being about divinely authorized leadership in the world, declaring that, contrary to the thinking of some, "polygamy is not the main issue. . . . [Rather] it is the rejection of the true gospel and its faithful clergy. . . . This keeps them [the Mormons] from the light."[37]

For Nutting, the Bible was the battlefield for religious discussions. However, he also realized that only rarely did a rational point, won or lost by proof-texting, make a difference to anyone's conviction. Trying to explain why Mormons could engage in rational discussion of the Bible and not see the light, an exasperated Nutting explained that the problem was because

---

movement, an ancient model for modern stability; and an insightful passage comparing the appeals of unstable revivalism with institutionalized restorationism in Sidney Ahlstrom, *A Religious History of the American People*, 357–358.

36. Mario S. DePillis, "The Quest for Religious Authority and the Rise of Mormonism," 68–88.

37. Nutting, *Light on Mormonism* 1(1): 132.

the ordinary Mormon mind is so soaked through and through with the untrue teachings of Mormonism, like a water-logged timber which has been in a pond for many years, that it is usually IMPOSSIBLE, even by the grace of God on most earnest efforts, to get the people to *see* saving truth enough to change radically. It must take a long process before the truth can get in enough to expel the errors which keep them from seeing Christ and Bible truth plainly.[38]

Another strategy of the wagon missionaries was to argue that faulty doctrine makes faulty people—i.e., Mormons were morally low compared to good Protestants.[39] This social argument also had a theological component: bringing the sinner to a conviction of his or her sinful state was the *sine qua non* of Evangelicalism. Protestant missionaries consistently argued that Mormon optimism about human nature revealed its tendencies toward pride, self-righteousness, and self-aggrandizement.[40]

Yet, like rational argument and biblical proof-texting, comparing the fruits of one religion to another often degenerated to ineffective stereotyping. The wagon missionaries would not allow that Mormons, who held "pagan beliefs in phallic gods of procreation," could live decent moral lives and raise exemplary families. When presented with statistical evidence showing that Mormons had healthy and stable families, above-average education, low crime rates, and a solid work ethic, Nutting explained it had nothing to do with their theology but revealed the lasting trace of their pre-Mormon backgrounds: "Enough genuine Christian influence had remained in the blood of the pioneers, and enough newly infused by converts of various Protestant denominations to raise Mormon society above the otherwise inevitable nadir to which its materialistic and heretical principles would otherwise thrust it."[41]

---

38. John Danforth Nutting, *Light on Mormonism* 5(4): 221.
39. John Danforth Nutting, "Awheel and Afoot in Mormonism," 37.
40. John Danforth Nutting, *Light on Mormonism* 2(2): 11.
41. Nutting, *Light on Mormonism*, 2(2): 11–12. Adverting to genetic explanation was typical social thinking of the time. The rage against immigration of European Catholics and Mormons was often expressed by describing the low quality of the human stock being imported. See B. Carmon Hardy, *Solemn Covenant: The Mormon Polygamous Passage*, 285, especially note 10; Robert Wiebe, *The Search for Order, 1877–1920*, 178. The experimental communities of the left and the Ku Klux Klan on the right agreed on one thing: heredity was destiny. See Lawrence Foster, *Religion and Sexuality: Three American Communal Experiments of the 19th Century*, 202–204. Eighty years ago, eugenics was commonly discussed in polite society. Ironically, the Mormons had frequently argued for eugenics to defend

The deep revulsion in Nutting's words above reveals that the doctrinal point of no compromise lay in his conception of a sovereign God of absolute power and gracious mercy versus Joseph Smith's Man of Holiness who, like his son Jesus, became flesh and descended below all things to win the human heart and became divine.[42] For their part, Mormons ridiculed other Christians who worshiped a spiritual God who was said to exist everywhere in general but no place in particular. Neither Protestant missionaries nor their LDS opponents showed mercy to false doctrine that led to divine debasement and unholy worship.

Comparing contradictory personal witnesses about religious truth likewise most often resulted in stalemate. Nutting and the wagon missionaries argued that Mormons hypnotized themselves into belief through repeating self-affirming prayers and testimonies, an argument that drew some support from scientific communities regarding the phenomenon of auto-suggestion. Nutting correctly pointed out that Mormon prayers sought divine confirmation only of the limited doctrines that they had already learned. Writing to his Protestant audience, Nutting described the Mormon methodology: "First postulate that Joseph Smith was a true oracle of God; then hypnotize yourself with your own testimony. . . . Like the [Muslim], the Mormon blinds himself to reason through the hypnosis of 'prayer' or what he thinks is prayer."[43] Nutting suggested that listeners should leave God a more open range of responses, at least one that allows them to pose an honest question about the truths that Nutting and his missionaries were preaching.

Nutting was correct in his basic critique. Each Saint was indeed taught to strive for a divine response to prayer on the truthfulness of Mormonism. No Mormon was mature until he or she had a testimony of

---

their polygamy as the solution "to the complicated knot of gender relations, family life, and racial decline. [Eugenic polygamy] could revolutionize the whole world." See Hardy, *Solemn Covenant*, 124n152.

42. This position is probably too starkly drawn. There was in the Book of Mormon and other Mormon scriptures a counter-argument to Pelagian optimism. "The natural man is an enemy to God, and has been from the fall of Adam" (Mosiah 3:18–19). "Now . . . I know that man is nothing, which thing I never had supposed" (Moses 1:9–10). Still, humans were free to rise or fall based on their uncreated status (D&C 93:29). See Harold Bloom, *The American Religion: The Emergence of the Post Christian Nation*, 124–26. Fundamentally, humans are open; they are neither depraved nor virtuous, but one choice leads to another.

43. Nutting, *Light on Mormonism* 4(3): 98.

God, Jesus, Joseph Smith, the Book of Mormon, and the current prophet leading the church. Personal testimony linked individual autonomy and communal solidarity. Brigham Young told his followers to sustain him as their prophet only on the basis of their personal revelation. Nutting undercut the certainty of personal gnosis by describing this method as a self-induced rite of passage into Mormon society that had little to do with God and very much to do with seeking community acceptance essential to any upward mobility.[44]

The wagon missionaries did not deny that emotional-spiritual feelings and experiences followed Mormons' prayers. However, they either responded that such revelation came from Satan or, more neutrally, that the process auto-hypnosis was at work.[45] This tactic required delicacy, since a Mormon who began to doubt that God answered their prayers about Mormonism might also question whether any truth could be ratified by prayer. The missionary thus had to quickly replace the newly created doubt with new faith based on either rational argument or a more persuasive experience. If the operation failed, the prospective convert might become an atheist.[46]

Despite the apparent scientific basis of his analysis, Nutting's choice of Muslim mesmerism to explain persuasive Mormon spiritual experience reflected a nineteenth-century trend for understanding the seduction of an otherwise rational people. The seductive Arabian Muslim had been for decades a common symbol of Mormon conversion of the naïve, and it remained an explanatory tool for missionaries in the early twentieth century.[47]

To Nutting and his rational proof-texting missionaries, the validity of the New Testament needed no additional corroboration, but Mormon belief in eternal personal agency required personal interpretation even in the

---

44. Nutting, "Difficulties of Work among the Mormons," 856.
45. Nutting, *Light on Mormonism* 4(3): 87.
46. John Danforth Nutting, Personal letter to F. S. Spalding, November 16, 1912.
47. For example, the best-selling anti-Mormon docu-novel, *Female Life among the Mormons: A Narrative*, by pseudonymous author Maria Ward, had matched the country's anti-slavery sentiments with the travesty of white female polygamous "slaves" in Utah. Ward attributed the proselytizing success of Mormon missionaries to their allegedly erotic-spiritual hypnotic powers. A victim in the book says "He [a Mormon missionary] exerted a mystical magical influence over me,—a sort of sorcery that deprived me of the unrestricted exercise of free will. It never entered into my brain that he could cherish impure motives. . . . No friendly voice was near to warn me, and I fell—." Quoted in Charles N. Cannon, "The Awesome Power of Sex: The Polemical Campaign Against Mormon Polygamy," 81.

presence of the Holy Spirit or God. The ultimate locus of authority was in the free mutual interpersonal responses between eternal persons (one of them being God). For Nutting, the priority in the locus of truth was always God, not the creature. Because the creature was fallen and depraved, he or she could not comprehend the actual divine presence. Sacred text became the earthly surrogate for God—it was as close as one could get to God. The Holy Spirit provided fiery confirmation of God's power or the quiet comfort of God's love; but God spoke through scripture. Any new personal revelation that came in the form of language could be seen as additional scripture, and God had given all scripture necessary for salvation. Anything more was superfluous, dangerous, and inherently prideful. Moreover, as Nutting experienced, what did new revelation ever achieve except further the argument over authoritative validity of interpretation, which in turn begged for more new revelation?

Nutting's Success

The Utah Gospel Mission counted a convert as one who signed and dated an engraved certificate card stating that he had confessed his sins, had accepted Christ as his savior, and would live a Christian life of careful Bible reading and prayer.[48] The wagon missionaries talked to thousands, calling them to a change of heart. Yet their revival-style tactics also sometimes worked against their ultimate success. Curious Mormons often attended summer revival meetings in tents used by the Gospel Missionaries.[49] Door-to-door approaches also gained the Evangelical missionaries admittance. But Protestant mass meetings often had to be held in schools, town halls, or, more frequently, Mormon churches. Although Mormon leaders were usually hospitable, they also attended these meetings, keenly noting Protestant arguments and observing the reactions of their flock, giving them the ability to provide specific counter-arguments to those who seemed ready to be persuaded. Sprinkled sparsely through Utah's small towns, Protestants could not support permanent pastors and meetinghouses; and Mormons avoided being seen in anything but a Mormon church service. Hence, those who did convert to Protestantism frequently left Utah, assuring that no nucleus of support grew in these small Mormon towns. The lack of

---

48. Terry, "John Danforth Nutting and the Utah Gospel Mission," 45–46.
49. Nutting, *Light on Mormonism* 2(4): 58.

social support from other believers was one of the primary reasons that so few people converted to Protestantism in Utah.[50]

It is difficult to say with any precision how successful Nutting's mission was because his newsletters never reported actual numbers of converts but rather pounds of brochures printed and distributed, numbers of meetings held, miles traveled, and speeches given. These seemed to be Nutting's preferred ways of measuring success. Conversions were so few that the Utah Gospel missionaries eventually concluded that Mormon aloofness to their message came from the Mormons' systematic slander of the missionaries and their avoidance of honest engagement with Protestant preaching of the Bible. Many missionaries also discussed feeling that an evil power had gripped Mormon believers, a belief that was a yet another obstacle to their being able to effectively communicate the Gospel message. After two decades in the field, Nutting acknowledged to his eastern supporters:

> No "big" things are possible, and no hasty work will do more than make temporary ripples; genuine, slow, plodding, spiritual work, as strongly as possible, is all that will tell. For this we have been working and praying all these years—it rests with others, still, to make full fruition possible, in both men and means![51]

A few years later, he sounded more optimistic, but still acknowledged the need for a steady approach to work among the Mormons:

> [Mormon] people are broader and more receptive to the truth; and eventually will receive it far more still, and Mormonism will become a somewhat peculiar but really Christian system. . . . This will be a long process, but all great movements move slowly; patience will be required for a long time yet, and constant diligence as well.[52]

A comparison of Nutting's early and later writings shows a shift of tone that signals a generational difference in his Mormon clients. In the early years of the ministry, the wagon missionaries approached first-generation Mormons who had typically converted from Protestantism. Hence, they were heretics who had rejected the truth and needed to hear pure Bible teachings. But second-generation Saints in the twentieth century were, to Nutting, heathens with a Judeo-Christian vocabulary. They were harder to engage in Protestant theological conversation, but easier to pity than the

---

50. Bruce Kinney, "Mormonism and Christianity," 90.
51. Nutting, *Light on Mormonism* 2(2): 58.
52. Nutting, *Light on Mormonism* 5(4): 239.

older heretics who had betrayed their own Protestant roots.[53] Over time, as Nutting encountered fewer heretics and more heathens, he employed a courteous tone with the latter that he had denied to the former. Still, his polemical content never changed. One of his last pamphlets was "Eight Reasons Why No One Should Be a Mormon by One Who Has Given over Fifty Years to Gospel Work among the Mormons."[54]

Reverend John Nutting died in 1949 in Cleveland, Ohio, with an estate of negligible worth, but he left a lasting missionary legacy. His methods of personal contacting continue to this day. In the early twenty-first century, each summer, missionaries from Protestant evangelical college seminaries fan out over the still remote small Utah Mormon towns to share the non-denominational Evangelical word. By stressing the need to convert individual Mormons rather than reform Mormonism itself, Nutting, despite using old revival-style tactics, ultimately created a viable long-term strategy. Converts from Mormonism could with integrity affirm that a shift in emphasis or greater clarity about Christianity had emerged from their own searching for truth—not unlike Joseph Smith had experienced. Perhaps on those terms, at least some reformation of Mormonism is always occurring.

---

53. Van Gorden, *Interview*, 1993.

54. John Danforth Nutting, "Eight Reasons Why No One Should Be a Mormon by one who has given over fifty years to gospel work among the Mormons."

CHAPTER SEVEN

William Mitchell Paden, Presbyterian Polemicist

Born on a Pennsylvania farm in 1854, William Mitchell Paden was raised by staunch Presbyterian parents. As a student at Princeton Theological Seminary, Paden attended a lecture by Dr. Duncan J. McMillan, a Presbyterian missionary to Utah's Great Basin, where McMillan spoke about his experiences as an evangelist working to bring the true gospel of Jesus Christ to the Mormons. The Presbyterian perspective on mission during the latter half of the nineteenth century was well summarized by missionary Wallace Radcliffe in 1899: "If Presbyterianism has a right for any existence, or any place, it has a right for every existence and for every place. If it is suitable for any condition or any age, it is suitable for all conditions and all ages."[1] Mormons felt equal ardor for their own expansion, and the Latter-day Saints in Utah resented the impertinence of being missionized by emissaries of the wicked they had left behind.[2] Despite such resistance, the dauntless McMillan had single-handedly opened parts of Utah to Presbyterian schooling during the 1870s. A history of Presbyterian work in Utah includes the following story about McMillan in action in Mt. Pleasant where he was setting up a mission school among the Mormons:

> [The locals] claimed that McMillan was guilty of sodomy, of living on beef stolen from the Mormons, and called him a vile, godless man, worse than an infidel, teaching sedition, infidelity and free love. One [Mormon] boasted that bullets were molded and ready for use at the first opportunity. Brigham Young himself commanded the people to unite to drive the intruder out of the community. [Consequently] McMillan had been warned that should he

---

1. Wallace Radcliffe quoted in James H. Moorhead, "The American Israel: Protestant Tribalism and Universal Mission," in *Many Are Chosen: Divine Election and Western Nationalism*, edited by William R. Hutchison and Hartmut Lehmann, 165.
2. Colin B. Goodykoontz, *Home Missions on the American Frontier*, 318, 403.

come to his own regular preaching service, his life would be in danger. When he did arrive—and he found a crowded house awaiting him—he was cautioned not to continue. . . . He took his place behind the pulpit, laid his revolver upon the open Bible where every eye could see it, sang a hymn alone, read the scriptures, poured out his soul in prayer and afterwards preached such a loving gospel that enmity for the time was disarmed.[3]

There is no corroborating evidence that this confrontation occurred. McMillan later said he went armed to the pulpit but never drew his pistol; however, he allowed the story to be told about him.[4] As the story began to prove itself as an excellent fundraiser, McMillan began telling it himself—with additional details. Either it or other stories like it must have made an indelible impression on young Paden.

Paden graduated from Princeton Theological Seminar in 1883, was ordained, and soon after served as pastor to the Holland Memorial Presbyterian Church in Philadelphia. In 1897, he resigned to become pastor of the First Presbyterian Church of Salt Lake City. He reported feeling drawn to this position "at the headquarters of Mormonism" because the Presbyterian Church stood "at the very head of the Gentile work among this peculiar people."[5] Paden had been successful in church building during his years in Philadelphia, and the now forty-three-year-old pastor saw opportunities for leadership among the various Protestant denominations grappling with the "Mormon problem." Utah would be "another big fight for my Master in one of His hard places."[6]

---

3. Theodore D. Martin and Marion E. Martin, compilers, *Presbyterian Work in Utah 1869–1969*, Books I–III.

4. Douglas R. Brackenridge, "Are You That Damned Presbyterian Devil?," 103–5; Douglas R. Brackenridge, June 28, 1993 Interview with Charles R. Paul regarding Presbyterian missions among the Mormons, June 28, 1993, Salt Lake City, Utah.

5. William M. Paden quoted in Paul J. Baird, *The Mystery of Ministry in the Great Basin*, 12. No biographer has treated the life of William Paden, but Baird's *The Mystery of Ministry in the Great Basin* provides a small amount of information on Paden's personal life. The William Paden files at Westminster College in Salt Lake City are partially indexed, as is the T. Ross Paden, Jr. Collection in Portland, Oregon. I have clustered some Paden quotations out of chronological sequence for thematic coherence. Paden's theology and attitude toward Mormonism did not change significantly as he aged.

6. William M. Paden, *The Holland Reminder*, Oct. 1897, Vol. VI, No. 11., n.p. Archives of the Presbyterian Historical Society, Philadelphia, PA, and copy in William Paden Collection, Westminster College Archive, Salt Lake City, UT.

Paden never married but was known to his close associates as a warm, intelligent bachelor. He loved to sit and chat about literature in his hotel apartment with a good friend and a good cigar. A sensitive passage in his diary reveals both his Christian commitment and his personal loneliness: "Our conversation conceals more than it reveals, represses more than it expresses, and usually hinders rather than helps real soul contact. . . . Our words are only words and move upon the topmost foam of thought. . . . As the artist travels alone who travels with one who has no relish of beauty, so the Christian lives alone who lives with those who make light of the wisdom of God and the beauty of holiness."[7]

The year before Paden's appointment, Utah had been rewarded with statehood after Mormons technically ceded the polygamy battle by withdrawing support for new plural marriages as well as abandoning a communal economy and their own political party. It might seem, then, that Paden was setting out toward an already conquered battlefield. But stopping polygamy was not enough; Paden hoped to help the Saints move from a disgraced church to a legitimate one. With his unalloyed enthusiasm, he found a means to do so when he discovered that Mormon leaders were quietly continuing plural marriage cohabitation after publicly stating they would cease the practice. In effort to embarrass the Mormon Church, Paden eventually took a public role in the Senate hearings to block Mormon apostle Reed Smoot from taking his elected seat. Paden investigated the alleged clandestine support of polygamy to bolster the argument made by ministers that no Mormon could be trusted, let alone Smoot who was an Apostle of the church. His tactic of engaging in religious conflict through the use of secular institutions was Paden's unique missionary tool. The theory seemed to be that by embarrassing and disenfranchising the Mormons, they would flock to Presbyterian arms.

Paden spent his first decade in Utah primarily concentrating on his duties to his flock. He built a new church for his congregation, which more than doubled from 200 to 500.[8] He also gave Bible lectures at the various Presbyterian schools that formed the backbone of that denomination's missionary program in Utah. In 1913, he was named head of the Utah Synod and became a traveling advisor to all the teachers and ministers. Paden was also active in the campaign that integrated the efforts of the Presbyterian, Methodist, Baptist, Congregationalists, Episcopalian, and sympathetic laymen committed to exposing Mormonism as a false religion.

---

7. William M. Paden, quoted in Paul Baird, *Mystery of Ministry*, 51.
8. Paul Baird, *Mystery of Ministry*, 115.

Because the costs of maintaining separate Presbyterian churches throughout Utah's far reaches were high, so Paden helped organize an ecumenical system that made any Protestant denomination fully acceptable to any other. Named the Comity Council of the Utah Home Missions Council, in 1916 this group became an ecumenical board that tried to ensure that there were no overlapping denominational efforts to serve Utah Protestants as well as to proselytize the Mormons.[9] Paden proudly noted that sixteen of Utah's twenty-nine counties had Presbyterian church representation, six were served by other denominations, and only seven had no permanent Protestant church within their borders. Local members paid about half of the cost of each local church (approximately sixty dollars per capita per year) while the Utah Home Missions Council paid the other half.[10] Paden's 1916 report to the Utah division of the Home Missions Council committee stated proudly: "We [Presbyterians] have the lion's share outside of Ogden, Logan, and Salt Lake. Upon our church is laid the whole responsibility for mission work in every field we occupy." No home mission force in the United States has such a free field and such entire accountability."[11] A perennial voice for the Protestant missions in Utah as late as 1930, Paden, then a seventy-six-year-old, was still negotiating with other denominations over which areas of the Utah mission should be expanded or cut back.[12]

The Smoot Hearings

Although Paden's work in nurturing Presbyterianism in Utah was noteworthy, it was his efforts to expose Mormonism as a fraudulent religion that earned national recognition. Upon his arrival in Utah, Paden had become a member of the Salt Lake Ministerial Association, which took him into the middle of ongoing efforts to fight theocratic politics in Utah. In 1899, three years after Utah achieved statehood, B. H. Roberts, a Latter-day Saint leader, was elected to represent Utah in the U.S. House of Representatives. Because Roberts was a polygamist with three living wives, the ministerial association successfully challenged his right to be

---

9. "The Utah Home Missions Comity Council Articles of Organization," William Paden Collection.

10. In 1908 the Protestant churches in American formed a jointly funded missionary effort, the Home Mission Council, to evangelize non-Protestant people in North America. The Utah subsidiary of the Home Mission Council focused on Mormon conversions.

11. William M. Paden, "Report of Home Missions Committee."

12. William M. Paden, "Notes for a Map of Allotment and Occupation in Utah."

seated. The association sent delegations to Washington and wrote numerous accusatory letters demanding that the House not recognize Roberts. They were successful in their efforts to block Roberts's seating, and only one Congressman served Utah that term.[13]

In January 1903, Utah's legislature elected Reed Smoot, a monogamist apostle, as U.S. Senator. Although the Senate eventually seated him, it responded to nationwide protests by ordering the Committee on Privileges to conduct a full investigation, which resulted in multiple hearings over the course of nearly four years. These hearings generated more than 3,000 published pages of testimony and registered the committee's recommendation (based on a seven to five vote) that Smoot be unseated. Smoot retained his seat, however, in no small part owing to U.S. President Theodore Roosevelt's positive reception of him at the White House. Smoot held his Senate position until 1932.[14]

During the investigations and hearings, Paden effectively and energetically organized protests against Smoot and formed national alliances with

---

13. Davis Bitton, *The Ritualization of Mormon History and Other Essays*, 150–70.

14. It required a two-thirds majority vote to expel a properly elected senator, and following a twenty-seven to forty-three vote, Smoot was seated. Kathleen Flake has analyzed the Smoot seating conflict as an event of agonizing assimilation whereby the Mormons were reluctantly accepted into American society. See Kathleen Flake, *The Politics of American Religious Identity: The Seating of Senator Smoot, Mormon Apostle*. My general historical thesis in this book is that the broader Protestant Christian community lagged substantially behind the broader political sector of American society in accepting the heretical Saints because the Mormons provided them with a solid and dangerous adversarial "Other" that helped the often-divided Protestants sustain a sense of unifying social power as pluralizing modern currents continually worked to erode their influence on national opinion. Indeed, resistance to the assimilation of Mormonism has not ceased. For example, as recently as the 2008 and 2012 Republican Presidential primary elections demonstrated. Many Evangelical Christians resisted supporting a highly qualified Mormon as candidate for U.S. President (Mitt Romney) until all the traditional Christians had dropped out of the race, openly stating that their reasons for not rallying behind him were due to his religion. However, once Romney was chosen as the Republican candidate in 2012, many Evangelicals got behind him. After the election Pew Forum data indicates that "white evangelical Protestants voted for Romney with as much enthusiasm as his other supporters did." "Evangelical 2012 Post Mortem: White Evangelicals and Support for Romney," http://www.pewforum.org/2012/12/07/election-2012-post-mortem-white-evangelicals-and-support-for-romney/ .

anti-polygamy groups. One of his first moves was to form a broad-based delegation, the Salt Lake Alliance, which included some of Salt Lake's prominent secular leaders to testify at the Smoot hearings.[15] The alliance delegation testified to the Senate committee that several Mormon leaders had flagrantly disregarded their agreement not to cohabit with their plural wives and also that the Mormon domination of Utah's economic life was un-American. Paden's role in the Smoot hearings illustrates the tactic of engaging in religious conflict through the use of secular institutions, a method he continued to use after the conclusion of the Smoot case.[16] The testimony and writings of the Salt Lake Alliance depicted the Mormons as duplicitous, claiming that they had never intended to break with polygamy. Hearing this alarm sounded in the national press during the Smoot hearings, many Americans felt betrayed, and more than four million signatures on petitions from various women's, Evangelical, and patriotic groups landed on the Senate hearing table.[17] In May 1903, four months after Smoot's election but one year before the formal hearings began, the General Assembly of the Presbyterian Church met in Los Angeles. Many of the delegates had passed through Salt Lake City on their way to the gathering, and Paden encouraged them to launch local petitions

---

15. To bolster support for their testimony before the Senate hearing, Paden did the research and organizational work and E. B. Critchlow, a prominent Salt Lake attorney, actually penned the protest against Smoot signed by many Utahns. The list of signers shows Paden's skill at mobilizing businessmen: P. L. Williams, counsel of the Oregon Short Line Railroad; E. W. Wilson, Commercial National Bank; Charles C. Goodwin, editor of the *Salt Lake Tribune*; W. A. Nelden, president of a wholesale drug company; Clarence T. Brown, pastor of a Congregational church; Esra Thompson, mining investor and former mayor of Salt Lake City; J. J. Corum, a real estate agent; George R. Hancock, a mining superintendent; W. Mont Ferry, a mining investor; J. L. Leilich, superintendent of Methodist Episcopal Missions; C. E. Allen, general manager of United States Mining Company; George M. Scott, businessman and former mayor of Salt Lake City; S. H. Lewis, master in chancery for the U.S. Court; H. G. McMillan, mining investor; and Abiel Leonard, bishop of the Protestant Episcopal church. See Thomas G. Alexander, *Mormonism in Transition: A History o the Latter-day Saints, 1890–1930*, 19. Because Brigham Young had forbidden his people to become involved in speculative mining, the Gentile mine owners and Mormon business leaders were not, as might be logically expected, Mormon political allies.

16. Milton R. Merrill, *Reed Smoot, Apostle in Politics*, 113.

17. Merrill, 96–97.

when they returned home.[18] Most of the resulting petitions came from Connecticut, Colorado, Indiana, Kansas, Michigan, New Jersey, New York, Pennsylvania, Utah, and Wyoming, with the mid-Atlantic states almost all represented, where the Presbyterian Church influence was strong.

Organizers opposed to Smoot's seating corresponded with Paden's Salt Lake Alliance, discussing strategies for convincing the Senate Committee on Privileges that Smoot's apostolic allegiance would override his patriotism. A particularly notable ally was Mrs. Frederick Schoff, a Presbyterian and the president of the National Congress of Mothers, an organization that helped assemble fifteen different women's groups on national, state, and local levels under the aegis of the National Union of Women's Organizations (NUWO). The latter organization sent in thousands of signed petition forms demanding that the Senate protect American families from Smoot's Mormon influence.[19] Schoff's NUWO union included the Interdenominational Council of Women, the Women's Home Missionary Society of the Presbyterian Church, the New York Women's Clubs Council, the General Federation of Women's Clubs, the New York Society for the Suppression of Vice, and, most importantly, the National Women's Christian Temperance Union (WCTU). With no affront to the ladies intended, The *Literary Digest* of Boston identified Paden as the instigator of the ladies' campaign:[20]

> People have lost sight of the modest little man who began the more recent crusade against Mormonism and instigated the direct charges against Senator Smoot. The women of the land, especially the members of the WCTU, have been conspicuous in claiming credit, but the one person to whom praise is due is Rev. W. H. Paden, a Presbyterian clergyman, formerly of Philadelphia, now of Salt Lake City.[21]

---

18. Brigham H. Roberts, *Defense of the Faith and the Saints*, Vol. 1, 121–22.

19. See "Women Unite Against Smoot" and "Petition to Oust Smoot."

20. The *Literary Digest* reference to Paden's leadership came in 1904, however the volume and page were illegible. According to a biographer of B. H. Roberts, two lesser-known Utah ministerial collaborators also deserve mention in organizing the campaign against Smoot's being seated: Thomas Illif of the Methodist Episcopal Church and Clarence T. Brown of the First Congregational Church, both of Salt Lake City. See Truman G. Madsen, *Defender of the Faith: The B. H. Roberts Story*, 244.

21. *Literary Digest*, fragment of newspaper magazine with no date or page found in Paden collection.

In addition to the petitions against Smoot, the Women's Union lobbied Congress to curtail Mormon immigration. The Mormon immigrants from Great Britain and Scandinavia were considered objectionable for religious, not ethnic, reasons.[22] Ethnic bias was strong in the early twentieth century. Twenty years later, a Protestant-led anti-Catholic lobby with a marked ethnic bias succeeded in passing the Johnson Immigration Act, which curtailed much traffic from eastern and southern Europe. However, Mormon immigrants from Great Britain and Scandinavia were considered objectionable for religious, not ethnic, reasons.[23] This approach launched an anti-Mormon crusade that lasted into the early 1920s, except for a lull during World War I when the Mormon soldiers proved to the nation that religious zeal in a non-traditional faith tradition could coexist with patriotism.[24]

It is no exaggeration to say that Paden set the anti-Mormon agenda for the twentieth century. Jan Shipps, a historian of Mormonism, observed that the Smoot hearings represented a political struggle more than a religious one, but it can be argued that after the political dust settled, the religious conflict with Protestantism increased.[25] Ministers feared that Mormonism would be accepted as a legitimate American denomination along with Utah's legitimacy as a state. After the Smoot hearings ended with a Utah Senator and Mormon Apostle sitting in Congress, the residual conflict into the 1920s was mainly motivated by religion.[26] Political

---

22. "Immigration Limits Set."
23. "Immigration Limits Set."
24. Jan Shipps, "From Satyr to Saint" in *Sojourner in the Promised Land: Forty Years among the Mormons*, 63–64.
25. Jan Shipps, "Difference and Otherness: Mormonism and the American Religious Mainstream," in *Minority Faiths and the American Protestant Mainstream*, edited by Jonathan D. Sarna, 81–103. Honored historian of Mormonism, Shipps says, "separating and following the various secular and religious strands of opposition to Mormonism is the best way to reconstruct the story of this peculiarly American minority faith and the American religious mainstream." Shipps claims that historians of American religious history have neglected the "manifestly religious reaction to the [Mormon conflict with the American government and people] as represented by the actions of the ecclesiastical bodies that made up the nations [cultural] mainstream."
26. Jan Shipps, "Difference and Otherness," 92. Shipps correctly points out that the interconnection of religious and political life in early-twentieth-century America was substantial and overt. The Mormons saw themselves as a people, not just a religious group, so their politics were unequivocally entwined with the

and personal revenge remained an indirect secondary motive as some non-Mormon Salt Lake businessmen, especially Thomas Kearns, editor of *The Salt Lake Tribune*, felt that Mormon leaders had hurt them politically or economically. As a result, they used their influence to criticize and embarrass Mormons, and they benefited from the cover of respectability that the sincere piety of the women and clergy gave their retaliation.[27]

After thirty months of sensational public hearings filled with material about clandestine polygamy, vote fixing, ecclesiastic big business, and secret temple oaths, the Senate's decision that Smoot was acceptable reflected this constituency's desire to downplay religious differences in Utah. After 1907, many Americans began to grow weary of what they thought to be nasty nit-picking over sectarian doctrinal differences. In response, evangelical Protestant religious leaders intensified their work to wake up the weary.

Writing in 1904 during the early days of the hearings, Paden explained that his purpose was not to ruin Mormon families but to expose Mormon dishonesty:

> None of the opponents of polygamy have ever asked that plural wives should be "turned out of doors." Nobody has objected to having plural wives and their children kindly provided for by the men who place them in this unlawful position. But the law . . . makes a wide distinction between providing for these plural wives and their children, and providing these same plural wives *with* children.[28]

Even though church president Joseph F. Smith had made excommunication a condition of new plural marriage in his "second manifesto" of 1904, he had been forced to testify under oath that he still cohabited with his plural wives. Not willing to cease and desist from advocating new marriages outside the U.S. jurisdiction, Apostles Matthias F. Cowley and John W. Taylor were dropped from the Twelve in April 1906 at Smoot's insistence. The next year, the First Presidency published a sixteen-page "Address . . . to the World" denying that the Church wished to dominate Utah politics or economics, affirming its loyalty to the United States, and also affirming the abandonment of polygamy.[29]

---

religion; and in the early twentieth century most of American politicians overtly owned their Protestant faith and claimed it as foundational for their political life.

27. B. Carmon Hardy, *Solemn Covenant: The Mormon Polygamous Passage*, 287–88.

28. William Mitchell Paden, "Letter to Editor," *Lewiston Journal*.

29. James B. Allen and Glen M. Leonard, *The Story of the Latter-day Saints*, 449. As a note of interest, by the turn of the twenty-first century an estimated 20,000 "fundamentalist Mormons," most but not all of them estranged from the

Mormons heartily disliked the missionary approach practiced by William Paden and others in his circle. The lurid national magazine articles that continued to be published after Smoot was seated repeatedly cited upstanding Protestant ministers residing in Utah as their sources for claims that Mormon leaders continued to secretly approve new plural marriages, control regional politics and economics, and be treasonous and disloyal Americans.[30] To be fair, Paden diligently promoted any embarrassment to Mormon leadership, but he scrupled at exaggeration—not only for ethical reasons but also because it destroyed his credibility. For instance, when Salt Lake Methodist mission leader Rev. John L. Leilich erroneously claimed that Smoot was a polygamist, the Salt Lake Alliance denounced him for it.[31]

A sworn statement of the Salt Lake Alliance to the U.S. Senate illustrates Paden's approach:

> We, your protestants, do further say and do earnestly and solemnly declare that we are moved hereto by no malice or personal ill-will toward Apostle Smoot, nor toward the people whom he seeks to represent in this high position. We wage no war against his religious belief as such. . . . We accuse him of no offense cognizable by law. . . . What we do deny to him is the right, either natural or political, to the high station of Senator of the United States from which to wage war upon the home—the basic institution upon whose purity and perpetuity rests the very government itself.[32]

Paden's personal image suffered when it was discovered that the indictments by Charles M. Owen, a chief informer on new polygamists

---

LDS Church, lived in plural marriages without government prosecution in Utah and northern Arizona. See Martha Bradley, "Changed Faces: The Official LDS Position on Polygamy, 1890–1990," 25–33.

30. From 1907 to 1911 polygamy as a religious doctrine was the main subject in *The Independent* and in *Colliers* in which authors advanced charges of new polygamous marriage. *Pearson's* discussed Mormon political and business control of Utah and polygamy. In *Everybody's* magazine, excommunicant and ex-Senator Frank Cannon wrote an eight-issue exposé that told stories about polygamy and power brokering in Utah; *McClure's* told of an inaccessible Mormon rural society that was duplicitous and suspicious of outsiders. The "Viper on the Hearth" series for *Cosmopolitan* magazine featured sordid stories of Mormon history that were "filled with murder and terror which held all in abject submission." See Alexander, *Mormonism in Transition*, 68–69; Terryl Givens, *The Viper on the Hearth: Mormons, Myths, and the Construction of Heresy*, for publishing details as well as a cultural critique of these articles.

31. Merrill, *Reed Smoot, Apostle in Politics*, 34–35, 38.

32. William Mitchell Paden, "A Protest of Citizens."

who testified in the Smoot hearings, were based on hearsay. Owen, who was employed by the Salt Lake Ministerial Association, had also posed for widely-distributed photographs wearing Mormon sacred temple garments, which had the double-edged effect of confirming Mormonism as bizarre but also leaving the distasteful impression that Paden was employing a bounty hunter of low character.[33] Despite this lapse, Paden's personal correspondence with several well-to-do Presbyterians in Salt Lake City nowhere suggests direct financial benefit through their attempts to diminish the Mormon leaders' political and economic influence.

Despite Paden's polemical attacks on Mormonism, there is no reason to doubt the sincerity of his regard for the Mormon people as individuals. His diary, never published, contains this affecting vignette:

> Several years ago I boarded with a Mormon family in a small Utah town. There were two daughters, one married with her husband living there . . . both quite intelligent, with a good education from Utah University . . . . One evening I was left alone with the daughter. We were sitting in front of the house, in a hammock, and she just opposite me on a settee. The evening was very warm and the air sultry, with flashes of sheet lightning continually sweeping the heavens. After a while, with a long breath she said, "I never thought much about religious matters until I went through the temple; after that my religion was everything to me." I said, "You refer to the marriage ceremony?" As she started to answer me, a flash of lightning illuminated her face and showed to me, I think, the most beautiful, enraptured, pure and earnest expression I have ever seen. Her eyes shined like stars as they looked into the heavens; her hair was like a halo of glory; her lips were slightly parted; a deep glow was over her face.[34]

Paden's Strategies after the Smoot Hearings

From the Presbyterians' point of view, it seemed incredible that Mormonism could continue to exist, let alone thrive, despite overwhelming national disbelief in their sacred story and the humiliating rejection of their offensive society and politics. They thought only the ignorant and gullible could give Mormonism any credence. But after observing the eroding national interest in defeating this resilient enemy, Protestant evangelists in Utah sought new ways to stop its growth. One local strategy was to continue to actively proselytize among individual Mormons in the

---

33. Merrill, *Reed Smoot, Apostle in Politics*, 61.
34. William Mitchell Paden Diaries, T. Ross Paden, Jr. Collection, n.d., n.p., circa spring of 1907.

hope that that exposure to pure doctrine would open their eyes to the truth. A second method was to use the still active Presbyterian school system, in operation since the 1870s, to provide Mormon youth a different way of seeing God and life's purposes than what they were learning in their homes. Paden's third and most controversial tactic was to stigmatize Mormonism as fundamentally anti-American and to discredit Mormon leaders through articles, brochures, and rallies in the hope of reducing national and international interest in the Mormon message.

To his great credit, Paden took the position of the forthright antagonist in these strategies, openly announcing his plans to diminish the social, political, and economic power held by Mormon leaders. Unlike Nutting and McMullin, Paden did not tell one story in front of the Mormons in Utah and spin things more negatively in Eastern fund-raising centers. He attacked Mormon leaders boldly in pamphlets and speeches, but always first declaring his good will toward Mormons as individuals. In a letter to the editor of the *Lewiston Journal* in Idaho he wrote:

I have had ample opportunity to study the Mormon system and its fruits. And I am prepared to say that, while I have never had anything but the utmost goodwill for the masses of the Mormon people, I am forced to join with other careful students in declaring that from a social, civil, and moral standpoint, no language is too strong to set forth the evil fruits of the Mormon system.

> Based on polygamy (even though they claim no longer to practice it), how could this system be otherwise than rotten? Its central idea of government being their priesthood, how could it be otherwise than anti-American? Having been founded . . . by as corrupt and immoral a man as the testimonies of Joseph Smith's acquaintances prove he was, how could its results be other than mischievous and immoral? . . . The Mormon Church will enjoy peace and harmony whenever its priesthood ceases to interfere with civil affairs and sets the example of obeying the laws of the land as loyally as they have always been obeyed by the great Christian denominations generally.[35]

In a pamphlet he published under the aegis of the Salt Lake Ministerial Association, he declared,

> Until the practices of the present leaders of the Mormon Church are radically changed, there can be no peace between them and pure Christianity; and that until the doctrines of the church are radically modified, it can never establish a claim to be even a part of the church of Jesus Christ.[36]

---

35. Paden, Letter to Editor, *Lewiston Journal*.
36. William Mitchell Paden, "Creed and Conduct of the Mormon Leaders."

Opening Mormon Eyes to the Truth

Although Paden blamed the Mormon leaders for Utah's political one-sidedness, he also sensed that Mormons affirmed the virtues of loyalty and cohesion by acting together as a united tribe. For him, their collective political action was more a manifestation of their loyalty to faith than subservience to authority. Hence, though he did not say so directly, many of Paden's tactics were an attack on this sense of Mormon loyalty to kinship and tribe. If their tribal bonds were weakened, then Christian denominations could find a greater welcome among them. Late in his life, Paden lamented:

> Oh for a Paul to arise among these people, to win them to the religion of Christ! The result of Paul's experience was not a reformed Judaism, but Christianity. And the result here would be, not a reformed kind of Mormonism still clinging to its false prophets and counterfeit scriptures, but an abandonment of all this, and an acceptance of the religion of Jesus.[37]

Even though Paden hoped for reform from within, and may have briefly entertained the illusion that Frank Canon, the wayward son of former Mormon Apostle George Q. Cannon, might fill that role, he again affirmed the need for aggressive proselytizing in 1914:

> We are chiefly concerned with the moral and religious beliefs of the Mormon people, and the effect of these beliefs and teachings on character and conduct. . . . During the past decade, Protestant methods have been pacific rather than polemic. This however, should not reflect on the value or necessity of combating false teachings and Mormon attempts to proselyte Gentiles in Utah and other states. Some of our missionaries are asking themselves, "Shall we be less aggressive in presenting the claims of the matter than the Mormons in pressing the claims of their prophet?"[38]

---

37. William Mitchell Paden, Personal Notes and Papers, T. Ross Paden, Jr. Collection, circa late 1920s.

38. Minutes of the Synod of Utah, 1914, 14. The debate over the aggressiveness and approach of Protestants in encounters with Mormons continues among Evangelicals. On the one hand, there are those who self-identify as "countercult" and who draw upon apologetic and polemical approaches in refuting Mormonism and other minority religions. On the other hand, there are those utilizing and advocating missions, dialogical, and religious diplomacy approaches. For a summary and assessment of these approaches by an Evangelical, see John W. Morehead, "Evangelical Approaches to New Religions: Countercult Heresy-Rationalist Apologetics, Cross-Cultural Missions and Dialogue," 4–14.

Paden's proselytizing advice to Utah Presbyterians was presented to his Home Missionary Committee in 1911 and 1912, which I abridge and summarize here:[39]

1. Every church member should be a missionary. They should not migrate to California, but remain where they are needed to be examples of good Christian men and women.
2. The missionaries sent to Utah should work with the local members as their force. They should try to reach every one in their parish area. Know who is who in your village and be bold in making friends.
3. Our mission is first to reach those who are sympathetic with our cause, next to touch the indifferent Gentiles looking for something better, and finally to convert apostate Mormons—and all the while leaven the great body of misguided but earnest Mormons.[40]
4. Attempt to contact people by going door to door and bringing the church into the home. Preaching in churches does not reach enough of the population. Not one in twenty Mormons know us at all. Visit people as friends but tell them what they must hear.

Also in 1913, Paden wrote a pamphlet to convince Protestant congregations to continue to support mission work in Utah:[41]

Q. What should be our attitude toward Mormonism?
A. We should understand its faith, study its specious presentation of its position, and tell others that which we have learned.

Q. Why should we do these things?
A. Because the evils [of Mormonism] are a blot upon our national life, and one that can be wiped out only by a public opinion so strong as to demand its extinction.

---

39. William Mitchell Paden, Personal letter to Miss C. E. Mason of Tarrytown, N. Y., May 8. 1911, Episcopal Diocese of Utah Collection; William Mitchell Paden, Personal letter to Isaac Russell of New York City, November 20, 1912, 1–10, The Library of the Episcopal Diocese of Utah, Spalding Collection.

40. Paden knew that his best prospects for conversion were those in transition and looking for new roots and relationships. Ironically, he scorned the Mormon missionary effort as being successful in converting merely "drifters, dissatisfied men and women who wanted something new in religion–not active church workers." See William M. Paden, "Questions and Answers on Mormonism," 6.

41. William Mitchell Paden, "Mormonism as a Political Power and Peril: Studies in Social Reform and What To Do."

Q. What further should we as Christians do?
A. We should generously support mission work among the Mormons.

Using Presbyterian Schools to Win Mormons to Christ

The Princeton pastor spent much of his ministry shaping Utah's Presbyterian schools to civilize and eventually convert young Mormons to the true gospel of Christ. The Presbyterian schools in Utah had been established in the 1870s during a raging debate among Christian educational missionaries about whether their main concern should be teaching Western civilization or the gospel, reflecting little angst over cultural imperialism.[42] The following 1909 argument by an African missionary reflects closely Paden's feelings, and its mention of polygamy makes it even more relevant:

> The older pagans are beyond the missionary's reach. They are polygamists to a man, and have not the slightest intention of changing their lives and embracing Christianity. . . . The majority of the young men and women are likewise past conversion. . . . It is . . . the children upon whom the missionary places his chief hope; but even these he cannot gain without some sort of school. Only by being together day by day, by frequent personal contact, instruction and exhortations can he be brought to see the wretchedness of the pagan state. . . . Without a school a missionary can do very little, so a school he must have. The native school is a means to the end.[43]

Although Mormons naturally mistrusted the motives of Presbyterian schools, they revered education. In spite of complaints and rebukes from their religious leaders, many Mormon parents still sent their children to these superior Presbyterian schools.[44] At the time of their establish-

---

42. Clayton G. MacKenzie, "Demythologizing the Missionaries: A Reassessment of the Functions and Relationships of Christian Missionary Education under Colonialism," 45–65.

43. Quotation of unnamed missionary in MacKenzie, "Demythologizing the Missionaries," 57.

44. Mark T. Banker, *Presbyterian Missions and Cultural Interaction in the Far Southwest, 1850–1950*. Banker corroborates missiological studies that show Christian-run schools played a major role in the evolution of national education by giving skills to the previously unemployable. As a result, it was often hard to differentiate between true converts to Christianity and those simply attracted by the hope of personal advantage or a political edge in overthrowing the current regime. See MacKenzie, "Demythologizing the Missionaries," 45–47. In this regard, Utah was little different from China or Africa.

ment, Mormon schools were operated in each Utah Mormon ward, run by church leaders or educational entrepreneurs of comparatively poor preparation and experience. In this, Utah was no different than most of the rest of the nation, leading Congress in 1888 to mandate the creation of public schools to replace these schools of admittedly uneven quality. In the early twentieth century, the Presbyterians reappraised the expense of operating their parochial system and decided that public schools were sufficiently liberal and Protestant and thus began closing them down. In Utah in 1900, there were twenty-five such schools, but only four in 1915 and three still running by 1920.[45] Though it was a practical move, closing the schools curtailed the Presbyterian influence in Utah.

In 1912, Paden spoke in a closed session of the Home Missions Committee about his plan to "conserve" the few Mormon students who passed through Presbyterian schools by making them better Christians and, in the end, disaffected Mormons.[46] One teacher at Wasatch Academy in Mt. Pleasant reported frankly about the faculty's approach to Mormon students in 1922: "It is our attempt to make the atmosphere of the academy so thoroughly Christian that the young Mormon making comparisons cannot help but weigh his own religion and find it wanting."[47]

These experiments were largely unsuccessful. As early as 1905, the *Home Missionary Monthly* discouragingly asserted: "Our Presbyterian schools [in Utah] have just produced more Mormon teachers, elders, bishops, and missionaries."[48] Ten years later, the 1915 Utah Presbyterian Synod report stated flatly: "A careful study of the present methods of work will reveal that results attained have not been commensurate with the labors of the missionaries and the expenditures of home mission funds."[49] A historian of Protestant schools summarized all the efforts thusly: "The

---

45. Banker, *Presbyterian Missions*, 165.
46. Minutes of the Synod of Utah, 1911–1915, 1912.
47. Martin and Martin, *Presbyterian Work in Utah, 1971*, Vol. 3, 320.
48. Article quoted in Banker, *Presbyterian Missions*, 134.
49. Banker, 163. See also, Bruce Kinney, *Mormonism: The Islam of America*, 165. Assessing the results of varying evangelistic efforts is another area of discussion and debate in contemporary circles. Evangelical counter-cult ministries assume their apologetic strategies result in converts when people express an interest in Evangelicalism, and while some converts can be demonstrated, there is no scientific survey data to confirm either the numbers involved or the reasons why these faith migrations take place. Claims by counter-cult spokespersons are at present anecdotal.

direct results of missionary work in Utah as measured by converts from Mormonism were so slight as to be almost negligible."[50]

Positioning Mormonism as Anti-American

With the closing of the Presbyterian mission schools and the demise of polygamy as a topic of active outrage, Paden needed a new strategy to focus continued attention and resources on the fight against the spread of Mormonism. This need for a new spotlight issue coincided with a broader crisis of identity and confidence American Protestantism was experiencing during the first years of the twentieth century. Approaching schism and decline, a new crusade had the potential to unify the denominations, and Paden, in concert with other groups, contributed to this effort by combining unease over Mormonism's "un-Christianness" with a new trend of increased American nationalism. After Smoot was confirmed, Paden worked to successfully position Mormonism in the national conscience as anti-Americanism and its leaders as abusive and exploitative. He had to maneuver with great care to avoid the label of persecutor, especially since the unsavory revelations about Charles Owen during the Smoot hearings had cost him dearly and his supporters did not want a repeat.

The National Reform Association (NRA), founded in 1863 and run by Protestant ministers from various denominations,[51] had developed into the *locus classicus* for nativist Protestant defensiveness by the turn of the century. In the mid-1920s, it switched its focus to national criticisms of moral laxity and secular humanism, but during the first two decades of the century it was the major national organization combating Mormonism. It was the first group to indict Smoot for his apostolic conflict of interest,

---

50. Goodykoontz, *Home Missions*, 318. Salt Lake City's Westminster College was clearly not instructing Mormon youth. During 1921–1922, only four of its 166 students were Mormons, forty-one were Presbyterian, thirty-four were Protestants, and eighty-seven claimed no church affiliation. See Banker, *Presbyterian Missions*, 175. This last group was probably from former Mormon families that wanted no more to do with any institutional religion and who were thus generally unsympathetic to the Presbyterian mission cause as well. See Banker, *Presbyterian Missions*, 105.

51. The NRA was led mainly by Reformed Presbyterian ministers but included clergymen from all the mainline denominations. These were well-educated men who gained support of some powerful laymen as trustees, including a US Senator, two governors, several federal judges, and college presidents. See Gary S. Smith, *Seeds of Secularization: Calvinism, Culture, and Pluralism in America, 1870–1915*, 58–59.

and was the major impetus behind a Constitutional amendment drafted to ban polygamy. The amendment, proposed in 1918, was stalled and quickly overtaken by the public interest in a drinking prohibition amendment that became law in 1920. The article read: "I. Polygamy and polygamous cohabitation shall not exist within the United States or any place subject to their jurisdiction. II. Congress shall have power to enforce this article by appropriate legislation."[52]

Neither the polygamy amendment nor other NRA efforts, such as an attempt to create national marriage laws and amend the preamble to the U.S. Constitution to make clear that the United States of America was a Christian nation, gained broad support.[53] Notwithstanding its failures, the NRA was a natural ally for Paden's new Presbyterian Utah plan.

The NRA's periodical, *The Christian Statesman,* was a major vehicle for anti-Mormon articles and was read by a national audience of Protestant clergymen and women reformists. Protestant home missions used their columns to sustain urgency in their reform mission. Paden was an occasional correspondent and contributor to the *Statesman* and served on its World Commission on Mormonism that lectured congregations and patriotic Protestant gatherings about the Mormon menace.[54] A 1914 editorial mission statement, published in the *Statesman,* articulated their resentment of Mormonism:

> Our crusade is against Mormon *treason* and the [Muslim] harem *system of the priests*. . . . The Mormons fight back with tracts and speeches uttering voluble endorsement of the thrift and industry of their people, but not ever meeting our specific charges. . . . Polygamy was never legal among them, and they would practice it still (as many do) without our constant vigilance. . . . *We must break the pretensions of the Mormon Church to be the righteous temporal ruler of this Republic.*[55]

---

52. "Editorials, Senate Joint Resolution 147," *The Christian Statesman,* May 1918, front page.

53. The NRA's proposal was to have the preamble to the Constitution changed to read: "We acknowledge the nation's dependence upon God and its submission to Jesus Christ its Supreme Ruler; the enactment of a code of laws in harmony with His civil teachings; and the administration of the government in accordance with His expressed will . . . There is but one way possible by which this nation may be preserved: SUBMISSION, AS A NATION, TO THE LORD JESUS CHRIST, ITS SUPREME RULER." See "Editorial," *The Christian Statesman,* 45. For the nation's reactions to radical changes in this era, see John W. Buenker, *Progressivism.*

54. William Mitchell Paden, "Mormon Pluralism," 172–176.

55. "Editorial," *The Christian Statesman*, April 1914, 146–47, 161; emphasis mine.

A second, lengthier mission statement two years later again articulated a view of Mormonism as anti-American:

> The lawful Christian Crusade against the aggressions of the leaders of the iniquitous, traitorous system of Mormonism in our country has claimed much of our attention because we deem the Mormon problem the most imminent of all the problems in our country—the one great evil which not only has in it the seeds of national destruction, but which also in recent years has been receiving the least attention from the great majority of the American people and which therefore has been *making the most rapid and manifest progress,* so much so indeed that it has become a veritable national menace. Moreover, this system, which blasphemously calls itself the Kingdom of God is . . . opposed to the progress of [our true] Kingdom of God, for the up-building of which, *in the civil sphere,* our Association is assiduously laboring.
>
> This Crusade is advancing into general acceptance. The high church courts have approved it. . . . Nearly all the organizations which are giving special attention to this work have recognized the National Reform Association as the leading agency. . . . All the religious press recognize . . . *by common consent [that] this Association is the responsible representative of the whole national movement.* More than 20,000 resolutions have gone into the departments in Washington. . . . Congressman Gillett of Massachusetts has introduced the proposed Anti-Polygamy Amendment. . . . We are expecting to reach all of the four hundred and eight congressional districts of the country to raise therein a local demand upon the Congressmen and Senators. . . . [The Mormons] are in a state of desperation. This is the first time they have had any fright concerning the national situation since 1890. . . . Today they recognize that a systematic effort conducted by this Association will assuredly arouse the conscience and intelligence of the whole Christian and patriotic people of the country.[56]

Additional measures being urged by NRA's petition against the Mormon Church included the unseating of any government official not swearing an oath to the United States as a higher allegiance than to an organized church, refusing use of the U.S. postal system for mailing Mormon literature, denying the LDS Church proselytizing privileges, prohibiting Mormons from immigrating into the country,[57] and auditing Mormon Church funds to assure that they were being used for publicly responsible

---

56. "Editorial," *The Christian Statesman,* January 1915, 44.

57. In addition to influencing temporary regulations restricting the immigration of Mormons, this American political action committee launched a European (especially British) anti-Mormon emigration program that likely slowed conversions there. See C. E. Mason, Personal letter to Bishop Spalding, March 29, 1911.

purposes.⁵⁸ Despite this sweeping agenda, the NRA's success appears to have been limited to relatively few cases in which local ministers were sufficiently influential to enact ordinances against distributing tracts by defining proselytizing as "peddling," which required special permits, and also by running a few Mormon missionaries out of town without injury.⁵⁹

Another *Christian Statesman* editorial shows the extreme vituperative tone of the NRA's rhetoric:

> I think one of the most effective ways of extirpating this enemy of liberty is to put upon it the brand of public odium, and to make that brand so large and deep and black that it may be seen . . . all over the world. . . . I propose to brand it as a sort of high treason against mankind; against government and law; against civilization and liberty; against the best hopes of men and women; and a bold defiant effort to build up and sustain an alien kingdom over the greatest Christian government in the world.⁶⁰

In consequence of its aggressive rhetoric, the NRA suffered the backlash of its own extremism. In 1920, *The Christian Statesman* published a highly imaginative speech delivered by an anti-Mormon novelist at the NRA's national convention. The Salt Lake Ministers Association then wrote a letter to *The Christian Statesman* expressing guarded objections to its publishing something that played so loosely with the facts.⁶¹ After this point, Paden apparently discontinued corresponding with *The Christian Statesman*. The Salt Lake Ministers Association's response was not unprecedented. Several Utah churchmen had grown weary of the exaggeration tactics employed by the NRA and others. An article in the *Home Mission Monthly* from one such Protestant Utah missionary two years earlier sarcastically asked: "Must we be fed tales of [old Mormon] atrocities in order to support our work in Utah?"⁶² The moderate press in the east had also begun to lose patience with NRA tactics, scoffing in a news report about

---

58. "Editorial," *The Christian Statesman*, January 1915, 22; "Editorial," *The Christian Statesman*, April 1917, 187.

59. "The Mormon Priests Must Leave Town," *Wellington Daily News*, Nov. 1, 1917; "Missionaries Are Peddlers," *New York Times*, September 4, 1918; "Anti-Mormon Activity on Increase?," *Ogden Examiner*, April 2, 1920. Although these developments doubtless made the Mormon missionaries feel persecuted, they were a far cry from, for example, the 1884 earlier murder of four Mormon missionaries in 1884 in Tennessee. See Madsen, *Defender of the Faith*, 144.

60. "Editorial," *The Christian Statesman*, January 1915, 21.

61. "Letters," *The Christian Statesman*, January 1920, 83.

62. Marshall Allaben, "The Challenge in Utah," 28.

a recent NRA fundraising meeting in Boston: "The talks would not have had any appreciable effect on educated people."[63]

Paden, who generally avoided the use of extreme rhetoric tactics, nevertheless complained against what he saw as cowardice by Christians and ex-Mormons to be more confrontational towards the Mormon threat to the nation. In an undated pamphlet, likely designed for an eastern audience seeking reassurance that their money was not being thrown away by supporting Utah mission efforts, Paden boldly tackled the question: "Missions Among the Mormons—Why?" by setting up unflattering comparisons between Mormonism, Islam, and Catholicism:

> There are those who have asked, "Why should we seek to Christianize the Mohammedans [Muslims]?" They believe in God and call upon His name. They accept in some fashion the teachings of the Old Testament, and give more or less honor to Jesus . . . but we protest against their formula, "There is no God but Allah, and Mohammed is His prophet." So with even more reason we protest against the Mormon credo: "There are many gods, and Joseph Smith is their prophet." The Mohammedan conception of God is higher than the Mormon . . . and while the religion of Mohammed may be carnal as regards its conception of the duties of man, it is far superior to the Mormon belief in carnal gods . . . male and female, like Baal and Ashtaroth. . . .
>
> Some of you will think that [Mormonism] is rather to be compared with medieval Romanism. But here again the comparison is in favor of Romanism that formally exalted the Cross and the death of Christ rather than angel Moroni . . . the Apostles Creed and the Lord's Prayer in favor of We Thank Thee O God For a Prophet. If reform was needed in the Roman Church, much more than reform is needed here in Utah.[64]

By positioning Mormonism as a greater threat to the nation than the two largest and most aggressive proselytizing religions in the world, Paden's strategy was to present Utah as an exotic yet familiar case. He knew it was not an urban ghetto, which home mission councils diligently

---

63. "Anti-Mormon Campaign In Boston," *Boston-Logan Journal,* April 20, 1920. One loyal vote of confidence for the NRA and *The Christian Statesman* was voiced as late as 1925 in a newsletter written by Rev. John Nutting. There Nutting speculated that one reason for a decrease in Mormon conversions during the prior year was "the National Reform Association . . . especially the very effective lectures of Mrs. Lulu Shepard and the articles in the *Statesman.*" See John D. Nutting, *Light on Mormonism* 4, no. 3: 131.

64. William M. Paden, "Missions Among Mormons-Why?"

supported.⁶⁵ He also knew it was not Egypt, China, Africa, or India, which foreign mission councils readily funded. Trying to appeal to both fronts, Paden attempted to portray Utah as a foreign nation and Mormonism as a pagan theology—but *inside* America! Adding these together, Paden was able to reignite fears that Mormons had audacious designs for the religious domination of the entire country and would doubtless restore polygamy as soon as the national vigilance relaxed. Writing to his Presbyterian supporters, he said:

> We recommend: I. That the policy of conducting the mission work in Utah be changed *to conform rather to the methods in foreign lands* than to the usual lines of work in other parts of our own country; II. . . . that the program shall emphasize the establishment and development of stations in strategic centers, rather than the present plan of maintaining a minister in a large number of isolated places.⁶⁶

This plan had the appeal of heroic foreignness while also reducing any lingering expectations for easy conversions. Earlier, Paden had wryly observed that the best analogue for Mormons in America was Ireland because in that country, two peoples of the same stock could intermarry, understand each other's government and language, but still remain separate peoples because of religion—even if they didn't practice it:

> Mormon men and women are often Mormons minus all care for the religious element of Mormonism. Usually, however, they have all the Mormon prejudices. As an Orangeman need not have any religion to be a Protestant, or a Dublin Irishman any religion to be a Catholic, so many Utahns do not have to have any religion to be Mormons.⁶⁷

---

65. The demands of the urban ghettos quickly overwhelmed the denominations' various mission programs. During the first decade of the twentieth century the United States absorbed seventeen million immigrants. The country's welfare program was shifting from voluntary, religious associations to a "welfare state" in the 1920s with professional, social, and government agencies supplanting the church missions. Robert Buroker presents a typical case in Robert L. Buroker, "From Voluntary Association to Welfare State: The Illinois Immigrant's Protective League, 1908–1926," 643–60. The shift from religious to civic assimilation programs for immigrants also occurred at this time. See Edward G. Hartmann, *The Movement to Americanize the Immigrant*.

66. Minutes of the Synod of Utah, 1911–1915, 1915, 14; my emphasis.

67. Minutes of the Synod of Utah, 1912, 25; a similar observation in "Report of Home Missions Committee," April 9, 1912, 2–5, William Paden Collection.

As to foreignness, Paden played on the exotic and erotic Muslim reputation of the era with innuendos about the hidden depravity in Mormon and Muslim polygyny—even if the Mormon practice had been relinquished. He added his voice to stories of clandestine immorality and obscene delights that flourished at the time.[68] Paden reported to the Home Mission Board in Philadelphia in 1924:

> Today the leaders of Mormonism are assuming a very militant attitude toward Christianity. The missionary doing work among the Mormon populations, feels that a wall of desolation has been placed between him and the community. The powers that be see to that. The missionary is not only isolated, but he feels that much of his effort is being check-mated because of the overwhelming alertness of the [Mormon] hierarchy. No missionary on foreign soil is any more cut off from access to the people than the devoted men and women who have been sent to Utah and the surrounding territory. . . . the closest parallel perhaps would be to work amongst the Mohammedans.[69]

In making such statements, Paden was joining with those who employed the Muslim image as a threat. Its connotations of rampant sexuality also suggested rapacious danger and triggered xenophobic reactions. In 1912, Bruce Kinney's *Mormonism: The Islam of America*, conjoined Mormon sexual immorality and female abasement as the inevitable results of a theology that posits sexually-active, polygamous gods.[70] Agreeing that Utah was the most difficult of missions because of the entrenched immorality and obstinacy of its religious system, Rev. Josiah Strong, a prime booster of Protestant America nativism, attacked Mormonism thus: "The civilized world wonders that such a hideous caricature of the Christian religion should have appeared in this most enlightened land . . . that the people who most honor womankind should be the ones to inflict on her this deep humiliation and outrageous wrong."[71]

Paden believed that Mormonism led to human debasement and sexual turpitude. Some of his personal views appear in argumentative

---

68. Craig L. Foster, "Victorian Pornographic Imagery in Anti-Mormon Literature," 115–132; Leonard Arrington and Jon Haupt, "Intolerable Zion: The Image of Mormonism in Nineteenth-Century American Literature," 243–260; Charles N. Cannon, "The Awesome Power of Sex: The Polemical Campaign Against Mormon Polygamy," 61–82.

69. William Mitchell Paden quoted in Clifford M. Drury, *Presbyterian Panorama: 150 Years of National Mission History*, 289–90.

70. Kinney, *Mormonism: The Islam of America*, 5, 109–11, 133–35.

71. Quotation in Kinney, *Mormonism: The Islam of America*, 160.

margin notes on every page of his personal copy of a book, *The Fruits of Mormonism,* which provided social statistics in favor of Mormon moral uprightness and civic responsibility.[72] Typical marginal comments from Paden's copy: "Mormon health excellent: Due to gentile doctors." "Divorce from adultery lowest in nation: They call it something else."[73]

Losing the Battle but Not the War?

Although the American people became less intrigued by Mormon doctrines and practices as the twentieth century progressed, Paden implored in a 1929 article that the country should still not assimilate the Mormon Church because it is only playing possum until it grows large enough to have things its own way again. Mormons had not repented of polygamy, polytheism, or priesthood domination of politics.[74] He believed Mormons would once again challenge the American Protestant system. He mistrusted a people who would suffer privation and humiliation for religious principle up to 1890 and then, within a decade, become docile citizens. In his mind, Mormon leaders were merely pretending to be solid Americans to placate the country while they built up their forces through deceptive proselytizing and lusty breeding.[75] While Paden and the NRA movement eventually lost momentum, Paden's strategy of branding the Mormons as misfit Christians has weathered many decades intact.

By 1925, American Protestantism was grappling with its own moral authority crisis amid the changing mores of sexual and ethnic diversity in urban America.[76] The national lack of enthusiasm for a sustained anti-Mormon movement was compounded by internal disunity among Protestant groups. The social gospel movement that rose to prominence in early-twentieth-century Christianity downplayed theology and became more interested in political and institutional initiatives, less as a form for influencing moral correctness than as a means for mobilizing community resources to help the less fortunate. Christian missions of every denomination were caught between the dilemma of whether it was more important to preach the saving word or extend a helping hand. The helping hand

---

72. Franklin S. Harris and Isaac B. Newbern, *The Fruits of Mormonism.*

73. William Paden's handwritten marginal notes are in a copy of *The Fruits of Mormonism* on the closed shelves of the Westminster College Archives.

74. William M. Paden, "Temple Mormonism," T. Ross Paden, Jr. Collection.

75. William M. Paden, "Is Mormonism Changing?," 19–27.

76. Robert T. Handy, *A Christian America: Protestant Hopes and Historical Realities,* 114–15.

won out. A convenient marker of this shift is the 1925 "Layman's Report" of the Baptist Church, which John D. Rockefeller Jr. and William E. Hocking, lay leaders of the Protestant central and liberal wings, helped edit and publish. The report stated, "The real battles are fought in the great transverse areas where spiritual and altruistic forces contend against materialism and cupidity, so Christianity needs to collaborate not compete with world religions."[77]

The social gospel approach also had its effects in Utah where, as early as 1920, the missionary teachers in the remaining Presbyterian schools decreased their direct attacks on Mormonism in favor of trying to do Christian service or improve education.[78] To the nation and even among some Christians working in Utah, most Mormons seemed to be as sincere as the billions of other non-Christian people around the globe. The theological and soteriological motivations for proselytizing waned.

Mormonism itself participated enthusiastically in progressive social movements, launching massive efforts to improve health care, pave streets and sidewalks, abate flies and mosquitoes, intervene to prevent juvenile crime, improve education, and sponsor dozens of parks, libraries, and recreational facilities. Both its small communities and urban centers fostered booster and civic clubs, and its enthusiastic and patriotic participation in World War I was impressive. Mormonism began to re-channel much of its religious energy into civic betterment. It held onto its religious flavor, but began emphasizing its adherence to health codes more than radical theo-social experimentation.[79]

Doubtless, many of its older members who had clung determinedly to their religious identities through the worst of government prosecution of polygamy felt stranded on the far side of this generational shift. Ironically, one of the people stranded there with them was William Paden. To his dismay, Paden was not able to sustain interest in the Utah mission. Mormon strangeness was camouflaged by Utah's Anglo Saxon Victorianism, and, compared to much other twentieth-century strangeness, was no longer a national interest.

Paden died in Salt Lake City in 1931, still believing that Mormonism needed to be destroyed and its people saved. Mormonism was as seductive

---

77. Quotation in Martin E. Marty, ed., *Pushing the Faith*, 90.

78. See selections from the 1920 *Home Mission Board Annual Report* in Banker, *Presbyterian Missions*, 172.

79. For a rich history of the twentieth-century Mormon transition from social misfits to acceptable citizens, see Alexander, *Mormonism in Transition*.

as it was false, and its eventual growth would be at the expense of true Christianity and even republican democracy.[80] He was an energetic leader of anti-Mormonism and pro-Presbyterianism. He wrote impressively, and his bibliography of known items includes scores of tracts and articles in periodicals distributed through the home mission networks in all parts of the United States.

Despite Paden's enduring vigilance against the evils of Mormonism, a year after his formal retirement the seventy-five-year-old warrior shared with his colleagues this uncharacteristically mellow advice about interacting with Mormons: "Find a warm spot in their hearts for the essential Christian faith. Avoid head-on collisions with the peculiarities of Mormonism which are not conducive to quiet talks of Christ's way of life."[81]

---

80. Paden, "Creed and Conduct of the Mormon Leaders"; Paden, "Is Mormonism Changing?," 19–27.

81. William Mitchell Paden, "Questions and Answers on Mormonism," 13.

CHAPTER EIGHT

Franklin Spencer Spalding, Episcopalian Diplomat

Franklin Spencer Spalding was born in 1865 and raised in Denver, Colorado, by his father, an Episcopalian minister. He attended Princeton University where, at age twenty-two, he entered the ministry as a vocation. After a year of teaching prep school, he entered General Theological Seminary in New York, graduating in 1891. He then moved back to Colorado where he was ordained by his father as a rector of small Episcopalian church in a Denver suburb. He was called to a larger rectorship in Erie, Pennsylvania, in 1897, where he served until 1904 when he was called to be a missionary bishop of Utah. He moved to Utah in early 1905, and served there until his death in an accident in 1914 at age forty-nine. Spalding was a vigorous and athletic man. At age thirty-three he led the first recorded ascent to the summit of Grand Teton in Wyoming in 1898. The route still bears his name and that of his climbing partner, William Owen.[1] Spalding never married.

Spalding's term of service in Utah was contained within the timeframe of John Nutting and William Paden, both of whom he knew, but neither of whose missionary strategies he followed. Known as "Old Pop" at Princeton because of his popularity among his classmates, he was a diplomat with a sense of humor—a trait that served him well working among the Mormon people.[2] One of his younger mission co-workers described him nearly fifty years following his death as follows: "A former Princeton football player, he was tall and spare, with a penetrating mind, skeptical of conventional ways and phrases, and a remarkable combination of fearlessness and personal humility."[3] Spalding's writing style was

---

1. Chris Boileau, "Utah Bishop First to Scale Grand Teton," 6–7; Leigh N. Ortenburger and Reynold G. Jackson, *A Complete Climbers Guide to the Teton Range*, 139.

2. John H. Melish, *Franklin Spencer Spalding: Man and Bishop*, 28.

3. Henry Knox Sherrill, *Among Friends*, 41.

lively, intelligent, and sophisticated. Writing with wry amusement to a young missionary the bishop was trying to recruit to Utah, he described what was probably not a typical Sunday:

> This is a small and difficult field. I drove a number of miles last Sunday to hold services in a shack. I was there before anyone else, lighted the fire in the stove, swept out the place. A little group came who thought I should thank them for the privilege of speaking to them. I spoke on one's duty to one's neighbor. A drunken woman interrupted and said that one should look out for oneself. As I tried to straighten her out, I recalled that two months before I had preached the same sermon in Grace Church in New York where everything was beautiful. All I can say is that God calls some of us to do this work. As for myself, I love it and would not be anywhere else.[4]

Spalding served as a traveling bishop to small churches in Nevada, Colorado, Idaho, Wyoming, and Utah, and to one Indian reservation in eastern Utah. He spent much of his time in Salt Lake City watching over his largest parish and overseeing the administration of a private Episcopalian preparatory school, Rowland Hall, founded in 1880 and still operating today. He also oversaw St. Marks Hospital, founded in 1872 by Episcopalian missionaries to Utah. For many years, its reputation surpassed that of LDS Hospital (founded in 1905) and was the most professional medical facility in Utah. He lamented having to administer the squabbles and budgets of these two institutions instead of having more time to minister to the more spiritual needs of his fellows. His ministry to the Mormons, he felt, was "the main job."[5]

Spalding's Proselytizing Plan

According to Spalding's biographer, a visiting banker from an eastern city asked the bishop, "What difference does it make what the Mormons believe? What harm does it do if they love Joseph Smith and his teaching? What business is it of ours?" Spalding replied, "Well, I must feel about their acceptance and teaching of what is intellectually and morally untrue, just as I suppose you would feel if you knew a group of people were coining and passing counterfeit money."[6] Spalding's reasoning was based on the notion of the purity of truth that had been dangerously diluted by well-meaning heretics. Rather than destroy those who held these degraded

---

4. Franklin Spencer Spalding quotation in Sherrill, *Among Friends*, 42.
5. Melish, *Franklin Spencer Spalding*, 228.
6. Melish, 170–71.

beliefs, however, he hoped to persuade a new generation to shift their erroneous views enough to be acceptable Christians.

Spalding believed Mormonism was a quasi-Christian religion with former Protestants as members. It was a theological heresy that could be rehabilitated as a new member of the Christian denominational fold. However, it was also a remarkably foreign misfit in American culture. In his first public talk on Mormonism, given to the Inter-Seminary Missionary Alliance in Cambridge, Massachusetts, in December 1905, he outlined the methods of dealing with Mormonism that were in vogue when he arrived in Utah: (1) The Protestant plan: to attack Mormons with opprobrium, (2) The Roman Catholic plan: to build a majestic cathedral, leaving the front door open, and (3) The Episcopalian plan: to avoid polemics and preach historic Christianity.[7] While Paden had worked to make Mormons disturbingly foreign, Spalding also compared the Latter-day Saints to a foreign mission but did so more sympathetically. Sensing Mormons had developed their own culture, he said the Saints deserved—but were not being offered—the same understanding and compassion most Christian missionaries hoped to show to Chinese, East Indian, or African peoples.[8]

Spalding cast the quarrel between Mormons and traditional Christians as a conflict between sincere religious groups each with firm religious convictions that might be influenced only in part by reason. He held that "infinite patience, unfailing courtesy, frank sympathy and consummate tact" were needed to make reason inoffensive and influential. Frequently in writing or speaking, he articulated his own ground rules: "It is all-important to get a man's point of view, and take it as seriously as he does, before we can hope to influence him. . . . Nobody accepts any truth until he thinks he thought of it himself."[9] Although Spalding thought that Mormons habitually exaggerated their own virtues and idealized their historical claims, he scrupulously attempted to avoid any exaggerated charges that they were disloyal or immoral, finding such an approach counterproductive.[10]

---

7. Melish, 164–65.

8. Melish, 165.

9. Franklin Spencer Spalding quoted in Melish, *Franklin Spencer Spalding*, 165–66, 174.

10. Melish, *Franklin Spencer Spalding*, 167; Franklin Spencer Spalding, a speech in the *Journal of Convocation*, 18–20.

Spalding thought the Saints were mostly naive, rustic, well-meaning heretics that possessed remarkably good religious "instincts."[11] However, he also believed most Evangelical Protestants had leaned too far toward Augustinian doctrine and temperament, so he positioned the Protestant Episcopal Church as the correct balance between the heresies of Mormonism and the excesses of Calvinism. Writing an article in 1913 to his Episcopalian readers interested in mission work, he spelled out in clear detail a comparison between his understanding of mainline Protestant orthodoxy and Mormonism's spiritual intuitions:

> Four general conclusions were final to the minds of the orthodox theology: (1) That Christianity is based upon a doctrine of the Atonement, (2) That the Church is invisible, (3) That the fear of Hell is the great motive for confessing Christ, (4) That Christ is to be worshiped only in spirit.
>
> We cannot escape from the feeling that the Latter-day Saints represent an ignorant, and from our point of view, a pathetically ignorant effort, to get back to the historic beliefs that (1) Christianity is based on the Incarnation and the Atonement, (2) That Christ founded a visible Church, (3) That everlasting punishment is not a necessary doctrine, (4) That there is room and need for ritual in the service of God.
>
> [On item 1)] In spite of much Protestant opinion to the contrary, the foundation of Christian truth, the basis of Christian theology is the doctrine of the Son of God in the man Jesus. I submit that the [Mormon] statement "What God is, man shall be; and what man is God once was" is a reaching out for the truth of the Incarnation of God in Jesus Christ, which St. Leo expressed in the words, "God became man that men might become the sons of God."
>
> [On item 2)] Though the claim that the Church of the Latter-day Saints is the only true Church of Jesus Christ is absurd, it is surely far better to try to enlighten them [regarding] the faith and order and worship of the Historical Church than to try to prove to them what an honest study of history will not prove, that the Apostolic Church may not have been in the mind of Jesus. . . .
>
> [On item 3)] When most theological thinkers feel that there is good ground in scripture and reason for an intermediate state, a paradise, that "in our father's house are many stations," ought there not to be a feeling of sympathy for the Latter-day Saint, who, with scant knowledge of the history of the development of the thought on the subject, made his own doctrine of the hereafter? . . .

---

11. Franklin Spencer Spalding, "What Is Left of Mormonism Without Polygamy?," 6.

[On item 4)] The Puritans did not use any decoration in the meeting houses of New England. . . . As a result Protestantism lost the immense value of aesthetics. . . . The combination wrought by Smith and his associates was a stroke of genius if not of religious art. It is hard to escape the feeling that had the Protestant churches not been too extreme the other way, the crude ritual of the Mormon temple would not have been so attractive.[12]

Mormon readers of his comments must have understood they were being praised and patronized simultaneously, but they also could sense that Spalding respected their genius for living a new form of Christian religion. Using this ironic method of chiding both Mormons and certain Protestants, Spalding tried to position himself as a fair critic, thus retaining both the Mormons' trust and the Protestants' sympathy.

In the February 1914 report to his Episcopal constituents, which he titled "The Proper Attitude toward the Mormon Church and People," Spalding focused on the development of individual "testimony," a topic that had also preoccupied Nutting. He observed:

If, at first, the child cannot give testimony to the divine mission of Joseph Smith he is required to testify to the goodness of his parents, his teacher, to God's love and so gradually is led on to bear testimony to the greatest of prophets. The result is a blind, unreasoned belief in the founder of Mormonism as a prophet of God, and in the truth of every claim he made. . . . Having been subject to this discipline their loyalty is unfaltering.

Now the first point I want to make is that a very large percentage of the members of all Christian Churches accept the creed and discipline of their several denominations and strengthen their faith and loyalty by precisely this same psychological process. The laymen in our Protestant and Catholic churches are too busy to study history and philosophy and theology. Nine-tenths of them know no more than they did when they went to Sunday School and a large number of those who remain loyal do it by a will to believe, not by a will to think. . . .

The Christian missionary has not always in the past tried to get the Mormon's point of view. The likeness I have ventured to insist on between Mormon belief and loyalty and the belief and loyalty of religionists shows the difficulty of the problem. . . . [Nevertheless] I confess . . . I cannot help feeling that I must point out to the Mormon what I feel are the untruths he believes as well as proclaim in his hearing, as convincingly as I can, the positive truth I hold. The theologian is a kind of philosopher who cannot avoid a sense of duty to proselytize. Yea, surely it is clear that sarcasm and ridicule are not only discourteous but stupid forms of argument. . . . We know that

---

12. Spalding, 3–7.

the sneer of the blatant infidel instead of shaking our loyalty, intensifies it, and in like manner the universal flood of derision which has been poured out upon Mormonism has only made Mormons more loyal.[13]

With this approach, Spalding established a persuasive tension between positive affirmation and negative critique. He did not want his attacks to increase Mormon defensiveness and resistance to change, nor did he desire to dissuade the Saints from their basic loyalty to their religion. His plan was to convert Mormonism itself to true Christianity, not convert Mormons into Episcopalians. Spalding wanted Mormonism to make some changes allowing its people to remain loyal enthusiasts, but to the orthodox Christian conception of God, not Joseph Smith's view. As Spalding's biographer summed it, his mission strategy "was to avoid the suspicion and hostility . . . but to accelerate the evolution . . . [Mormonism] was gradually assuming of an ordinary Christian sect."[14]

The bishop seemed to especially respect two Mormon practices that he adopted in his effort to convert the Saints. The first was evangelizing other Christians; the second, their belief in continuous revelation. He defended his own aggressive counter-proselytizing efforts with an argument for reciprocity: "We are not here in Utah to attack but to assist, and being full of the missionary spirit themselves [the Mormons] will not blame us if we try to share with them what we think Christ has given us."[15] He made the same reciprocal argument regarding new revelations:

> It is clear that the whole subject of historical development of Christianity has no interest to the Mormon. . . . [However,] I cannot but feel that the thoughtful Saint must see that his [exclusionary] pride is not justified because it leads to narrowness, and even on the principles of his own creed is inconsistent. A God who has still many things to reveal to His people did not keep silent for hundreds of years and does not now limit Himself in inspiring prophets for His children to the hierarchy residing in Salt Lake City. This is written in no spirit of unkindness but with a sincere feeling that this Church of ours has something to give our brethren in Utah.[16]

He also drew on the Mormon belief in continuous revelation, arguing that it was logically inconsistent with their claim of a universal Christian

---

13. Franklin Spencer Spalding, "The Proper Attitude toward the Mormon Church and People," 16–17.
14. Melish, *Franklin Spencer Spalding*, 165.
15. Franklin Spencer Spalding's speech in *Journal of Convocation*, 18–19.
16. Franklin Spencer Spalding's speech in *Journal of Convocation*, 19–20.

apostasy that had left the earth without revelation between the death of the ancient apostles and the revelations of Joseph Smith.[17]

Spalding distinguished between a purposeful conspiracy of Mormon leaders who covered the truth to preserve their own power and the culturally induced blindness of irrational belief. In Spalding's view, the Mormon people—including their highest officials—do not lie, their system does. In a handwritten, untitled speech prepared presumably for an Episcopalian sermon or report, he wrote:

> The time has come that the real Evil of Mormonism be laid bare, namely, that it is a lie, and it teaches men to lie. . . . If they want to believe in the divine authorization of their priesthood, a divided Christendom cannot complain . . . but [we must] fearlessly and hopefully try to make them see that it is a lie they are holding in their right hand.[18]

Spalding refused to claim that designing and exploitive men led Mormonism, but he noted the faults of many individuals—but with a sense of humor. He recorded an instance of Mormon hypocrisy at the little Episcopal Church in Vernal, Utah:

> The Mormons are peculiar in their moral ideas. Nobody ever locks his doors . . . but we noticed our collection hat was almost empty. . . . Earlier in the evening a young man came in to cordially ask for a Prayer Book, and gave us two nickels . . . said he was tired of Mormonism and deeply impressed with Episcopal religion. It proved later that this same pious youth had taken all the money in the hat but the two nickels; and the Prayer Book dodge was a precaution to prevent discovery . . . The Mormons are very polite.[19]

Following his own credo that it is impossible to influence people unless you take them as seriously as they take themselves, the bishop decided that he would engage B. H. Roberts, one of the best-known Mormon intellectual apologists of his time and a senior church leader, in a respectful exchange.[20] Information about the relationship between Spalding and Roberts is limited to a few letters and newspaper articles from which it appears that in 1912, Spalding, then forty-seven, engaged and befriended B. H. Roberts, then fifty-five.[21] Given Spalding's goal of influencing the

---

17. Franklin Spencer Spalding's speech in *Journal of Convocation*, 20.
18. Franklin Spencer Spalding, Untitled speech, handwritten, 6.
19. Franklin Spencer Spalding, Personal travel journal, March 3, 1905, entry.
20. Franklin Spencer Spalding, Letter to Dr. H. V. Hilprecht, University of Pennsylvania, April 23, 1910.
21. B. H. Roberts was the closest thing to a theologian and philosopher in Salt Lake City. Roberts was a full time ecclesiastical leader, simultaneous husband

up-coming intelligencia of Mormonism, any influence on Roberts would have had broad ramifications.

In the brief correspondence dating about the time Spalding published a critique of Joseph Smith's translation of The Book of Abraham, Roberts and Spalding are very cordial. Indeed, it seems from their correspondence that they both understood that their interactions were in fact a serious contestation over the true church of Christ, and at the same time a demonstration of their true Christianity. Each showed by word and tone that he wanted victory only on fair terms—in a way that the opponent would agree was fair. Even if they both doubted the possibility of fundamentally moving the other, their eristic encounters remained patient and good-hearted.

It appears they would write each other seeking clarification on doctrines or practices. Roberts once even asked Spalding for help in selecting and critiquing a reading list on Christian history. On another occasion, after receiving from Spalding some materials that contained Spalding's criticisms of Mormonism, Roberts responded to the Bishop with this note:

> I discover myself your debtor to the extent of two notes, one very excellent book treating of a most important historical question, two copies of a brochure by yourself treating a Mormon issue with the very best of intentions I am sure, and out of a desire to be helpful rather than offensively critical—for all which I desire to express my appreciation which is none the less real for being long delayed.[22]

Another time when Roberts corrected Spalding for misquoting him in a public statement regarding polygamy, Spalding wrote a public apology, which the newspaper printed:

> I regret exceedingly that I have quite unintentionally misstated Mr. Roberts's opinion on this matter. . . . Upon many matters of theological belief I cannot agree with Mr. Roberts, but I have perfect confidence in his honesty and

---

of three, elected (unseated) Congressmen, prolific writer and historian, and by consensus then and now, one of the brightest Mormons who ever lived. He walked across the plains to Utah as a pioneer boy, never had formal college training, worked in mining camps, and as a blacksmith, served in WWI as a chaplain, and became the major intellectual apologist for Mormonism. See Truman G. Madsen, *Defender of the Faith: The B. H. Roberts Story*; Stan Larson, "Intellectuals in Mormon History: An Update," 187–89.

22. Brigham H. Roberts, Personal note to F. S. Spalding. From the context it appears the note was likely written in 1912.

sincerity. I deeply regret that I have—without intending to do so—reported incorrectly on his opinion.²³

Tellingly, on November 1, 1914, Roberts was the first to speak to an audience of two thousand people at Spalding's memorial funeral service in the Salt Lake Theatre.²⁴ Among other things, Roberts said, "Bishop Spalding was an honorable opponent . . . who dedicated himself to the betterment of mankind irrespective of their beliefs. . . . He was intellectually honest, a quality as big and precious as it is rare. . . . His death has left us with broken harmonies."²⁵

Spalding's Approach to Polygamy

One rarely wins the heart and mind of an opponent by embarrassing him. To win the Mormons to more traditional Christianity, Spalding tried to find a way for the Mormon people to save face even if they were to be convinced their founding Prophet had not been fully inspired or made mistakes. Thus, Spalding aimed to allow Joseph Smith to remain an honored prophet with human limitations and errors in his legacy.²⁶ In Spalding's view, Smith might have been inspired in some things, sincerely mistaken in many, but well-intended in most if not all. Spalding set up an intellectually and morally consistent dichotomy for the Mormons: either live your religion taking Joseph Smith as completely prophetic with all the consequences—including potential prosecution for illegal bigamy and cohabitation—or admit that dubious part of your religion was a human mistake and make adjustments. He quoted Joseph Smith's statement, "A prophet is only a prophet when acting as such."²⁷ Spalding then argued with considerable sophistication that a true prophet might err without los-

---

23. Franklin Spencer Spalding, Letter to the Editor, *Deseret News*, March 14, 1914.

24. Melish, *Franklin Spencer Spalding*, 295.

25. "Glowing Tributes Paid to Bishop Spalding's Memory: Notable Gathering is Held at the Salt Lake Theater in Honor of the Departed Churchman," 1.

26. Richard Mouw has argued similarly and presented contemporary Evangelicals with an interpretive possibility beyond the true prophet vs. false prophet dichotomy in Richard J. Mouw, "The Possibility of Joseph Smith: Some Evangelical Probings," in Reid L. Neilson and Terryl L. Givens, eds., *Joseph Smith Jr.: Reappraisals after Two Centuries*.

27. Joseph Fielding Smith, ed. *Teachings of the Prophet Joseph Smith*, 278.

ing his or her overall authority. A true church, like a true believer, should admit its errors, repent, and constantly move toward perfection.[28]

Spalding used this argument to tackle the topic that was thorny for Mormons and anti-Mormons alike: polygamy. He sent a letter to Isaac Russell, a friendly correspondent at *The New York Times,* containing Spalding's essay *The Honest Way Out of a Difficult Situation* that the newspaper published.[29] In this essay, Spalding deftly suggested that Joseph Smith had erred in his timing, not in his morality. The ancient polygamist patriarchs like Abraham and Jacob, upon whom Smith based his practice, were not dishonored by practicing this form of marriage since polygamy was a cultural and historical marriage custom, not an act of absolute immorality as many ministers argued. However, the Mormon practice of ongoing revelation should have updated its marriage practices to meet the needs of modern society. It was a prophetic mistake by Joseph Smith to revive the outdated practice, but that did not prove Smith was uninspired in other matters. The essay concluded that a people cannot be faulted for loyally supporting their good-hearted though sometimes mistaken leaders. Though mistaken, Mormons who practiced modern polygamy were courageous not immoral.[30] Russell, himself a lapsed Mormon, showed sympathy with the idea:

> Following a long period in which the Mormon problem in Utah has been a center of bitter controversy with the Presbyterian and Methodist Churches leading the anti-Mormon assaults, the Protestant Episcopal Church has taken a hand in the hope of effecting permanent peace in the intermountain sector. . . . The bishop of Utah has offered the Mormons, especially their confused youth, 'An Honest Way Out of a Difficult Situation.' . . . Religious

---

28. Though he was the most compelling, Spalding was not the first to criticize the Mormons this way. Many early critics had tried to reform Mormonism from within by disregarding Joseph Smith's more controversial doctrines. An example from Spalding's era was David Williams who wrote a brochure called "Will the Mormon People Become Christians?" that made a similar argument: "Throw away all the strange doctrines that have crept into the [Mormon] church, no matter by whom they came, and hold fast to the fullness of the gospel as it was given by Jesus Christ Himself, according to the New Testament and the Book of Mormon, which are one. Let all that love the doctrine of Christ come together as one man and the standard of Christ to the nations." See David M. Williams "Will the Mormon People Become Christians?," 34.

29. Franklin Spencer Spalding, "The Honest Way Out of a Difficult Situation: A Friendly Word to the Latter-Day Saints."

30. Spalding, "The Honest Way Out."

beliefs which are not put into practice produce moral and intellectual confusion. . . . Belief ought to justify and inspire conduct, and therefore when practice contradicts creed, honest men are bound . . . either to revise their belief or else persist in conforming to it. . . . Quite clearly honesty requires a definite choice between the two: either, in spite of civil law and opposing religious opinion, polygamy still be practiced, or else the creedal statement concerning polygamy be revised. . . .

It is a truth that the followers of Jesus secured a change in the civil law only by courageously practicing their beliefs in spite of that law. It seems, therefore, that the time has come when the Mormons should carefully consider the belief itself. . . . In ancient days women and children were considered as chattel, and there was no reason not to possess a number of wives. . . . Women are not chattel today, but man's equal. Plural marriage, therefore, *today* does become immoral and corrupt. . . . It would seem that the right way out of the dilemma for sincere [Mormons] is to frankly admit that the prophet who gave them the revelation was mistaken. . . . This was the opinion of David Whitmer, who maintained his testimony of the Book of Mormon even "after Brother Joseph had drifted into error and blindness."[31]

Spalding's suggestion that it might be an act of courageous faith to live polygamy in the face of criticism was a bold move that risked offending both sides, implying the Mormons might be cowards to have quit it, or that they might have been admirable to live it. This implication also demonstrates Spalding's distinctive method, tone, and intellect.

Spalding's Use of Scholarly Authority

By avoiding unsavory speculations on the Mormons' motives, Spalding distanced himself from Paden's tactic of attacking LDS leaders. Instead, he made a major contribution to the religious dialogue by critiquing Mormonism's historical claims based on verifiable facts. Spalding was sure that the Book of Mormon's narrative of Hebrews who migrated to America and were visited by the resurrected Christ would be so inconsistent with pre-Columbian history that he urged intelligent Saints to change their view of it from history to "sacred story."[32] For the most part, he avoided engaging in trench warfare and concentrated on lecturing to and writing

---

31. Isaac Russell, "Shows Mormons How To Drop Polygamy."

32. Spalding, *Journal of Convocation*, 19. Spalding thought as a perspectivalist that as history and sacred stories tend to be revised when new perspectives come to view, both history and sacred story could be seen as true and malleable—at least from a moral viewpoint.

for well-educated Mormons.[33] Over the nine years of his Utah ministry, he participated in debates, lectured at university student-sponsored events, authored newspaper articles, published a short book and various pamphlets, not counting the writings and speeches designed for his own congregation that did not deal with competing religious claims. His tone was patient and sympathetic but confident and unabashed. Because he saw young educated people generally becoming more liberal in their views, he thought Mormonism would change as its new generation matured.

His own model for true religion was one of gradual historical adaptation: "All churches outgrow . . . the distinctive dogmas and observations upon which they were historically founded," he wrote in a tract, and "Mormonism is no exception to this rule."[34] He wrote tolerantly to a cousin in 1908, "Many of the older doctrines are not taught openly because the young people would not accept them. . . . To charge the present Mormons with all that Smith and Young taught is almost as bad as charging the Presbyterian Church with all that Edwards preached."[35] He hoped, by sound argument based on Mormon doctrines, to "accelerate the natural process of Mormon evolution . . . toward the likeness of an ordinary Christian sect." For example, acknowledging Mormon belief in continuous revelation, he argued that Mormons ought to look forward to changing their views if the light of the Spirit expanded them. Of course, he had no doubt the Spirit would incline them toward upholding a more traditional Christianity.[36]

Spalding also performed important analyses of the Book of Mormon and the Book of Abraham—both scriptures produced by Joseph Smith. Perhaps drawing from William James's treatise on various types of religious paranormal behavior, he concluded that Joseph Smith had produced the book by automatic writing—not by ruse or direct imagination:

> I am more and more convinced . . . that the Book of Mormon is an example of automatic writing . . . and if so the time has come when the book must be tested carefully and critically. This I have been trying to do. Fortunately,

---

33. Franklin Spencer Spalding, *The Annual Report of the Bishop*, 19.
34. Franklin Spencer Spalding quoted in John R. Sillito and Martha Sonntag Bradley, "Franklin Spencer Spalding: An Episcopal Observer of Mormonism," 346.
35. Franklin Spencer Spalding quoted in Melish, *Franklin Spencer Spalding*, 169.
36. Franklin Spencer Spalding, speech in the *Journal of Convocation*, 20.

we have—accepted by the Mormons—Joseph's replica of some lines of the text. . . . Why not go to [ancient language experts] for verification?[37]

This refusal to call Mormonism a purposeful hoax led Spalding to carefully consider the Book of Mormon and other Joseph Smith writings on their own merits, thus making Spalding the co-founder, along with B. H. Roberts, of textual criticism of the Mormon scriptures. Spalding, familiar with scholarly work of higher biblical criticism, in 1901 submitted copies of some of the Egyptian hieroglyphs and demotic text that Joseph Smith likely used for his translation of The Book of Abraham to several scholars of ancient languages for their textual analysis. To the scholarly experts he chose, Spalding confided his hope of enlightening the Mormons:

> Now what we want is to secure a statement of a few great authorities as to the value of [The Book of Abraham]. I believe the time is ripe for such a method of giving light to the Mormons. It is easy, of course, to consider the whole thing as beneath notice, but you must remember that from 1830 when the Mormon church was founded until now, the sect has grown from nothing to nearly half a million adherents and this very moment 2,000 young men are preaching Mormonism all over the world. It is impossible to influence anyone unless you take him as seriously as he takes himself, and there can be no doubt that the Mormon people most seriously and sincerely believe in the authenticity of these sacred books. Most denied the text's comprehensibility and/or authenticity but did not try to produce an authoritative, alternative translation.[38]

Spalding was searching for scientific authority to bolster his rhetorical persuasion tactics. He was clearly leading his witnesses, but he no doubt assumed they could still speak their minds without consulting each other, thus providing a semi-controlled experiment that would hold rhetorical weight even if it did not have methodological rigor.

The Book of Abraham included several poorly copied facsimiles of the papyri that Smith used to inspire his translation. Spalding assumed Smith's translation of the text, if valid, would be replicated and confirmed by professionals. When the Orientalists each separately called Smith's work erroneous fabrication, Spalding published his evidence in a short book, *Joseph Smith, Jr. as a Translator*, indicating Smith to be a poor translator and, by inference, an imperfect prophet, as well.[39] If Joseph did an inspired *mis*translation of the Book of Abraham, why then should anyone

---

37. Franklin Spencer Spalding, Letter or notes on Joseph Smith's translation methods, handwritten. It appears the notes might be before 1910 by context.
38. Spalding, Letter to Dr. H. V. Hilprecht.
39. Franklin Spencer Spalding, *Joseph Smith, Jr. as a Translator*.

trust the results of his inspiration in translating the Book of Mormon? While this potent criticism seems to have caused only a few to flee their faith, it helped move a subsequent generation of Mormon apologists to work seriously on ancient studies.[40]

Such research made Spalding a Protestant missionary hero, even among those who found his conciliatory style too soft. Evangelical missionaries in Utah extensively used his book on Smith as translator. According to the Women's Home Missionary Society:

> The armor of the Mormon Church has been pierced. It has been discovered and acknowledged that their historical theory of the miraculous and infallible translation of the Book of Mormon is absurd and incredible. . . . Nothing that has occurred . . . so emphasizes the triumphal march and influence of Christian teaching and example among these people. When the foundation disintegrates, the superstructure must fall.[41]

B. H. Roberts's initial response to Spalding was a counter-critique of the certainty of modern criticism of scriptural texts. He quipped that Spalding, who had been appreciatively studying higher textual biblical criticism, should not waste effort searching for the undiscoverable accuracy of any ancient agglomerations of words by unknown authors.[42] Spalding took Roberts's jab with good humor saying in a private letter to a friend that while Roberts used old-fashioned forms of exegesis and argument, Spalding was uncomfortable wrestling with new textual and historical critical approaches to the Bible. Such approaches allowed, ironically, for the "ongoing revelation" with which Mormons would have been at ease; however, they challenged traditional—and still prominent—Evangelical

---

40. Spalding's criticism of the Book of Abraham had long-range effects on Mormon intellectuals. It began an effort among the Mormons to learn from serious scholarship how to critically analyze some of the Latter-day Saints' historical claims. Fragments of the original four scrolls of papyri along with several hieroglyphic illustrations (which had been sold by Joseph Smith's family after his death) were located in 1967 in the archives of the New York Metropolitan Museum of Art. For an overview of the various professional opinions regarding the original Smith translation and its relation to the rediscovered fragments and other hieroglyphs, see John Gee, "A History of the Joseph Smith Papyri and Book of Abraham." It discusses wide differences of opinion on how to interpret the Book of Abraham from outright hoax to pseudepigraphal expansion to miraculous inspiration.

41. Women's Home Missionary Society of the Methodist Episcopal Church. The date is possibly 1912 by context.

42. Brigham H. Roberts, "Remarks on Joseph Smith, Jr. as a Translator."

Christian view, arising as a response to scholarly and scientific criticism of the Bible in relation to Old Testament development and the creation narratives respectively, and in connection with the result of the Modernist-Fundamentalist controversies, that the Bible was inerrant. "One feels the only thing that can save Mr. Roberts and his friends from error is the frank acceptance of the precepts of Higher Criticism," Spalding wrote, "but if we ask Mr. Roberts to accept the principles of Modern Bible study surely we must accept them ourselves."[43]

Spalding also expanded the reach of his critical book by working with Isaac Russell at the *New York Times* to comment positively on the respectful tone and rational approach of his critique of the Book of Abraham translation. Russell thought Spalding could help both clear-thinking Mormons and non-Mormons in the controversy over the respectability of Mormonism in America. He wanted the Mormons to liberalize and the Protestants to allow them space to do so. He told the bishop in a personal letter: "I cannot possibly feel that in aim or purpose they [Mormon leaders] were consciously tricky or dealt crookedly with their followers. I have resented attacks upon them based on this premise. . . . I am keen for using my vantage ground here to trip up every falsifier who comes against them in bitterness of heart and fraudulence of data."[44]

In early 1913 Roberts wrote a lengthy review of Spalding's critique in the local *Deseret News* in which he admitted that the Bishop had done a service by raising good questions; however, Roberts entered a "plea in bar" deferring final conclusions until it could be determined what Joseph Smith had meant by "translation," and until the experts could themselves agree on the meaning of the facsimiles. Roberts concluded that the Bishop's book showed only that if Joseph Smith had not been given divine direction to offer a correct translation, then Smith was not acting as a prophetic scribe in this case; but that the scholarly opinions were too tentative as to the meaning of Egyptian religion to say that anything final had been proven.[45]

In his earlier response to Spalding, Roberts had defended Smith's prophetic authenticity with a simple statement of personal belief: "I believe in the translations Joseph Smith has given to the world—confessedly not by scholarship but by inspiration, by his own spirit being quickened by contact with God's spirit—and that in those translations are truths that

---

43. Franklin Spencer Spalding, Personal letter to Isaac Russell of New York City.
44. Isaac Russell, Personal letter to Franklin Spalding.
45. Brigham H. Roberts, "A Plea in Bar of Final Conclusions," 309–25.

are parts of a mighty system of truth, the like of which is not found elsewhere among men."[46]

Spalding's Protestant Critics

Spalding offended some Mormons, but his careful rhetoric truly upset many Evangelical missionaries. Telling Spalding he was naive to think Mormons would be frank with him, John Nutting penned this paternal and condescending personal letter:

> Unless you have had many years of experience among the people, you do not know what you are saying . . . for it is one of the most painful facts about the Mormon people that almost all of them will lie, especially to further the interests of their religion. . . . Everyone who gets beneath the surface comes to this view, which is that of every experienced pastor or other person I know. And nothing else can be expected but such blurring and obliterating of moral distinctions when one prays to a god who was once a human sinner and liar of course; [enjoying] polygamy now in his heaven. . . . Mormonism can only be vanquished by enlightening its people about Christianity, and letting the outside world know about Mormon paganism. . . . Neither can be done without battle, for the foe will fight you in proportion to [your] prospect of success for God. If you still doubt my positions . . . a month in our work [in the field] would satisfy you, if not one week.[47]

Roberts's commentaries on Spalding's findings also irked the Evangelicals because it sidestepped the implications of the actual accuracy of Smith's translation. Referring specifically to Roberts's 1913 replies, Nutting again wrote Spalding:

> But what do you think of their intellectual honesty now? . . . What a contrast between Roberts' sarcasm or ridicule and your even too-catholic and generous spirit[!] If it be too much to expect them to give up at once, would it be so if they were really candid and honest with the truth? . . . The whole matter is . . . whether *you* will see only an imaginary [Mormon] character, only

---

46. Brigham H. Roberts, "Remarks on *Joseph Smith, Jr. as a Translator*." One hermeneutical approach used among a minority of Latter-day Saints in the twenty-first century reflects Roberts's analysis. It allows that Joseph Smith was inspired by viewing the text to write a new inspired commentary that he loosely called a translation. This way of thinking does not delight traditional scholars or exegetes on either side of this argument.

47. John Danforth Nutting, Personal letter to F. S. Spalding, November 16, 1912.

slightly influenced by their terrible doctrines, and hence will do them great harm by unintentional flattery, or by opposing those who know the facts.[48]

Further opposition to Spalding's comparatively soft approach came from the International Council for Patriotic Service (ICPS), a multi-denominational adjunct committee serving the women's mission boards of various Protestant denominations. For many years, the ICPS had provided articles for publication to raise awareness and money for missionary work in Utah and to warn Americans against the Mormons who were interested in eventually replacing the government with a theocracy. ICPS had initially been formed to publicize the threat of Mormon influence in America and to help unseat B. H. Roberts in 1898. It did not disband when Roberts was dispatched but instead broadened its scope of defending the nation and its homes against the evils of Mormonism. This council increased its proselytizing efforts to the Mormons after apostle Reed Smoot was seated in the Senate by providing articles to the Women's Home Mission Council to publish in its monthly magazine. These articles typically contained extremely critical exposés of alleged incidents of new plural marriages and vague charges of economic conspiracy and theocratic control. In 1911, one year before Spalding published his studies of Joseph Smith as translator, the ICPS president at the time, Miss C. E. Mason of Tarrytown, NY, expressed her displeasure over Spalding's diplomatic liberality toward the Mormons who still professed polygamy though claiming no longer to practice it, and who would take over the country if given the chance. Mason happened upon an article Spalding had written containing an implied critique of the ICPS's sensation-seeking approach and wrote the bishop a personal twenty-page typed letter that defended her organization, cited Rev. William Paden as its source for information about polygamy and Mormonism's continued theocratic intentions, and sketched out both a strategy that was adopted by the National Reform Association and a buy-out real estate plan that would have dispossessed Mormon property-holders:

> Our information can be corroborated by Dr. Paden and other Utah Christian ministers who have aided us in the past by their counsel. . . . [We] have just heard of Mormon Elders arriving from Europe with a band of fifty young women converts . . . and of their distributing tracts to our high school girls as they come out of school buildings . . . We cannot condone the indecency of their system. . . . We women do not believe lectures on socialism or on the

---

48. John Danforth Nutting, Personal letter to Bishop F. S. Spalding, Jan. 4, 1913. Emphasis mine.

Psalms of David [Spalding's favorite text] will cure this evil, not even when presented by a Bishop so beloved as the bishop of Utah. We believe there are two ways to stop this evil; first and quickest, by a national marriage law or by an anti-polygamy amendment to the Constitution . . . and the second way is slower but also a surer way than has ever been tried to correct the situation in the Mormon states, viz. to buy up lands and sell them in small tracts to Christian settlers without cash, giving them a long term of years to pay for them, such settlers knowing clearly in advance that they are going there just as College settlement workers go, to exemplify Christian homes in a community with benighted ideas of family life.

I have talked this matter over in a preliminary way with highly enlightened people in Scotland and Holland, and so forth. Steadfastness to his religion has been a characteristic of the Dutchman throughout his history; Scotch, English, and Scandinavian Christians are equally desirable, though they do not come with as much money to buy homes as the Dutch. . . . It will take capital, but it can be raised by your clergy, and your gentile citizens. . . . A tide of immigrants would aid in neutralizing the voting power of the Mormons, and maintain higher ideals of marriage. We would thus fight the Mormon with his own weapons . . . for it is not the religion of the Mormon, but the hunger of man in other nations for land, for homes and for opportunity which primarily brings the converts here. . . . ignorant, degenerate, psychologically unsound types which the Mormons too often bring . . .

If our polemics cause family division among the faithful Protestants, just as the fight over slavery caused, we will never be silent until this curse is swept away.[49]

Of all the proposals to solve the Mormon problem, Mason's was clearly the boldest.[50]

Bishop Spalding responded to Mason with a practical defense of his stance. He concluded courteously but firmly:

Perhaps the real difference in our points of view is that I know the Mormons as individuals, you know them as a group. I know many young Mormon missionaries personally and they are not white slave traders—but are very much like other young men. You know them impersonally as advocates of a false religious system. No doubt our work supplements each other, and

---

49. C. E. Mason, Personal letter to Bishop Spalding, March 29, 1911.

50. The Dutch Plan that Mason mentions is an example of minoration (dilution of one group's majority population by another group's greater birthrate or inmigration) explained in D. W. Meinig's geopolitical theory as a strategy favored by imperial managers, and used by the U.S. government in its overwhelming, though never assimilating, treatment of troublesome, indigenous minorities. See D. W. Meinig, "The Mormon Nation and the American Empire," 36–39.

though my personal knowledge may prevent my adopting your somewhat harsh methods of criticism, I do not think it makes me a coward nor do I think your knowledge of me is accurate enough to justify you in suggesting such a charge.[51]

For his part, Spalding criticized Utah ministers who were unable to agree on their Christian doctrines but were united in their contempt for Mormonism. He distanced the Episcopalian and Roman Catholic churches from extreme anti-Mormonism, eschewed faith-destroying antagonism, and took the position that Christians should help Mormonism improve by "thinking of the Latter-day Saints at their best."[52]

To Spalding, one unacceptable result of the antagonism between Protestants and Mormons was that it left disillusioned Mormons with no place to go: "A good many have apostatized from the Mormon Church, but few have been persuaded to join other religious societies." Spalding reasoned that some of this religious homelessness resulted from the inability of disillusioned Mormons to separate religion in general from Mormonism in particular, observing "that when that [Mormon] expression is rejected interest in all religion ceases."[53] A second reason for Spalding taking the approach he did was his prediction based on his study of history that a mass disillusionment would someday sweep over Mormonism. "We can

---

51. Franklin Spencer Spalding, Personal letter to Miss C. E. Mason of Tarrytown, NY, May 8, 1911.

52. Franklin Spencer Spalding quotation in Melish, *Franklin Spencer Spalding*, 169. Also see Franklin Spencer Spalding, Annual Report of the Bishop of the Missionary District of Utah, 1908; Franklin Spencer Spalding, "Our Church in Mormonland."

53. Spalding, "Our Church in Mormonland." Here parallels could be drawn to Mormons who go through a process of religious disaffiliation, many times to skepticism, but also reaffiliation with other religious organizations. See Stan L. Albrecht and Howard M. Bahr, "Patterns of Religious Affiliation: A Study of Lifelong Mormons, Mormon Converts, and Former Mormons," 373; Howard M. Bahr and Stan L. Albrecht, "Strangers Once More: Patterns of Disaffiliation from Mormonism," 180–200. For an up-to-date reading based on a comparison of U.S. Mormon membership as reported by the Glenmary Research Center in contrast with the National Survey of Religious Identification and the American Religious Identification Survey, the Mormon Social Science Association has concluded that the Mormon Church attracts a large number of converts (in-switchers), but also loses a large a number of apostates (out-switchers). See John W. Morehead, "Divine Disenchantment: Transitions, and Assisting Those in Religious Migration," 116–31.

meet this situation as no other religious body can. . . . because there are so many points of contact between the 'Church idea' and sacraments of [both our religions]."[54] The Bishop was forced to be nimble, trying to work on the narrow ground of reason between strident, emotional pro- and anti-Mormon crusaders, neither of whom he could afford to offend.

In 1914 Spalding published a controversial article titled "The Proper Attitude toward the Mormon Church and People" in the *Utah Survey,* an Episcopalian newsletter distributed to Protestants supporting his efforts in and outside Utah. He urged patient understanding and the cessation of critical remarks about Mormon motives:

> Not only are polygamous marriages not multiplying, but polygamy was never practiced by the Mormons to the extent popularly supposed, and if the Churches are even half awake, they have nothing to fear from the proselytizing efforts of the two thousand Mormons scattered over the earth, most of whom are school boys, who only know a few little speeches and few Bible texts and who look at the call to a mission quite as much as a chance to see the world as to convert it. . . . . We [missionaries to Mormons] must be on our guard lest we yield to the temptation actually to regret that the Mormons are improving—to be almost sorry that we have lost our old thunder because we can no longer honestly repeat the stories of the sensationalists who are not held back by either truth or charity. . . . The days in which interest in foreign missions was aroused by dreadful tales of brutality, lust and ignorance have happily passed. . . . The attitude toward the Mormon seems to be the sole exception to this philosophical method and approach.[55]

Spalding continued the article with a status report of changes in Mormonism. He thought Mormons were using the Bible much more than the Book of Mormon, were speaking of God in less anthropomorphic terms, and were educating more intellectuals who might potentially reform the church if they did not leave it first. Spalding begged his Protestant constituents to be patient, to praise any positive change in Mormonism, and to cease the polemical diatribes. In short, he recommended that missionaries "convert Mormonism slowly—do not strengthen it by attempting to destroy it."[56]

The National Reform Association targeted Spalding directly by reprinting Spalding's "The Proper Attitude Toward the Mormon Church

---

54. Franklin Spencer Spalding, paraphrased in Jesse Herbert Dennis, *The Work of the Church Among the Mormons,* 33.

55. Spalding, "The Proper Attitude," 21.

56. Spalding, 20, 22–23.

and People" in its September 1914 edition of its magazine, *The Christian Statesman*, accompanied by a critique that attacked Spalding's patient, naive, non-polemical approach to Mormonism:

> If "The Proper Attitude" is right, our crusade against the Mormon Kingdom is wrong. If our crusade is right, "The Proper Attitude" is wrong. We state the case bluntly. . . . Our crusade is not an attack on religion . . . but any further attempt to substitute Mormonism for our Christian government we must resist [and thus] wage this crusade.[57]

The *Statesman* piece went on to emphasize its stand by demanding that the LDS Church excise all revelations regarding polygamy from its sacred scriptures and withdraw from any commercial ventures. It also advocated that no Mormon leader be allowed to hold public office.[58]

In spite of Spalding's call for patience, those who had been committed to eliminate the menace of Mormonism continued to work in an aggressive mode. Two years after the bishop's death, the ICPS was sounding brassy warnings about a treasonous Mormon theocratic conspiracy in the monthly journal of the Women's Board of Missions of the Presbyterian Church of America. With polygamy no longer a lively issue, Elizabeth Vermilye, then President of the ICPS, reported boldly (and incorrectly) that in the Mormon temple every Mormon pledges before God and angels "to do all in my power to crush the United States Government and to defeat its purposes. I promise to will this to my children and my children's children as a sacred legacy."[59] The ICPS was right that most Mormons wanted to remain apart from what they saw as fallen Christendom and to stand alone as the only true and living church on the earth; but in spite of any bloc voting in Utah, the great majority of Latter-day Saints envisioned theocracy as something that would be instituted only by God at the Second Coming of Christ. Compared to the salaciousness of polygamy and the threat of forced theocracy, Spalding's diplomatic approach proved too light-handed to the NRA and ICPS.

Spalding the Educator

Spalding reinforced his practice of sound argument with good works, becoming a dynamic community leader in the process. In addition to

---

57. "An Attitude for Christians," 219.
58. "An Attitude for Christians," 219–25.
59. Elizabeth B. Vermilye, "Are Christians Justified in Combating Mormonism?" 283–86.

leading the works of mercy performed at St. Mark's Hospital and the works of intellectual advancement at Rowland Hall School, the Episcopal diocese also sponsored Emory House, the Episcopalian Club house at the University of Utah, financed by a generous $25,000 grant from a New York donor.[60] Spalding personally oversaw the construction and enjoyed the comfortable ambiance of this building, giving frequent lectures there and informally discussing any religious and secular matters interesting to the students who dropped in.[61] He used these lectures and discussions to provide any interested Mormon students with information about inconsistencies in Mormon doctrines or histories that would shake them from a lethargic acceptance of their religion and dissuade them from their desire to serve missions to convert Protestants out of state. Spalding wrote a short pamphlet, *The Missionaries and the Wise Man* (circa 1913), which suggests how he likely approached these students. In the parable he developed in the pamphlet, the wise man was a university professor of psychology whom Mormon missionaries encountered. After they told him of Joseph Smith's theophany, the wise man said:

> These are indeed wonderful descriptions of psychic phenomena, but really you young men seem too intelligent to believe them to be other than the peculiar mental experience of Joseph Smith. You do not really believe, do you, that God the Almighty, infinite and eternal, has a bodily form as described by Joseph Smith? . . . All thoughtful scholars are agreed that the descriptions of God in early Hebrew writings are natural to men in the childhood of the race, but impossible for men who live today. . . . I have looked into Mormonism with much interest—your church has not for forty years produced a thinker.[62]

The wise man then proceeds to explain that faith in life after death is good, but that the notions Mormons entertain about the various mansions in hierarchical degrees of glory that humans might inhabit are fanciful. He adds that Joseph Smith and his colleagues blurred the difference between poetical truth and propositional truth in scripture. By this time in the story, the missionaries understood from the kindly wise man that Joseph Smith believed he had seen God and Christ, but had only seen "sensations stored up in his own mind." The wise man then concludes,

> Go home, young men, and study. Prepare yourselves to be teachers before you presume to teach. I am sure you know in the bottom of your hearts that

---

60. Dennis, *Work of the Church Among the Mormons*, 25.
61. Melish, *Franklin Spencer Spalding*, 158.
62. Franklin Spencer Spalding, "The Missionaries and the Wise Man," 5–8.

only the very ignorant can be influenced by the inaccurate and unscientific teaching you give. You have a good state university. Instead of spending the money of your parents and friends on these profitless [mission] journeys, spend it securing a good college education. Stop trying to persuade men to believe what no intelligent man can possibly believe.[63]

Episcopal records do not note success at converting Mormons through this patronizing approach but, like most polemical tracts, its intended audience was not for the Mormons alone. Spalding likely could have been speaking to his own more traditional Protestant constituents who took the Bible poetry too literally—or fancifully from his point of view—with similar results.

Spalding and a New Testament Social Model

Although Spalding certainly felt no joy from Mormonism's proselytizing successes, he generously praised Mormon communitarianism and lay participation.[64] In a review of his work to the Episcopal Church he wrote, "Do we not envy the system of the Latter-day Saints, which makes little boys deacons and sets them to work, and has 6,700 in other orders of the Seventies, hundreds of whom are preaching their faith outside of Utah, while the rest, as part of their duty, are preaching it within the state?"[65] His eager embrace of religion's role in social betterment not only themed his missionary work but also revealed his politics. Taking his lead from the communal ways of the earliest New Testament Christians, Spalding was an adamant socialist and pacifist, who was considered too politically and philosophically liberal by some of his constituents.[66] Spalding's passionate legacy so influenced his suc-

---

63. Spalding, 11–12.

64. Spalding was not alone to view the Latter-day Saints' social-economic communal towns as a possible new way of developing America. Ruth and Reginald Kauffman, two American socialist journalists, published a study of the Mormon economic system that criticized what they thought was wide-spread anti-Mormonism in the press and further analyzed the social-economic benefits of the Mormon system compared to capitalistic new communities. See Ruth Kauffman and Reginald Wright Kauffman, *A Study of the Mormons in Light of Economic Conditions*. The best overview and analysis of Mormon social-economic planning and execution is Leonard J. Arrington, *Great Basin Kingdom*; and Leonard J. Arrington, Feramorz Y. Fox, and Dean L. May, *Building the City of God*.

65. Spalding, "What Is Left of Mormonism Without Polygamy?," 7.

66. Spalding apparently was philosophically pragmatic, and an early follower of the process philosophy in the mode of William James and Alfred N. Whitehead.

cessor, Bishop Paul Jones, that the Diocese leadership asked Jones to resign in 1918 due to his strong advocacy of pacifism during World War I.[67]

But Spalding was not an impractical idealist. A. J. Simmonds, a historian and archivist at Utah State University, admired Spalding's fund-raising acumen: "He had a gift. Any man who can denounce the private ownership of property in the morning and in the evening talk eastern capitalists and financiers into building mission churches in Utah, certainly had something going for him."[68] Spalding's skill was apparently an acquired one, for he abhorred the fund-raising requirements of his job and wistfully compared his paltry $4,000 annual budget in 1910 from the headquarters church to that of "the superintendent of Methodist Missions [who] has twenty-five clergy in Utah and $16,000 for his work." Spalding concluded ruefully, "We certainly do a great deal on our name and distinguished ancestry."[69] A younger missionary colleague acknowledged that Spalding "was a Christian Socialist and had a passion for social reform. In those days missionary bishops largely raised their own funds through sermons, addresses, and personal solicitations. Bishop Spalding's strong political views did not make his task any easier."[70]

Bishop Spalding's interest in social betterment stemmed directly from his belief that a true Christian converted best by exemplary behavior, and he hoped his people could humbly show good works to the Mormons. Rev. George Townshend, paraphrasing Spalding's thought on the importance of example, explained in a brochure to Episcopalian on Mormonism:

> We believe that the preaching in Utah of the Historic Gospel, and of a more reasonable and spiritual Faith, will put to shame the old Mormonism and compel [them to make] further eliminations and further substitutions. "The Latter-day Saints" have an admiration for the good and the true as well as other men; and if the lives of our Church people are more clean and kind than those of the Mormon people, if our ministers are more courageous and intelligent than the Mormon ministers, if our Church has in it more of the idealism and heroism of Jesus than the Mormon system, if our religion gives purer light to the soul in its aspirations after the Divine than does the Mormon religion, then there will be little need to decry Mormonism, for

---

See A. J. Simmonds, "Speech to the 81st Convention of the Church in the Utah Diocese," June 20–22, 1986.

67. A. J. Simmonds, "Speech to the 81st Convention," 15.
68. Simmonds, 13.
69. Simmonds, 14.
70. Henry Knox Sherrill, *Among Friends*, 41.

its eclipse will be manifest to all seeing eyes and it will stand convicted and condemned by the minds and consciences of its own votaries.[71]

Although he enjoyed an intellectual tangle, Spalding offered his belief that Christian mission success generally depended on Christians getting their house in order through common service to humanity: "Christian unity will never come until followers of Jesus Christ realize that his religion depends not upon exact thinking but upon Christ-like living."[72] Spalding's service was cut short when he was struck and killed by an automobile in Salt Lake City in 1914, nine years after he began his mission there.

Final Thoughts on Spalding

Despite Spalding's magnanimity, he could not avoid conflicts over his gracious treatment of people who disagreed with him over universal religious truth claims. Had Spalding lived longer, his stance as a fair, respectful, and uncompromising antagonist may well have become a viable model. Spalding found the Mormons an honest, intelligent people and their practical and optimistic theology an understandably seductive lie. He could understand the practical and spiritual appeal of Mormonism and treated its adherents with more sympathy than did other missionaries to Utah during this period.

Spalding did not try to overturn the Mormon penchant for new, inspired texts or hermeneutics. Nor could he attack faith without injuring his own position. Indeed, he seemed to understand that aside from an outright confession of fraud by the writer, no historical evidence has ever been uncontestable, and thus there is no final universally acceptable proof that any textual prophetic statement (Mormon or otherwise) is or is not interpreted by divine inspiration. Spalding, who knew how dangerous counterfeit doctrines could be, took more stock in the persuasive evidence of fruitful Christian living.

Though he penned it two years before Spalding's death, Isaac Russell wrote a fitting tribute to the way Spalding conducted himself during his Utah ministry. In a letter to the bishop, he expressed his opinion that "the best I can hope for the Mormons is that all who come against them would do so in the spirit you have exercised, and with such a powerful showing of data to back them up."[73]

---

71. George Townshend, *The Conversion of Mormonism*, 75–76.
72. Franklin Spencer Spalding quoted in Melish, *Franklin Spencer Spalding*, 285.
73. Isaac Russell, Personal letter to Franklin Spalding, 1912.

CHAPTER NINE

Comparing Mission Methods of Nutting, Paden, and Spalding

Summary Observations

Stereotyping any of these complex missionaries is difficult, but each utilized a preferred method that can be descriptively categorized. They often disagreed with each other's methodology but were friends in a common cause. Nutting saw Paden as a helpful ally on the national scene, but an unenthusiastic supporter of his peripatetic Utah mission. Nutting thought Spalding to be naive and aloof from the real people but was complimentary to the Bishop regarding his book on Joseph Smith's mistranslation. Paden considered Nutting irrelevant and Spalding a bother. Spalding saw Paden and Nutting as allies, but in hopeless campaigns with flawed strategies.

In a direct proselytizing encounter, any one of these missionaries might normally begin with a critique of Mormonism's exclusive truth claims, arguing that Mormons needed to humble themselves before the longstanding Christian truth in the Bible. It usually ended with the proposition that Mormons enter orthodox Christendom by accepting Christ and the orthodox interpretation of the Bible; this required them to repudiate among other things their ideas of plural gods with active sex lives, their optimistic belief in the human ability to secure salvation via good works, their elaborate secret temple ordinances, and their claim to be the only religion with a true priesthood authorized to receive new scripture and other revelations from God. They would effectively call the prospective convert to repent of pride evidenced in Mormon exclusivist claims and their Pelagian belief that salvation required good works in addition to faith. Humility was the remedy and was attained after a stark realization of the falseness of the Mormon heresy. Then the pure and simple gospel of Christ, faith in the only mediator with heaven, would have ground to grow.

As proselytizing approaches are compared, perhaps the strongest distinction was between a missionary who thought Mormons could be convinced by logical means to repudiate their new faith and convert again to the old one, and a missionary who hoped to influence Mormonism without converting its members to mainline Christianity. The former assumed that anyone claiming to have objectively discovered the one true church would hold that belief because of an ideal correspondence between the ancient truth of Christ as witnessed in the Bible and the actual church they had joined. To break the link in that correspondence would show the church to be false. However, as Richard Hughes observed in his comparison of early Mormonism with the nascent evangelical Churches of Christ:

> It is manifestly the case that Joseph Smith searched for a church that was objectively true. But objectivity for Joseph . . . was not a matter of rational and scientific precision, as it was for Alexander Campbell and the Churches of Christ, and as it is for the modern mind today. It rather was a matter of the immediate power of God which carried for Latter-day Saints fully as much objective truth as the Bible carried for Alexander Campbell. When all is said and done, that was the critical difference between the Mormons and the Churches of Christ in nineteenth-century America.[1]

That crucial tension remained between evangelical Protestantism and Mormonism in the twentieth century. While both groups relied heavily on their family religious traditions and their social/temperamental compatibility with their church organizations, the Saints were converted and sustained mainly by their feelings of spiritual confirmation, while the evangelicals were sustained mainly by confidence in their coherent interpretation of the biblical texts.

Mormons believed deity was free to pronounce new instructions to their leaders for each new problem. Theirs was a method of truth tested by coherence to principles and feelings more than correspondence with biblical text or precedent. God's caring love never changed for the Mormons, but His actions and pronouncements were always in motion with the rest of the universe. They put great stock in living prophets. After a few years, even The Book of Mormon was less important than what Brigham Young had spoken. This method allowed a flexibility that strict biblical constructionists found sloppy and dangerous but turned out to be remarkably compatible with American ways of thinking.[2]

---

1. Richard T. Hughes, "Two Restoration Traditions: Mormons and Churches of Christ in the Nineteenth Century," 51.

2. Michael Novak claimed that Max Weber's theory of a Protestant work and save ethic in a rationalized bureaucratic society was insufficient to explain the innovative American business and religious culture. Expanding on Daniel Boorstin's thesis in *The Creators*, Novak argued that Americans sensed themselves

Christian religion generally has been viewed as a method of gaining joyful everlasting salvation. Nutting wanted to simplify and systematize the correct method of salvation through rational arguments supporting scriptural warrants. Protestant doctrines and worldview provided for him such a system. The following is from a letter he wrote to Spalding defending his approach:

> Not a very large proportion of Mormons [know the whole of their doctrine] . . . though I can get some to deny the non-Christian aspects which are inevitable logical parts of the system; and when I think it wise (seldom), I can usually make them acknowledge belief in many gods (if not in Adam as god) *or repudiate the logic they see. There is far more logical connection in their system than we usually think.*[3]

Nutting saw the logical connections between aspects of various Mormon doctrines and assumed the Saints could be brought to see they did have a closed system of theology; and further, that if any part of their system were wrong, then the whole had to be called into question. However, Mormonism was an open, always unfolding system, and Nutting was often frustrated in his attempt. The open system of Mormon revelation—never completely finished—allowed too much room for evasive interpretation of his irrefutable scriptural arguments.[4] Paden was more pragmatic than

---

as creators in the Biblical image of God the creator. See Michael Novak, "The Secularist Faith," 60. Thus, a religion that found doctrinal warrants for continuous revelation and change might reflect the American penchant for new and improved everything. Older than this American spirit was the ancient religious desire for personal progress through resurrection and everlasting life. This, in its Christian form, raised the classic problems of *samsara,* change—even in heaven—without surcease, and *nirvana,* the long-sought end of all self and change, yet without annihilation. Of course, the Mormons pushed this problem as far as they could theologically—continually debating how God might be *perfect,* yet could continually *progress.* Daniel H. Ludlow, ed. *The Encyclopedia of Mormonism* Vol. 2, 465–66. This belief in continuous revelation and change was also perhaps why a Mormon school of theology never developed. Stated extremely, rather than retrieve and systematize what God has been, said, and done, the Latter-day Saints wanted to observe what God will become next as revealed through new revelation.

3. John Danforth Nutting, Personal letter to F. S. Spalding, 1912; emphasis mine.

4. The ninth LDS Article of Faith states, "We believe all that God has revealed, all that He does now reveal, and we believe that He will yet reveal many great and important things pertaining to the kingdom [or system] of God." Mormons juggled a perspectival theory of interpreting truth with an exclusivist claim that

Nutting and more concerned with results of the Mormon system than its logical validity. But he and Spalding were organization men who accomplished things by knowing the right people. Nutting was the most prolific polemical writer of them all, and used persuasive argument as his major tool, distrusting personal relationships. He left Utah about six months each year to raise money in the east and to take a vacation from the fray.

Another impediment to missionary success among Mormons that was perhaps subtler than allegiance to prophetic leadership was their belief that each individual had to receive divine manifestations of truth in response to prayer. Mormons were taught from youth that they needed to be converted to the truthfulness of their own religion. Each was to repeat in his own way the sacred experiences of Moses and Joseph Smith: to kneel and make contact with deity. Open revelation not only allowed for the prophet to receive new scripture, it required each individual to follow the promptings of God in his or her personal life and to confirm directly any new revelation given to the leaders. As in any church of charismatic prophecy, too many prophets can cause confusion. An established system in Mormonism allowed God to speak to anyone, but only to the president of the Church for official church-wide pronouncements. Individuals were charged with gaining a personal confirmation of the prophet's on-going dicta. Conversion was thus never quite finished because God was not yet finished revealing all the truth.

John Nutting argued that all of this emphasis on divine communication to the soul allowed the leaders of the LDS Church to manipulate the naive members to experience self-hypnosis, during which they would hear affirmative answers to their prayers about the truthfulness of Mormonism. Their answers had to be devilish whispers or auto-suggestions.[5] As a conciliator, Spalding would not dare to judge the source of another's answer to sincere prayer, but he could attack the person's interpretation. Thus, he focused on the textual and historical results of Mormon revelation, avoiding the idea that Mormons were self-deceived, or that Satan was answering most prayers in Utah.

Nutting, trying to show by syllogistic proof-texting that grace was more important than works, was just not as interesting as a prophet who was thought to talk with God personally in the temple—at times face to face. Like Gnostics who knew directly from God, Mormons often toyed with

---

theirs was "the only true and living church on face of the whole earth with which [God was] well pleased" (D&C 1:30).

5. John Danforth Nutting, "Present Day Mormonism and Its Remedy."

their opponents' arguments over biblical interpretation. Both Protestants and Mormons would have agreed that rational, historical evidence was necessary to establishing the reality of Jesus Christ's mission as well as Joseph Smith's; but only a personal spiritual confirmation direct from the Holy Ghost was sufficient to bring and maintain conversion to the gospel.

Finally, Protestant forms of polity were represented variously from Nutting's democratic non-denominational Congregationalism, to Paden's representative rule of elected presbyters, to Spalding's top-down authority of bishops. No particular form of polity seemed to provide more or less attraction to potential converts. In the remote Utah setting with so few Protestant church members, none of these polities were strongly evident to the Saints who tended to group them all as Protestants. Mormon Church governance was quite complex and seemed to include all aspects of the Protestant ways, though if forced to choose the Episcopalian notion of higher authority would likely have appealed to many prophet-heeding Saints.

Given the purposes for which this book was written, the theoretical analysis that follows is intended to be useful for formulating actions that can improve the manner in which rival religious groups engage in ideological contests. No parsimonious single theoretical system is adequate to explain the complex dynamics involved in social conflicts, so an array of disciplinary tools, deftly employed, is needed. In this analysis, we compare the idiosyncratic approaches of the three missionaries as occurring more or less simultaneously during the first decades of the twentieth century.

From the view of religion as a social organization, religious groups that have lasted beyond a generation have developed their own complex sub-culture, meshing the doctrinal and ecclesiastical with all other aspects of practical life. This was the case for the Mormon people who had isolated themselves as a sub-group from the United States and from Protestant Christianity. Sub-culture identity theory, then, provides a useful framework to begin to understand the conflict described in this history.[6]

---

6. Similar to "cultural meaning" theories like Gaetano Mosca's theory of political formula and Peter Berger's theory of plausibility structure, "sub-culture identity" theory has been more recently employed by Christian Smith for his study of the sub-culture he calls American Evangelism. Armand Mauss has propounded a similar theory with respect to the Mormons whereby the Saints' strong identity as disreputable critics of the surrounding culture oscillates in counter-point to their weaker identity as respectable citizens. The theory, based in perceived meanings, claims that in pluralistic societies, the religious sub-groups that succeed best created both clear distinctions from and significant tension with other relevant outgroups,

Protestants saw the Mormons as a sub-culture of Anglo-Saxon American Protestant heretics, and Mormons gave Protestants the identical title. Sub-culture identity theory sustains the observation that Protestants and Mormons needed to engage each other for their mutual benefit. Each proved to be mutually useful out-group opponents that provided identity limits without threatening their long-term group viability by persuasive or violent counter-measures. We can learn from American religious history that unless reformers give respectful space for resistance from their critical rivals, resentment and violence eventually result.

In this chapter, the focus is on how these two rivals engaged in their battle. Social psychology, theology, and missiology will be used to categorize the proselytizing methods employed by these opponents.

Social-psychological domain

Conflict Over Scarce Resources?

Traditional conflict theory in the Marxist mode assumes human's battle over scarce resources can apply in several ways to the proselytizing contests.[7] A great irony had occurred in Utah. American Protestant hegemony had, through federal government action, successfully cut off the LDS Church's economic, legal, and political resources in the late 1880s to the point that the Church president felt inspired to capitulate to federal demands on polygamy and Church involvement in politics.[8] However, in twenty years the

---

short of becoming genuinely counter-cultural subversives. Sub-culture identity theory attempts to challenge, or better, envelope, the assumptions of other recent social theories used to explain the sustained success of certain American religions. See Armand L. Mauss, *The Angel and the Beehive: The Mormon Struggle with Assimilation*. Thus, the sheltered enclave theory of Berger and Hunter, the status discontent theory of Hofstadter and Gusfield, the strictness theory of Kelly and Iannaccone, and the competitive marketing theory of Finke and Stark are all appreciated, but considered too limited for the cases of many religious type social groups. See Malcom Magee, review of *American Evangelicalism: Embattled and Thriving*.

7. Political, social, and religious power coercively deployed to produce and distribute scarce resources has been the main focus of conflict theory from Machiavelli to Marcuse. It has been assumed that human nature was fundamentally geared for survival amid a population with limited life resources. Conflict theorists never quibbled over struggles for scarce resources, but about who might win or lose these struggles. James T. Duke, *Conflict and Power in Social Life*, 84.

8. B. H. Roberts, in surprise and dismay at the 1890 Manifesto to end polygamy, wrote he was sure the Saints were ready to endure and hold out much

tables were turned as Utah and the Mormons had attained control over their resources once again. Amid a statewide Mormon hegemony, the Utah Protestants were now the minority supplied with barely enough resources in funding and manpower to sustain their own congregations, let alone provide social and physical ecclesiastical resources to rival those of the large number of tithe-paying Saints in Utah. The LDS Church's material facilities, including financial assistance for needy families, were substantially stronger among the Mormons in their home state. Further, by 1910 the Mormons had increased the quality of their public school system to near parity with the Presbyterian private schools that had upstaged the Saints since the 1870s. The convenient ubiquity of Mormon ward chapels—fully staffed with lay ministers and youth leaders and adequate financial means—made it difficult for the local Protestant clinics to attract adherents based on better ecclesiastical or economic resources. Even so, the difference in material resources was not the main issue of scarcity. Social resources were the true center of conflict—who had the most social capital?

The Mormon proclivity to educate their young in the faith, and to see that they courted and married only Latter-day Saints, effectively snubbed non-Mormons from enjoying deep social friendships that might lead to courtship and marriage. In Utah, even a high-class Episcopalian was an untouchable.[9] Religion is a social organization, and Mormons with

---

longer. See Ronald W. Walker, "B. H. Roberts and the Woodruff Manifesto," 365. Indeed, the brooding question of Mormon social history was blatantly asked by Senator Joseph Bailey during the Smoot hearings: Given the gravity of Mormon attachment to polygamy as a true doctrine of salvation, why would the Mormon people not, just as the ancient Christians, "go to the stake" instead of politically compromise? B. Carmon Hardy, *Solemn Covenant: The Mormon Polygamous Passage*, 38n121, 376; citing Smoot *Proceedings* 1:322. The Mormon prophet who issued the Manifesto said he was inspired to do so to save the temples from being desecrated by escheatment to the gentiles, but there quickly developed two explanations among the Mormon people. First, they were not righteous enough to deserve the support of Heaven in their trial, or second, the Manifesto was only a temporary set-back to allow for stronger Mormon entrenchment among the Gentiles. See Thomas G. Alexander, *Things in Heaven and Earth: The Life of Wilford Woodruff, A Mormon Prophet*, 287; see also Hardy, *Solemn Covenant*, 43–44. Just as to many religious Confederates the South would rise again, so many Mormons planned to practice their true doctrines again.

9. Augustine Kanjamala reported that over half the Roman Catholic converts in India have been Dalits (untouchables) who have found an increase in their social status among Christians of the world if not amid the Hindu population.

their strong family structures had the social resources cornered, forcing Protestants (many of whom were single volunteers to the mission field or single workmen in Utah mines) to gather in smaller enclaves to seek their close friends and potential marriage partners. The deep resentment over this religious caste system cannot be over-estimated. No matter how friendly Mormons tried to be towards visitors to Utah, their rebuff of deeper social ties hurt the pride of Americans who were first class citizens in most other communities. Though denominational lines were quite easily transgressed as Methodists and Presbyterians schooled together, and eventually inter-married, Mormons kept apart from the American denominational system to maintain high numbers of Saint-to-Saint marriages. It should be noted, however, that there was no apparent evidence that this religious conflict in Utah derived from resentments over differences in socio-economic class status.[10]

Aesthetic Temperament and Group Attractiveness

In *The Denominational Society* Andrew Greeley compared "high" and "low" churches in various aspects of religious life, namely theology, ritual, liturgy, organization, clergy, piety, ethics, and worldview.[11] Following Nietzsche, he utilized Apollonian and Dionysian modes to describe gen-

---

See William R. Burrows, *Redemption and Dialogue: Reading Redemptoris Missio and Dialogue and Proclamation*, 201. Even in India where Christian Dalits attempt to assist each other, their economic status can improve. Rex Cooper, an anthropologist doing private research of Mormon conversions in various countries, has found that the Latter-day Saints grow most rapidly and maintain stronger memberships in countries where joining the Mormon Church increases their social status. The largest population of Latter-day Saints in the world as a percentage of total population is in Tonga (approximately fifty-percent vs. the United States two-percent). One is "more Tongan" if one is a Mormon than if not. See personal interview with Rex Eugene Cooper.

10. The socio-economic class distinctions for the Utah Mormons at the turn of the twentieth century seemed to reflect similar stratification lines as those of the evangelical Protestants in the West. Though broadly spread along the bell curve most were between upper-lower and lower-middle class members of society. Eugene A. Nida, "The Roman Catholic, Communist, and Protestant Approach to Social Structure." There were no abnormal differences in the sociological cohorts of age, gender, education, wealth, marriage, or employment. However, Utah did have a disproportionate concentration of English and Scandinavian immigrant stock due to the nineteenth-century Mormon mission success in those places.

11. Andrew M. Greeley, *The Denominational Society*.

eral proclivities within various Christian religions and as well as between different religions. Followers of Apollo tend toward subdued worship without much emotion, enjoying formal, cerebral rites, orderly doctrines, and practices. Dionysians worship through their emotions thriving on informal physical rites, and untamed, exuberant practices. Greeley's later work categorized different believer's images of God to correlate with various behaviors and attitudes, including what might be called religious temperament. For example, a Catholic raised with a pleasant religious image of Mary often believes God is a warm and nurturing being. Contrarily, being raised with a judgmental, patriarchal image of God, an adult often feels at home with a strict authoritarian religious group. Greeley's theory even allows researchers to predict social behaviors like marriage success and career happiness based on different divine images.[12]

Greeley followed on the initial insight of William James that the social-psychological temperament of a person is more compatible with the distinct aesthetic aspects of some religious philosophies and not with others. He also was inspired by David Tracy in his introducing the imagination as integral to rationality and all rigorous disciplines.[13] Greeley extols the imaginative human faculty—the poetic, story making, beauty sensing self—that is the experiential nexus for one's religious doctrines and practices. Harold Bloom has also expounded on the attraction of the imaginative theological narratives of various American religions for their typical members.[14] This aesthetic, temperamental, narrative, imaginative approach to proselytizing differences is a fruitful way toward understanding what occurred when Protestants attempted to engage Mormons in serious proselytizing.

William James distinguished different religious temperaments as the most important influence on the choice of a religious way of life. Temperament trumped any doctrinal beliefs or promised institutional perquisites. James classified two basic temperaments vis-a-vis one's orientation toward the presumed unseen reality of undergirding the universe.

---

12. Andrew M. Greeley, *Religion: A Secular Theory*, 53–70, 97–106.

13. See David Tracy, *The Analogical Imagination: Christian Theology and the Culture of Pluralism*, 28–31. In his *Lectures on Ideology and Utopia*, Paul Ricoeur said "Social imagination is constitutive of social reality itself." See Paul Ricoeur, *Lectures on Ideology and Utopia*, xxxiv. The imagination works as part of the interpretive act in all sentient experience including the rational, emotional, and willful meanings created for inter-personal and inter-group activity. This is also elaborated on in Andrew M. Greely, *Religion as Poetry*.

14. Harold Bloom, *The American Religion: The Emergence of the Post Christian Nation*.

One orientation, "the healthy minded," assumed the cosmos to be a friendly place, appearing basically safe and open to receive human creative activity. This temperament leaned toward optimistic risk-taking and a pluralistic view of reality and God. The other orientation, "the sick soul," sensed that everything was constantly falling short of something better. Unrequited love and injustice hung over creation with bad news almost every hour; in short, the world and the self were broken and needed fixing. Only through re-birth into a higher reality could one get beyond this vale of tears.[15] Considering these two temperaments, Mormons more often seemed healthy minded optimists while Protestants seemed to focus on the pessimistic view that humans should see themselves as sick souls. Given this, there was a social psychological proclivity to avoid communion due to discomfort with each other's naive optimism or morbid pessimism.

Whether their doctrines attracted the temperaments or the temperaments developed the doctrines, there was a remarkable alignment. The practical, romantic Mormons weighed what they thought to be a bland Protestant gospel against what they felt to be a full-bodied faith and found the former wanting, even if the latter was imperfect. Protestant missionaries reported that Mormon converts to Protestantism were primarily those personally disillusioned with the Mormon community, and only secondarily disillusioned with their heretical doctrines. There may have been cases of conversion of Mormon rational idealists who temperamentally belonged in Protestant denominations, but as the missionaries above witnessed, most ex-Mormons became atheists or deists, enjoying no church affiliation after leaving Mormonism.

What stands out in this history is that the solid Apollonian Protestants thought they were dealing with solid Apollonian Mormons who had merely lost their bearings in a heretical society away from mainstream American religious life. They hoped to approach Mormons with rational philosophical and theological arguments to awaken their truth-seeking minds to reality. The missionaries did not grasp that the Latter-day Saints had developed an American blend of disciplined Apollonian industry and passionate Dionysian excess—the former being their exoteric comportment, the latter being their esoteric imaginative life. They were not seekers of truth, but questers for godhood. Their normal routine was a front for a life-long mythical ascent drama with inter-personal sexual love as its centerpiece; and they preferred their own play over the Protestants' theologi-

---

15. William James, *The Varieties of Religious Experience*, 77–154. Originally the Gifford Lectures, 1901 and 1902.

cal argumentation or historical criticism of Mormonism. On this topic of aesthetic temperament, the viewpoint bias is all-important. The lives of Protestant missionaries were not stodgy, but often artfully creative as the speeches and writings of the missionaries attest.[16] Indeed, the rhetoric of frontier missionary work was that of high adventure, especially for those back east who were told of the exploits of their missionaries in the desert.[17]

Group Loyalty and Resistance

There are two social-psychological experiences in any group, one based in desire for loyalty and the other in desire for autonomy. Affirming unity and resisting suspicion must find an acceptable balance for long term group orderly survival.[18] Protestants provided the order of skeptical resistance for their Mormon clients, but were unable to provide an order of loyalty that could compare to the Saints' current loyalties to religious kith and kin. Most of the Mormon converts to Protestantism came from those who had already breached the order of loyalty usually because of inter-personal offenses or incompatibilities before the missionaries arrived, and who were looking for a new social and religious life.

Rodney Stark emphasized rigorous personal sacrifice as the social psychological linchpin for success in religious movements.[19] Mormons and Protestants both understood that fact and both groups were heavily vested in their religious commitments. This made their proselytizing encounters more defensive engagements than honest inquiries that explored doubts as well as affirmations. Their loyalties were compatible with their personal and social identities. That is not to say they believed their religious organizations were above criticism, but even the critical members within either group found an opponent in common in the offensive proselytizers. Further, when under attack, one can claim to be persecuted, which is a

---

16. The writings of each of the ministers contained entertaining and artful allusions. William Paden's speeches and sermons were especially poetic. See for example Paden's 1900 and 1901 speeches to the Ladies' Aid Society in Salt Lake City.

17. Francis C. Kelly, *The Story of Extension*.

18. I derived these categories of loyalty and skepticism obliquely from Paul Ricoeur's categories of hermeneutical retrieval and suspicion. Loyalty rather than retrieval seemed to reflect better my observations of social psychological behaviors in groups.

19. Rodney Stark, "Why Religious Movement Succeed or Fail: A Revised General Model," 134–37. This theory is controversial, but it is a healthy amendment to rational choice theory that emphasizes the current material benefits of affiliation.

sign of any powerful religion or movement. Mormons found a way to feel like they were forced to sacrifice by enduring Protestant opprobrium without having to actually sacrifice their lives, friends, and families as the ancient martyrs were required to do. Protestants used Mormon heretics as a firm border that gave shape to Protestant fissiparous diversity.

The relationship of Mormon and Protestant loyalty and skepticism within their respective religions also deserves attention. Although the Saints were subject to prophetic authorities who might speak *ex cathedra* from time to time, their theologies were not so systematically orthodox that an individual was kept from skeptical speculation. As long as one did not criticize the leadership publicly, they could believe a wide range of possible interpretations. Small though it was, Mormonism retained a measure of tolerance for those loyal to church authority and ritual though somewhat deviant in their personal beliefs.[20] Both Protestants and Mormons might be slightly critical of their own religions, but it was the criticism of loyal insiders with no second thoughts about their desire to remain within their religious communities. Exceptions to this had already left the Mormon fold before being proselytized by the Protestants, and were often allies with them in their opposition to Mormonism, though rarely converts to any other religion.[21] Mormons called their lapsed members "inactives," or "Jack Mormons," and those that actively condemned Mormonism after leaving it, "apostates."[22] The apostates were often helpful witnesses for the

---

20. On this point Richard Neuhaus has said, "Differences that in Protestantism produce myriad denominational divisions are accommodated by Catholicism within an expansive understanding of the rule of faith (*regula fidei*) and ecclesial communion, with the latter anchored in the bishops who are in communion with the bishop of Rome." Richard Neuhaus, "On Catholic Catholicism," 80. This is the evident genius of religious orders wherein, for instance, "Franciscan can break with Franciscans and Jesuits can condemn Dominicans without the question ever arising as to whether they are members of the one Church. Of course they are."

21. Franklin Spalding reported, "A good many have apostatized from the Mormon Church, but few have been persuaded to join other religious societies. [Afterward] all interest in religion ceases." See Franklin Spencer Spalding, "Our Church in Mormonland," 38. In the twenty-first century interest at least in institutional religious affiliation has decreased substantially among millennials.

22. Anson Shupe, scholar of new religious movements, uses the term apostate like the Mormons used it, for someone who is involved in a counter-movement after leaving a religion. However, many sociologists of religion use the term more generally to mean one who has withdrawn from a religious group. James A. Beckford, *Cult Controversies: The Social Response to New Religious Movements*, 140–41.

Protestant cause outside Utah, but riled the local Saints too much to be suitable proselytizers because they were viewed as vindictive traitors.

Both Protestants and Mormons believed that divine truth, once known and/or experienced, was irresistible to good-hearted intelligent folks. If one were to leave a religion, it was because they had never really known it as true or were a foul traitor to the truth. Both Protestants and Mormons agreed among themselves that almost all who did convert to Protestantism were already disaffected members who were looking for some radical alternative to their prior religion—not ruling out agnostic non-affiliation, experimental spiritualism, or atheism. In any case, it was black and white rhetoric: you could leave naively or traitorously, but never intelligently or honestly. This rhetoric was problematic when thinking of converts from other religions. Were they sincere and intelligent folks, or dupes and turncoats? Succinctly, we all live in groups and any convert to a new group appears as an apostate to the group left behind. People subtly feel that adult converts are tainted with disloyalty even if they have come to the right side.[23]

Lacking the authority of pope or prophet and relying on consensual unity of scriptural interpretation for their solidarity, Protestants developed a denominational system of authorized schisms to allow for deviancy. Systematic theologies of strict scriptural readings and distinct ecclesiastical governing styles (Episcopal, Presbyterian, Congregational) narrowed the room for deviancy. Among Protestants, it was not considered apostasy to join another Protestant denomination that better reflected one's beliefs about the scriptures and church government. If considered as a single body comprising separate denominations, then Protestantism was as open as Catholicism and Mormonism. However, this fungibility of membership never looked so benign at the ground level. No council of churches could or would feign equivalency to the twelve apostles' authority like the Roman Catholics and Mormons did with their highest authorities.

Social Solidarity vs. Doctrinal Unity

Antonio Gramsci maintained that the cultural sphere must be won before political hegemony can be secured. Arguably, religious hegemony can likewise only be secured when the cultural sphere has been won.[24] Solidarity is the main attribute of a culture. Religious programs that aim to

---

23. Jesse Herbert Dennis, *The Work of the Church Among the Mormons*, 32.

24. My thoughts on this subject coalesced after reading Jan Nederveen Pieterse, *Christianity and Hegemony: Religion and Politics on the Frontiers of Social Change*, 22–24.

change the world need to win one culture at a time by somehow becoming the major influence on cultural solidarity. Missionaries have traditionally assumed that a person comes to a belief about the ultimate purpose of life first, and then adopts a religion coherent with that purpose. Thus, the rhetoric of theological persuasion was the main method of conversion for most Christian missionaries.[25] However, modern cultural linguistic analysis shows that both speech-acts and non-verbal acts are equally productive of meanings. Therefore, recent missionaries have taken a more inductive approach to broad cultural observations before proclaiming or experientially manifesting their truth. They have hesitated to translate religious meanings in advance of a personal immersion in the culture of potential converts. To immerse is not necessarily to saturate, however, and the level of empathic understanding of missionaries can differ greatly. Knowing a language never equaled understanding the religion of a people—and this worked both ways for the potential converts as well as the missionaries. In Utah, Mormons and Protestants spoke the same language and came from similar cultural backgrounds, so they believed they understood the full meanings of each other's communications about religion. But they rarely seemed to engage at a level of mutual understanding that allowed for serious sharing of the fullness of each other's religious beliefs and experiences.

The Protestant belief in simplicity created a cultural change problem of subtracting without replacing. Spalding sensed this more than his partners, and hoped to subtract very little, leaving Mormon culture intact. Nevertheless, as anthropologist Paul Hiebert has observed:

> Protestants in their rebellion against ritualism have often overlooked its importance in the maintenance of faith and the transmission of religious beliefs. Too often missionaries have been guilty of destroying a people's traditional symbols and rituals without providing them with meaningful substitutes.[26]

For Mormons, their sacred ritual ordinances were order-yielding activities around which quotidian life was arranged. Further, though they believed each soul was personally responsible for its salvation, their ordinances inevitably included their families and friends. Thus, personal salvation was attained for inter-personal enjoyment. Protestant individualism with Jesus

---

25. This method was warranted by the original apostles' logic in Acts 17:2, 18:4, Romans 10:14, and 1 Peter 3:15, in which reasoning over the correct interpretation of the scripture, or over the ramifications of seeing Jesus resurrected, was the preferred means of proselytizing.

26. Paul G. Hiebert, "Introduction: Mission and Anthropology," xxi.

seemed too sparse to fill the social void that conversion would have created for the Mormon.

One wonders what would have been persuasive for conversion of a person who was content with his or her religion? Martin Marty reported this story about the barbarian noble Radbod of Frisia who was a converted Christian king of a pagan state in the area of modern France: at his baptism, he asked the attending bishop whether he would meet his ancestors in Heaven to which the bishop replied "no." Wherewith, the old king stepped back out of the font, preferring to live in Hell with his great ancestors than share Heaven with lower-class persons like the bishop.[27] Joseph Smith in like manner said, "Let me be resurrected with the Latter-day Saints, whether I ascend to heaven or descend to hell, or go any other place. And if we go to hell, we will turn the devils out of doors and make a heaven of it.... What do we care where we are, if the society be good? ... Friendship is the grand fundamental principle of Mormonism."[28]

Though the Saints formed a young religion, they believed it was the oldest of all, and quickly developed a mythos of deep loyalty to their traditions and predecessors who had gone before. Of course, they had never heard of the apostolic fathers, or saints of the Middle Ages, and they had just barely figured the Reformation into their sacred past. The Protestants who knew the serial church history saw Mormons as deluded by their myths that rejected the facts of history. They never quite addressed "Mormon time" as Jan Shipps, a Methodist scholar living years among Mormons, came to understand it: as sacred time that vaulted over eighteen hundred years of Western civilization to make sense of dispensational revelatory breakthroughs from Adam to the present day.[29]

Anti-religious Proselytizing

While Nutting and Paden would have preferred Mormonism to collapse, and Spalding would have liked it to reform, the polemics these ministers engaged in were usually based on fact as they saw it. Only rarely did they pass on fabricated rumors or blatant distortions of Mormon doctrines and practices. Though for political, economic, and religious reasons,

---

27. Martin E. Marty, *The One and the Many: America's Struggle for the Common Good*, 7, 685–719.

28. Andrew F. Ehat and Lyndon W. Cook, eds., *The Words of Joseph Smith*, 228; Joseph Fielding Smith, ed., *Teachings of the Prophet Joseph Smith*, 316.

29. Jan Shipps, *Mormonism: The Story of a New Religious Tradition*, 51–53.

some citizens of Utah had been and still were "anti-Mormon" in the truest sense of the term, and Nutting and Paden did become involved in some low anti-Mormon hyperbole, albeit for high motives. Primarily, the missionaries desired to save souls, which from their viewpoint justified offensive eristics. Of course, when under attack, group members care little about the motive of one's adversary. Thus, the tone of much religious polemical engagement feels offensively negative. I have found it useful to compare the Protestant work in Utah with the anti-cult activity later in the twentieth century to show the strong distinction between missionary work and anti-religious action.[30]

Using Edward Shils's center/periphery theory of social differentiation, combined with Ernst Troeltsch's theory of social organization of religious groups, Anson Shupe has made another categorical distinction between normal proselytizing and anti-cult missionary work.[31] His analysis of American religious history shows the following standard tactics have been used to slow or kill growth of new religious movements. I summarize his findings as follows: Anti-cult practitioners a) use cult apostates to reveal their dark motives and deeds; b) claim a take-over conspiracy evidenced by secret rites and rapid growth; c) cast guilt-by-association with well-known, norm-perverting, marginal groups; d) attempt legal repression of cult practice or proselytizing; e) discredit the cult leaders, showing they

---

30. Louis Midgley has provided a brief history and up to date analysis with copious bibliographical notes of anti-Mormon proselytizing activity—the countercult culture of Protestantism that was born at the end of the nineteenth century and is still quite alive at the beginning of the twenty-first century. See Louis Midgley, "Anti-Mormonism and the Newfangled Countercult Culture," 271–340. Mormons, Moonies, Masons, Catholics, New Agers, and other new religious movements are the typical targets for this effort to cleanse the world of heretical or devilish cults. Midgley's critique is that of a Latter-day Saint political scientist.

31. Troeltsch presented a developmental group theory of religion in three stages. First, the cult, a small group that commenced with some unique religious experience or charismatic founder seeing itself as separate from society; then the sect, a larger group that developed traditions and leadership based on the original experience or the cult founder but with more resources and more acceptable social integration in society; and finally the church, a large group with long-standing traditions and leaders that have gained respect generally and been integrated into normal society. See Ernst Troeltsch, *The Social Teachings of the Christian Churches*. This scheme has been replaced with the theory of new religious movements (NRMs) that allows fluidity between Troeltsch's more rigid categories, and avoids the negative connotation of cult or sect.

cannot be trusted; f) issue enough indictments that the public thinks there must be some fire from all the smoke.[32] Other analysts add that anti-cult strategies avoid discussing anything positive about their adversary, claiming, for example, that any conversions are based on hypnotism or trickery that captivates the converts and makes them helpless victims. Often, they call for and urge vigilante teams to liberate those who have been brain-washed into believing they need no liberation.[33]

Anti-cult activity has sometimes resulted in an unintended collusion between antagonists. The interaction allows the new religious movement to attain recognition as a counter-cultural deviant that is being persecuted, while the anti-cult workers attain recognition for their no non-sense orthodox stand against deviancy.[34] The identity of both groups has been vitalized by the interaction; and if the cult can withstand the negative onslaught long enough to attain name brand status, it might eventually become a legitimate religious group. Such anti-cult methods were used in late-nineteenth-century anti-Mormonism, anti-Catholicism, and anti-Masonry movements.[35]

Though some analysts might consider the missionaries to Utah deprogrammers of Mormon cult brain-washing, the model only works if one believes the missionaries really believed that 400,000 Latter-day Saints had been mesmerized into servile submission over two generations. Paden and Nutting were not opposed to using some anti-cult tactics to embarrass what they believed to be duplicitous leaders, but they believed Mormons to be in possession of their faculties. To them, Mormons had learned the wrong doctrines, but had not been brainwashed under duress. Nor did the Saints look to enjoy much benefit from public exposure as a cult in 1910. They had received all the notoriety they needed for name brand recogni-

---

32. Anson Shupe, Jr., *The Anti-cult Movement in America*.

33. See James R. Lewis, "Apostates and the Legitimation of Repression: Some Historical and Empirical Perspectives on the Cult Controversy," 390–92. This analysis eerily implicates the U.S. Government as potentially anti-cultist in its approach to the David Koresh affair in Waco, Texas. Brainwashing and group hypnotism were the techniques of choice to explain Joseph Smith's ability to get converts and signed witnesses to the golden plates. See Fawn M. Brodie, *No Man Knows My History*, 77.

34. Annette P. Hampshire and James Beckford, "Religious Sects and the Concept of Deviance," 211.

35. David Brion Davis, "Some Themes of Counter-Subversion: An Analysis of Anti-Masonic, Anti-Catholic, and Anti-Mormon Literature," 216–22.

tion during the prior twenty-five years, and were hoping to be viewed as normal American citizens.[36]

The Mutual Assumption of Bad Faith

If the object of social-psychological group therapy can be summed up in a word it would be "trust." The therapist knows that strangers or opponents are suspicious of each other and cannot build trust until they desire to risk granting each other the benefit of the doubt. This also applies to conflicts over religion. A frequent reciprocal allegation made by the Protestants and Mormons was that their words were true, but their hearts were wrong. They quoted Isaiah at each other accusatorily: "This people draw near unto me with their mouth, and their lips do honor me, but have removed their heart far from me" (Isa. 29:13). This impugned the integrity of the other's religious life. With both opponents assuming bad faith as the foundation for the other's position, little wonder proselytizing rarely moved either side.

We can surmise from the record of their conflict that many Mormons and Protestants believed their opponents who rejected their teachings were ignorant, lazy, cowardly, duped, or evil. William Paden seemed to assume the Saints were poorly educated folk from the lower strata of society whose only hope was an education that would lift those who had the mental capacity to see the silliness of their current religious position and convert to something better— preferably Presbyterianism. Franklin Spalding seemed to believe that the Saints were intelligent and sincere in most things, but imprisoned their trusting loyalty to a few religious traditions that kept them from true Christian salvation. They were dupes of their upbringing, and afraid to face the truth that would force them to admit the faults of past leadership. John Nutting, while accepting the possibility that Paden's and Spalding's above judgment might be correct in some cases, also seemed to believe that the devil was alive and well among the Mormon people, and that many Saints had chosen to reject the true Christian religion for the evil delights of materialism which Mormonism rationalized under the evil whisperings of diabolical influences on the hearts and minds of those who preferred wickedness to truth.

As we finally review the missionary methods of Nutting, Paden, and Spalding we see a pattern of unintended bad faith that developed between

---

36. See Thomas G. Alexander, *Mormonism in Transition: A History of the Latter-day Saints, 1890–1930* for the history of the Mormon reactive move toward harmonious relations with the American people after the years of trauma.

each of them and their Mormon prospects. Nutting's approach allowed that his hearers might have a diabolical resistance to the truth of the divine Spirit. Paden's approach emphasized how their leaders and traditions duped the people. Spalding, as empathetic as he tried to be, assumed that the rustic Mormons were just not smart enough to see the light, so he put all hope in persuading the few intellectuals among Saints to lead the rest to modern theological views. None of these approaches were complementary towards their prospective converts.

Though there was no violence between opponents in this history, there was not much respect between noble adversaries either. Given their belief in a singular economy of God that allowed sincere seekers to find the truth, there seemed to be no logical alternative available for the opponents to judge each other in a positive way when they rejected the truth and refused to convert. At the conclusion of this chapter, I will address the difficulty that assumptions of bad faith create in religious conflicts, and suggest a possible alternative that allows an evangelical missionary to think of one's opponent as intelligent, aware, brave, and good-hearted, even if he or she has rejected clear and adequate proselytizing efforts.

Theological Domain

Monotheism, Trinitarianism, and Henotheism

Theologically speaking, the Mormon/Protestant argument over the eternal non-created existence of matter, intelligent beings and God(s) was the most profoundly important. However, in the early twentieth century, the most salient theological difference seemed to be the issue of polytheism—demoting God by giving him a social life among divine persons in the Godhead and beyond.

All three missionaries seemed to agree theologically on their differences with Mormon perspectives regarding the fundamental nature of deity; and all three felt compelled to apologetically engage the Saints to persuade a conversion of belief about God. The issue of monotheism and polytheism was a prime doctrinal difference.

The Christian doctrine of the divine incarnation in Jesus of Nazareth created a difficulty for the strict monotheists among the Christians. The doctrine of the triune God developed as an attempt to avoid espousing even a limited notion of polytheism. The issue of superiority between the three aspects of a singular deity was ultimately settled by the irrelevance of the question because one God is one God. All other so-called deities were figments of unenlightened or wrongly inspired human imagination. Had the Latter-day Saints rested with three separate deities united in one purpose in the Christian Godhead, evangelicals might have winked at this social Trinitarian heresy; but the notion of potentially billions of deities existing in henotheistic relationships was just too far from conventional belief.

The perceived difference in doctrines of deity was substantial enough to claim that the religions believed in and worshiped different kinds of Gods, despite their common usage of biblical monotheistic vocabulary. Their proselytizing conflict, in light of the differing fundamental notions of deity, took the form of a superiority contest between their divinities. In the end, one God would eventually prove to be the highest or the only God. Until that ultimate end, the two groups attempted to show signs of their deity's superiority by other means. Because the standard format of proof-texting from Biblical sources continually ended with interpretive disagreements, it became evident that other methods than textual argument would be required to prove their interpretations right or wrong. The authority of the interpreter became the main issue. Resorting to the New Testament assertion that by his or her fruits we could know a true or false prophet, the missionaries tried to compare the observable fruits of allegedly divine influence in the present lives of believers. Protestant missionaries attempted to display how the true God helped true believers by increasing their levels of social and personal well-being in terms of low crime rates, material prosperity, better health, and higher education rates. However, since God let the sun shine on both the righteous and the wicked very often, these signs might admittedly be coincidental, and thus not sufficiently convincing of divine authority.

Spiritual gifts from deity to humanity were thought to be more impressive, as it would be difficult to label frequent and notorious repetitions of miracles as being merely coincidental. Frequent and notorious was the problem. A science of accounting for miracle contests has never been developed. Complicating the matter further, both Mormons and Protestants agreed that the devil could perform miracles to fool humans to follow false paths. Nevertheless, Mormons tended to look for charismatic gifts as divine authoritative warrants.[37] They quietly looked for miraculous healings, visions, angelic visitations, and prophecies to manifest among their own people and to accompany anyone else who claimed divine authority. Latter-day Saints tended to rely on personal events that were reported privately by the parties involved, with rumors often in the air regarding their

---

37. The seventh LDS Article of Faith states: "We believe in the gift of tongues, prophesy, revelation, visions, healing, interpretations of tongues, and so forth."

prophet's latest communication with the Almighty, or reports of helpful visits from angels or the dead being raised. Protestants had many years earlier found that miracles needed authoritative interpretation as much as texts. While not opposed to or unfamiliar with charismatic gifts, they found the intervening hand of their God displayed in their frequent and notorious ability to raise funds to build hospitals and schools staffed with angelic nurses, who healed many a Mormon, or teachers, who revealed visions of U.S. history, scientific laws, or sound Christian teachings to those in dark ignorance. It was as if the grace and works dichotomy were reversed with respect to proving the true God's authoritative presence. Mormons talked of and practiced more spiritual charisma; the Protestants proved they were real Christians by material works that served the community.

Still, neither convinced the other of their God's prowess by these methods. Indeed, they could not even admit they were trying to do so because any contest of comparison might admit they considered the other's deity legitimate enough to warrant comparison with theirs. The contest and the results can only be sensed by reading their private reports, and by observing their incessant willingness to devote their lives and resources trying to convert each other to the true Christianity—meaning the real God.

Revealing True Deity

Remarkably, all agreed that proselytizing was *de rigor*, but they disagreed on the persuasive power of different methods of proselytizing.[38] Though charismatic Protestants abounded, the evangelical missionaries in Utah were college-graduated ministers that followed an Enlightenment approach to apologetics that relied on rational argument and observable facts to support their spiritual convictions. Mormons engaged in the polemical discussions but were ultimately moved by what they felt and observed as spiritual power, no matter if the argument was won or lost. The question was not so much, "are you following God's lawful order set out in the scriptures," as it was "do you demonstrate the power of God now like the ancients did?" If Protestant missionaries had been healers and speakers in tongues and visionary charismatics, they would have caused great interest and perhaps converted a few Mormons who were feeling that their

---

38. A fine case study of this problem of intelligible criteria for adjudicating truth claims or experiences in an African/European missionary encounter in which a dichotomy of natural and supernatural realms did not clearly exist for the Africans was reported in William Reyburn, "The Missionary and Cultural Diffusion."

own people had become lax in using the spiritual gifts. However, it is too easy to say that the Protestants sent the wrong team to Utah or that they should have sent the Pentecostals to fight fire with fire instead of conservative evangelicals that tried to pour cold water on the fervent Saints. One senses that the Saints and Protestants had already decided against their opponents regardless of any evidence that might be provided.

Though it was never explicitly claimed, one senses that while the evangelicals and Saints both were awaiting the proof of their God's superiority at the final eschaton, they desired at the turn of the twentieth century to bolster their patience with an early henotheistic victory measured by growth in their membership—mainly through converts. Was not the human heart the true battleground for religion after all? Both Protestants and Mormons were under pressure to show a domestic success as the former was being diluted by religious pluralism generally, and the latter had been refused the right fully to practice their religion in America. With no pillar of fire marking the divine presence among them for all to see, proselytizing success was one way of providing a faith sustaining proof that their Lord was the Most High God. Proselytizing failure, however, could not be accounted to the impotence of God, nor could the sincere missionary be blamed. That left the potential convert as the culprit.

Missiological Domain

Categories of Proselytizing Strategies

To further distinguish the differences between the missionaries in this study, I will employ a typology of proselytizing strategic methods that I have assembled from scholars of missiology who have developed a critical understanding of social science and theology in the study of missionary work.[39] Modern missiology, like ethno-methodology, is usually inductive,

---

39. The cross-disciplinary aspect of this analysis is evident, along with the strain between generalizing and particularizing that typifies social science. This book combines history, theology, social theory, and social science to grasp a more complete understanding. I want to make clear why comparative personality analysis is not a part of this study. Without diminishing the persuasive influence of personalities and unique interpersonal relationships, I chose not to employ the typology of Raven and Kruglianski, which lists seven types of interpersonal power used in persuasion that Newton Malony has already applied to proselytizing strategies. See B. H. Raven, "Conflict and Power," 180–88; H. Newton Malony, "The Psychology of Proselytism," 136–37. This analysis tends

extrapolating theory from case studies. A cluster of missiological categories from several missiological case studies will serve to typify the methods and purposes displayed by missionaries of most religious persuasions. There is no intention of claiming diametrical opposition between the symmetrical conceptual poles of these categories. They form a continuum of primary purpose that distinguish the typical group motives. They are as follows:

Conciliator-Confrontationist.[40] The conciliator attempts to maintain feelings of mutual acceptance during the proselytizing process, even if the missionary must compromise the message to do so. A confrontationist attempts to overpower the potential convert with persuasive comparative evidence that conversion to a new allegiance is the only appropriate step.

Diffusionist-Communalist.[41] The diffusionist desires to spread the word broadly making individual conversions without concern for the local culture, and thinks a short-term personal contact is sufficient to warn or teach. A communalist believes a long-term community support system is required to teach adequately, and aims to establish an ongoing organization that changes the culture in the long run.

Romantic-Rationalist.[42] A romantic seeks for imaginative possibilities and favors charisma over legalism, using cognition as one tool, but not as a rational truth template to measure various incommensurate realities. A

---

to be so conditioned on particular situations that it has less potency in making categorical generalizations. Of course, this "inter-personal uniqueness factor" makes all social scientific analysis subject to contextual understanding. Raven and Kruglanski's power types are as follows: coercion, the use of harmful threats; connection, the influence of important personal relations; expert, the skill of problem solving or task performance; information, the use of new knowledge or logical argument; legitimate, the influence of office or position of status; referent, the force of personal attractiveness or social charm; reward, the reinforcement of positive incentives or gifts. Applying these categories quickly to this study, except for information power and perhaps expert power with respect to teaching schools, the Protestant missionaries felt overpowered by their Utah opponents.

40. A clear case of this analytical dimension is in the International Bulletin of Missionary Research: Clinton Bennett, "Victorian Images of Islam," 115–19.

41. For an example of this dimension see David R. Heise, "Prefatory Findings in the Sociology of Missions," 49–58; and Jon Miller, "Missions, Social Change, and Resistance to Authority: Notes toward an Understanding of the Relative Autonomy of Religion," 29–50.

42. The emphasis on "romantic" immediate revelation versus "rationalist" interpretation of scripture is striking in Hughes, "Two Restoration Traditions."

rationalist is one who seeks after the perfect form of things, and assumes that orderly cognition reflects an ideal reality beyond the constant flux.

Colonizer-Assimilator.[43] The colonizer works to alter the permanent cultural behaviors of another assuming religious attitudinal change will follow cultural change. An assimilator is satisfied with attitudinal changes, and does not attempt to alter cultural habits. The few habits that need to change will do so if the religious attitude is correct.

Typifying Nutting

John Nutting was a rationalist of the right, using Bible-based formulas that would bring one to Christ and personal salvation—the Lord willing. He followed a diffusionist method compatible with his belief that he was not responsible to convert people, only to testify strongly to the Word of God. God would graciously persuade those who were predestinated to become true Christians. Nutting was also a confrontationist, and an anti-cultist and an energetic Jamesean twice-born sick soul. His concept of God was that of a strict disciplinarian with mercy shown to those who have earned it by repentance or those whom God chooses to save for reasons of His own.

The Utah Gospel Mission plan was to convert souls in rural towns on their own turf. Rather than convert Mormons into denominational Christianity, the wagon missionaries converted them to their view of Christ and allowed them to maintain their cultural identities as Mormons. Their nomadic life allowed for no established community churches, but their God cared mainly about the state of an individual's heart and thought church hierarchies and social life were extraneous to true worship. Focus on scripture study alone was a pious act. No beautiful buildings or artwork stirred the evangelical soul of Nutting's converts. They had submitted to God's grace, and that was sufficient. Nutting's goal could be achieved by the prospects merely hearing the Word. For him, the fundamental conversion moment occurred only after someone was convinced they were innate sinners and needed Christ's saving grace. This required a deconstruction of the Mormon idea of human nature and man's relationship to God. Nutting had to attack and prove Mormon doctrine wrong before a Mormon would feel convicted of being hopelessly lost without Christ.

---

43. The example and analysis of this dimension is clear in Clayton G. MacKenzie, "Demythologizing the Missionaries: A Reassessment of the Functions and Relationships of Christian Missionary Education under Colonialism," 45–65.

Whatever was instrumental in converting Mormon souls was good for them. Thus, anti-cult strategies were the best hope of awakening them to their wretched state and leading them to ultimate heavenly bliss. Mormons were asleep and needed to be awakened by any loud means before it was too late. Timeliness was crucial to Nutting's thought. God had a time limit for saving souls. Nutting's image of a strict God was emphasized by the idea that those heathens and Mormons who died without being saved were damned in hell. God's judgment was only assuaged by the certain knowledge that Christ had interceded for one's soul before the bar of God. The saved evangelicals were trying to inoculate as many Mormons as possible from the coming scourge of God's wrath on those who had not confessed Christ.

Nutting's personal conversion approach focused on converting individuals by personal witnessing door to door, preaching at small town tent meetings, and distributing Bible tracts by hand or mail. The goal was to bring a change of church affiliation—exchanging old Mormonism for a new Protestant identity. The individual, once converted and saved, could stay in Utah as a quiet example or move on to a more Protestant civilization, usually in California. Interestingly, given his strategy, a convert might privately sign up for Nutting's Utah Gospel Mission salvation and even remain in the closet as an inactive Mormon among their family and associates. Nutting's approach allowed the local culture to function, so his confrontational proselytizing directness was less threatening to the community. On one level, Nutting could be trusted because he openly proselytized the way Mormons did, and he required so little of his converts that they did not appear different from less-active Saints.

Typifying Paden

William Paden desired to eliminate a false religious institution. He hoped to prove to Mormon adherents that their leaders were false prophets and their doctrines erroneous. Further, he supported the nineteenth-century plan to teach the true gospel and American culture to the Saints' children in Presbyterian private schools. Paden hoped that humbled and enlightened younger Saints would fall gratefully into Presbyterian arms, the old Mormon leaders would be left with no congregations, and the institution would collapse. Paden came to Utah as a warrior with a confrontational-changer role. He was an anti-cultist, and a concentrator. Paden's Utah plan was based on a theological assumption that Mormon heresy required a change in the Mormon culture. He chose to accomplish this by a confrontationist approach. For constructive proselytizing results, Paden tried to destroy the old cultural foundation before building anew.[44] In this respect, his followed the way of anti-cult missionaries today. His method of proselytizing his potential converts was indirect—teaching Protestant ideals to Mormon students in Protestant schools while they learned about American democracy and mores; and teaching Mormon associates by exemplary Christian service honestly offered to needy individuals in the community.[45]

He was also proud of being part of a great organization with the pedigree that the Presbyterian provided. Indeed, as a confrontational-changer, he tried to give Mormons whose world was Utah a broader perspective, namely that Mormonism was a small cult compared to the Presbyterian Church and Protestantism generally. He thought Mormons would be wise enough to see what the majority of Christians saw, to disenthrall themselves from their parochial reliance on self-interested religious leaders, and to join a mainstream denomination that would put their zeal to better Christian use.[46]

As a concentrator, Paden wanted to establish a permanent Presbyterian Church presence, believing that a church helped save souls and that sacraments were important to salvation. The erosion of Protestantism in general, and Presbyterianism specifically in Utah, bothered him greatly. Nutting's non-denominationalism kept him immune from the institutional pressure Paden felt to competitively perform as a church. Paden felt like an executive in charge of a territory under scrutiny from the home office. He took responsibility to warn as many as possible about Mormonism. His warning went primarily to Protestants who might meet Mormon missionaries in their homes in the east. His was a broader, public relations approach because he observed little return on direct proselytizing of Saints in Utah.

---

44. Paden truly believed that some cultural disruption was required to get the Saints' attention. Paden was not alone in this tactic. Another turn of the century missionary (a Jesuit) speaking of his work in Zambia, said his goal was to create disharmony in the indigenous culture in order to bring it to the truth. That meant publicly criticizing the local gods. Paden would have agreed with the Jesuit in this case: "If Christ be the Son of God, no heathen deity can be of God . . . there can be no compromise between Him and false deities . . . the Catholic's form of Christianity is the only true form and the only true religion. This is the power behind the Catholic Missioner." See Brendan P. Carmody, *Conversion and Jesuit Schooling in Zambia*, 26.

45. Mark T. Banker, *Presbyterian Missions and Cultural Interaction in the Far Southwest, 1850–1950*, 163–65; and Colin B. Goodykoontz, *Home Missions on the American Frontier*, 403.

46. "Minutes of the Synod of Utah," Fragments and Paden notes.

Wanting to make the Saints into Presbyterians, he faced a tougher conversion task, because Mormons had to overtly join Presbyterianism in front of their disapproving neighbors. They had to publicly turn traitor for Paden, and Mormons were just not disposed to retro-conversion back to the Protestantism that their parents had left, considering it an inferior form of Christianity. As a theologian, his concept of the divine was not easy to assess because his language in polemical writings differed so greatly from his beautiful sermons and private personal writings. However, his doctrine supported the absolute sovereignty of God and the loving mercy of that Sovereign.

His propositional truth arguments against Mormonism were so polemical that few individuals would heed his reason without sensing its passionate bias. Thus, without individual "clients" his modis operandi was to employ the power of social and government institutions to attack the credibility of Mormonism as an institution. Paden also attempted to build a stronger institutional presence in Utah to impress the Saints with the size and power (spiritual and temporal) of the Presbyterian Church.[47] He hoped to effect a change in local mores and ultimately religion by building schools and churches that would outshine the Mormon counterparts.[48] He was a cultural colonizer par excellence.

Typifying Spalding

Spalding was a conciliator and a communalist who desired to change a few of the most offensive doctrines and practices of Mormonism by influencing the Saints' intellectual leaders to consider where Joseph Smith was—and was not—truly inspired. He hoped that over time the leaders would stop emphasizing the erroneous doctrines and replace them with orthodox correctness. Once done, Mormons were welcome as any new Christian denomination with a rare blend of communal and industrial social ethics.[49]

Spalding, a socialist desiring a peaceful economic revolution in the world, was torn between admiration for the social and economic collective

---

47. Heise, "Prefatory Findings," 49–59.
48. William M. Paden, *The Holland Reminder*.
49. Spalding employed an approach often used by the Mormon missionaries—namely, claiming the potential convert could keep all the truth that he or she had gained from the prior religion while adding thereto. Spalding was less demanding than the Mormons too, allowing converts to remain in their religion with some modified beliefs. The Saints' focus on exclusive religious authority and saving ordinances required converts to leave their old unauthorized church for the only truly authorized one.

experimentation of the Mormons and disappointment at their unwillingness to think freely and act except in lockstep with church leadership. He was sympathetic to their notion of setting up a new world community that integrated their spiritual and economic lives in Utah, but was dismayed that its foundation was largely false myth.[50] He was a conciliator-changer who established a long-term friendly relationship with those he wished to influence. He shunned anti-cult strategies. His concept of God seemed that of a patient, benevolent parent who would not destroy all the non-Christians. If God could be patient with the sincere Mormons, why could the missionaries not be so? As a high churchman on the mountain desert frontier, he saw the irony of his humble position, using humor to soften almost every communication. He never planned to demolish Mormonism, but thought it would collapse as soon as its historical claims of special revelation were disproved. Nutting and Paden considered his attitude a hindrance to their work, a backbiting critique used by the opposition to discredit their efforts. He, in turn, was convinced anti-cult work would only cause greater solidarity among Mormons. He needed the Saints to relax non-defensively for his intellectual persuasions to be considered.

Spalding's approach to his prospects via polite debate did catch the attention of some Mormon intellectuals, but he died before he could follow up in a personal way with students that he might have influenced in Salt Lake City. He thought that to change Mormonism, he would have to convert its intellectuals. To gain the ear of the latter, he made public statements defending Mormon morality and integrity, then wrote criticisms of Joseph Smith that intellectual Saints would take seriously.

---

50. As Jon Miller points out in his study of Christian social movements, the Mormons were another of a long chain of those who felt small agrarian based communities were the ideal way of life, Martin Luther being a prime theoretical exponent. See Jon Miller, *The Social Control of Religious Zeal*.

CHAPTER TEN

Contestational Rivalry Without Coercion or Violence

Practical Results of the Utah Missions

In analyzing this religious conflict in the United States, a public health metaphor of a plague is useful. Each opponent sees the other as carrying a plague of false religion that might overrun the world if not checked by doctors of the truth. Latter-day Saints had interpreted the past 1800 years as a spiritual devastation for Christianity. They believed the Protestant reformers had attempted to heal the Christian world from the plague of Catholic apostasy, but ultimately failed to improve matters much, so the Mormons were called to restore the pure doctrines and true priesthood to the earth. The evangelical Protestants at the turn of the twentieth century were worried about spiritual plagues too—especially in America where Catholics, Mormons, Masons, and Jews were spreading their contagion that would change the nation from a Protestant society to a pluralistic mélange of spiritual corruption. Mormons were particularly creating a seductive epidemic of spiritual pride that would bring many souls to grief when the day of judgment came. They decided that in order to truly love humanity they had to be intolerant of the contagious Saints.[1]

The perennial way to stem the spread of a dangerous plague has included three intolerant and effective strategies. The contagion was eradicated, quarantined, or cured. In religious conflict terms, analogous strategies were followed. The offending proselytizers were annihilated, exiled, or converted. These strategies were employed at one time or another between European

---

1. Intolerance was one aspect of Jesus's own critical way. He even resorted to physical aggression in cleansing the temple of money changers. This in turn gave the establishment an excuse to attempt to destroy him (Mark 11:15–19). On the difficult virtue of counter-plague intolerance, I re-quote Nietzsche: "Not their love of men but the impotence of their love of men keeps the Christians of today from—burning us [whose heresies lead legions into eternal damnation]." Friedrich Nietzsche, *Beyond Good and Evil* and *On the Genealogy of Morals*, 84.

Americans and native Americans, abolitionists and slaveholders, and Americans and Mormons. The three Protestant missionaries here focused directly on a conversion strategy in an attempt to overcome the previous Mormon-American strategy of exile to the Great Basin. Protestants understood that exile and peaceful co-existence would never contain the aggressive proselytizing of Mormons who, unlike native Americans, could easily infiltrate and influence the culture beyond their western reservation.

The missionaries' pre-emptive strike in Utah was a remarkable example of non-violent eristics or contestation whereby persuasive means remained in the modes of proselytizing and public service. Violence or extortion were avoided in the twentieth-century period of the Mormon conflict because it had lost its political and economic elements and become essentially religious. With a voluntary conversion strategy, neither side could press beyond persuasive means without risking the very goal of the effort: unforced conversion. The temptation to use the asymmetrical power advantages that Mormons had in Utah and Protestants had nationally was tempered by the continual desire to convert one's opponent. One did not wish to offend potential converts so deeply that proselytizing would be impossible. The doctor had to be nice to the patient or there would be no chance to give the inoculation. Proselytizing and counter-proselytizing came to be engaged with the goal of free willed conversion. Though it could become nastily over-heated at times, the engagement stopped shy of violence because conversion, rather than exile nor annihilation, was the goal. The conversion strategy of aggressive proselytizing thus ironically yielded a peace-sustaining political result.

What about converting the saints? This history has not chronicled many conversions.[2] Historian Timothy Yates summarized the three basic missiological strategies for twentieth-century Protestant missions:

---

2. Historian Ferenc Szasz's summary analysis of Protestant missions to the American Southwest concluded that what limited success the Protestants had at converting the Saints came from providing a friendly home to those who had already dissented from Mormonism. "The Gentile population of Utah showed little increase over the years. The 1870 census, for example, noted 730 Protestants out of 100,000; 1884 accounted for 1,848 out of 169,000; 1890, 4,645 of 208,000; 1906, 7,432 of 335,000; and 1914, 8, 767 of 404,000. The Protestant population continued to rise, but only in the same proportion as the Gentile immigration to Utah. . . . [By 1915] of the eighty Protestant churches in Utah, only eight had become self-supporting." See Ferenc M. Szasz, *The Protestant Clergy in the Great Plains and Rocky Mountain West, 1865–1915*, 171–173.

Individual conversion based on personal change in belief; church planting based on local congregations self-governing, self-supporting, and self-extending; and national church building based on widely accepted ethnic or countrywide customs.³ Though Nutting might have emphasized individual conversion, and Paden national church building, and Spalding local church governing, it is evident that all three of these strategies would have been approved by each of the missionaries. However, in Utah these strategies had to be implemented among a singularly religious people that had already rejected Protestantism a generation before and had established a majority Latter-day Saint base camp in Utah from which it launched aggressive missions among all Christians who would listen. It was a daunting task to make enough converts for self-sustaining local churches, and to bring Utah into the perceived Protestant national hegemony. As the prior three chapters demonstrate, the Utah Protestant missionaries attempted several alternate strategies to influence a few of the Saints to consider listening to the traditional message of Christianity and leave Mormonism.

Scott Appleby helps us understand the Utah missions by contextualizing Protestant missionary work among Catholics and Jews at the turn of the century, concluding that missionaries were either too offensive or too innocuous to make many actual conversions. The missionaries turned out to be their own best converts.

> The ordeal of civility led to strengthening of enclave cultures in turn-of-the-century America, in part because many missions produced two ironic results. First, *they were far more successful in deepening the faith and commitment of the missionary band itself and their lapsed coreligionists than in winning new converts to the religion.* Second, they sounded the alarm bell for the target group, leading that denomination to redouble its efforts to meet the social and spiritual needs of its people.⁴

James Beckford has studied recruitment strategies used by new religious movements.⁵ These he categorized in three types: the first, offering isolating *refuge* to a convert from the miseries or evils of the world; the second, providing a *revitalization* program for the convert and a mission of transformation of the world; and the third, assisting the convert to obtain a therapeutic *release* from undesirable obstructions to personal fulfillment. These categories did not quite fit the Utah proselytizing contest in

---

3. Timothy Yates, *Christian Mission in the Twentieth Century*, 34.
4. R. Scott Appleby, "Missions and the Making of Americans," 269; my emphasis.
5. James A. Beckford, *Cult Controversies: The Social Response to New Religious Movements*, 118–29.

1910. Protestant missionaries did not view themselves as representing new religious movements, though Mormonism was still viewed that way and indeed had used the strategies of offering both refuge and revitalization to the Protestants in the nineteenth century. Protestants were attempting to revitalize the country and their own congregations with a utopian notion of American Christian unity at the time; but they had no new and improved story to excite their compatriots to enthusiasm. The Protestant missionary war cry was for faithful retrenchment to set a good example for the world. However, Protestant probity proved of little interest to new generations of Americans, least of all the Mormons who were still smarting from religious defeat in 1890 at the hands of Protestant legislators and were regrouping their resources to plan their own revitalizing proselytizing counter attack later in the century.

As Episcopalian historian A. J. Simmonds reported, the Saints left Mormonism only if they were unhappy in their social relations with their Mormon neighbors or family members.[6] And when they left, it was not on account of conversion to Protestantism by proselytizing. The lapsed Mormons either left town completely, or left religion completely, but rarely did they join another local Christian church. For reasons I have set out above, none of their missiological strategies were effective in accomplishing these goals. Still, John Nutting and William Paden lived long enough to pass judgment on their long years of Utah service, Nutting serving fifty and Paden thirty. They both retired feeling a mixture of success at having maintained the standard of truth, and disappointment at the continued growth in Mormonism and the diminished missionary zeal of Protestantism.[7]

Mormon group solidarity proved an enormous obstacle to the missionary work of the Protestants at the turn of the twentieth century. The inertia of rest cannot be overestimated either. Friendships and mating patterns were intensely in-group oriented. Even unbelieving Mormons did not want to limit their social chances since the majority community intermarried and raised up children in the faith.[8] A Latter-day

---

6. A. J. Simmonds, *The Gentile Comes to Cache Valley*.

7. John Danforth Nutting, "Eight Reasons Why No One Should Be a Mormon by one who has given over fifty years to gospel work among the Mormons"; William Mitchell Paden, "Is Mormonism Changing?," 23.

8. Research suggests that about thirty-percent of American adults during their lifetimes have switched religions; moving out of organized religion completely is the most frequent switch. See Frank Newport, "The Religious Switcher in the United States," 582–83. He found that the most frequent factors correlating with

Saint who chose to convert to Presbyterianism would be breaking with the family covenant, as well as drastically reducing the pool of potential spouses. Replacing his or her Mormon friends would likewise be a daunting proposition.[9] In 1900, the greater Salt Lake City area had about 100,000 people and was approximately eighty-percent Mormon.[10] The other twenty-percent was split among unaffiliated citizens and members

---

change were shifts in socio-economic status, adopting the religion of a spouse, and religious conversion of young people. In Utah, most switching occurred out of religion completely. Darren Sherkat and John Wilson have also studied religious switching and have concluded that children from close families usually switched to liberal traditions and congregations, while children from distant families switched to conservative sects. See Darren E. Sherkat and John Wilson, "Preferences, Constraints, and Choices in Religious Markets: An Examination of Religious Switching," 1012–25. Both the Protestants and the Mormons in this study were conservative, raising the untested possibility that Mormons from close families who desired to switch found nowhere new to go. Sherkat and Wilson's study also reports that religious switching is substantially influenced by the potential switcher's proximity to home, access to mating prospects, and other recreational activities. In early-twentieth-century Utah, all of these factors would have worked to keep the potential switcher Mormon.

9. Related to this, Rodney Stark has noted the significance of social capital to the rise of Mormonism and other religious movements. Stark defines this as incorporating two aspects, culture and emotions, and he sets it forth in the following proposition: "Religious capital consists of the degree of master of and attachment to a particular religious culture." Over time people invest more and more of themselves into religious culture and thus have a high level of religious capital that results. This has ramifications for continued involvement in a given religious culture which leads to two additional propositions: First, "In making religious choices, people will attempt to conserve their religious capital"; and second, "The greater their religious capital, the less likely people are to either re-affiliate or convert." See Rodney Stark, *The Rise of Mormonism*, 65. The mission strategy employed by the Episcopal bishop to Utah allowed Mormons to become acceptable Christians en mass, maintaining their social capital.

10. Kevin Christiano's research shows Salt Lake City as the most religiously uniform city in America. In 1890, eighty-two-percent of the population was Mormon; in 1906, seventy-percent—the decrease due to in-migrating Gentiles after Utah statehood in 1896. Christiano's study shows that the main cause of the changes in the relative numbers of Catholics, Protestants, and Jews in Utah was immigration, especially from Southern and Eastern Europe, from which half of American immigrants came in 1906. See Kevin J. Christiano, *Religious Diversity and Social Change: American Cities, 1890–1906*, 172–75. The most recent demographic studies show Salt Lake City in 2017 is less than half Mormon. See

of various other denominations and faith traditions, none having a large minority. The Latter-day Saints were not merely another fungible denomination, but an insular society with their own church education system, businesses, and close social and family circles. In Utah, the first question was, "Who are your family connections around here?" ahead of the standard American question, "What do you do [for a living]?" Protestant missionaries were establishing small clinics, but to compete culturally in Utah they needed substantial rival colonies.[11] That has begun to occur in the twenty-first century when Salt Lake City became more than half non-Mormon. However, the main rival culture to Mormonism became pluralistic secularism, not Protestantism.

Missionaries: Contaminators and Contaminated

In studying cases of proselytizing engagement, none of them reflect purely one-sided influence. The missionary cultural contaminators were often also contaminated by the culture that was their target. When engaged with a potential convert the latter often took the role of resisting skeptic or even counter-proselytizer. Resistance can also be indirect in the case of a host culture that resists the conversion of any of its members but does not deploy a direct missionary force of its own.[12]

The Mormon/Protestant contest in Utah was complexly affected by the general rule established by Brigham Young requiring the Saints to be hospitable to the Protestants while resisting their proselytizing intrusions, rather like inviting someone to a dance but refusing to dance with him or her. The potential Mormon convert often perceived himself as an unofficial counter-proselytizing missionary. Because the primary proselytizing

---

Matt Canham, "Salt Lake County Is Becoming Less Mormon—Utah County Is Headed in the Other Direction."

11. Sociologists and missiologists Lofland and Richardson define "clinics" as cognitive orientations among converts or adherents who are not yet institutionally organized to participate in society. "Colonies" are as fully rounded societies within a greater society that provide economic support, collective belief systems, and an "ideal organization" plan for the adherents to follow. See James Beckford, ed., *Religious Organization: A Trend Report and Bibliography*, 810.

12. An illuminating set of studies on this subject is David E. Young and Jean-Guy Goulet, *Being Changed by Cross Cultural Encounters*, 72–88, 330; especially a western anthropologist's experience with spiritualism and healing in the bush and the concluding argument to take informants' experience more seriously than one's ideology.

action by Protestants is the topic of this study I did not do a double analysis, but another analysis might have been applied to the subtle counter-proselytizing efforts of Mormon resisters who would have liked nothing more than to convert the eastern missionaries.

All missionaries are aware of the possibility of identity change, for it is their stock and trade. That awareness—that a person can change religions—is a profound realization that ironically opens the missionary to the possibility of profound personal change. However, the missionaries' commitment year after year did convert some, and helped to avoid erosion from the existing Protestant community until it grew to a self-sustaining level from Protestant Utah immigrants. The missionaries had chosen religious vocations because they felt called to a task of high and holy purpose. They saw themselves during the early-twentieth century as the last American frontiersmen and women. Frontier missionaries received ambivalent support from Protestant hierarchies in the East.

Missionaries work out on the religious frontiers, positioning themselves on the very border. At one moment they are intrusive colonizers of the natives' traditions—at the next, assimilators of the local culture.[13] To remain pure meant to have little influence; to have influence meant to become contaminated. There, on that edge, missionaries would at times look for middle ways between different cultures; and in so doing the messenger who came to translate became the translated, returning home a changeling.[14]

Missionaries went to righteously contaminate a strange culture, did so, and returned carrying a new contamination themselves. Thus, their supporting church in the East risked a certain amount of contamination whenever a missionary was sent to the field. With all the stories of cultural and theological strangeness that were sent home, one thing was abundant-

---

13. Treatments of this problem by Clayton G. MacKenzie and Lian Xi describe contemporary proselytizing as a delicate balance between imperial colonization and syncretistic absorption. See Clayton G. MacKenzie, "Demythologizing the Missionaries: A Reassessment of the Functions and Relationships of Christian Missionary Education under Colonialism," 45–65; Lian Xi, *The Conversion of Missionaries: Liberalism in American Protestant Missions in China, 1907–1932*.

14. Lamin Sanneh reported the effects of translating the Christian scriptures into the vernacular on both the indigenous culture and the missionary translators. The former was more receptive because it was validated as equal to the European linguistic Biblical culture, and the latter often took up local causes against the European interests from which they came. See Lamin Sanneh, "Christian Missions and the Western Guilt Complex," 333.

ly communicated: the people in the mission field were also human beings living lives of integrity and fullness even without the Protestant religion. Might they have something to teach Protestant Yankees? Missionaries had the dual potential to crossbreed new strength into the old tradition, or to syncretistically dilute the old tradition into impotence. For frontier Protestant missionaries, their border crossing would change their own religion if they were not careful to maintain a certain antipathy for the alien culture. Yet without respecting it, they had no chance of penetrating deeply enough to convert anyone. Nutting and Paden were able to keep the wall up high enough to avoid much sympathy towards Mormonism, but Spalding found himself sincerely admiring Mormons in ways that made his own home leaders uncomfortable.

Coda: Religious Rivalry as You Like It

What follows are summary judgments about the way humans can with integrity and without coercion engage in contestation over immeasurable matters of greatest importance. Civility without wholeness of human expression is too weak to build and sustain cooperative community. Respect and trust, the foundation for social order, derives from fuller disclosure of diverse beliefs and respect for different practices. Communities that last, even those that have one religion or ideology, do so by finding respectful ways to disagree about truth. Humans have different points of view even within orthodox groups, and with diverse religions in a community it is even more obvious that agreement over ultimate truth cannot be the glue that keeps people together. But a community of silent conflict-avoiders is impossible to maintain. The contestation over ultimate truth needs to be a normal practice in the mode of peaceful and patient persuasion without threat of coercion. This is the lively experiment that Roger Williams initiated and that the Protestants and Mormons awkwardly but eventually adapted into their way of living together in America. It is lively because it is never finished; and it requires re-acquaintance by voices on the right and the left within each generation.

Between cultural totalism and cultural relativism, Peter Berger and later Lee Yearley imagined the possibility of a fruitful campus for cultural contestation.[15] In recent decades their theories have been enriched by the

---

15. Peter Berger has promoted inter-religious contestation to replace traditional proselytizing: "Contestation means an open-minded encounter with other religious possibilities on the level of their truth claims. Put differently,

work of Belgian secular political conflict theorist Chantal Mouffe whose focus is on the usefulness of the never-ending rivalry for hegemonic power that is sustained by democratic persuasion, not coercion.[16]

Authentic two-way proselytizing is a mature, non-coercive, persuasive form of religious contestation. This would not be a place for dialogue where people chat about their differences and similarities, nor a place for polemical engagement with the goal to convert the opponent, nor a place to form coalitions of groups with similar community interests. It would be a field for non-violent contestations between competing truth claims on the assumption of the possibility of finding and agreeing on commensurate religious truths. It is a dangerous place unless one is very clear and confident of one's own experience of truth. The only requirements for entry are honest malleability and no desire to convert others. One must not enter the contest with covert missionary motives, and one must be open to the possibility of personal change. The contestation method is existentially risky, intellectually and emotionally unpredictable, and sometimes socially awkward.

Berger wisely sensed the need for something in the religious domain like a sporting field that allowed tough contact but rejected violence. He had the right idea, but his barring of missionaries stereotyped as totalitarian colonizers would keep the best teams from entering his stadium. Apparently, he found no plausible structure in contemporary society for the engagement of missionaries who honestly desire to convert each other. He could imagine no missionary that desired a contest with the express aim of converting the other who would also be open to the possibility of experiencing personal, even radical, change during the engagement.

---

one seriously engages another religion if one is open, at least hypothetically, to the proposition that this other religion is true. . . and to be prepared to change one's own view of reality. Anything short of this, however valuable it may be, is less than the contestation called for by the present situation. It is this kind of contestation that is as yet in an embryonic phase." Peter Berger, *A Far Glory*, 76–77; see also Peter Berger, *The Heretical Imperative*, 167. Berger wanted to get beyond apologetic missionizing and beyond academic comparison to achieve authentic contestation. Berger, 185. In this field Lee Yearley promotes a "virtue of spiritual regret" that attempts to enact deep empathy, then feeling regret that one cannot be two people—fully committed to two opposing worldviews. See Lee Yearley, "Conflicts Among Ideals of Human Flourishing"; Lee Yearley, "New Religious Virtues and the Study of Religion."

16. Chantal Mouffe, *Agonistics: Thinking the World Politically*.

While there may be some who resist any influence of those they engage, the practical result of engagement is mutual change.

Marc Gopin, peace-building practitioner, has gone even further than Berger in warning against violence derived from proselytizing:

> Many religious values, both within and between cultures, are bound to contradict each other. . . . There is great danger in the future even from nonviolent religious institutions that have difficulty recognizing the limits of evangelism.[17]

> [Consider now] the drive to convert as many people as possible to one's beliefs. . . . [T]he very drive, nonviolent though it may be, will likely create more and more pretexts for violence in the crowded world of today. In particular, the corporate institutions of religion, for whom power is dependent upon the number of adherents, tend to vie with each other in increasingly hostile ways when this issue is not confronted. . . . *More thought needs to be given to why some people find deep religious fulfillment through a particular tradition that exists side-by-side in their minds or hearts with an abiding respect for other religious traditions.*[18]

Gopin wisely suggests that everyone involved in social persuasion should consider the potential negative effects of their motives and methods on those they are trying to influence. But he should leave open a radical possibility that forthright persuaders of any stripe might call each other's ways into question and invite change without provoking or taking offense. This seems to be the only authentic way for humans—persuaders all—to live side by side with integrity. We cannot wait for the apparition of unconditional respect. We can engage now with honesty in the persuasive contest over the highest way for social and spiritual change without choosing to take offence at our rivals. There is even the practical possibility of building more respect, trust, and even friendship in the process.

Evangelizing typically describes a one-way conversation in which a missionary teaches a hearer with no expectation that the missionary will be taught in return. The missionary, believing themself called by God, feels ethically bound to speak the full truth that God has put in his or her heart. However, the most effective communication is a two-way exchange that includes open mutual expression and mutual listening. This openness includes full disclosure of motives to persuade change in a rival as well as to learn from him or her.

---

17. Marc Gopin, "Religion, Violence, and Conflict Resolution," 24.
18. Gopin, 21; emphasis added.

We set the tone for this study with a magnanimous quote from Sir Thomas More, a classical Christian who sensed the potential nobility of a worthy religious opponent. Let us end with a statement of Joseph Smith, Jr. in the same spirit:[19]

> If it has been demonstrated that I have been willing to die for a Mormon, I am bold to declare before heaven that I am just as ready to die for a Presbyterian, a Baptist or any other denomination. It is the love of liberty that inspires my soul . . . . If I esteem mankind to be in error, shall I bear them down? No! I will lift them up, *and in their own way too, if I cannot persuade them my way is better!* — And I will not compel any man to believe as I do, only by the force of reasoning, for truth will cut its own way. . . [We] should cease wrangling and contending with each other, and cultivate the principles of union and friendship.

Religious integrity moves some unusual souls to engage in aggressive contests of religious persuasion—attempting to move others to see a higher truth—while eschewing contentious wrangling or coercion that would offend either friendship or freedom of conscience. Friendship is bound by complex cords of trust-building co-resistance and collaboration. Such will be the foundation of any peaceful tension we can sustain. Well-married couples know this; and committed religious rivals, if they are persuaded by this study, will come to know it too.

Crucial to this study of religious conflict is this fact: the intensity of the conflict between Mormons and Protestants was substantial, but neither side was inclined to coerce by means of violent force. That had not been the case in the prior century. Mormons had exited the United States for the yet-to-become Utah territory under threat of mob violence over their aggressive political-theocratic organization and social-theological practices. In the early twentieth century, the fight was more clearly over souls and the means of engagement mainly persuasive.

Spalding was not intensely resisted by the Mormons, nor did the Episcopalians maintain a long and vigorous proselytizing effort after the first part of the century, though their hospitals served the community con-

---

19. This is an edited extract from a scribe's notes of a speech given on July 9, 1843. See Andrew F. Ehat and Lyndon W. Cook, eds., *The Words of Joseph Smith*, 229; and Smith, *Teachings of the Prophet*, 313; my emphasis. Note that Smith highlights the tension within a regime of perpetual friendly persuasion—namely, that we desire to help the other pursue the good while attempting to persuade that there is a higher and different good to pursue. More, the desire for mutuality of this contestational and cooperative engagement presumes, even after conversion, further desire for change is inevitable within the orthodox community.

tinuously. Paden was rarely engaged at all by potential proselytes because neither his school approach nor his polemical public relations approach was directly focused on religious conversion. While the fine schools endeared his church to many Mormons, at times his vitriolic polemics incurred distrust. There was no long-term proselytizing engagement sustained by the Presbyterians after their early-century investment. Nutting did engage the Saints in a personal fashion that was similar in method to their manner of proselytizing. His emphasis on individual conversion allowed him to meet the Mormons face-to-face in witnessing matches that were potentially meaningful to both opponents who hoped spiritually to persuade the other party. Nutting's program was sustained well into mid-century, and still has methodical vestiges with certain evangelical witnessing missions to Utah today. Had Nutting also included a local social church community to which his converts might attach, the intensity of the engagement with the Saints would no doubt have been even greater, but a critical mass of converts in small town areas was very difficult to assemble and sustain a community.

The lack of violent responses to these approaches might stem from the perceived impotence in recruiting a threatening number of Mormon converts. However, it also might be the case that religious diversity was the new expectation in Utah as well as the United States, and that strategies of annihilation and exile were deemed inappropriate during this period of increased religious pluralization. The strategy of persuaded conversion came to be the preference from both theological and practical standpoints. Proselytizing methods that focused more on personal conversion were also congenial with the American way of adjudicating moral and religious questions by the voice of individual conscience.

In conclusion, let us recall the deeply religious cultural wars in America during the nineteenth century. There was horrible violence between European and native Americans over valuable land control, between Northern and Southern sections of the United States over the legality of slavery, and to a lesser extent between the United States and the Mormons over local political control and the legality of polygamy. After polygamy and major Church involvement in politics were publicly disbanded in Utah, the twentieth-century conflict between the mainline Protestant religions of the United States and the Mormons lacked a broader economic, political, and moral relevance. It became mainly a religious contest of proselytizing. Given the turbulent, often violent, ideological and religious conflicts elsewhere in the country and the world at the time, perhaps the most remarkable legacy of Protestant missions to Utah was the relatively peaceful manner in which Protestant missionaries engaged inflammatory religious topics. Christian historians of the American West can look back at these unique missionaries and affirm that they had "fought a good fight, finished the course, and kept the faith . . . henceforth to receive a crown of righteousness" (2 Tim. 4:7–8). These missionaries would have sympathy with the handwritten motto over Mother Teresa's door in her Calcutta hospice mission office that said God does not expect us to be successful—only to be faithful.

Another book might study how the evangelical Protestants' continual critique of non-traditional Christian doctrines and practices influenced Mormon leaders in the late twentieth century to emphasize Jesus Christ and his gracious atonement in all their public messaging and their internal curriculum. Spalding, at least, would be satisfied that the Saints had moved toward more classical Christian discourse within their community. Yet another book might explore the rising influence in the twenty-first century of Mormon theology that emphasizes the familial relationship between an embodied God and humanity on some Protestant and Catholic theologians. Today with pervasive and quick communication, the cross-contamination, co-resistance, and collaboration between rival groups continues and compounds. In our troubled times of ideological conflicts, contestants of all stripes—including secular proselytizers—should learn from this study that persuasive means of contestational engagement that, alas, allow no *final* resolution of all perspectives will outperform strategies of isolationism or coercion if the goal is to enhance long-term influence on future generations within and outside their communities.

Bibliography

Ahlstrom, Sidney E. *A Religious History of the American People*. Vols. I and II. New Haven: Yale University Press, 1972.
Albrecht, Stan L., and Howard M. Bahr. "Patterns of Religious Affiliation: A Study of Lifelong Mormons, Mormon Converts, and Former Mormons." *Journal for the Scientific Study of Religion* 22, no. 4: 373.
Alexander, Thomas G. "The Reconstruction of Mormon Doctrine." *Sunstone* 22, nos. 3–4 (June 1999): 15–29.
———. Interview, July 22, 1993. With Charles R. Paul.
———. *Mormonism in Transition: A History of the Latter-day Saints, 1890–1930*. Urbana: University of Illinois Press, 1986.
———. *Things in Heaven and Earth: The Life of Wilford Woodruff, a Mormon Prophet*. Salt Lake City: Signature Books, 1991.
Allaben, Marshall. "The Challenge in Utah." *Home Missionary Magazine* 33 (December 1918): 26–29.
Allen, James B. and Glen M. Leonard. *The Story of the Latter-day Saints*. Salt Lake City: Deseret Book, 1976.
Ammerman, Nancy T. "Fundamentalists Proselytizing Jews." In *Pushing the Faith*, edited by Martin Marty, 109–22. New York: Crossroads, 1988.
"An Attitude for Christians." *The Christian Statesman* 48, no. 9 (September 1914): 209–25.
Anderson, Gerald H. "American Protestants in Pursuit of Mission: 1886–1986." In *Missiology—An Ecumenical Introduction*, edited by F. J. Verstraelen, 374–420. Grand Rapids, MI: William B. Eerdmans, 1995.
"Anti-Mormon Activity On Increase?" *Ogden Examiner* (April 2, 1920).
"Anti-Mormon Campaign In Boston." *Boston-Logan Journal* (April 1920).
Appleby, R. Scott. "Missions and the Making of Americans." In *Minority Faiths and the American Protestant Mainstream*, edited by John D. Sarna. Urbana: University of Illinois Press, 1998.
———. *Spokesman for the Despised: Fundamentalist Leaders of the Middle East*. Chicago: University of Chicago Press, 1997.
Arendt, Hannah. *Between Past and Future: Eight Exercises in Political Thought*. New York: Penguin Books, 1954.
Arrington, Leonard J. *Great Basin Kingdom: An Economic History of the Latter-day Saints, 1830–1900*. Lincoln: University of Nebraska Press, 1966.
Arrington, Leonard J., and Davis Bitton. *The Mormon Experience: A History of the Latter-day Saints*. New York: Alford A. Knopf, 1979.
Arrington, Leonard J., Feramorz Y. Fox, and Dean L. May. *Building the City of God:*

Community and Cooperation Among the Mormons. Salt Lake City: Deseret Book, 1976.

Arrington, Leonard, and Jon Haupt. "Intolerable Zion: The Image of Mormonism in Nineteenth-Century American Literature." *Western Humanities Review* 22 (Summer 1968): 243–60.

Asad, Talal. *Genealogies of Religion: Discipline and Reasons of Power in Christianity and Islam*. Baltimore: Johns Hopkins University Press, 1993.

Bahr, Howard M., and Stan L. Albrecht. "Strangers Once More: Patterns of Disaffiliation from Mormonism." *Journal for the Scientific Study of Religion* 28, no. 2: 180–200.

Baird, Paul J. *The Mystery of Ministry in the Great Basin*. Globe, AZ: Pabsco Printers, 1978.

Banker, Mark T. *Presbyterian Missions and Cultural Interaction in the Far Southwest, 1850–1950*. Urbana: University of Illinois, 1993.

Barlow, Philip L. "Unorthodox Orthodoxy: The Idea of Deification in Christian History." *Sunstone* 8, no. 5 (September–October 1983): 13–18.

Barry, John M. *Roger Williams and the Creation of the American Soul*. New York: Penguin Books, 2012.

Beckford, James A. *Cult Controversies: The Social Response to New Religious Movements*. London: Tavistock Publications, 1985.

———, ed. *Religious Organization: A Trend Report and Bibliography*. Hague: Mouton, 1975.

Beckwith, Francis J., and Stephen E. Parrish. *The Mormon Concept of God: A Philosophical Analysis*. Lewiston, NY: Edwin Mellen Press, 1991.

Bederman, Gail. "'The Women Have Had Charge of the Church Long Enough': The Men and Religion Forward Movement of 1911–1912 and the Masculinization of Middle Class Protestantism." *American Quarterly* 41 (September 1989): 432–65.

Bennett, Clinton. "Victorian Images of Islam." *International Bulletin of Missionary Research* 5 (July 1991): 115–19.

Berger, Peter. *A Far Glory*. New York: The Free Press, 1992.

———. *The Heretical Imperative*. Garden City NY: Anchor Press/Doubleday, 1979.

Beringer, R. E., Herman Hattaway, Archer Jones, and William Still, Jr. *Elements of Confederate Defeat: Nationalism, War Aims, and Religion*. Athens: University of Georgia Press, 1988.

Berkhofer Jr., Robert. *The White Man's Indian: Images of the American Indian from Columbus to the Present*. New York: Alfred A. Knopf, 1978.

Bernstein, Richard. *Beyond Objectivism and Relativism: Science, Hermeneutics and Praxis*. Philadelphia: University of Pennsylvania Press, 1983.

Biallas, Leonard J. *World Religions: A Story Approach*. Mystic, CT: Twenty-third Publications, 1991.

Bitton, Davis. *The Ritualization of Mormon History and Other Essays*. Urbana: University of Illinois Press, 1994.

Blasi, Anthony, and Michael Cuneo. *Issues in the Sociology of Religion*. New York: Garland Publications, 1986.

Blomberg, Craig L., and Stephen E. Robinson. *How Wide the Divide?: A Mormon and An Evangelical in Conversation*. Downers Grove, IL: InterVarsity Press, 1997.

Bloom, Harold. *The American Religion: The Emergence of the Post Christian Nation.* New York: Simon and Schuster, 1992.

———, ed. *John Milton's Paradise Lost.* NY: Chelsea House Publishers, 1987.

———, ed. *William Blake's The Marriage of Heaven and Hell.* NY: Chelsea House Publishers, 1987.

Boileau, Chris. "Utah Bishop First to Scale Grand Teton." *Utah's Diocesan Dialogue* (January 1992): 6–7.

Boorstin, Daniel. *The Creators.* New York: Random House, 1993.

Bowden, Henry W. *American Indians and Christian Missionaries: Studies in Cultural Conflict.* Chicago: University of Chicago Press, 1981.

Bracht, John L. *Man of Holiness: The Mormon Search for a Personal God.* Salt Lake City: Sacred Tribes Press, Electronic Edition, 2010. Expanded edition of 1988 M.A. Thesis, University of Sydney.

Brackenridge, R. Douglas. "Are You That Damned Presbyterian Devil?" *Journal of Mormon History* 21, no. 1 (Spring 1995): 80–105.

———. Interview with Charles R. Paul, June 28, 1993.

Bradley, Martha. "Changed Faces: The Official LDS Position on Polygamy, 1890–1990." *Sunstone Magazine* 14 (January 1990): 25–33.

Bringhurst, Newell G. *Saints, Slaves, and Blacks: The Changing Place of Black People Within Mormonism*, 2nd ed. Salt Lake City: Greg Kofford Books, 2018.

Bringhurst, Newell G., and John C. Hamer. *Scattering of the Saints: Schism Within Mormonism.* Independence, MO: John Whitmer Books, 2007.

Brodie, Fawn M. *No Man Knows My History.* New York: Alfred Knopf, 1971.

Brown, Dee A. *Bury My Heart at Wounded Knee.* New York: Bantam Book, 1972.

Bruns, Gerald. *Hermeneutics, Ancient and Modern.* New Haven: Yale University Press, 1992.

Buenker, John W. *Progressivism.* Rochester, VT: Schenkman Books, 1977.

Bunker, Gary L., and Davis Bitton. *The Mormon Graphic Image: 1834–1914.* Salt Lake City: University of Utah Press, 1983.

Buroker, Robert L. "From Voluntary Association to Welfare State: The Illinois Immigrant's Protective League, 1908–1926." *Journal of American History* 58 (December 1971): 643–60.

Burrows, William R., ed. *Redemption and Dialogue: Reading Redemptoris Missio and Dialogue and Proclamation.* Maryknoll, NY: Orbis Books, 1993.

Canham, Matt. "Salt Lake County Is Becoming Less Mormon—Utah County Is Headed in the Other Direction." *The Salt Lake Tribune*, July 16, 2017.

Cannon, Charles N. "The Awesome Power of Sex: The Polemical Campaign Against Mormon Polygamy." *Pacific Historical Review* 4 (February 1974): 61–82.

Carmody, Brendan P. *Conversion and Jesuit Schooling in Zambia.* Leiden, Netherlands: E. J. Brill, 1992.

Christiano, Kevin J. *Religious Diversity and Social Change: American Cities 1890–1906.* Cambridge, UK: Cambridge University Press, 1987.

Christy, Howard A. Book Review of John Alton Peterson, *Utah's Black Hawk War. Journal of Mormon History* 26, no. 1 (Spring 2000): 281–89.

———. "Open Hand and Mailed Fist: Mormon-Indian Relations in Utah, 1847–52." *Utah Historical Quarterly* 48 (Summer 1978): 32–53.

---. "The Walker War: Defense and Conciliation as Strategy." *Utah Historical Quarterly* 49 (Fall 1979).

Churchill, Ward. *Struggle for Land: Indigenous Resistance to Genocide, Ecocide, and Expropriation in Contemporary North America*. Monroe, ME: Common Courage Press, 1993.

Clark, Joseph. *Leavening the Nation: The Story of American Home Missions*. New York: Baker and Taylor, 1903.

Clymer, Kenton J. "Methodist Missionaries and Roman Catholicism in the Philippines, 1899–1916." *Methodist History* 18, no. 3 (1980): 171–78.

Coleman, Michael C. *Presbyterian Missionary Attitudes Toward American Indians, 1837–1893*. Jackson, MS: University Press of Mississippi, 1985.

Constant, Benjamin. "The Liberty of the Ancients Compared with that of the Moderns." In *Benjamin Constant*, translated by B. Fontana. Cambridge: Cambridge University Press, 1988.

Cooke, Jacob E., ed. *The Federalist*. Middletown, CT: Wesleyan University Press, 1961.

Cooper, Rex Eugene. Interview with Charles R. Paul, June 17, 1997.

---. *Promises Made to the Fathers: Mormon Covenant Organization*. Salt Lake City: University of Utah Press, 1990.

Cowan, Douglas E. *Bearing False Witness? An Introduction to the Christian Countercult*. Westport, CT: Praeger, 2003.

Curtis, Susan. *Consuming Faith: The Social Gospel and Modern American Culture*. Baltimore: Johns Hopkins University Press, 1991.

Dallek, Robert. "National Mood and American Foreign Policy: A Suggestive Essay." *American Quarterly* 34 (1982): 229–61.

Davis, David Baryon. "Some Themes of Counter-Subversion: An Analysis If Anti-Masonic, Anti-Catholic, and Anti-Mormon Literature." *Mississippi Valley Historical Review* 47 (September 1960): 216–22.

Dennis, James S. *Christian Missions and Social Progress: A Sociological Study of Foreign Missions*. New York: Revell, 1897.

Dennis, Jesse Herbert. *The Work of the Church Among the Mormons*. Milwaukee: Morehouse Publishing, 1921.

DePillis, Mario S. "The Quest for Religious Authority and the Rise of Mormonism." *Dialogue: A Journal of Mormon Thought* 1 (Spring 1966): 68–88.

Dillenberger, John. "Grace and Works in Martin Luther and Joseph Smith." In *Reflections on Mormonism: Judaeo-Christian Parallels*, 176–86, edited by Truman G. Madsen. Salt Lake City: Bookcraft, 1978.

Drescher, Elizabeth. "Yet Another Survey Shows 'Nones' Growth at Record Levels," *Religion Dispatches*, March 14, 2013, http://www.religiondispatches.org/dispatches/elizabethdrescher/6925/yet_another_survey_shows__nones__growth_at_record_levels.

Drury, Clifford M. *Presbyterian Panorama: 150 Years of National Mission History*. Philadelphia: Presbyterian Church of America, 1952.

Duke, James T. *Conflict and Power in Social Life*. Provo, UT: Brigham Young University Press, 1976.

Dumézil, Georges. *The Destiny of a King*. Chicago: University of Chicago Press, 1973.

Dummelow, J. R., ed. *The One Volume Bible Commentary*. New York: Macmillan Publishing, 1908.
"Editorials, Senate Joint Resolution 147." *The Christian Statesman*, May 1918.
Ehat, Andrew F., and Lyndon W. Cook, eds. *The Words of Joseph Smith*. Salt Lake City: Bookcraft, 1980.
"Elliot Patronizes Mormons." *The Boston News*, March 26, 1892.
Faulconer, James E. "Divine Embodiment and Transcendence: Propaedeutic Thoughts and Questions." *Element: The Journal of the Society for Mormon Philosophy and Theology* 1, no. 1 (Spring 2005): 1–14.
Flake, Kathleen. *The Politics of American Religious Indentity: The Seating of Senator Reed Smoot, Mormon Apostle*. Chapel Hill: The University of North Carolina Press, 2004.
Flanders, Robert B. *Nauvoo: Kingdom on the Mississippi*. Urbana: University of Illinois Press, 1965.
Foster, Craig L. "Victorian Pornographic Imagery in Anti-Mormon Literature." *Journal of Mormon History* 19, no. 1 (Spring 1993): 115–32.
Foster, Lawrence. *Defenders of God: The Fundamentalist Revolt Against the Modern Age*. New York: Harper & Row, 1989.
———. *Religion and Sexuality: Three American Communal Experiments of the 19th Century*. New York: Oxford University Press, 1981.
Fowler, Robert Booth. *Religion and Politics in America*. Metuchen, NJ: Scarecrow Press, 1985.
Franclot, Jenny. *Roads to Rome: The Antebellum Protestant Encounter with Catholicism*. Berkeley: University of California Press, 1994.
Frye, Northrup. *The Great Code: The Bible and Literature*. New York: Harcourt, 1981.
Fulton, John. *The Tragedy of Belief: Division, Politics, and Religion in Ireland*. Oxford: Oxford University Press, 1991.
Gadamer, Hans-Georg. *Truth and Method*. New York: Seabury Press, 1975.
Garraty, John A., and Peter Gay, eds. *The Columbia History of the World*. New York: Harper & Row, 1972.
Gaustad, Edwin S. *Dissent in American Religion*. Chicago: University of Chicago Press, 1973.
Girard, René. *Things Hidden From the Foundation of the World*. Stanford, CA: Stanford University Press, 1987.
———. *Violence and the Sacred*. Baltimore: Johns Hopkins University Press, 1977.
Givens, Terryl L. *The Viper on the Hearth: Mormons, Myths, and the Construction of Heresy*. New York: Oxford University Press, 1997.
Gleckner, Robert. "The Road of Excess." In *The Marriage of Heaven and Hell*, edited by Harold Bloom, 103–17. New York: Chelsea House Publishers, 1987.
Glendon, Mary Ann. "The Man Who Loved Women and Democracy." Book review of *Women and the Common Life: Love, Marriage and Feminism* by Christopher Lasch. *First Things*, no. 70 (February 1997): 40–43.
"Glowing Tributes Paid to Bishop Spalding's Memory: Notable Gathering is Held at the Salt Lake Theater in Honor of the Departed Churchman." *The Salt Lake Tribune*, November 2, 1914, 1.

Goen, C. C. *Broken Churches, Broken Nation: Denominational Schisms and the Coming of the Civil War*. Macon, GA: Mercer University Press, 1985.
Goodykoontz, Colin B. *Home Missions on the American Frontier*. Caldwell, IN: The Caxton Printers, 1939.
Gopin, Marc. "Religion, Violence, and Conflict Resolution." *Peace and Change* 22, no. 1 (January 1997): 1–31.
Gottschalk, Paul. *The Earliest Diplomatic Documents of America*. Berlin: P. Gottschalk, 1978.
Gramsci, Antonio. *Selections from the Prison Notebooks*, edited and translated by Q. Hoare and G. Nowell Smith. London: Lawrence & Wishart, 1971.
Greeley, Andrew M. *Religion As Poetry*. New Brunswick, NJ: Transaction Publishers, 1995.
———. *Religion: A Secular Theory*. New York: The Free Press, 1982.
———. *The Denominational Society*. Glenville, IL: Scott, Foresman, 1972.
Hackett, David G. "Gender and Religion in American Culture, 1870–1930." *Religion and American Culture* 5 (Summer 1994): 127–57.
Hagen, William T. *American Indians*. Chicago: University of Chicago Press, 1993.
Haidt, Jonathan, and Gregg Lukianoff. "Why It's a Bad Idea to Tell Students Words Are Violence." *The Atlantic*, July 18, 2017.
Hale, Van. "Defining the Mormon Doctrine of Deity." *Sunstone* 10, no. 1 (1985): 23–27.
———. "The Doctrinal Impact of the King Follett Discourse." *BYU Studies* 18, no. 2 (1978): 209–23.
———. "The King Follett Discourse: Textual History and Criticism." *Sunstone* 8, no. 5 (1983): 5–12.
Hamilton, Edith, and Huntington Cairns, eds. *Plato: The Collected Dialogues Including the Letters*. Princeton, NJ: Princeton University Press, 1961.
Hampshire, Annette P. *Mormonism in Conflict: The Nauvoo Years*. New York: Mellon Press, 1985.
Hampshire, Annette P., and James Beckford. "Religious Sects and the Concept of Deviance." *The British Journal of Sociology* 34, no. 2 (June 1983): 208–26.
Handy, Robert T. *A Christian America: Protestant Hopes and Historical Realities*, 2nd ed. New York: Oxford University Press, 1984.
———. *Undermined Establishment*. Princeton, NJ: Princeton University Press, 1991.
———. *We Witness Together: A History of Cooperative Home Missions*. New York: Friendship Press, 1956.
Hansen, Klaus J. *Quest for Empire: The Political Kingdom of God and the Council of Fifty in Mormon History*. East Lansing: University of Michigan Press, 1967.
Hardy, B. Carmon. "Self Blame and the Manifesto." *Dialogue: Journal of Mormon Thought* 24, no. 3 (Fall 1991): 43–57.
———. *Solemn Covenant: The Mormon Polygamous Passage*. Urbana, IL: University of Illinois Press, 1992.
Harris, Franklin S., and Isaac B. Newbern. *The Fruits of Mormonism*. New York: MacMillan, 1925.
Hartmann, Edward G. *The Movement to Americanize the Immigrant*. New York: Columbia University Press, 1948.
Hartshorne, Charles. *A Natural Theology for Our Time*. LaSalle, IL: Open Court Publishing, 1967.

Haurwas, Stanley, and L. Gregory Jones, eds. *Why Narrative? Readings in Narrative and Theology.* Eugene: Wipf & Stock, 1997.

Haws, J. B. *The Mormon Image in the American Mind: Fifty Years of Public Perception.* New York: Oxford University Press, 2013.

Heelas, Paul, and Linda Woodhead. *The Spiritual Revolution: Why Religion is Giving Way to Spirituality.* Oxford: Blackwell, 2005.

Heise, David R. "Prefatory Findings in the Sociology of Missions." *Journal for the Scientific Study of Religion* 6 (1967): 49–58.

Hexham, Irving, Stephen Rost, and John W. Morehead II, eds. *Encountering New Religious Movements: A Holistic Evangelical Approach.* Grand Rapids, MI: Kregal Academic & Professional, 2004.

Hiebert, Paul G. "Introduction: Mission and Anthropology." In *Readings in Missionary Anthropology II*, edited by William A. Smalley, xv–xxv. South Pasadena, CA: William Carey Library, 1978.

Hill, Marvin S. *Quest for Refuge: The Mormon Flight from American Pluralism.* Salt Lake City: Signature Books, 1989.

Hofstadter, Richard. *Social Darwinism in the United States, 1860–1914.* Philadelphia: University of Pennsylvania Press, 1945.

Hoxie, Frederick E., ed. *Encyclopedia of North American Indians.* Boston: Houghton Mifflin Harcourt, 1996.

Hughes, Richard T. "Two Restoration Traditions: Mormons and Churches of Christ in the Nineteenth Century." *Journal of Mormon History* 19, no. 2 (Spring 1993): 51.

Hutchison, William R. "Christianity, Culture, and Complications: Protestant Attitudes toward Missions." In *Pushing the Faith*, edited by Martin Marty, 78–92. New York: Crossroads, 1988.

Hutchison, William R., and Hartmut Lehmann. *Many Are Chosen: Divine Elective and Western Nationalism.* Minneapolis, MN: Augsburg Fortress Press, 1994.

Hymnal of the Protestant Episcopal Church in the United States of America, The. New York: The Church Pension Fund, 1940.

Hymns: Church of Jesus Christ of Latter-day Saints. Salt Lake City: Deseret Book Company, 1964.

"Immigration Limits Set." *The New York Times*, January 1, 1904.

Irving, Gordon. "The Law of Adoption: One Phase of the Development of the Mormon Concept of Salvation." *BYU Studies* 14, no. 3 (Spring 1974): 291–314.

Irwin, Lee. "Native Voices in the Study of Native American Religions." In *Critical Review of Books in Religion.* Atlanta, GA: Scholars Press, 1998.

James, William. *The Varieties of Religious Experience.* New York: First Vintage Books/ The Library of America Edition, 1990.

Jefferson, Thomas. *The Declaration of Independence.* First published July 4, 1776.

Jenkins, Philip. *Mystics and Messiahs: Cults and New Religions in American History.* New York: Oxford University Press: 2001.

Jesse, Dean C. "Joseph Smith's 19 July 1840 Discourse." *BYU Studies* 19, no. 3 (1979): 392–94.

———. "The Early Accounts of the First Vision." *BYU Studies* 9, no. 3 (1969): 275–94.

Jones, Christopher C. "The Power and Form of Godliness: Methodist Conversion

Narratives and Joseph Smith's First Vision," *Journal of Mormon History* 37, no. 2: 88–114.

———. "The Worst Fights are Behind Relatives: Mormons and Methodists in the Nineteenth Century." Paper presented to "At the Crossroads, Again: Mormon and Methodist Encounters in the Nineteenth and Twenty-First Centuries," Mormon Chapter of the Foundation for Religious Diplomacy conference held at Wesley Theological Seminary, Washington, DC, February 2012.

———. "We Latter-day Saints are Methodists: The Influence of Methodism on Early Mormon Religiosity." MA Thesis, Brigham Young University, 2009.

Kauffman, Ruth, and Reginald Wright Kauffman. *A Study of the Mormons in Light of Economic Conditions*. Urbana: University of Illinois Press, 1994.

Keller, Robert H., Jr. *American Protestantism and United States Indian Policy 1869–1882*. Lincoln: University of Nebraska Press, 1983.

Kelly, Francis C. *The Story of Extension*. Chicago: Extension Press, 1922.

Kinney, Bruce. "Mormonism and Christianity." *The Intercollegian*. (January 1909): 88–90.

———. "The American Mohammedanism." *The Missionary Review of the World* (January–December 1899): 844.

———. *Mormonism: The Islam of America*. New York: Flemming H. Revell Company, 1912.

Lamar, Howard R. "National Perceptions of Utah's Statehood." *Journal of Mormon History* 23, no. 1 (Spring 1997): 42–65.

Larson, Gustive O. "Brigham Young and the Indians." In *The American West: An Appraisal*, edited by Robert G. Ferris, 176–87. Sante Fe: Museum of New Mexico, 1963.

———. *The "Americanization" of Utah for Statehood*. San Marino, CA: Huntington Library, 1971.

Larson, Stan. "Intellectuals in Mormon History: An Update." *Dialogue: A Journal of Mormon Thought* 26, no. 3 (Fall 1993): 187–89.

Launius, Roger D., and Spillman, W. B. *Let Contention Cease: The Dynamics of Dissent in The Reorganized Church of Jesus Christ of Latter Day Saints*. Independence, MO: Graceland/Park Press, 1991.

"Letters." *The Christian Statesman*, January 1920, 83.

Lewis, James R. "Apostates and the Legitimation of Repression: Some Historical and Empirical Perspectives on the Cult Controversy." *Sociological Analysis* 49 (1989): 386–96.

Lincoln, Bruce. "Commentary on *Genealogies of Religion* by Talal Asad." Unpublished remarks at the American Academy of Religion Convention, Chicago, IL, Nov. 21st, 1994.

Lindbeck, George. *The Nature of Doctrine: Religion and Theology in a Postliberal Age*. Philadelphia: The Westminster Press, 1984.

"Literary Digest." "Missionaries are Peddlers." *The New York Times*, September 4, 1918.

Loughlin, Gerard. *Telling God's Story: Bible, Church and Narrative*. Cambridge: Cambridge University Press, 1999.

Ludlow, Daniel H., ed. *The Encyclopedia of Mormonism*, 5 vols. New York: Macmillan Publishing Company, 1992.

Lyman, Edward Leo. *Political Deliverance: The Mormon Quest for Statehood.* Urbana: University of Illinois Press, 1986.
Lyon, T. Edgar. "Evangelical Protestant Missionary Activities in Mormon Dominated Areas, 1865–1900." PhD diss., University of Utah, 1962.
MacKenzie, Clayton G. "Demythologizing the Missionaries: A Reassessment of the Functions and Relationships of Christian Missionary Education under Colonialism." *Comparative Education* 29, no. 1 (1993): 45–65.
Madsen, Truman G. *Defender of the Faith: The B. H. Roberts Story.* Salt Lake City: Bookcraft, 1980.
Madsen, Truman G. *Reflections on Mormonism.* Salt Lake City: Bookcraft, 1985.
Magee, Malcolm. Review of *American Evangelicalism: Embattled and Thriving,* by Christian Smith. *H-AmRel, H-Net Reviews,* March 1999, http://www.h-net.org/reviews/showrev.php?id=2912
Malony, H. Newton. "The Psychology of Proselytism." In *Pushing the Faith,* edited by Martin Marty, 125–42. New York: Crossroads, 1988.
Martin, Theodore D., and Marion E., compilers. *Presbyterian Work in Utah 1869–1969.* Salt Lake City: Wheelwright Lithography, 1971. Books I–III. Typed mss. In the Presbyterian File, Drawer 3, Westminster College Archive, Salt Lake City, UT, 1971.
Marty, Martin E. "A God To End All Gods." *Context,* August 15, 1997, 4.
———. "The Spirit Behind Pentecostalism." *Context,* May 1, 1997, 6–7.
———. *Fundamentalism and Evangelicalism.* New York: K. G. Saur, 1993.
———. *Modern American Protestantism and its World: Missions and Ecumenical Expressions.* New York: K. G. Saur, 1993.
———. *Modern American Religion I: The Irony of it All.* Chicago: University of Chicago, 1986.
———. *Modern American Religion II: The Noise of Conflict.* Chicago: University of Chicago, 1991.
———. *Pushing the Faith.* New York: Crossroads, 1988.
———. *Religion and Republic: The American Circumstance.* Boston: Beacon Press, 1987.
———. *Righteous Empire: The Protestant Experience in America.* New York: Dial Press, 1970.
———. *The One and the Many: America's Struggle for the Common Good.* Cambridge, MA: Harvard University Press, 1997.
———. *When Faiths Collide.* Malden, MA: Blackwell Publishing, 2005.
Mason, C. E. Personal letter to Bishop Spalding, March 29, 1911. Episcopalian History Collection, Box 12, Folder 5, Marriott Library Special Collections, University of Utah, Salt Lake City, UT.
Mather, Cotton. *Magnalia Christi Americana: or the Ecclesiastical History of New England, from its First Planting in the Year 1620, unto the Year of our Lord, 1698,* Vol. 1. London: Thomas Parkhurst, 1702.
Mauss, Armand L. *The Angel and The Beehive: The Mormon Struggle with Assimilation.* Urbana: The University of Illinois Press, 1994.
May, Dean. "Dissent and Authority in Two Latter-day Saint Traditions." *Sunstone* 17, no. 1, (June 1994): 16–20.

May, Henry F. *The End of Innocence: A Study of the First Years of Our Own Times, 1912–1917*. New York: Alfred Knopf, 1959.
McComas, Henry C. *The Psychology of Religious Sects*. New York: Fleming H. Revell, 1912.
McConkie, Bruce R. *Mormon Doctrine*. Salt Lake City: Deseret Book, 1966.
McDannell, Colleen, and Bernhard Lang. *Heaven: A History*. New Haven: Yale University Press, 1988.
McMurrin, Sterling M. "Comments on the Theological and Philosophical Foundations of Christianity." *Dialogue: A Journal of Mormon Thought* 25, no. 1 (1992): 37–47.
———. *Theological Foundations of Mormon Religion*. Salt Lake City: University of Utah, 1965.
Mead, Sidney E. "Denominationalism: The Shape of Protestant America." *Church History* 23 (December 1954): 125–36.
———. *The Nation with the Soul of a Church*. New York: Harper and Row, 1975.
Meinig, D. W. "The Mormon Nation and the American Empire." *Journal of Mormon History* 22, no. 1 (Spring 1996): 33–51.
Melish, John H. *Franklin Spencer Spalding: Man and Bishop*. New York: MacMillan, 1917.
Merrill, Milton R. *Reed Smoot, Apostle in Politics*. Logan: Utah State University Press, 1990.
Meyer, Eduard, Heinz F. Rahde, and Eugene Seaich. *The Origin and History of the Mormons, with Reflections on the Beginnings of Islam and Christianity*. Salt Lake City: University of Utah, 1961.
Meyers, Gustavus. *History of Bigotry in the United States*. New York: Capricorn, 1943.
Midgley, Louis. "Anti-Mormonism and the Newfangled Countercult Culture." In *FARMS Review of Books* (1998): 271–340.
Miller, Jon. "Missions, Social Change, and Resistance to Authority: Notes Toward an Understanding of the Relative Autonomy of Religion." *Journal for the Scientific Study of Religion* 32, no. 1 (1993): 29–50.
———. *The Social Control of Religious Zeal*. New Brunswick, NJ: Rutgers University Press, 1994.
Miller, Randall M., Harry S. Stout, and Charles Reagan Wilson, eds. *Religion and the American Civil War*. New York: Oxford University Press, 1998.
Millet, Robert L. "Joseph Smith and Modern Mormonism: Orthodoxy, Neoorthodoxy, Tension, and Tradition." *BYU Studies* 29, no. 3: 49–68.
Millet, Robert L., and Gerald R. McDermott. *Claiming Christ: A Mormon-Evangelical Debate*. Grand Rapids, MI: Brazos Press, 2007.
Mills, Edward L. "One Hundred Years of Mormonism." *The Missionary Review of the World* (December 1930): 917–20.
Milton, John. *Paradise Lost*. New York: W.W. Norton, 1975.
Minutes of the Synod of Utah. Fragments and Paden notes, 1911–1915. In William Paden Collection, Westminster College Archive, Salt Lake City, UT.
Moore, R. Laurence. *Selling God: American Religion in the Market Place of Culture*. New York: Oxford University Press. 1994.
Moorhead, James H. "God's Right Arm? Minority Faiths and Protestant Visions of America." In *Minority Faiths and the American Mainstream*, edited by John D. Sarna. Urbana: University of Illinois Press, 1998.

———. "The American Israel: Protestant Tribalism and Universal Mission." In *Many Are Chosen: Divine Election and Western Nationalism*, edited by William R. Hutchison and Hartmut Lehmann, 145–66. Cambridge: Harvard Theological Studies, 1994.
Morehead, John W. "Divine Disenchantment: Transitions, and Assisting Those in Religious Migration." In *From Fear to Faith: Stories of Hitting Spiritual Walls*, edited by Joel Watt and Travis Milam, 116–31. Gonzales, FL: Energion Publications, 2013.
———. "Evangelical Approaches to New Religions: Countercult Heresy-Rationalist Apologetics, Cross-Cultural Missions and Dialogue." *Evangelical Interfaith Dialogue* (Fall 2013): 4–14.
"Mormon Elder Attacked." *The Ogden Examiner*, March 19, 1920, 1.
"Mormon Priests Must Leave Town, The." *The Wellington Daily News*, November 1, 1917.
Mormon Puzzle: Understanding and Witnessing to Latter-day Saints, The. Alpharetta, GA: Northern American Mission Board of the Southern Baptist Convention, 1997.
Mosser, Carl, and Paul Owen. "Mormon Apologetic, Scholarship and Evangelical Neglect: Losing the Battle and Not Knowing It?" *Trinity Journal* 19, no. 2 (1998): 179–205.
Mouffe, Chantal. *Agonistics: Thinking the World Politically*. London: Verso, 2013.
Mulholland, Kenneth R. "Indian Carried Christianity: Wampanoag Christianity on Martha's Vineyard, 1643–1690." PhD diss., University of Utah, 2010.
Murphy, Paul V. *The Rebuke of History: The Southern Agrarians and American Conservative Thought*. University of North Carolina, 2001.
Neill, Stephen. *A History of Christian Missions*. New York: Penguin Books, 1990.
Neilson, Reid Larkin, and Terryl Givens, eds. Joseph Smith, Jr.: Reappraisals after Two Centuries. Oxford: Oxford University Press, 2008.
Neuchterlein, James. "Sin, Theodicy and Politics." *First Things* (November 1998): 7.
Neuhaus, Richard. "Christ and Creation's Longing." *First Things* (December 1997): 22–25.
———. "On Catholic Catholicism." *First Things* (November 1998): 80.
Newport, Frank. "The Religious Switcher in the United States." *The American Sociological Review* 44, no. 4 (1979): 528–52.
Nibley, Hugh W. *Approaching Zion*. Salt Lake City: Deseret Book Company, 1989.
———. *Mormonism and Early Christianity*. Salt Lake City: Deseret Book Company, 1987.
Nida, Eugene A. "The Roman Catholic, Communist, and Protestant Approach to Social Structure." In *Readings in Missionary Anthropology II*, edited by William A. Smalley. South Pasadena, CA: William Carey Library, 1978.
Nietzsche, Friedrich. *Beyond Good and Evil* and *On the Genealogy of Morals*. Translated by Walter Kaufmann. New York: Vintage Books, 1989.
———. *The Birth of Tragedy* and *The Case of Wagner*. Translated by Walter Kaufmann. New York: Vintage Books, 1967.
Norman, Keith E. "Divinization: The Forgotten Teaching of Early Christianity." *Sunstone* 1, no. 1 (Winter 1975): 14–19.
———. "Mormon Cosmology: Can It Survive the Big Bang?" *Sunstone* 10, no. 9 (1985): 19–23.
Novak, Michael. "The Secularist Faith." A review of *The Wealth and Poverty of Nations:*

Why some are so Poor by David S. Landes in *First Things*, Vol. 85, August/September 1998, 58–61.

Nussbaum, Martha. *Liberty of Conscience: In Defense of America's Tradition of Religious Equality*. New York: Basic Books, 2008.

Nutting, John Danforth. "A Study of the Present Mormon Problem." *The Independent* 54 (April 17, 1902): 930–34. West.

———. "Awheel and Afoot in Mormonism." *The Home Missionary* 74, no. 2 (May 1905): 37–45. West.

———. "Difficulties of Work Among the Mormons." *Missionary Review of the World* 26 (1903): 855–58. Funk & Wagnalls, New York. West.

———. "Eight Reasons Why No One Should Be a Mormon by one who has given over fifty years to gospel work among the Mormons." Cleveland, OH: Utah Gospel Mission. Pamphlet. 1952.

———. *Light on Mormonism*. Cleveland, OH: Utah Gospel Mission, Publisher, 1923–29.

———. "Mormonism Today and its Remedy." *Missionary Review of the World*, May, Funk & Wagnalls, New York. Reprint and revision distributed by Utah Gospel Mission, Cleveland, OH. West. 1913.

———. "Paul's Method of Dealing with False Religionists." Cleveland, OH: Utah Gospel Mission. 1927.

———. Personal letter to Bishop F. S. Spalding, Jan. 4, 1913. Episcopalian Church History File, Box 12, Folder 10, Marriott Library Special Collections, University of Utah, Salt Lake City, UT.

———. Personal letter to F. S. Spalding, November 16, handwritten, Episcopal Diocese of Utah, Acc. # 426, Box 12, Folder 10, Marriott Library Special Collections, University of Utah, Salt Lake City, UT. 1912.

———. "Present Day Mormonism and Its Remedy." Cleveland, OH: Utah Gospel Mission, Publisher. Pamphlet. 1923.

———. "The Secret Oaths and Ceremonies of Mormonism: The Secret Temple Work Which Binds Mormons Together Under the Power of Their Priestly Leaders." Cleveland, OH: Utah Gospel Mission, 1912. Pamphlet.

———. "The Truth About God." Cleveland, OH: Utah Gospel Mission, Publisher, 1909. Pamphlet. West.

———. "Why I Could Never Be A Mormon." Cleveland, OH: Utah Gospel Mission, 1913. Pamphlet. West.

Olson, Roger E. *The Mosaic of Christian Belief: Twenty Centuries of Unity & Diversity*. Downers Grove: InterVarsity Press, 2002.

Ortenburger, Leigh N., and Reynold G. Jackson. *A Complete Climbers Guide to the Teton Range*. Palo Alto, CA: L. N. Ortenberger and R. G. Jackson, 1990.

Ostler, Blake T. "Review of The Mormon Concept of God: A Philosophical Analysis by Francis J. Beckwith and Stephen E. Parrish." *FARMS Review of Books* 8, no. 2 (April 1994): 99–146.

———. "The Idea of Pre-existence in the Development of Mormon Thought." *Dialogue: A Journal of Mormon Thought* 15, no. 1 (1982): 59–76.

———. *Exploring Mormon Thought: Of God and Gods*. Salt Lake City: Greg Kofford Books, 2008.

Paden, William Mitchell. "A Protest of Citizens." A petition form, T. Ross Paden Jr. Collection, Calvin Court, Portland, OR. 1903.

———. "Creed and Conduct of the Mormon Leaders." Salt Lake Ministerial Association, Publisher, Salt Lake City, UT. Pamphlet. 1907.

———. *The Holland Reminder* 6, no. 11 (October 1897).

———. "Is Mormonism Changing?" *The Biblical Review* 14, no. 3 (July 1929): 19–27.

———. Letter to Editor, *Lewiston Journal*, Lewiston, Idaho. In clipping file, T. Ross Paden, Jr. Collection, Calvin Court, Portland, OR.

———. "Liberty, Law, and Loyalty," Salt Lake City: Ladies' Aid Society of the First Presbyterian Church, 1901.

———. "Minutes of the Synod of Utah." Fragments and Paden notes, William Paden Collection, Westminster College Archive, Salt Lake City, UT.

———. "Missions Among Mormons-Why?" New York: Board of Home Missions of the Presbyterian Church in the USA., Publisher. Copy in William Paden Collection, Westminster College Archive, Salt Lake City, UT.

———. "Mormon Pluralism." *The Christian* 69. Statesman. Pittsburgh, PA: National Reform Association, Publisher, Special Collections, Harold B. Lee Library, Brigham Young University, Provo, UT.

———. "Mormonism as a Political Power and Peril: Studies in Social Reform and What To Do." August, New York, American Institute of Social Service, Publisher. Pamphlet. 1913.

———. "Notes for a Map of Allotment and Occupation in Utah." October 16, 1930. William Paden Collection, Presbyterian File, Item 15, Westminster College Archive, Salt Lake City, UT.

———. Notes on the story of Westminster College, Salt Lake City, UT, December 6, 1913. William Paden Collection, Westminster College Archive, Salt Lake City, UT. Westminster folder.

———. Personal Notes and Papers, T. Ross Paden, Jr. Collection, Calvin Court, Portland, OR.

———. "Questions and Answers on Mormonism." *Bulletin of National Missions*, Presbyterian Church USA, New York. Copy in William Paden Collection, Westminster College Archive, Salt Lake City, UT. 1929.

———. "Report of Home Missions Committee." September 1, Salt Lake City, typed, William Paden Collection, Westminster College Archive, Salt Lake City, UT. Missions folder. 1916.

———. "Report of Home Missions Committee." William Paden Collection, Westminster College Archive, Salt Lake City, UT. 1912.

———. "Temple Mormonism." Salt Lake City: Gentile Bureau of Information. T. Ross Paden, Jr. Collection, Calvin Court, Portland, OR. Pamphlet.

———. William Mitchell Paden Diaries, T. Ross Paden, Jr. Collection, Calvin Court, Portland, OR.

Pannenberg, Wolfhart. "How to Think about Secularism." *First Things* 64 (June/July 1996): 27–32.

———. *Basic Questions in Theology: Collected Essays*, Vols. I & II, translated by George H. Kehm. Philadelphia: Fortress Press, 1970–71.

Parkin, Max H. *A History of the Latter-day Saints in Clay County, Missouri, from 1833 to 1837*. PhD diss., Brigham Young University, 1976.
Parvin, Earl. *Missions U.S.A*. Chicago: Moody Press, 1985.
Pascal, Blaise. *Oeuvres Complète*. Edited by Louis Lafuma. Paris: Aux Éditions du Seuil, 1963.
Paul, Charles Randall. "Four L.D.S. Views on Harold Bloom: A Roundtable." *BYU Studies* 35, no. 1 (1995): 189–97.
Paulsen, David L. "The Doctrine of Divine Embodiment: Restoration, Judeo-Christian, and Philosophical Perspectives." *BYU Studies* 35, no. 4 (1995): 6–94.
Perrin, Nicholas. *Jesus the Temple*. Grand Rapids: Baker Academics, 2010.
Peterson, Daniel C. "Shall They Both Not Fall in the Ditch? What Certain Baptists Think They Know about the Restored Gospel." *FARMS Review of Books* 10, no. 1 (1998): 12–96.
Peterson, John Alton. *Utah's Black Hawk War*. Salt Lake City: University of Utah Press, 1999.
"Petition to Oust Smoot." *New York World*, January 9, 1905.
Pieterse, Jan Nederveen. "Christianity, Politics and Gramsciansim of the Right." In *Christianity and Hegemony: Religion and Politics on the Frontiers of Social Change*, edited by Jan Nederveen Pieterse, 1–31. New York: Berg, 1992.
Plato. *Plato: The Collected Dialogues Including the Letters*. Edited by Edith Hamilton and Huntington Cairns. Princeton, NJ: Princeton University Press, 1961.
Pratt, Orson. *The Essential Orson Pratt*. Salt Lake City: Signature Books, 1991.
Pratt, Parley P. *The Autobiography of Parley P. Pratt*. Salt Lake City: Deseret Book, 1950.
Prucha, Francis Paul, ed. *The Indian in American History*. New York: Holt, Rinehart and Winston, 1971.
Prucha, Francis Paul. *The Great Father: The United States Government and the American Indians, Vols. 1 and 2*. Lincoln: University of Nebraska Press, 1995.
"Questions and Answers on Mormonism." New York: Women's Board of Home Missions of the Presbyterian Church, 1912. Special Collections, Harold B. Lee Library, Brigham Young University, Provo, UT.
Rauschenbusch, Walter. *Christianity and the Social Crisis*. New York: Macmillan, 1907.
Raven, B. H., and W. Kruglianski. "Conflict and Power." In *The Structure of Conflict*, edited by P. G. Swingle, 177–219. New York: Academic Press, 1975.
Redfield, James. "The Origins of Philosophy." University of Chicago, January 1993, unpublished manuscript of lecture.
Reed, Michael G. *Banishing the Cross: The Emergence of a Mormon Taboo*. Independence, MO: John Whitmer Books, 2012.
Reeve, Paul. *Religion of a Different Color: Race and the Mormon Struggle for Whiteness*. New York: Oxford University Press, 2015.
Reherd, Herbert Ware. "An Outline History of the Protestant Churches of Utah." In *Utah Centennial History*, edited by Wain Sutton, 649–90. Chicago: Lewis Historical Publications, 1948.
Reyburn, William D. "The Missionary and Cultural Diffusion." In *Readings in Missionary Anthropology II*, edited by William A Smalley, 198–222. South Pasadena, CA: William Carey Library, 1978.

Rice, Claton. *Ambassador to the Saints*. Boston: The Christopher Publishing House, 1965.
Ricoeur, Paul. *Interpretation Theory: Discourse and the Surplus of Meaning*. Fort Worth, TX: Christian University Press, 1976.
———. *Lectures on Ideology and Utopia*. Edited by George H. Taylor. New York: Columbia University Press, 1986.
———. *The Conflict of Interpretations: Essays in Hermeneutics*. Edited by Don Ihde. Evanston: Northwestern University Press, 1974.
Roberts, Brigham H. *The Autobiography of B. H. Roberts*. Edited by Gary Bergera. Salt Lake City: Signature Books, 1990.
———. *Defense of the Faith and the Saints* Vol. 1. Salt Lake City: Deseret News Press, 1907.
———. Personal note to F. S. Spalding. Episcopal Diocese of Utah Collection, Box 12, Folder 7, Manuscripts Division, Special Collections, University of Utah Marriott Library, Salt Lake City, UT.
———. Personal letters to Bishop Franklin Spalding. Episcopal Diocese of Utah Collection, Box 12, Folder 7, Manuscripts Division, Special Collections, University of Utah Marriott Library, Salt Lake City, UT. 1909–11.
———. Personal letters to Bishop Franklin Spalding. The Historical Archives of the Church of Jesus Christ of Latter-day Saints, Salt Lake City, UT. 1912–14.
———. "A Plea in Bar of Final Conclusions." *Improvement Era* 16, no. 4 (February 1913): 309–25.
———. "Remarks on Joseph Smith, Jr. as a Translator." *The Salt Lake Tribune*, December 15, 1912.
———. *The Truth, The Way, The Life: An Elementary Treatise on Theology*. Edited by John W. Welch. Provo, UT: *BYU Studies* Monographs, 1994.
Robinson, Stephen E. *Are Mormons Christian?* Salt Lake City: Bookcraft, 1991.
Roosevelt, Theodore. "Mr. Roosevelt to the Mormons." *Collier's Magazine* 47, April 15, 1911, 28.
———. *The Strenuous Life*. New York: Macmillan, 1901.
———. *The Winning of the West*, Vol. 1. New York: G. P. Putnam's Sons, 1948.
Rorty, Richard. *Objectivity, Relativism, and Truth: Philosophic Papers*, Vol. 1. New York: Cambridge University Press, 1991.
Russell, Isaac. Personal letter to Franklin Spalding, Dec. 3, 1912. Episcopalian History Collection, Box 12, Folder 6, Marriott Library Special Collections, University of Utah, Salt Lake City, UT.
———. "Shows Mormons How To Drop Polygamy." *New York Sunday Times*, July 17, 1910. Episcopalian History Collection, Box 12, Folder 6, Marriott Library Special Collections, University of Utah, Salt Lake City, UT.
Sanneh, Lamin. "Christian Missions and the Western Guilt Complex." *The Christian Century*. April 8, 1987, 331–34.
Sarna, Jonathan D., ed. *Minority Faiths and the American Protestant Mainstream*. Urbana: University of Illinois Press, 1998.
Schmitt, Karl M. "American Protestant Missionaries and the Diaz Regime in Mexico: 1876–1911." *Journal of Church and State* 25, no. 2 (1983): 253–77.
Sherkat, Darren E., and John Wilson. "Preferences, Constraints, and Choices in

Religious Markets: An Examination of Religious Switching." *Social Forces* 73, no. 3 (March 1995): 993–1026.

Sherrill, Henry Knox. *Among Friends*. Boston: Atlantic Monthly Press Book, 1962.

Shipps, Jan. "Difference and Otherness: Mormonism and the American Religious Mainstream." In *Minority Faiths and the American Protestant Mainstream*, edited by Jonathan D. Sarna, 81–103. Urbana: University of Illinois Press, 1998.

———. "From Satyr to Saint." In *Sojourner in the Promised Land: Forty Years among the Mormons*, 50–66. Urbana: University of Illinois Press, 2000.

———. "From Satyr to Saint: American Attitudes Toward the Mormons, 1860–1960." Paper presented at the Chicago Meeting of the Organization of American Historians. April, 1973.

———. "In the Presence of the Past: Continuity and Change in Twentieth Century Mormonism." In *After 150 Years: The Latter-day Saints in Sesquicentennial Perspective*, edited by Thomas Alexander and Jessie Embry, 11–35. Provo, UT: Charles Redd Center, 1983.

———. "Is Mormonism Christian?: Reflections on a Complicated Question." *BYU Studies* 33, no. 3 (1993): 439–65.

———. *Mormonism: The Story of a New Religious Tradition*. Urbana: University of Illinois Press, 1985.

Showalter, Elaine. *Sexual Anarchy: Gender & Culture at the Fin de Siècle*. New York: Viking/Penguin Press, 1990.

Shupe, Anson Jr. *The Anti-cult Movement in America*. New York: Garland Publishing, 1984.

Sillito, John R., and Martha Sonntag Bradley. "Franklin Spencer Spalding: An Episcopal Observer of Mormonism." *Historical Magazine of the Protestant Episcopal Church* 54 (December 1985): 339–49.

Simmel, Georg. *On Individuality and Social Forms*. Compiled and translated by Donald N. Levine. Chicago: University of Chicago Press, 1971.

———. *Conflict and The Web of Group-Affiliations*. Translated by Kurt Wolff and Reinhard Bendix. London: The Free Press of Glencoe, 1964.

Simmonds, A. J. "Speech to the 81st Convention of the Church in the Utah Diocese." June 20–22, 1986. Library of the Episcopal Church, Spalding File, Salt Lake City, UT.

———. *The Gentile Comes to Cache Valley*. Logan: Utah State University Press, 1976.

Smith, Christian. *American Evangelicalism: Embattled and Thriving*. Chicago: University of Chicago Press, 1998.

Smith, Gary Scott. *Seeds of Secularization: Calvinism, Culture, and Pluralism in America, 1870–1915*. Grand Rapids: Eerdmans, 1985.

Smith, John A. "Ecclesiastical Politics and the Founding of the Federal Council of Churches." In *Missions and Ecumenical Expressions*, edited by Martin Marty. New York: K.G. Saur, 1993.

Smith, Jonathan Z. *Drudgery Divine: On the Comparison of Early Christianities and the Religions of Antiquity*. Chicago: University of Chicago Press, 1990.

Smith, Joseph Fielding. *Teachings of the Prophet Joseph Smith*. Salt Lake City: Deseret Book Company, 1969.

Smith, William Victor. *Textual Studies of the Doctrine and Covenants: The Plural Marriage Revelation*. Salt Lake City: Greg Kofford Books, 2018.

Snay, Mitchell. *Gospel of Disunion*. New York: Cambridge University Press, 1993.
Snow, Lorenzo. "Column Article." *Deseret News Weekly*, December 8, 1869.
Spalding, Franklin Spencer. Annual Report of the Bishop of the Missionary District of Utah. Episcopal Diocese of Utah Collection, Box 4, Folder 5, Manuscripts Division, Special Collections, University of Utah Marriott Library, Salt Lake City, UT. 1907–10.
———. "The Honest Way Out of a Difficult Situation: A Friendly Word to the Latter-Day Saints." Historical Archives of The Church of Jesus Christ of Latter-day Saints, Salt Lake City, UT. 1910.
———. *Joseph Smith, Jr. as a Translator*. Salt Lake City: Arrow Press, 1912.
———. Journal of Convocation, 18–20. Episcopal Diocese of Utah Collection, Box 1, Folder 3, Manuscripts Division, Special Collections, University of Utah Marriott Library, Salt Lake City, UT. 1907.
———. Letter or notes on Joseph Smith's translation methods, handwritten. The Library of the Episcopal Diocese of Utah, Spalding File, Salt Lake City, UT.
———. Letter to Dr. H. V. Hilprecht, University of Pennsylvania, April 23, 1910. The Library of the Episcopal Diocese of Utah, Spalding Collection, Salt Lake City, UT.
———. Letter to the Editor, *Deseret News*, March 14, 1914. The Library of the Episcopal Diocese of Utah, Spalding Collection, Salt Lake City, UT.
———. "The Missionaries and the Wise Man." Salt Lake City: The Arrow Press. Historical Archives of The Church of Jesus Christ of Latter-day Saints, Salt Lake City, UT.
———. "Our Church in Mormonland." *The Churchman*, May 1, 1909..
———. Personal letter to Isaac Russell of New York City, November 20, 1912. The Library of the Episcopal Diocese of Utah, Spalding Collection, Salt Lake City, UT.
———. Personal letter to Miss C. E. Mason of Tarrytown, NY, May 8, 1911. Episcopal Diocese of Utah Collection, Box 12, Folder 5, Marriott Library Special Collections, University of Utah, Salt Lake City, UT.
———. Personal travel journal, March 3rd entry. Episcopal Diocese of Utah Collection, Box 12, Folder 1, Manuscripts Division, Special Collections, University of Utah Marriott Library, Salt Lake City, UT. 1905.
———. "The Proper Attitude toward the Mormon Church and People." *The Utah Survey* 1, no. 6 (February 1914): 14–24.
———. "What Is Left of Mormonism Without Polygamy?" *The Utah Survey* 1, no. 3 (November 1913): 1–8.
———. Untitled speech, handwritten. The Library of the Episcopal Diocese of Utah, Spalding File, Salt Lake City, UT.
Stark, Rodney. "Why Religious Movement Succeed or Fail: A Revised General Model." *Journal of Contemporary Religion* 12 (1996): 133–57.
———. *The Rise of Mormonism*. Edited by Reid L. Neilson. New York: Columbia University Press, 2005.
Stenger, Mary Ann. "Gadamer's Hermeneutics as a Model for Cross-Cultural Understanding and Truth in Religion." In *Religious Pluralism and Truth:*

Essays on Cross-Cultural Philosophy of Religion, edited by Thomas Dean, 151–68. Albany: State University of New York Press, 1995.

Strauss, Leo. *The Rebirth of Classical Political Rationalism: Essays and Lectures by Leo Strauss*. Chicago: University of Chicago Press, 1989.

Strong, Josiah. *Our Country: Its Possible Future and Its Present Crisis*. New York: American Home Missionary Society, 1885.

Szasz, Ferenc M. *The Divided Mind of Protestant America, 1880–1930*. Tuscaloosa: University of Alabama Press, 1982.

———. *The Protestant Clergy in the Great Plains and Rocky Mountain West, 1865–1915*. Albuquerque: University of New Mexico Press, 1988.

Tanner, Jerald, and Sandra Tanner. *Answering Mormon Scholars*, Vol. I & II. Salt Lake City: Utah Lighthouse Ministry, 1994.

Teich, Mikulás, and Roy Porter, eds. *Fin de Siècle: Its Legacy*. New York: Cambridge University Press, 1990.

Terry, Brendan. "John Danforth Nutting and the Utah Gospel Mission." Masters thesis, Brigham Young University, 1992.

Thernstrom, Stephan, Ann Orlov, and Oscar Handlin, eds. *Harvard Encyclopedia of American Ethnic Groups*. Cambridge, MA: The Belknap Press, 1994.

Thoreau, Henry David. "Let Such Pure Hate Still Underprop." Henry David Thoreau Online. Accessed May 2, 2018. http://www.thoreau-online.org/let-such-pure-hate-still-underprop.html

Thorson, Craig L. *Adam-God*. Aurora, Colorado: Publishment, 1994.

Tinker, George E. *Missionary Conquest: The Gospel and Native American Cultural Genocide*. Minneapolis: Fortress Press, 1993.

Tocqueville, Alexis de. *Democracy in America*. Translated by George Lawrence. New York: Harper and Row Publishers, 1988.

———. *L'Ancien Regime*. Edited by G.W. Headlam. Oxford: Clarendon Press, 1969.

Townsend, Luther Tracy. "Manifest Destiny from a Religious Point of View." An Address Delivered before the Boston Music Hall Patriotic Association, November 6, 1898. Baltimore, MD.

Townshend, George, M.A. *The Conversion of Mormonism*. Hartford: T. B. Simonds, Soldier and Servant Series. In Episcopalian History Collection, Box 12, Folder 16, Marriott Library Special Collections, University of Utah, Salt Lake City, UT.

Tracy, David. *The Analogical Imagination: Christian Theology and the Culture of Pluralism*. New York: Crossroad, 1989.

Troeltsch, Ernst. *The Social Teachings of the Christian Churches*. Translated by Olive Wyon. New York: Harper Press, 1960.

Turner, Bryan S. *Religion and Social Theory*. London: Sage Publications, 1991.

Tuveson, Ernest Lee. *Redeemer Nation: The Idea of America's Millennial Role*. Chicago: University of Chicago Press, 1968.

"Utah Home Missions Comity Council Articles of Organization, The." William Paden Collection, Presbyterian Church file, Item 17, Westminster College Archive, Salt Lake City, 1916.

Utter, Jack. *Wounded Knee and the Ghost Dance Tragedy*. Lake Ann, MI: National Woodlands Publishing Company, 1991.

Van Gorden, Kurt. Two telephone interviews in August and September with Charles Randall Paul regarding the life history of John Danforth Nutting. 1993.
Van Hoak, Stephen P. "And Who Shall Have the Children? The Indian Slave Trade in the Southern Great Basin, 1800–1865." *Nevada Historical Society Quarterly* 41, no. 1 (Summer 1998): 3–25.
Van Wagoner, Richard S. *Mormon Polygamy: A History*. Salt Lake City: Signature Books, 1986.
Varg, Paul A. "Motives in Protestant Missions, 1890–1917." *Church History* 23, no. 1 (1954): 68–82.
Vermilye, Elizabeth B. "Are Christians Justified in Combating Mormonism?" *Home Mission Monthly* 30, no. 12 (October 1916): 283–86.
———. "Non-Christian Faiths in America." In leaflet, November 14, 1912. The International Council for Patriotic Service. Library of the Episcopal Diocese of Utah, Spalding File, Salt Lake City, UT.
Voegelin, Eric. "History and Gnosis." In *The Old Testament and Christian Faith: A Theological Discussion*, edited by Bernhard W. Anderson, 64–89. New York: Harper & Row, 1963.
Walker, Ronald W. "B. H. Roberts and the Woodruff Manifesto." *BYU Studies* 22, no. 3 (1982): 363–66.
———. "Toward a Reconstruction of Mormon Indian Relations, 1847–1877." *BYU Studies* 29, no. 2 (1989): 23–42.
Walls, Andrew F. *The Missionary Movement in Christian History*. Maryknoll, NY: Orbis Books, 1995.
Wangler, Thomas E. "The Birth of Americanism: Westward the Apocalyptic Candlestick,."*Harvard Theological Review* 65, no. 4 (1972): 415–36.
Ward, Maria. *Female Life among the Mormons: A Narrative*. New York: Derby & Jackson, 1857.
Weaver, Jace, ed. *Native American Religious Identity: Unforgotten Gods*. Mary Knoll, New York: Orbis Books, 1998.
Webber, Timothy P. *Living in the Shadow of the Second Coming*. Grand Rapids, MI: Academie Books, 1983.
Weber, Max. *From Max Weber*. Translated and edited by Gerth and O. Mills. Oxford: Oxford University Press, 1946.
———. *Ancient Judaism*. Translated by Hans Gerth and Don Martindale. New York: Free Press, 1952.
Weber, Timothy P. *Living in the Shadow of the Second Coming: American Premillennialism, 1875–1925*. New York: Oxford University Press, 1979.
Welter, Barbara. "She Hath Done What She Could: Protestant Women's Missionary Careers in Nineteenth-Century America." In *Women in American Religion*, edited Janet Wilson Jones, 111–25. Philadelphia: University of Pennsylvania, 1980.
White, O. Kendall. *Mormon Neo-orthodoxy: A Crisis Theology*. Salt Lake City: Signature Books, 1987.
Wiebe, Robert. *The Search for Order, 1877–1920*, American Century Series. New York: Hill and Wang, 1976.

Williams, David M. "Will the Mormon People Become Christians?" Harold B. Lee Library, Brigham Young University, Provo, UT. 1900.

Wind, A. "The Protestant Missionary Movement, 1789–1963." In *Missiology—An Ecumenical Introduction*, edited by F. J. Verstraelen, 237–52. Grand Rapids, MI: William B. Eerdmans Publishing Company, 1995.

"Women Unite Against Smoot." *New York Times*, November 15, 1903.

Women's Home Missionary Society of the Methodist Episcopal Church. n.d.: Report, New York City. Found in the Archives of the Church of Jesus Christ of Latter-day Saints, Salt Lake City, UT.

Woodard, Colin. *American Nations: A History of Eleven Rival Regional Cultures of North America*. New York: Viking Press, 2012.

Wright, Christopher J. H. *The Mission of God: Unlocking the Bible's Grand Narrative*. Grand Rapids: InterVarsity Press, 2006.

Wuthnow, Robert. *After Heaven: Spirituality in America Since the 1950s*. Berkeley: University of California Press, 1998.

Xi, Lian. *The Conversion of Missionaries: Liberalism in American Protestant Missions in China, 1907–1932*. University Park: Pennsylvania State University Press, 1997.

Yates, Timothy. *Christian Mission in the Twentieth Century*. Cambridge, UK: Cambridge University Press, 1994.

Yearley, Lee. "Conflicts Among Ideals of Human Flourishing." In *Prospects for a Common Morality*, edited by G. Outka and J. Reeder, Jr., 233–53. Princeton: Princeton University Press, 1993.

———. "New Religious Virtues and the Study of Religion." Fifteenth Annual University Lecture in Religion, Arizona State University, Tempe, Arizona, 1994, 1–26.

Yohn, Susan M. *A Contest of Faiths: Missionary Women and Pluralism in the American Southwest*. Ithaca, NY: Cornell University Press, 1995.

Yorgason, Ethan, and Chiung Hwang Chen. "Geopolitical Imaginations about Mormons in News and Popular Magazines." Paper presented at the Association for Education and Journalism and Mass Communication in Toronto, Canada, August. 2005.

Young, David E., and Jean-Guy Goulet. *Being Changed by Cross Cultural Encounters*. Peterborough, Ontario: Broadview, 1994.

Index

A

aesthetic temperament, 200–201
American century, 23–25
American Civil War, 41–43
American religious experiment, 1–2, 6–8, 10–11
anti-American Apostle, 28–29
anti-cult strategies, 209
anti-Protestantism, 72–73
authority, 117, 119, 133

B

Berger, Peter, 228
Blake, William, xxiin9
Bloom, Harold, xi, 68, 103, 109n49, 132n32, 201
Book of Abraham, 174, 178–81
Book of Mormon, 178

C

Christian Statesman, The, 158–60
civil disobedience, 29
concluding summation, 232–33
conversion of missionaries, 223
Comity Council of Utah Home Missions, 144
cross-cultural contamination, 226–28
cultural conflict, 47

D–F

divine sociality, 110–112
doctrinal conflicts, 87–103

Flake, Kathleen, 46n16, 145n14
Frye, Northrup, 6n4

G

Givens, Terryl, 46n16, 150n30
Gopin, Mark, 230
Gramsci, Antonio, 205
Grand Teton, 167
Greeley, Andrew, 81, 104, 108n47, 200–202

H

henotheism, 211–12
Heavenly Parents, 111
Hughes, Richard, 194

I–L

International Council for Patriotic Service, 183–84
James, William, xix, 55n47, 87n7, 201–2
Lincoln, Abraham, 25, 69

M

Madison, James, xxi, 4, 13–15
Madsen, Truman, xi
Marty, Martin, xi, 30, 207
Mather, Cotton, 59
McMillan, Duncan, 141–42
Meinig, D. W., 19–20
missiology, 214–16
Moore, Laurence, 77, 108

More, Thomas, 231
Morehead, John, xii, 153n38, 185n53
Mormon population in Utah, 226
Mormon Wars, 26–29
Mouffe, Chantal, xxi, 229
"Muslim" Mormons, 136, 156n49, 161, 163

N

National Reform Association, 157–58
National Union of Women's Organizations, 147
Native American Religious Wars, 30–34
Neuchterlein, James, 98
new religious movements, 223–24
Nibley, Hugh, xi
Novak, Michael, xiii–xiv, xvii–xix, 194n2
Nussbaum, Martha, 17n22

P

Pope Alexander VI, 12
proselytizing, xvii–xix, 49–51, 122n2, 133n32, 171
Protestant mission success, 138, 168, 186, 191, 204, 224–25

R

Rauschenbusch, Walter, 45
religious bigotry, 66
Roberts, B. H., 97n25, 144, 173–75, 180–82
Romney, Mitt, 145n14
Roosevelt, Theodore, 34–35, 44n9, 47n21, 67–68, 145
Russell, Isaac, 176, 181, 191

S

sacred narratives, 83–86
Salt Lake Ministerial Association, 122, 125, 144, 151–52
Shipps, Jan, 54n44, 60n3, 63n11, 109n49, 148, 207

Shupe, Anson, 209–210
Simmel, Georg, 100
Smith, Jonathan Z., 54
Smith, Joseph F., 149
Smith, Joseph, Jr., 71, 74–75, 86, 92–96, 101n32, 102, 107, 175, 188, 231
Smoot, Reed, 63, 143, 145, 151
Snow, Lorenzo, 59
social capital, 199
social conflict theory, xvi–xvii, xx–xxi, 8–11
social gospel movement, 45, 164–65
Stark, Rodney, 203
styles of religiosity, 103, 109
sub-culture identity theory, 197
symbols and rites, 104

T

Thoreau, Henry David, 5
Tocqueville, Alexis de, 8–11, 31, 38, 46, 69
Tracy, David, xi, 201
tribal loyalty, 207
true church controversy, 54

U

Utah Gospel Mission, 122, 125, 131, 137–38
Utah Home Missions Council, 144

W

Wasatch Academy, 156
Williams, Roger, 4–5, 17n22, 228
Winthrop, John, 12
women's missions, 52–53, 147
World Council of Churches, 56

Y

Yearley, Lee, 228
Young, Brigham, 36

Also available from
GREG KOFFORD BOOKS

Mormonism in Transition: A History of the Latter-day Saints, 1890–1930, 3rd ed.

Thomas G. Alexander

Paperback, ISBN: 978-1-58958-188-3

More than two decades after its original publication, Thomas G. Alexander's Mormonism in Transition still engages audiences with its insightful study of the pivotal, early years of the Churcah of Jesus Christ of Latter-day Saints. Serving as a vital read for both students and scholars of American religious and social history, Alexander's book explains and charts the Church's transformation over this 40-year period of both religious and American history.

For those familiar with the LDS Church in modern times, it is impossible to study Mormonism in Transition without pondering the enormous amount of changes the Church has been through since 1890. For those new to the study of Mormonism, this book will give them a clear understanding the challenges the Church went through to go from a persecuted and scorned society to the rapidly growing, respected community it is today.

Praise for Mormonism in Transition:

"A must read for any serious student of this 'peculiar people' and Western history." – STANLEY B. KIMBALL, *Journal of the West*

"Will be required reading for all historians of Mormonism for some time to come." – WILLIAM D. RUSSELL, *Journal of American History*

"This is by far the most important book on this crucial period in LDS history." – JAN SHIPPS, author of *Mormonism: The Story of a New Religious Tradition*

"A work of careful and prodigious scholarship." – LEONARD J. ARRINGTON, author of *Brigham Young: American Moses*

"Clearly fills a tremendous void in the history of Mormonism." – Klaus J. Hansen, author of *Mormonism and the American Experience*

Mormonism at the Crossroads of Philosophy and Theology:
Essays in Honor of David L. Paulsen

Edited by Jacob T. Baker

Paperback, ISBN: 978-1-58958-192-0

"There is no better measure of the growing importance of Mormon thought in contemporary religious debate than this volume of essays for David Paulsen. In a large part thanks to him, scholars from all over the map are discussing the questions Mormonism raises about the nature of God and the purpose of life. These essays let us in on a discussion in progress." —RICHARD LYMAN BUSHMAN, author of *Joseph Smith: Rough Stone Rolling*.

"This book makes it clear that there can be no real ecumenism without the riches of the Mormon mind. Professor Paulsen's impact on LDS thought is well known.... These original and insightful essays chart a new course for Christian intellectual life." —PETER A. HUFF, and author of *Vatican II and The Voice of Vatican II*

"This volume of smart, incisive essays advances the case for taking Mormonism seriously within the philosophy of religion–an accomplishment that all generations of Mormon thinkers should be proud of." —PATRICK Q. MASON, Howard W. Hunter Chair of Mormon Studies, Claremont Graduate University

"These essays accomplish a rare thing—bringing light rather than heat to an on-going conversation. And the array of substantial contributions from outstanding scholars and theologians within and outside Mormonism is itself a fitting tribute to a figure who has been at the forefront of bringing Mormonism into dialogue with larger traditions." —TERRYL L. GIVENS, author of *People of Paradox: A History of Mormon Culture*

"The emergence of a vibrant Mormon scholarship is nowhere more in evidence than in the excellent philosophical contributions of David Paulsen." —RICHARD J. MOUW, President, Fuller Theological Seminary, author of *Talking with Mormons: An Invitation to Evangelicals*

Common Ground—Different Opinions:
Latter-day Saints and Contemporary Issues

Edited by Justin F. White
and James E. Faulconer

Paperback, ISBN: 978-1-58958-573-7

There are many hotly debated issues about which many people disagree, and where common ground is hard to find. From evolution to environmentalism, war and peace to political partisanship, stem cell research to same-sex marriage, how we think about controversial issues affects how we interact as Latter-day Saints.

In this volume various Latter-day Saint authors address these and other issues from differing points of view. Though they differ on these tough questions, they have all found common ground in the gospel of Jesus Christ and the latter-day restoration. Their insights offer diverse points of view while demonstrating we can still love those with whom we disagree.

Praise for *Common Ground—Different Opinions*:

"[This book] provide models of faithful and diverse Latter-day Saints who remain united in the body of Christ. This collection clearly demonstrates that a variety of perspectives on a number of sensitive issues do in fact exist in the Church. . . . [T]he collection is successful in any case where it manages to give readers pause with regard to an issue they've been fond of debating, or convinces them to approach such conversations with greater charity and much more patience. It served as just such a reminder and encouragement to me, and for that reason above all, I recommend this book." — Blair Hodges, Maxwell Institute

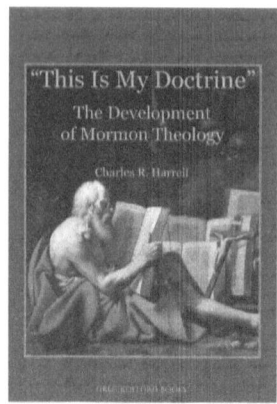

"This is My Doctrine": The Development of Mormon Theology

Charles R. Harrell

Hardcover, ISBN: 978-1-58958-103-6

The principal doctrines defining Mormonism today often bear little resemblance to those it started out with in the early 1830s. This book shows that these doctrines did not originate in a vacuum but were rather prompted and informed by the religious culture from which Mormonism arose. Early Mormons, like their early Christian and even earlier Israelite predecessors, brought with them their own varied culturally conditioned theological presuppositions (a process of convergence) and only later acquired a more distinctive theological outlook (a process of differentiation).

In this first-of-its-kind comprehensive treatment of the development of Mormon theology, Charles Harrell traces the history of Latter-day Saint doctrines from the times of the Old Testament to the present. He describes how Mormonism has carried on the tradition of the biblical authors, early Christians, and later Protestants in reinterpreting scripture to accommodate new theological ideas while attempting to uphold the integrity and authority of the scriptures. In the process, he probes three questions: How did Mormon doctrines develop? What are the scriptural underpinnings of these doctrines? And what do critical scholars make of these same scriptures? In this enlightening study, Harrell systematically peels back the doctrinal accretions of time to provide a fresh new look at Mormon theology.

"*This Is My Doctrine*" will provide those already versed in Mormonism's theological tradition with a new and richer perspective of Mormon theology. Those unacquainted with Mormonism will gain an appreciation for how Mormon theology fits into the larger Jewish and Christian theological traditions.

The End of the World, Plan B: A Guide for the Future

Charles Shirō Inouye

Paperback, ISBN: 978-1-58958-755-7

Praise for *End of the World, Plan B*:

"Mormonism needs Inouye's voice. We need, in general, voices that are a bit less Ayn Rand and a bit more Siddhartha Gautama. Inouye reminds us that justice is not enough and that obedience is not the currency of salvation. He urges us to recognize the limits of the law, to see that, severed from a willingness to compassionately suffer with the world's imperfection and evanescence, our righteous hunger for balancing life's books will destroy us all."
— Adam S. Miller, author of *Rube Goldberg Machines: Essays in Mormon Theology* and *Letters to a Young Mormon*

"Drawing on Christian, Buddhist, Daoist, and other modes of thought, Charles Inouye shows how an attitude of hope can arise from a narrative of doom. The End of the World, Plan B is not simply a rethinking of the end of our world, but is a meditation on the possibility of compassionate self-transformation. In a world that looks to the just punishment of the wicked, Inouye shows how sorrow, which comes from the demands of justice, can create peace, forgiveness, and love."
— Michael D.K. Ing, Assistant Professor, Department of Religious Studies, Indiana University

"For years I've hoped to see a book that related Mormonism to the great spiritual traditions beyond Christianity and Judaism. Charles Inouye has done this in one of the best Mormon devotional books I've ever read. His Mormon reading of the fourfold path of the Bodhisattva offers a beautiful eschatology of the end/purpose of the world as the revelation of compassion. I hope the book is read widely."
— James M. McLachlan, co-editor of *Discourses in Mormon Theology: Philosophical and Theological Possibilities*

Perspectives on Mormon Theology: Apologetics

Edited by Blair G. Van Dyke and Loyd Isao Ericson

Paperback, ISBN: 978-1-58958-580-5
Hardcover, ISBN: 978-1-58958-581-2

This volume in the PERSPECTIVES ON MORMON THEOLOGY series is an exploration of Mormon apologetics—or the defense of faith. Since its very beginning, various Latter-day Saints have sought to utilize evidence and reason to actively promote or defend beliefs and claims within the Mormon tradition. Mormon apologetics reached new levels of sophistication as believers trained in fields such as Near-Eastern languages and culture, history, and philosophy began to utilize their knowledge and skills to defend their beliefs.

The contributors to this volume seek to explore the textures and contours of apologetics from multiple perspectives, revealing deep theological and ideological fissures within the Mormon scholarly community concerning apologetics. However, in spite of deep-seated differences, what each author has in common is a passion for Mormonism and how it is presented and defended. This volume captures that reality and allows readers to encounter the terrain of Mormon apologetics at close range.

For the Cause of Righteousness: A Global History of Blacks and Mormonism, 1830-2013

Russell W. Stevenson

Paperback, ISBN: 978-1-58958-529-4

**2015 Best Book Award,
Mormon History Association**

"In Russell Stevenson's *For the Cause of Righteousness: A Global History of Blacks and Mormonism*, he extends the story of Mormonism's long-standing priesthood ban to the broader history of the Church's interaction with blacks. In so doing he introduces both relevant atmospherics and important new context. These should inform all future discussions of this surprisingly enduring subject."
 — Lester E. Bush, author of "Mormonism's Negro Doctrine: An Historical Overview"

"Russell Stevenson has produced a terrific compilation. Invaluable as a historical resource, and as a troubling morality tale. The array of documents compellingly reveals the tragedy and inconsistency of racial attitudes, policies, and doctrines in the LDS tradition, and the need for eternal vigilance in negotiating a faith that must never be unmoored from humaneness."
 — Terryl L. Givens, author of *Parley P. Pratt: The Apostle Paul of Mormonism* and *By the Hand of Mormon: The American Scripture that Launched a New World Religion*

"You might wonder what a White man could possibly say to two Black women about Black Mormon history. Surprisingly a whole lot! As people who consider ourselves well informed in African-American Mormon History, we found a wealth of new information in *For the Cause of Righteousness*. Russell Stevenson's well-researched exploration of Blacks and Mormonism is an informative read, not just for those interested in Black history, but American history as well."
 — Tamu Smith and Zandra Vranes (a.k.a. Sistas in Zion), authors, *Diary of Two Mad Black Mormons*

Voices for Equality: Ordain Women and Resurgent Mormon Feminism

Edited by Gordon Shepherd, Lavina Fielding Anderson, and Gary Shepherd

Paperback, ISBN: 978-1-58958-758-8

Praise for *Voices for Equality*:

"Timely, incisive, important—this book teaches us that our sometimes very personal struggles with gender and equality in Mormonism have profound and far-reaching significance. In these pages, some of Mormonism's finest researchers and thinkers bring a richness of historical and scholarly perspective and a powerful new survey of tens of thousands of Mormon people to bear on headline-making issues like women's ordination, sister missionaries, church discipline, the internet and faith, and change in the LDS church. They offer us a rare and precious opportunity to grasp the full significance of this moment. This book is a much needed mirror for our time."

— Joanna Brooks, co-editor of *Mormon Feminism: Essential Writings* and author of *The Book of Mormon Girl: A Memoir of an American Faith*

"*Voices for Equalty: Ordain Women and Resurgent Mormon Feminism* is a very important contribution to the discussion of Mormon feminism and the struggle for the ordination of women to the priesthood in the LDS Church. Anyone interested in this subject, any library concerned to be up-to-date on these issues, needs to have this book."

— Rosemary Radford Ruether, world-renowned feminist scholar and Catholic theologian, author of *Sexism and God-Talk: Toward a Feminist Theology* and *Women-Church: Theology* and *Practice of Feminist Liturgical Communities*

www.ingramcontent.com/pod-product-compliance
Lightning Source LLC
Chambersburg PA
CBHW020224170426
43201CB00007B/305